THE FAILURE OF THE FOUNDING FATHERS

BRUCE ACKERMAN

The Failure *of the* Founding Fathers

JEFFERSON, MARSHALL, AND THE RISE OF PRESIDENTIAL DEMOCRACY

THE BELKNAP PRESS OF

HARVARD UNIVERSITY PRESS

CAMBRIDGE, MASSACHUSETTS

LONDON, ENGLAND

2005

Library of Congress Cataloging-in-Publication Data

Ackerman, Bruce A.
The failure of the founding fathers : Jefferson, Marshall, and the rise of presidential
democracy / Bruce Ackerman.
p. cm.
Includes bibliographical references (p.) and index.
ISBN 0-674-01866-4 (alk. paper)
1. United States—Politics and government—1801–1809.   2. United States—Politics
and government—1797–1801.   3. Jefferson, Thomas, 1743–1826.   4. Marshall, John,
1755–1835.   5. Presidents—United States—History.   6. United States. Supreme
Court—History.   7. Constitutional history—United States.   8. Constitutional law—
United States—History.   9. Federal government—United States—History.   10.
Seperation of powers—United States—History.   I. Title.

E331.A15   2005
320.973'09'034—dc22   200504034

For Cody and Sofia—
and the day after tomorrow

CONTENTS

THE FAILURE OF THE FOUNDING FATHERS

PART ONE

The People's President

INTRODUCTION

America on the Brink

For a week in February 1801, America teetered on the brink of disaster. The electoral college had deadlocked, and the job of picking the next president fell to the House of Representatives. Vote after vote was leading nowhere—after thirty-five ballots, still no president of the United States.

Inauguration Day was less than three weeks away. President John Adams's term would end, and the Constitution did not specify what was to happen next if the impasse in the House continued. For ordinary Americans, it was clear enough what ought to happen: the Republican party and its presidential candidate, Thomas Jefferson, had won the election, and the House should recognize this fact. But the Federalist party was powerful in Congress, and many Federalists were trying to throw the presidency to Aaron Burr, a political chameleon who might well make great concessions to gain the prize. If this gambit failed, the Federalists might have pushed John Marshall, their newly appointed chief justice of the Supreme Court, into the president's chair. While Marshall was the nation's most popular Federalist politician, he was utterly unacceptable to the Republicans. Jefferson detested him, despite—because of?—the fact that they were cousins.

Danger signs were everywhere. The Republican governors of Pennsylvania and Virginia were preparing their state militias to march on Washington if the Federalists used a legal trick to steal the presidency. A mob surrounded the half-built Capitol in Washington, D.C., threatening death to any Federalist pretender to the office. Leading Federalist newspapers conjured up the prospect of "the militia of Massachusetts consisting of 60,000 *(regulars let us call them)* in arms" crushing the force of some "factious foreigners in Pennsylvania, or a few *fighting* bacchanals of Virginia."[1]

If hotheads had had their way, the 1787 Constitution would have disintegrated. American history would have moved in a Latin American

3

direction. We would have seen military clashes, ending, most probably, with another constitutional convention, this time with Thomas Jefferson in the chair. Rather than proving an enduring feature of the American order, written constitutions would have begun to seem ephemeral things—with the Constitution of 1802 replacing the Constitution of 1787, which had only recently replaced America's first constitution: the Articles of Confederation of 1781.

Three constitutions in twenty years! How many more crises and constitutions were in store for an unruly infant republic on a vast continent? Would the United States ever reach any kind of equilibrium?

Thanks to some unsung heroes—including the deviously resourceful Thomas Jefferson, the surprisingly cool-headed John Adams, the much maligned Aaron Burr, and the otherwise forgotten James Bayard—the republic weathered its first great crisis. On the thirty-sixth ballot, the House of Representatives selected Thomas Jefferson and cut off the cycle of violence. Though John Adams refused to show up at the inaugural ceremony, Federalist Chief Justice Marshall swore Jefferson in as president of the United States.

This was no easy victory. If the nation survived the crisis, it wasn't because the Constitution provided clear rules for the political game. The Framers of 1787 made an alarming number of technical mistakes that invited partisans to inflame an already explosive situation. I will be setting the constitutional stage so that you can appreciate the evolving choices confronting the protagonists in this great drama, as well as the complexities of their responses.

While they managed to save the republic, our heroes do not emerge with clean hands. Statesmanship turns out to be a tricky business, displaying incongruous combinations of self-restraint and self-interest, public concern and petty patronage. But in the end these complexities cast a flickering light on a fundamental question: How did Americans manage their first democratic transition without descending into a cycle of violence?

Given our inveterate tendency to read history backwards, we haven't taken this question seriously. The entire crisis has been treated as if Jefferson's victory was inevitable. Most contemporary historians go further and downplay the traditional focus on great events in Washington, choosing to emphasize social, not political, developments.

Constitutional lawyers have also trivialized the crisis. For them, the House election of Jefferson serves as prologue to a series of flare-ups in the electoral college that have struck the nation over the centuries. When yet another disaster hits, as in Bush v. Gore in the 2000 election, the profession dusts off the old precedents to see whether they contain some lessons. But during ordinary times, constitutional lawyers are happy to let sleeping dogs lie while turning their attention to the exciting goings-on at the Supreme Court.

This is a mistake. I will be viewing the crisis as symptomatic of a much deeper constitutional transformation in American history, and one that reverberates to the present day. February 1801 marks the birth-agony of the plebiscitarian presidency: for the first time in American history, a president ascended to the office on the basis of a mandate from the People for sweeping transformation. The great engine for change was the invention of recognizably democratic political parties—with Federalists and Republicans ferociously competing with each other for electoral supremacy. The presidency became the obvious institutional focus for this competition, making it plausible for the electoral winner to claim a popular mandate. Thomas Jefferson was the first president to make such a claim, and this assertion generated a series of shattering challenges to the rest of the system. Although America pulled back from the brink in 1801, the rise of the plebiscitarian presidency triggered institutional confrontations that transformed basic constitutional arrangements by the end of the decade, and in ways that remain relevant today.

I begin with the Philadelphia Convention of 1787 and its failure to foresee the development of democratic party competition. Following the teachings of classical republican thought, the Convention equated parties with factions and considered them unmitigated evils. Two-party competition is at the core of modern democracy, but the Convention had a very different aim. It sought to create a republic that transcended faction, not a democracy in which parties rotated in office. Its complex constitutional machine aimed to encourage the selection of political notables to govern in the public interest, and to disdain the arts of faction.

When they looked at the presidency, the Convention feared a demagogue, and it designed the electoral college to reduce the chances that a political opportunist could ascend to power. But the onset of party competition undermined its basic premises. In 1787 the Convention delegates could reasonably suppose that their electoral college had been engineered to select a statesman who transcended petty factionalism as president; but in the course of a decade their clever design had disintegrated into a jumble of antiquated legalisms that threatened to frustrate the choice of the People. Through inspired statesmanship and plain good luck, the leaders of 1801 managed to avoid a disaster by picking Thomas Jefferson. In solving their immediate problem, however, they created a new challenge to the constitutional order.

With Jefferson at its head, the Republican party was not content with gaining the presidency. It aimed for nothing less than a sweeping repudiation of the Federalist past—both its governing philosophy and its governing personnel. There was one large obstacle to this "revolution of 1800": the six Federalists sitting on the Supreme Court, led by John Marshall. For these men, the Jeffersonians' claim of a mandate from the People was sheer demagoguery. The supreme act of popular sovereignty was the ratification of the Constitution of 1787, not the election of 1800, and the Court's job was to put the Republicans in their place.

The result was a decade of grim institutional struggle between the men of 1800 and the men of 1787—between the president, whose mandate from the People was backed by Congress, and the Court, whose mandate was backed by a piece of paper. At the end of our story, neither side would gain total victory. They would instead pass on to the next generation a fragile synthesis of the constitutional meanings of both 1787 and 1800.

The Jeffersonians' struggle with the Marshall Court inaugurated a complex institutional dance that can be seen as one of the great leitmotivs of American constitutional development. Over the next two centuries there would be many presidents who would claim a mandate from the People on the basis of their party's victory at the polls; and there would be many Courts that would look upon these large claims with skepticism, seeking to put the president in his place even when his plebiscitary authority was backed by sweeping majorities in Congress. And these later struggles often ended in a manner similar to the first—with neither side achieving total victory, and both finding themselves enmeshed in an evolving synthesis of the plebiscitarian assertions of the present with the constitutional achievements of the past.

In the early years of the republic, the ongoing institutional struggle displayed an inner logic, with one conflict setting the stage for the next. I will be presenting this drama in five acts. Part One of this book deals with Act I, exploring how democratic party competition smashed the old electoral college and transformed the nature of the presidency. Part Two shows how the triumph of the plebiscitarian presidency triggered a series of confrontations over the next decade between the revolutionaries of 1800 and the constitutionalists of 1787.

Act II: The Assault on the Old Constitution. The story continues with the entry of the newly elected Republican Congress onto the scene in December 1801. With the encouragement of the president, Congress begins its revolutionary work by repudiating one of the most vulnerable portions of the Federalist inheritance. During its lame-duck session earlier in the year, the Federalist Congress had used its final days of power to create a new and powerful set of circuit courts to dispense federal justice throughout the nation. Before handing over the presidency to Jefferson, Adams filled these new courts with dedicated Federalists eager to fulfill their nationalizing mission.

For the Jeffersonians, these "midnight judges" were an affront to the American people. When they created and filled these judgeships, the lame-duck president and Congress knew that the voters had repudiated the Federalist party. Nevertheless, they chose to appoint a host of Federalists to intrude upon the administration of justice in the states. The People had elected their new president and Congress to put an end to such incursions on state prerogatives. If the Republicans were to remain faithful to their mandate, they would at once repudiate this final Federalist assault on popular sovereignty.

Within weeks the new congressional majority was pushing through legislation that would destroy the new courts and purge the midnight judges from office. The Federalist minority responded by invoking the Constitution as a bar. In the Federalists' view, the text of 1787 spoke for the People in a higher sense than did the Jeffersonians, and the Judiciary article of that great text protected the midnight judges from political interference. Unless and until the Jeffersonians managed to amend the Constitution, the judges' appointments were sacrosanct.

The Republicans overwhelmed these Federalist objections by party-line votes in Congress, but the Supreme Court posed a very different problem. No party-line vote could help the Republicans there—all six justices were Federalists. How would these remaining representatives of the old regime respond to the Republican claims of a mandate from the People?

Act III: The Court Retreats. Enter John Marshall and his famous opinion in Marbury v. Madison, known throughout the world as an epoch-making statement vindicating the power of judges to lay down the law to politicians in the name of the Constitution.[2] Modern constitution-builders have entirely lost sight of *Marbury*'s relationship to the crisis that gave it birth. Once we set the historical stage more fully, *Marbury* will take on a different appearance. Rather than a ringing vindication of judicial power, it was part of a large strategic retreat, rationalizing a stunning judicial concession to the Republicans' proud claim to a mandate from the People.

To glimpse the bigger picture, consider William Marbury's very distant relationship to the Republican assault on the old regime portrayed in Act II. He wasn't one of the new circuit judges who were the Republicans' main targets. He was merely seeking his commission for the inconsequential post of justice of the peace in the District of Columbia. Marbury got caught up in the larger controversy only because Adams awarded him his petty post at the last minute, and Jefferson took the broad view that Adams was wrong to give out any jobs, however small, once he had lost his bid for reelection. As a consequence, the new president ordered his secretary of state, James Madison, to refuse to hand Marbury his commission as JP. If he hoped to gain his commission, he would have to go to the courts for relief.

Before considering Marbury's effort further, we should first consider the fate of the cadre of Federalist judges purged by the Republican Congress. In contrast to the hapless Marbury, Adams made sure that these distinguished gentlemen got their commissions before his presidential term came to an end. Indeed, the new judges were already holding court throughout the United States at the time the Republican Congress kicked them out of office. Their struggle to keep their jobs involved the constitutional independence of all future judges of the United States. Nothing similar was at stake in Marbury's lawsuit.

The justices of the Supreme Court were well aware of this point. They seriously contemplated a judicial strike to protest the purge of their colleagues on the circuit courts—playing with legal arguments they later found persuasive in *Marbury*. Nonetheless, they finally decided to accept the legitimacy of the Jeffersonian purge in a little-known opinion, Stuart v. Laird, handed down a week after *Marbury* in 1803. Despite Marshall's strong conviction that the Jeffersonians were acting unconstitutionally, and despite the ready availability of techniques that would have allowed the justices to resist, the Supreme Court refused to follow up on *Marbury* by defending the circuit judges against the Jeffersonian purge. Instead, the Court allowed the Jeffersonians to claim a mandate from the People to deliver a powerful blow to the ideal of judicial independence. On this crucial matter, it was the presidentialist revolution of 1800, not the Founding of 1787, that served as the basis for future constitutional development.

If we look at what the Marshall Court did, and not merely what it said, it is wrong to treat *Marbury* as the main event and *Stuart* as an historical curiosity. *Marbury* is better viewed as a footnote to *Stuart*. As a first approximation, an integrated reading of the Stuart and Marbury decisions goes something like this: *Stuart* stands for the proposition that the Supreme Court should give way to the central claims made by a victorious president and his party in the name of the People. *Marbury,* in turn, holds out the prospect that on matters of less central concern to the People of the present day, earlier achievements of popular sovereignty may appropriately inform constitutional development.

Act IV: The Struggle for Judicial Independence. The justices' decision to throw the circuit judges overboard failed to pacify the Jeffersonians, who embarked upon an escalating assault against the Federalists on the Supreme Court. Their constitutional weapon of choice was impeachment. Jefferson selected Justice Samuel Chase as his first target, and by 1804 the House went along with a bill of impeachment. The danger to the Court was so grave that, at one point, Marshall considered surrendering *Marbury*'s assertion of the power of judicial review. But when the moment of truth came at the Senate impeachment trial, enough Republican senators joined the Federalist minority to acquit Chase.

The Marshall Court's strategic retreat in *Stuart* was beginning to pay off. A couple of years is an eternity in politics. If the justices had gone to the mat in defense of the Federalist circuit judges in 1802 or 1803, the Republicans would have reacted immediately with an impeachment campaign to clear out the obstructionists from the Court. By ceding constitutional ground to the Republicans on their central issue, the justices bought themselves time, and time is a precious commodity for life-ten-

ured judges in their ongoing struggle with a mobilized political movement. Justices live on, but political movements can disintegrate, and by
the time of Chase's Senate trial in 1805, the president's leadership of Congress had begun to weaken.

Despite the failure of impeachment, Jefferson continued to plot further assaults on the Court. But his capacity for presidential leadership diminished over time, and a new institutional equilibrium was emerging:
president and party would count for a great deal in the constitutional order that the Founders had never imagined; but judicial independence
would survive and perhaps the justices might make good on *Marbury's*
claim to power at some remote moment in the future.

Act V: Judicial Synthesis. Marshall did not live to see the day when the
Court would follow up on *Marbury* and again strike down a federal statute. He watched with alarm, though, as his fellow Federalists began to resign from the bench, giving Jefferson a much easier way to change the
course of constitutional law. Although a frontal assault on judicial independence was institutionally difficult and politically costly, there was nothing to stop the president from naming sympathetic Republicans to vacancies. Time might have been on the side of the Marshall Court in the short
run, but the longer run was shifting in the presidentialist direction.

Both Jefferson and his successor, James Madison, occasionally faltered
in their determination to name committed Republicans to the Court. But
as the years passed, their strategy of transformative appointments began to
make a real difference. During its early years the Marshall Court almost always spoke with a single voice, and that voice was almost always Marshall's. Over time, though, more Republican voices began to be heard.
And by the end of the decade power began to shift.

By 1812 only three of the Court's seven justices were holding commissions signed by Federalist presidents. And once Marshall lost his solid
Federalist majority, the Court's jurisprudence took a Jeffersonian turn. In
United States v. Hudson and Goodwin, its great decision of 1812, Marshall was no longer writing for the Court. His accustomed place had been
occupied by William Johnson, Jefferson's first appointee, who ordered a
sweeping cutback in the power of the federal courts. Our story ends with
the Court weaving a complex web of doctrine that promised a synthesis of
Federalist and Republican principles.

This moment is missed in standard accounts, which emphasize a later period in the long life of the Marshall Court. In this book I do not chronicle the doctrinal twists and turns of the Marshall Court over its long history. We have more than enough of these court-centered accounts. In focusing on the Court's first decade, I want to locate the changing role of the judiciary as a response to an even more fundamental constitutional transformation—the rise of a democratic party system which enabled the president to claim a mandate from the People for constitutional change. Within this setting, my five-act drama elaborates a distinctive model of constitutional change that relies on judges both to refine presidential claims of a mandate and to integrate these new mandates into the fabric of constitutional law.

I want to contrast this form of interaction between president and Court with the forms of constitutional change developed earlier in the Founding period. In elaborating their own ideas about constitutional change, the delegates to the Philadelphia Convention did not seriously consider the executive branch as an appropriate bearer of a ringing mandate from the People. Within their Whiggish understanding of history, the chief executive, aka THE KING, was the great enemy of the People. If the People mobilized to assert their rights, they did so through representative assemblies. The paradigm was the Glorious Revolution of 1688, with its Westminster Convention demanding that future kings swear allegiance to a newly fashioned Bill of Rights.[3]

The Philadelphia Convention of 1787 saw itself as a proud successor of this Whig tradition, and when it looked to the future, it naturally supposed that assemblies would once again take the lead in speaking for the People. When drafting Article V dealing with constitutional amendments, the Philadelphians envisioned a process involving a dialogue between assemblies on the national and state levels—either a new constitutional convention or two-thirds of Congress was authorized to propose amendments, and three-fourths of state conventions or legislatures could ratify them. There was no suggestion that presidents might play a constructive role in higher lawmaking.

This was a perfectly sensible decision in 1787—nothing in the English-speaking tradition suggested that presidents might serve as bearers of popular mandates for fundamental constitutional change. But the ink on the Constitution was hardly dry before history played one of its many tricks: starting with the election of 1800, presidents would often claim mandates, and the legitimacy of these claims would be adjudicated through a dialogue in which both the Supreme Court and the Congress would play fundamental roles. The electoral college crisis of 1801 inaugurated a model of presidential leadership that would coexist and compete with the Philadelphia Convention's model of assembly leadership for the next two centuries.

To mark this point, I propose a new way of defining the Founding's contribution to the American constitutional experience. To prepare the ground for redefinition, I propose a naive question: When precisely did "the Founding" occur?

The received wisdom begins with the Philadelphia Convention of 1787 but does not end there. Everybody recognizes that the proposal and ratification of the Bill of Rights were essential parts of the original deal— and so the common understanding of "the Founding" proceeds into the 1790s. At that point things become a little hazy,[4] but one final event stands out: Marbury v. Madison is presented as the triumphant conclusion of the story. With the great chief justice announcing the ascendancy of judicial review, all the really important pieces of the constitutional puzzle are in place: the Constitution, the Bill of Rights, and the Supreme Court dedicated to their enforcement. Constitutional history leaves Jefferson's administration with a sense of resolution—a conviction that, though the unknowable future would place immense strains on our early inheritance, the Founders built better than they knew (or we deserve).

"The Founding," in short, is conventionally understood as if it were a (rather primitive) moving picture rather than a single epic painting. In editing our early history, however, we have left some essential scenes scattered on the cutting room floor.[5]

I have no problem with the first two acts in the Founding drama: the Constitution and the Bill of Rights are indeed tributes to the capacity of assemblies—conventions in the first case, legislatures in the second—to gain mandates for constitutional change in the name of We the People. Only our preoccupation with Marbury v. Madison in the third act is misguided. The last phase of the Founding should begin in 1800, with Jefferson's electoral victory marking a mandate for fundamental change. Though *Marbury* remains important, it is only one part of a complex dialogue between the Court and the political branches. Rather than celebrating a single decision, we should see *Marbury* as part of a decade-long effort by which the Supreme Court began to weave all three great acts of popular sovereignty—the Constitution, the Bill of Rights, and the Republican revolution of 1800—into a living doctrine of higher law.

My revision is less harmonious, emphasizing continuing institutional crises and provides only a tenuous sense of resolution. But is it more revealing?

For starters, it permits a deeper appreciation of some fundamental historical truths. Considered in its largest outlines, the Founding was a great debate between centralizers and decentralizers—with the centralizers winning big in 1787, and their opponents regaining the initiative with the Bill of Rights and the revolution of 1800. The conventional narrative reveals a pro-Federalist bias because it focuses exclusively, in its triumphalist conclusion, on Marshall's effort to put Jefferson in his place in Marbury v. Madison. Although the Marshall Court did manage to sustain important centralizing themes into the Jeffersonian era, it is wrong to ignore the decentralizing thrust of this last phase of Founding politics. Yet this is precisely the consequence of emphasizing *Marbury* at the expense of other great events of the early 1800s.

Paradoxically, the conventional narrative also blinds us to the importance of nationalizing tendencies in our early history: most notably, to the way the rise of national political parties generated a new understanding of the president as the choice of the People. Once we eliminate the electoral college crisis from our view of the Founding, we will have trouble recognizing the powerful impact of plebiscitarian presidencies over the entire course of American constitutional development. Of course, it would be wrong to ignore this point when treating the particular cases of Jackson or Lincoln or Roosevelt, but it is easy to treat these presidentialist initiatives as special cases, not as examples of an ongoing dynamic emerging from the Founding itself.[6] And the same is true when it comes to legal discussions of particular efforts by the Supreme Court to integrate presidentialist mandates into the living doctrine of American constitutional law. In contrast, my revision of the Founding's final act places these points at the very center of our constitutional understanding.

There are large intellectual gains in making this turn, but it inevitably raises bigger issues. For Americans at least, there is more at stake in revisionist accounts of "the Founding." So long as the republic lives, the Founding is our fate. In our politics, in our law, in our deepest self-understandings as a nation, we are forever returning to consult its meaning. There is a Sisyphean character to the enterprise—but that will never deter the effort, nor should it. Americans are right to suppose that decisions made long ago by Enlightenment revolutionaries continue to shape the range of our present opportunities—if only through a complex process of historical mediation over two centuries. By cutting out crucial scenes from the Founding, the conventional narrative damages America's capacity to understand itself.

And we need all the self-understanding we can get. History can't serve as a cookbook, providing us with definitive recipes for solving twenty-first-century problems of statecraft. The early republic was a very different place from the hegemonic nation we call America. Nevertheless, our first constitutional encounter with the plebiscitarian presidency remains a relevant source of reflection on contemporary dilemmas. And apart from any particular insights, the story provides an antidote to a characteristic disease of intellectual life in an imperial republic: an all-too-pervasive tendency to treat the Founders as demigods, almost divinely inspired to discharge their task of steering the infant Republic on the path to future greatness.

This is not how the Founders appear here. There was no miracle at the Philadelphia Convention. In designing the presidency, the Framers made blunder after blunder—some excusable, others not. These mistakes set the stage for many awkward moments.

Item: The Framers designated the president of the Senate to preside over the counting of the presidential ballots, but the Senate president in 1801 turned out to be Thomas Jefferson himself—who used his power to eliminate his Federalist rivals from contention in the House runoff.

Item: The Framers mistakenly allowed the retiring president and Congress to control affairs for an extended lame-duck period after they lost an election. This gave the Federalists a chance to use their last days in power to push for a statute that would have authorized their new chief justice to displace Jefferson as president of the United States.

Item: As lame-duck secretary of state, Marshall blundered and forgot to give some of the president's appointees their commissions for office. When the disappointed office-seekers went to the Supreme Court for relief, Marshall, in his new position, did not do the right thing and disqualify himself from the decision. Instead, he used the case as an opportunity to berate the incoming administration for failing to correct his blunder. The case is Marbury v. Madison.

With the vice president counting his rivals out, and his rivals pushing the chief justice toward the presidential chair, with Marshall responding to Jefferson's election by abusing his position as chief justice to rebuke the new administration—there is more than a whiff of the banana republic in our story. The protagonists do not take on the appearance of neo-classical demigods. They are human, all too human. And yet, for all their misadventures, they managed to pull their nation back from the brink and pass on to their successors a fragile sense of constitutional order that transcended their bitter partisan disagreements.

May the same be said of us.

1

The Original Misunderstanding

Begin with the Founding, and its Enlightenment pretensions. The Constitutional Convention had its share of compromises, but it was also betting on ideas. Men like James Madison and James Wilson were trying to base their constitution on the best political science of their time. But this simple point provokes an unasked question: What if the Framers' political science turned out to be just plain wrong?

The answer could be crisis. If the Founding scheme was a clever effort to design an institutional machine in the light of scientific predictions about American politics, the machine could easily run amok if the predictions ran awry.

This is just what happened, and with bewildering speed.

From Revolution to Democracy

There is a wide gap separating the Founding conception of political life from our own. Two words, "revolution" and "democracy," mark the distance of two centuries. The men of 1787 were very proud of being revolutionaries, but talk of democracy made them nervous. Nowadays everybody is a democrat, but revolution makes us edgy. If we are to glimpse the constitutional crisis of the 1790s, we must look beyond our contemporary sensibilities and see the Founders as they saw themselves—the glorious victors of the first modern war of independence.[1] George Washington came to the Convention as a triumphant rebel leader, and Alexander Hamilton as his clever and energetic adjutant. The most important moment in the lives of James Madison and James Wilson had been when they cast their lot against the British.

These revolutionaries were not about to abandon their commitments in midstream. Without passionate devotion to the cause, they would never have had the audacity to speak in the name of "We the People" at Philadelphia. The Convention was in fact an illegal assembly; and it defiantly called for ratification by another round of illegal assemblies meeting in the states.[2] These actions seemed plausible only because of the revolutionary precedents that Washington and others had established in repeatedly breaking fundamental laws in their struggle against the English.

They were revolutionaries with a difference—the last to live before the French Revolution. None of these gentlemen yet suspected that modern revolutions would consume their children voraciously in spasms of violence and oppression. To be sure, they feared a Caesar or a Cromwell. But they did not realize that they stood on the threshold of a quarter-century of mass mobilizations and murderous warfare in the name of revolution. When they looked to their own past, the Glorious Revolution of 1688 suggested a very different possibility. Revolutions were tricky but manageable affairs, in which the mass of citizens would recognize, and defer to, the superior virtue of the landed and commercial elites who led the struggle for liberty.

Of course, the Glorious Revolution had not lasted forever; nor would their own. History demonstrated the ease with which virtue could be corrupted by concentrated power. This set the problem for the Founders' Enlightenment political science: How to organize power to avoid degeneration into despotism?

Here is where the Founders' answer deviated from our own. Most obviously, they were blind to the claims of women and slaves and native Americans to equal participation in the electoral process—without votes, how could these groups protect themselves? But they were also oblivious to a second important check on power. Apart from the vote, moderns place their trust in fair competition between political parties as the great engine for disciplining despotic power. For us, an election without party competition is no election at all. Not so for the Founders. They equated parties with factions, which they saw as evils. Worse yet, they did not reach this judgment after soberly considering the democratic case for party competition. Nothing resembling the modern party system had yet emerged as an historical reality. Even in England, the words "Whig" and "Tory" marked extended groupings of elite families, locked in factional struggle for power and patronage.[3]

Nor did the classical theory of republican government help the

Founders glimpse the future. The great republican writers of the past—
Aristotle and Cicero and Machiavelli and Harrington—equated party division with factional strife. As they saw it, republics died when leaders separated into factions, each cabal placing its narrow interests ahead of the
public good. The result was an escalating cycle of instability and incivility,
culminating in the despotic ascendancy of a Caesar or a Cromwell. The
fundamental challenge was to induce leaders to put the public good ahead
of their own—and to sustain the unity of the Commonwealth against the
ever-present dangers of factional disintegration.[4]

These classical teachings resonated with the Founders' revolutionary
experience. During their struggle against England, political division meant
weakness before the imperial foe, and bordered on betrayal: We will all
hang separately if we do not hang together. This attitude, once formed,
was hard to break.

Even Madison did not try. His work at the Convention, and in the
Federalist Papers, linked party with faction and condemned it as evil. He
merely looked to Enlightenment political science for help in designing a
better constitutional machine to control the beast. According to him, the
creation of a big republic would multiply the number of factions and make
it easier for large-spirited notables like Washington and himself to dominate the electoral competition over petty factional leaders. The clever
design of the separation of powers would further diffuse factional strife
and enhance the capacities of the elite to reason together with relative
dispassion about the public good.[5]

Within this framework, it is easy to see why the Founders were wary of
"democracy." If common folk were given real power, they might abandon
the elites and cede political control to petty politicians who would fail to
impose the stringent self-discipline needed to place the public interest
over factional desire. Rather than helping petty demagogues join together
into large parties, the aim of constitutional design was to break them into
innumerable squabbling bands—and thereby allow notables like Washington to transcend factional intrigue altogether.

Washington's presence at the head of the Convention assured the delegates that their larger vision was no pipe dream. Here was a man who had
already proved his large-souled character through years of selfless service
on the battlefield. This demonstration of "public character," not any display of partisan wiles, would predictably win him the presidency without

his stooping to petty politics. Once he had set the republic on the right course, wouldn't the constitutional machine assist his successors in sustaining his example of nonpartisan statesmanship?

The Meaning of Party

Washington was grimly determined to try. He included both Hamilton and Jefferson in his first cabinet, and desperately sought to keep these great rivals in harness. But it was not to be. By the end of his first administration, Jefferson and Hamilton were already locked in bitter conflict.[6] And by the time Washington left office, the division between Federalists and Republicans was dominating the political scene, in at least four ways.

First, the two parties developed *well-articulated ideologies* that ramified across the political agenda at home and abroad: Republicans were for revolutionary France and against monarchical England; Federalists were against atheistic France and for a realistic accommodation with England. Republicans were for a strictly limited central government; Federalists advanced an ambitious national agenda of economic and social development. Networks of party newspapers trumpeted these differences in the major cities, elaborating themes that were endlessly rehearsed in churches, in taverns, and at dinner tables throughout the land.[7] To put this point in a single line, Americans were constructing *parties of public opinion.*

Second, the ideological struggle took on concrete organizational form in the nation's capital. This new sociological reality is especially noteworthy because it arose despite the sincere determination of the leading protagonists—President Adams and Vice President Jefferson—to sustain the Washingtonian model of nonpartisan statesmanship.

When viewed from a certain angle, Adams and Jefferson were more alike than different. Both had made their mark as thinkers, writers, and diplomats—revolutionaries of the pen, not the sword. Both vividly recalled the days when they had been fast friends and leading diplomatic spokesmen for the American cause in Europe—memories that would provide an important resource when the written constitution obstructed the transition of power in 1801. But both men were now thoroughly enmeshed in the new world of party politics. As president and vice president, Adams and Jefferson made continuing gestures of public fealty to the ideal of nonpartisanship. This only meant that they left others in charge of the grubby business of day-to-day partisan organization, with very different results. Jefferson and Madison worked hand in glove; Adams and Hamilton were increasingly at odds.

These personal relationships should not distract attention from the larger party network that increasingly dominated day-to-day politics in the nation's capital. Gone were the days of the First Congress, when members primarily viewed themselves as local notables trying to mediate regional and state interests for the common good. This older view was never entirely displaced, but it came to be dominated by a different political reality. Congressional Federalists and Republicans were caucusing, and voting together, on the basis of common ideologies. Comprehensive statistical analyses reveal "extremely high" rates of party voting during the Adams administration, "well above levels . . . in modern times."[8] Call this the construction of *parties of central government.*

Third, as the struggle for the presidency loomed in 1800, the terms of partisan combat shifted. In contrast to previous elections, Thomas Jefferson was not content to present himself, in eighteenth-century fashion, as a man of character who modestly allowed others to draft him for high office. He also elaborated a campaign platform behind the scenes, sending letters to party leaders throughout the country defining Republican political principles. While these letters were formally "private," he expected them "to circulate beyond the persons to whom they were addressed, and there is ample evidence that they did so. The principles and issues that he stressed appeared repeatedly in Republican newspapers, broadsides, and party leaflets throughout the campaign. The Republican party took a clear stand on the issues in 1800, and it was Jefferson more than anyone else who articulated the positions." The Federalists replied in kind, making the election seem a contest of ideals, and not merely a contest between notables.[9]

But national coordination went beyond the realm of ideas. Both Federalists and Republicans held party caucuses to name vice-presidential running mates for Adams and Jefferson respectively, and managed to make these choices stick. In 1796 electors scattered their second-place votes among a variety of candidates. Four years later they refused to stray from the straight and narrow, and proved remarkably faithful to their party slates.[10] Call this the mobilization of state elites into *presidential parties.*

Fourth, the presidentialist mobilization of state elites began to transform the nature of local elections—though these continued to differ greatly from those of later periods. Political leaders did not yet think of themselves as professionals concerned with the nuts-and-bolts of party building, patronage management, and winning elections—this didn't happen until the 1830s. Within the prevailing eighteenth-century framework, candidates generally presented themselves as gentlemen modestly accepting positions tendered to them by a local community impressed with the superiority of their character.

This form of public presentation did not prevent them from scheming endlessly behind the scenes—but this to-ing and fro-ing was part and parcel of the general social competition among community leaders, and was not understood as the province of a specialized political class. As a consequence, candidates were often unopposed, and when they did compete, they did so more on the basis of their character and connections than on the basis of rival political ideals.

But this pattern was fractured by the ideological pressures of the presidential contest. Politicians like Aaron Burr and Alexander Hamilton pioneered new forms of popular mobilization in the mid-Atlantic states, where party competition was already fairly well developed.[11] Even in Federalist New England and the Republican South, there was a perceptible increase in partisan modes of campaigning and self-understanding.[12]

This rippling ideological contest invited Americans to view the elections of 1800 in a distinctive way. They were not simply contests among local notables for the privilege of representing their constituents; nor did they merely raise strictly local issues. They were becoming forums for a larger debate over national political ideals, competing visions of national development. Call this the *partisan transformation of local elections.*

The rise of parties of public opinion, the organization of parties of central government, the mobilization of state elites into presidential parties, the partisan transformation of local elections—these features combine into a distinctive whole, but they should not be confused with the party-machine formations that arose at later points in American history. To mark the difference, I will call the Republicans a *movement-party,* in which common ideals played a central role in mobilizing the protagonists on a national basis.[13]

This was hardly the last time that a movement-party would come to the fore, but it was the first, and its victory encouraged participants to give a distinctive understanding to the election returns. As the ballots surrounding the presidential and congressional contests rolled in, citizens around the country came to see them as manifestations of a collective choice between the rival principles of Federalism and Republicanism. As a consequence, the Republicans in the nation's capital could begin to claim that their electoral victories gave them *a popular mandate*—both for their presidential candidate, Thomas Jefferson, and for further legislative moves in their party's ideological direction once the new Congress came to power.

Two Responses to Party

Americans of the twenty-first century are familiar with efforts by parties to claim popular mandates on the basis of electoral victories. But such a claim caught the revolutionary generation unprepared. The philosophy of 1787 did not recognize that ongoing and organized party opposition was a legitimate, indeed an indispensable, part of democratic life. It had no room for the thought that the opposition party might pretend to a popular mandate in its effort to displace the party in power. Instead, it presented the participants with two different ways of understanding their situation— both with potentially disastrous consequences.

The first diagnosis was initially more congenial to the likes of Washington, Hamilton, and Adams—the men in power. If parties are factions, and factions destroy republics, it makes perfect sense to challenge the very legitimacy of a rising party—as Washington did in disparaging the Republicans in his Farewell Address:

> Let me . . . warn you in the most solemn manner against the baneful effects of the spirit of party generally.
>
> This spirit, unfortunately, is inseparable from our nature, having its root in the strongest passions of the human mind. It exists under different shapes in all governments, more or less stifled, controlled, or repressed; but in those of the popular form it is seen in its greatest rankness and is truly their worst enemy.
>
> . . .

It serves always to distract the public councils and enfeeble the public administration. It agitates the community with ill-founded jealousies and false alarms; kindles the animosity of one part against another; foments occasionally riot and insurrection. It opens the door to foreign influence and corruption, which find a facilitated access to the government itself through the channels of party passion. Thus the policy and the will of one country are subjected to the policy and will of another. [Read this as accusing the Republicans of being disloyal Frenchmen.]

There is an opinion that parties in free countries are useful checks upon the administration of the government, and serve to keep alive the spirit of liberty. This within certain limits is probably true; and in governments of a monarchical cast patriotism may look with indulgence, if not with favor, upon the spirit of party. But in those of the popular character, in governments purely elective, it is a spirit not to be encouraged. From their natural tendency it is certain there will always be enough of that spirit for every salutary purpose; and there being constant danger of excess, the effort ought to be by force of public opinion to mitigate and assuage it. A fire not to be quenched, it demands a uniform vigilance to prevent its bursting into a flame, lest, instead of warming, it should consume.[14]

There are paradoxes aplenty here. On the one hand, Washington was undoubtedly distressed by the transformation of his second administration into a party regime dominated by Federalists and denounced by Republicans. His address also stands as one of the greatest acts of nonpartisan statesmanship in the history of the republic—it announced that he would refuse a third term in office, thereby creating a precedent against the pernicious tendency toward presidencies-for-life.

On the other hand, partisan politics also stood behind Washington's grave denunciation of party. The passage was ghostwritten by Alexander Hamilton, the Federalist party leader; and it came at a time of maximum partisan advantage. Washington held off his announcement until September 17, 1796, keeping the Republicans off-balance in the presidential election campaign—since Jefferson was unprepared to oppose Washington if he decided to continue in office. Now the chief magistrate had given the Federalists a wonderful electioneering tool, enabling them to denounce the Republicans as factionalists in opposing the election of John Adams. So far as Federalists were concerned, Adams was no mere party man. He was the great revolutionary leader who would continue the nonpartisan tradition exemplified by Washington.[15]

Jefferson and Madison disagreed, but not on grounds that seem obvious to modern democrats. They did not try to explain that the Republicans played a vital role in an ongoing two-party system. They tried to justify their mobilizational activities within the established, nonpartisan understanding of politics. Despite their pervasive distrust of faction, all protagonists recognized an all-important exception to the non-party rule. Call it the *revolutionary proviso*.[16] The men of the 1790s had spent the better part of their lives in a glorious act of revolutionary dissent against King George and his evil ministers. And all agreed that further acts of revolutionary defiance might be justified in response to similar efforts at centralizing oppression. All that was necessary was an analogy between the Federalists of the 1790s and the Tories of yesteryear.

We can see Madison reorienting his thought at the very dawn of party competition. In a crucial early decision, he and Jefferson had helped establish a party newspaper, the *National Gazette,* to engage in nationwide competition with the paper that served as the mouthpiece of the administration, the *Gazette of the United States.* The latter newspaper, not yet understanding itself in party terms, presented itself as an impartial voice (similar, for all the differences, to the voice of the *New York Times* today).

But the *National Gazette,* under its incendiary editor Philip Freneau, changed all that. After a few months of decorous indecision, Freneau began viciously attacking the Hamiltonian policies of the administration in the name of the "republican interest." The two *Gazettes* soon found themselves in a partisan newspaper war with national circulation. During the start-up phase, Madison was filling Freneau's pages with anxious questions about the meaning of the new politics. A brief essay on "Parties" took a large step beyond his more famous reflections on faction in the *Federalist Papers.* As in *Federalist* no. 10, he said that parties were both "unavoidable" and "evil," but here he proposed a different cure. He no longer hoped that the Constitution would proliferate the number of quibbling factions and thereby enable nonpartisan statesmen to transcend petty politics. He now recognized that there would be only two parties, and proposed "to combat the evil" by "making one party a check on the other."[17]

This remark contained the seeds of a more modern understanding. But it was not taken up in Madison's more elaborate "A Candid State of the Parties," published in the *Gazette* as partisanship heated up with the approaching 1792 elections. Madison now endowed the emerging party system with a distinctive history. During the Revolution, he explained, the party in favor of independence set itself against the party of loyalists; then in 1787 the proposal of the Constitution once again split the people into two parties; and this party system had now been succeeded by a "third division, which being natural to most political societies, is likely to be of some duration in ours":

> One of the divisions consists of those, who from particular interest, from natural temper, or from the habits of life, are more partial to the opulent than to the other classes of society; and hav[e] debauch[ed] themselves into a persuasion that mankind are incapable of governing themselves . . . Men of those sentiments must naturally wish to point the measures of government less to the interest of the many than of a few, and . . . by giving such a turn to the administration, the government itself may by degrees be narrowed into fewer hands, and approximated to an hereditary form.
>
> The other division consists of those who, believing in the doctrine that mankind are capable of governing themselves, and hating hereditary power as an insult to the reason and outrage to the rights of man, are naturally offended at every public measure that does not appeal to the understanding and to the general interest of the community.[18]

This is the rhetoric of the revolutionary proviso. Madison is already demonizing his opponents as covert monarchists tempted by "hereditary" government. In the years ahead, Republicans would elaborate this theme with a vengeance.[19] They did not merely disagree with Hamilton's public finance; they saw it as an insidious effort to corrupt American politics by English methods. They did not merely disagree with the administration's pro-English foreign policy; they saw it as a betrayal of the liberal republican principles that the French had borrowed from the American Revolution.[20] As time went on, it became increasingly clear to the Republicans that the Washington-Adams regime was dominated by "monocrats"—Jefferson's neologism—who were hell-bent on the destruction of the republic.[21]

Within this framework, the Republicans easily acquitted themselves of the charge of factionalism by advancing onto the political stage as saviors of the republic. They were embarked—and legitimately so—on the next American Revolution, fighting the good fight against the poorly disguised successors of King George and Lord North.

The Cycle of Suppression

As the Federalist-Republican contest reached new intensity during the election of 1800, the protagonists were facing a genuinely unprecedented problem: How to reconcile the reality of party division with the anti-party understandings inherited from the past?

This question seems even more intractable when viewed in historical perspective. After two centuries, it is easy to identify the Founders' predicament as characteristic of successful colonial revolutionaries.[22] As a general rule, the retreat of the imperial power permits the ascendant revolutionary elite to indulge in the luxury of disagreement. During the period of national liberation, these disagreements are suppressed by the ever-present threat of defeat; but after the revolution, they take on a pressing urgency as the new nation defines its affirmative direction.

And yet the models of revolutionary legitimacy inherited by the elite make it terribly difficult for them to manage these disagreements in a mutually respectful fashion—with the "ins" decrying faction just as they did in the old days of revolutionary struggle, while the "outs" charge the "ins" with betraying the revolution and secretly siding with the old imperial power. The result, all too often, is a bloodbath, as the once-unified elite destroys itself in an orgy of mutual recrimination and escalating violence.

This dynamic is perfectly visible in the American case. Before 1800 the Federalists put the law behind Washington's warnings about faction by passing the Sedition Act of 1798 and launching a series of criminal prosecutions against leading Republicans, especially editors of the party's newspapers in Philadelphia, New York, Boston, and Richmond. All of these prosecutions, vigorously endorsed by Federalist judges in their charges to the grand jury, come up for trial in the election year of 1800.[23]

The Republicans responded in self-defense from their southern bas-tions of political power. In 1798 Jefferson and Madison ran the Kentucky and Virginia Resolutions through the state legislatures—challenging the Federalists' constitutional understanding of the Union, and preparing the way for more rounds of recrimination.

As the election of 1800 approached, the auguries were not auspicious for a peaceful transfer of power, and the fact that this transfer occurred at all is a great achievement—especially since the text of the original Constitution made the task harder, not easier.

The Original Understanding

The 1787 text reveals the Founders at their Enlightenment best—and worst. If politics had evolved as they expected, the Founders' design of the electoral college would have proved to be very clever. But unfortunately their scheme was not very robust and quickly collapsed under the weight of the rising party system.

Selecting a president posed one of the toughest problems for the Convention. Time and again, the delegates struggled in vain to find a solution that would command enduring support.[24] Eager to get out of Philadelphia, they finally pushed the problem onto the docket of a special committee called the "Committee of Postponed Parts," chaired by David Brearley and charged with solving previously irresolvable issues.[25] Despite the pressures of time, the delegates spent most of two days—September 5 and 6—on the Brearley proposals.[26] As we shall see, their final solution reveals telltale signs of inattention to crucial details. Though their eyes may have wandered toward the exits, the Philadelphians did display a good deal of intelligent institutional engineering. We shall never appreciate their ingenuity unless we see the problem within their anti-party framework.

Since the Founders were clueless about the operation of a two-party system, they did not hit upon the solution that seems obvious to us: design a system under which each party nominates a presidential ticket. Instead of delegating the nomination function to the parties, they supposed the Constitution itself had to provide a non-party mechanism that picked out the best candidates.

Grandees like Washington were the ideal. Notables of this caliber did not gain prominence by making demagogic appeals to the public. They proved their high "public character" by years of selfless service to the republic. Yet there was no assurance that such figures would be in great supply. Politics was emphatically local. Commercial and landed elites might compete endlessly for attention in each of the states, but few local leaders had a chance to prove their mettle on a nationwide basis. As the Framers well understood, the war against England gave them exceptional opportunities to project themselves onto the continental stage. By serving in the patriots' army, Washington and others could demonstrate their republican virtue—or lack of it—to an attentive audience in all thirteen states; the problems of wartime coordination also required civilian politicians to engage in extraordinary levels of interstate interaction—and mutual assessment. But in more normal times, would there be a steady supply of "continental characters"?[27]

The optimists believed that "Continental Characters will multiply as we more & more coalesce";[28] but others were not so sure.[29] Unless some steps were taken, wouldn't each state's electors get together and vote for a favorite son, leading to a scattering of regional favorites when all the votes were counted?

Here is where the Founders tried to economize on the short supply of truly national leaders through clever institutional engineering. Why not give *two* votes to each elector, but allow him to cast only one for a citizen from his own state. Gouverneur Morris explained: "as one vote is to be given to a man out of the State, and as this vote will not be thrown away, 1/2 the votes will fall on characters eminent & generally known."[30]

At this point a second ingenious feature of the original machinery appears to view. Suppose, as was the case in 1800, that the electoral college contained 138 members, who cast 276 votes. Under the 1787 Constitution, the top choice would become president provided that his name appeared on 70 of the 276 ballots; and the second choice would become vice president.[31] In other words, the aim of this Enlightenment machine was to create the artificial impression that the president was a man of truly national character even if the pickings were pretty slim. A man could become president if he was the second choice of a bare majority of the electors.

Even this expedient might sometimes fail to produce the simulacrum of a George Washington. Politics might become so state-centered that nobody could gain a minimal level of national support. How, then, to proceed?

The Brearley Committee proposed a backup procedure under which the president would be selected by the Senate from the top five vote-getters in the electoral college.[32] But this was resisted on the ground that the Senate had already been given many special powers, and that granting it additional prerogatives would give the entire system an "aristocratic complexion."[33] The objection proved persuasive, leading to the adoption of the most peculiar voting system known to the Constitution.

The Convention shifted the locus of authority from the Senate to the House, but retained the Senate's principle of equality in state voting power. For presidential purposes only, each state delegation in the House would cast a single vote—Delaware's single representative and Virginia's large delegation counting equally[34]—and the balloting would proceed until a candidate received the votes of an absolute majority of the states.[35]

This transformation of the People's House into a state-centered assembly may seem odd to us, but it made quite a bit of sense in the eighteenth century. To put the point in numerical terms: If no single candidate in 1800 could garner 70 of the 276 votes cast by 138 electors, this suggested that American politics had taken an emphatically decentralizing turn. As a consequence, shouldn't the backup mechanism also take a decentralizing turn by giving an equal vote to each state in the Union?

Perhaps, but strong nationalists like Madison and Hamilton weren't convinced. They wanted to eliminate the backup procedure, or at least reduce the frequency of its use.[36] These efforts were successfully resisted by the small states—who feared that electors from the largest states might otherwise dictate the choice of the president when a broader consensus on a suitable candidate was lacking.[37]

The small states won this particular battle, but the debate diverted the Convention from a second design issue. This involved a mathematical oddity arising from the complexities of the emerging design. Since each elector could vote for two candidates, it was now mathematically possible for several names to turn up on a majority of ballots—indeed, two could even end up in a dead heat, with each winning, say, 73 votes. How, then, to break *this* type of tie?

The question raises very different issues from those involved when *no* presidential candidate has gained widespread support. In the no-majority case, the small states could reasonably suppose that the electoral college leader would be a "favorite son" from one or another big state—after all,

these local candidates could fish from a larger pool of electors than notables from small states. Since the small states would not play a major role in
nominating candidates, they might plausibly insist on greater importance
in the House runoff.

The small states had much less of a grievance when two candidates
tied with the same majority vote. Under this scenario, it was highly likely
that *both* candidates gathered their 73 votes by collecting electors from
states of all sizes. In contrast to the no-majority case, there was a vanish-
ingly small bias against the small states in the tied-majority case. In other
words, the Founders' weird voting rule—under which each House delegation cast a single ballot to select a president—made very little sense when
two broad-based candidacies gained precisely the same number of votes.

The delegates might have noticed this point if they had given themselves more time. They were formidable issue-spotters, and had identified
an analogous problem in an earlier debate.[38] But time was running short
in September when the Brearley proposals came to the floor, and nobody
focused on the question in the rush to resolve more contentious issues.

The Founders' lapse may be extenuated if we recall that they were leg-
islating for a world without national political parties. In such a world, centuries might go by without a dead heat between two candidates who both
won a majority vote. Didn't the Convention have better things to do than
design a brand-new system for such an unlikely possibility?

In any event, the Convention merely changed a single rule to take this
odd case into account. If two candidates tied with a majority vote, the
Constitution provided that only these two would enter the House runoff.
When all candidates fell short of a majority, the five leading candidates
would enter the runoff, even if the top two were tied.

This minor tweak would cause big trouble in 1800, putting Thomas
Jefferson in a deeply compromising position at a crucial moment in the
vote count. Before turning to this fascinating story, consider the deeper
reasons for the failure of the Founders' intricate mechanism.

The Machine that Failed

To sum up, the rise of national parties had turned the Convention's pretty
piece of Enlightenment machinery upside down. There was no longer a

need for a complicated procedure to give each state's politicians an incentive to transcend localism and select a leader of truly continental standing. Congressional caucuses of Republican and Federalist loyalists could do this work on their own by nominating a national ticket and campaigning for competing slates of partisan electors who would enter the names of their party's favorites on their ballots.

Worse yet, the Founders' machine would systematically malfunction in the new environment. Each party would designate a candidate for president and another for vice president. But the Founders had made it impossible for the electors to rank their two choices. To tame the beast of localism, they had required each elector to cast two votes for the presidency, insisting that at least one choice come from out of state. Unless the parties took special care, the Founders' odd case of a tie vote would become the standard case—with each party's electors casting their votes for the same two party favorites. The winning ticket would end in a dead heat, throwing the election into the House—with the single representative from Delaware counting as much as the entire delegation from Pennsylvania or Virginia.

The states were also unprepared for the onslaught of party competition. Their methods for selecting electors were very much in flux—in 1796 six states had opted for popular election and ten had given the job to the legislature. They also differed on whether the winning candidate was allowed to take all the electoral votes, with some devising systems for splitting the vote in rough proportion to popular sentiment.

The approach of the elections of 1800 provoked fierce partisan jockeying. The Republicans in Virginia changed their system to deprive the Federalist minority of any electoral votes; the Federalists in New England responded in kind. Partisanship led to a sustained deadlock in Pennsylvania, threatening to disable the state from casting its fifteen votes. (In the end, the Federalist Senate and the Republican House struck a deal to split the vote 8 to 7.) After all this partisan maneuvering, the electoral college count probably provided a less reliable indicator of voter sentiment in 1800 than in 1796.[39]

The election was a drawn out and bitterly partisan affair. Since each state chose its own election day, the selection process began with New York in April and ended with South Carolina in early October.[40] It was a horse race right down to the wire. After South Carolina's Federalists swept

Charleston, the overall result was too close to call—with the final decision on electors made by the state legislature, not by the voters directly. In a chaotic legislative session, the Republicans managed to win all eight of the state's electoral votes, pushing the Jefferson-Burr ticket over the top by an electoral college vote of 73 to 65.[41]

Unfortunately the Republicans lost sight of the Founders' obsolete "two vote" rule. None of the party's electors contrived to give Jefferson a one-vote victory over Burr by voting for a different candidate in his second spot.[42] The Federalists were craftier—they made sure that John Adams received one more electoral vote than their vice-presidential candidate, Charles Cotesworth Pinckney, by arranging for a single Federalist elector to cast his second ballot for John Jay.

As a consequence, Jefferson and Burr each received 73 votes. This would have been a minor inconvenience but for another Founding blunder. The Republicans had not only won the presidency but swept into the House as well. If the newly elected House had gotten the chance to resolve the runoff, the Republican majority would have awarded Jefferson the presidency on its first ballot. But in a fit of inadvertence, the Founding Fathers had allowed the lame-duck House of Representatives, elected in 1798, to serve the tie-breaking function, and thereby set the stage for a major crisis.

The Jeffersonians had suffered a big defeat in 1798. As spirited defenders of the French Revolution throughout the decade, they paid a heavy political price when the revolution lurched out of control, especially when the French began to seize increasing numbers of American ships on the high seas. The crowning insult came with the XYZ Affair, precipitated by the French foreign minister's demand of a bribe before he would even consider American complaints. The Federalists skillfully exploited the wave of patriotism that followed, winning a landslide victory in the House elections.[43]

All that was in the past. Although the Republicans were now winning the House elections, the Constitution allowed the lame-duck Federalist House to choose the next president. This blunder—whose genesis I will explain in due course—transformed a minor mismanagement of the Republican electors into a recipe for a major crisis. As a shocked Jefferson told Monroe: "[A]fter the most energetic efforts, crowned with success, we remain in the hands of our enemies by want of foresight in the original arrangement [that is, by having failed to instruct one elector to leave Burr off his ballot]."[44]

Paradoxically, the worst effects of this Founding blunder were somewhat ameliorated by another curious aspect of the Convention's design: its adoption of the special "one state–one vote" rule. By sheer accident, this unique mechanism had a positive effect on the outcome: though Federalists were in solid control of the House under the normal voting rules, their members were concentrated in the North. When the presidential balloting began, Federalists controlled only six states, while the more diffusely distributed Republicans controlled eight, with two (Vermont and Maryland) split evenly and failing to cast a ballot.[45]

Eight states were not enough to elect a president. The Constitution required the winning candidate to gain the affirmative votes of an absolute majority: since sixteen states were then in the Union, nine votes were needed. If a very few Republicans could be seduced, the presidency would fall to Burr, who might run a coalition government with moderate Federalists. Even if the Federalists did not elect Burr, they could block Jefferson by remaining steadfast—opening the way, as we shall see, to a variety of constitutional manipulations that might end in depriving both Jefferson *and* Burr of the presidency.

For the Republicans, the right way to resolve the impasse was clear enough. The Federalists should stop playing constitutional games and listen to the voice of the People—who, by supporting the Republican party in the elections, had *obviously* intended Jefferson to be president, Burr vice president: "If the voice of the people of America be at all regarded, Mr. Jefferson will be preferred to Mr. Burr," as "Aristides" explained in the Republican *National Intelligencer*.[46]

Aristides was unsparing in his critique. The Federalist lame ducks simply had no authority to displace the considered judgment of the American people: "the House of Representatives chosen two years ago, as it at present stands on the verge of political dissolution, is not the Representative of the people at this time." And the Convention's concession to small states made the distortion even worse: "voting by states, [the House] would be the representative, not of the people, but of the states only."[47] Jefferson had a mandate from the People, and that was that—"the real representatives of the people hold opinions absolutely in collision with their present nominal representatives." The emerging system of two-party competition had generated a form of democratic authority superior to the merely legal legitimacy derived by the manipulation of constitutional forms.

The Federalists were not convinced. As their newspapers repeatedly pointed out, the Republicans owed their narrow victory in the electoral college to the Constitution's notorious compromise with slavery, under which the South gained an electoral college bonus equal to three-fifths of its slave population. In the election of 1800 this provision gave Jefferson and Burr extra electoral votes for their sweep of the South. Federalist papers proffered their readers mathematical calculations establishing that Adams and Pinckney would have come out ahead were it not for the nefarious compromise with slavery:

> Thus we have proved, by numerical calculation, that a majority of the freemen, of the United States have *really* elected Mr. Adams, to the Presidency, and Mr. Pinckney, to the Vice Presidency. But the absurd policy of representing the neg[r]oes of the southern states . . . will probably elevate to the presidential chair, two citizens, who as they are the *men of the people,* and the *guardians of liberty,* will feel neither gratified nor honored, by the reflection, that they are about to ride into the TEMPLE OF LIBERTY, upon the *shoulders of slaves.*[48]

The impending deadlock in the House was pushing both sides beyond the constitutional rules to the foundational ideal of popular sovereignty—twisting the principle in partisan directions. The Republicans, after all, were the partisans of states' rights, but this wasn't preventing them from decrying the operation of the "one state–one vote" rule in the House runoff. They were insisting instead that the House recognize that Jefferson, not Burr, was the considered choice of the American people.

The Federalists' counterargument was more in character, since their unease with the constitutional compromise with slavery was real, if intermittent.[49] Their strategic aim in raising the issue was clear enough—to carve out moral and political space to give them a large degree of freedom in the pushing and shoving that lay ahead. If Republican talk of a popular "revolution" was disingenuous poppycock, poorly disguising the victory of the slave power, the Federalists were well within their rights to demand reassurances from Jefferson on policy and personnel before handing him the presidency. And if he refused to deal, there was nothing wrong with using the constitutional rules to deny him power entirely and give the Federalist party a new lease on life.

After all, the rules of the game are the rules of the game, aren't they? And wouldn't Jefferson be a spoilsport if he refused to accept defeat, merely because he had won the election?

2

John Marshall for President

The lame-duck Congress was the first to forsake cosmopolitan Philadelphia for the humble village that bore the proud name of Washington. Albert Gallatin, the sober leader of the House Republicans, described the dismal scene to his wife: "Our local situation is far from being pleasant or even convenient. Around the Capitol are seven or eight boarding-houses, one tailor, one shoemaker, one printer, a washing-woman, a grocery shop, a pamphlets and stationery shop, a small dry-goods shop, and an oyster house. This makes the whole of the Federal city as connected with the Capitol."[1]

The lame-duck session began on November 22, but Congress was officially scheduled to count the electoral votes and move into the tie-breaking procedure on Wednesday, February 11, 1801—giving the protagonists ten weeks to wheel, deal, and demonize one another. Gallatin was soon feeling stir-crazy, writing to his wife:

> As to politics, you may suppose that being all thrown together in a few boarding-houses, without hardly any other society than ourselves, we are not likely to be either very moderate politicians or to think of anything but politics. A few, indeed, drink, and some gamble, but the majority drink naught but politics, and by not mixing with men of different or moderate sentiments, they inflame one another. On that account, principally, I see some danger in the fate of the election which I had not before contemplated. I do not know precisely what are the plans of the New England and other violent Federals, nor, indeed, that they have formed any final plan; but I am certain that if they can prevail on three or four men who hold the balance, they will attempt to defeat the election under pretence of voting for Burr.[2]

Federalists, for their part, were already discussing the distribution of ministries in a Burr government. Timothy Pickering sized up the situation in the first week of January: "I am rather inclined to think that Mr. Burr will be preferred . . . General Marshall will then remain in the department of state; but if Mr. Jefferson be chosen, Mr. Marshall will retire."[3] General Marshall is, of course, John, who had been named secretary of state in 1800 after a fierce partisan struggle, but had not yet been favored by President Adams with the chief justiceship. At that time he was probably the most popular Federalist politician on the national stage. A Burr-Marshall coalition would have been a formidable political force.

While the Federalists' effort to amass nine states for Burr provided the centerpiece for all the scheming, a second question loomed ominously in the background. Even if the Federalists were unsuccessful in seducing the small number of Republicans they needed to win nine states for Burr, they were in a very strong position to deprive Jefferson of victory, and thereby throw the House proceeding into unending deadlock: if neither Jefferson nor Burr won nine votes by March 4, who would become president at the end of Adams's term in office?

In its rush to the finish line, the Convention missed this issue entirely. In a breathtaking show of incompetent draftsmanship, the delegates failed to provide an explicit answer to this obvious question—"open[ing] upon us an abyss," said Jefferson, "at which every sincere patriot must shudder."[4]

But the legal mind abhors a vacuum. While the protagonists recognized that the Convention had blundered, this did not prevent them from searching through the constitutional text for bits and pieces that might be used to construct the legal foundation for a default solution.[5]

The Interpretive Options

The key provision turned out to be in section 1 of Article II:

> In case of the removal of the President from office or of his death, resignation or inability to discharge the power and duties of the said office, the same shall devolve on the Vice President, and the Congress may by law provide for the case of removal, death, resignation or inability, of both President and Vice President, declaring what of-

ficer shall then act as President, and such officer shall act accordingly
until the disability be removed or a President shall be elected.

This provision was originally intended to authorize congressional action
if some physical "inability" prevented both president and vice president
from completing the terms to which they were elected. Since President
John Adams and Vice President Thomas Jefferson were both hale and
hearty on March 4, 1801, their "inability" to continue in office was not
physical but legal—their four-year terms had expired. But this inability
was no less real than the physical kind, and since it caused a vacancy,
shouldn't the text be read broadly, authorizing Congress to fill the vacancy by statute?

A well-drafted Constitution would have made such tea-leaf reading
unnecessary. Partisans on both sides were stuck with what they had, and—
surprise, surprise—they disagreed about its constitutional meaning.

Those who adopted the broad textual reading had one great advantage—they could point to a path for resolving the crisis that, all things
considered, was about as sensible as circumstances allowed. The solution
was part of a more general effort by Congress to regulate presidential selection. When the first group of presidential electors convened to select
Washington in 1789, Congress had not yet met; but as the next election
approached, Congress passed a statute in 1792 that confronted many of
the obvious problems left by the text, including the question of what
should happen if both president and vice president were unable to discharge their offices.[6]

And remarkably enough, this statutory solution turned out to be pe-
culiarly suitable for use in the looming deadlock. It did not simply name
an official—say, the secretary of state or the speaker of the House—to
serve out the rest of the term vacated by the president and vice president.
It provided that a double vacancy should trigger a brand-new election for
the presidency. The statute gives a detailed description of the special procedure—instructing the secretary of state to call the new election, solving
a number of problems that might come up in its administration, and providing that the newly elected president and vice president would not
merely fill out the previous incumbents' terms in office, but would serve
an entire four-year term (sec. 12). No less important, it provided for a
smooth transition by naming the president pro tem of the Senate as interim president (sec. 10).

Given this statutory structure, a broad reading of the Constitution seemed to provide a sensible stopgap if the House failed to name a president by March 4. Rather than yielding chaos, a House deadlock could simply trigger a special election, with the president pro tem of the Senate serving as president in the meantime. But was it proper to stretch a constitutional provision intended for dying or disabled officials to cover a case of a legal vacancy generated by a deadlock in the House?

Different participants gave different answers. Many Republicans predictably denounced any Federalist effort to invoke the statute. So far as they were concerned, Jefferson had already won a mandate from the People, and it was up to the Federalists in the House to recognize this fact. Federalists took a different view, and only abandoned the statutory option under pressure and with reluctance.[7]

Or more precisely, the Federalists had two statutory options. On the one hand, they could simply invoke the 1792 statute and put the president pro tem of the Senate into the president's chair during the special election. On the other, they could use their majorities in the House and the Senate to pass a new succession statute naming somebody else as interim president—for example, John Marshall, thereby giving their most popular candidate the advantage of campaigning for the presidency as the incumbent.

Republicans who denounced the Federalists' statutory options as unconstitutional also confronted a good deal of strategic complexity. During the run-up to March 4, they would predictably use their "strict construction" of Article II as a weapon in the struggle to get the House to name Jefferson as president: "Unless you Federalists end the deadlock, and allow Jefferson's election, the presidency will fall vacant and the federal government will come to an end!" But if this game of chicken failed and the House remained deadlocked on March 4, the strict constructionists would then be in a bind. On their reading, the presidency would be vacant, and the Constitution provided no way of filling it. What should happen next?

After all, Americans would have to get out of the Founding morass, somehow or other. Even though their proposal might not be legal or constitutional, didn't the Republicans owe the nation a way out of the dilemma? I will call this their search for an *unconventional solution*.

It is, I suppose, a tribute to the vitality of the American legal mind that *all* these themes—and many ingenious variations—were vigorously developed in the days and weeks to come. Would any of them manage to contain the bitter struggle that loomed ahead?

Madison's Proposal

As sitting vice president, Jefferson was in Washington when he heard the news of the electoral college deadlock, and in his first letter to Madison he was already focusing on the proliferating possibilities. On December 19 he was reporting: "[T]here will be an absolute parity between the two republican candidates. This has produced great dismay and gloom on the republican gentlemen here, and equal exultation on the federalists, who openly declare they will prevent an election, and will name a President of the Senate, *pro tem.* by what they say would only be a *stretch* of the constitution."[8] A week later Jefferson wrote to Madison about the alternative statutory scenario: "The federalists appear determined to prevent an election, and to pass a bill giving the government to Mr. Jay, reappointed Chief Justice, or to Marshall as Secretary of State."[9]

As the new year dawned, Madison wrote back to explore unconventional responses:

> On the supposition of . . . an interregnum in the Executive, or of a surreptitious intrusion into it, it becomes a question of the first order, what is the course demanded by the crisis. Will it be best to acquiesce in a suspension or usurpation of the Executive authority till the meeting of Congs. in De^r. next, or for Congs. to be summoned by a joint proclamation or recommendation of the two characters havg a majority of votes for President. My present judgment favors the latter expedient. The prerogative of convening the Legislature must reside in one or other of them, and if both concur, must substantially include the requisite will. The intentions of the people would undoubtedly be pursued. And if, in reference to the Constn: the proceeding be not strictly regular, the irregularity will be less in form than any other adequate to the emergency; and it will lie in form only rather than substance; whereas the other remedies proposed [by the Federalists] are substantial violations of the will of the people, of the scope of the Constitution, and of the public

order & interest. It is to be hoped however that all such questions will be precluded by a proper decision of nine States in the H. of R.[10]

Madison's strategic objective is clear. If the lame-duck House refuses to elect Jefferson, let's get the new one into town as soon as possible— since Republicans would outnumber Federalists by two to one in the new House, they would have no trouble delivering nine states to Jefferson as soon as they came to Washington.

To be sure, the written Constitution did not give the Republican front-runners any legal authority to summon Congress, nor did it legally empower the new House to name a new president. But these "irregularit[ies] . . . lie in form only" while the Federalist "remedies . . . are substantial violations of the will of the people, of the scope of the Constitution, and of the public order & interest."[11] This letter to Jefferson is dated January 10, but similar Madisonian missives were already circulating among politicians of both parties in Washington, D.C.[12]

The Federalists' Reply

As the Republicans began contemplating unconventional action, Federalists were publicly wrapping themselves in the written Constitution. A powerful essay, appearing under the name "Horatius," was printed twice in newspapers circulating in the Washington area—on January 2 in the *Alexandria Advertiser,* and on January 6 in the *Washington Federalist.* Provocatively entitled "The Presidential Knot," the essay proposes to cut through the impending constitutional crisis with 2,500 words of finely honed legal argument.

After describing the likely prospect of a House deadlock, Horatius sets out to eliminate the Madisonian solution from the field of play. The written Constitution, he emphasizes, provides that "the House of Representatives shall *immediately* chuse, by ballot, one" of the contenders: "The choice is required to be *immediately made,* in order that the result may be declared in the presence of the Senate, and to prevent the possibility of intrigue and corruption. The choice must be therefore made before the house adjourns or disperses, and after the convention of the Senate and

House of Representatives terminates, the house cannot at a future day act upon this subject."

Horatius does not explicitly describe Madison's proposal, but any knowledgeable politician would have understood the point: Madison's opinions notwithstanding, the Republican effort to resolve the deadlock by an appeal to the newly elected House is nothing less than an all-out assault on the Constitution.

After giving Madison's unconventional ruminations the back of his hand, Horatius confronts the Republicans' efforts to create a constitutional crisis: "Some gentlemen," he explains, are "over zealous for the success of Mr. Jefferson, [and] utter threats that unless he is elected the government shall be at an end. Menaces of this kind are always unbecoming and at no time to be regarded, and the writer of these observations, being by no means inclined to give the preference to Mr. Burr, regrets that they were not repressed."

In contrast to Republican hotheads, Horatius casts himself as a cool legalist seeking to resolve the crisis through the power of reason alone. He begins with the relevant provisions regulating presidential succession in Article II, and predictably opts for a broad reading of the key phrase: "inability to discharge the power and duties of said office." On his view, there is no reason to restrict this term to physical incapacity: "[I]n the interpretation of a written constitution or form of government, that interpretation is never to be made which will frustrate the end of the . . . constitution," which in this case is "self preservation."

Having cleared a constitutional path for congressional action, Horatius then takes a surprising turn. As we have seen, the succession statute of 1792 required new elections to fill vacancies—a procedure that seemed to be the best possible way of resolving an impasse in the House. What is more, that statute would have allowed the Federalist Senate to appoint one of their partisans as interim president—a prospect that the *Washington Federalist* ought to have found pleasing.

And yet Horatius rejects this obvious solution. According to him, Congress had not only made a bad choice in 1792 in designating the president pro tem of the Senate as interim president; it had acted *unconstitutionally,* and as a consequence, the lame-duck Congress was absolutely required to pass a new statute to fill the resulting gap.

To make his case, Horatius once again returns to the text, emphasizing that the language of Article II limits succession to "officers." On his view, this term signifies only federal officials who have "received their commissions and appointments from the President, according to which criterion the President of the Senate pro tempore is not an officer." He buttresses this claim by citing the Senate's refusal to impeach one of its colleagues, William Blount, on the ground that he was a member of Congress and not an "officer of the United States" as required by the impeachment clause. By parity of reasoning, the senator chosen as president pro tem does not qualify as an "officer" and so cannot constitutionally succeed to the presidency.

Horatius also denies that the statute of 1792 can be saved by recourse to the great residual source of congressional power: the "necessary and proper" clause. Where, as here, there is a clause explicitly directed to the problem of presidential succession, it should serve as the exclusive source of constitutional authority—especially when the necessary and proper clause would authorize Congress to appoint a "member out of their own body [who] may continue in office for the whole term of the ensuing four years, or perhaps longer."

There is only one way to cut the "presidential knot." If the House deadlocks, the lame-duck Federalist Congress and president should, as one of their final acts, pass a new statute naming an "officer of the United States" to serve as president instead of Thomas Jefferson. And who might that "officer" be?

Horatius is silent on this matter, but there could be little doubt that the palm would go to Secretary of State John Marshall. As a matter of protocol, his cabinet position was the first created in 1789, and so Marshall served as the senior "officer" of the United States; as a matter of politics, Marshall was the most popular Federalist leader of the moment—probably the only man acceptable both to the Adams and Hamilton wings of the party.[13] Once he took up residence in the President's House, he would have been the obvious man for the Federalists to rally a round in a last desperate campaign to prevent the atheist and Francophile Jefferson from coming to power.[14]

The *Washington Federalist* was, in short, offering to cut two presidential knots at once. It was not only denouncing as revolutionary any Jeffersonian effort to resolve the deadlock by an unconventional appeal to the next House of Representatives. It was telling the Federalists of the existing

Congress that the Constitution, properly construed, imposed on them the high responsibility to take statutory action to promote their own leading presidential candidate to the President's House!

It would be a bad mistake to dismiss Horatius's aggressive conclusions as the ravings of a heated partisan. To the contrary, the legal argumentation is of the highest quality, and the best modern scholarship suggests that Horatius had a very good legal point. There are indeed powerful reasons against allowing Congress to promote one of its own members to the presidency. His insistence that Congress appoint an "officer" appointed by the president makes good constitutional sense.[15]

Whatever its abstract legal merit, Horatius's conclusion could not have been more inflammatory in the context of 1801. Republicans were already denouncing Federalist efforts to place Burr into the presidency in defiance of their party's campaign for Jefferson. But their protests would have escalated to dangerous levels if their opponents denied *both* candidates the electoral prize and exploited legal technicalities to enable John Marshall to sit in the President's House and run for a full term in a special election.

The written Constitution was fast becoming a partisan weapon in the new world of party politics.[16] Rather than smoothing the path of democratic transition, it was disrupting an already tense situation. Part of the problem was bad draftsmanship, which allowed Horatius to play the game of legalistic reasoning without an adequate set of rules to cover the case at hand. This point, while important, should not lead us to ignore the deeper source of the potential conflict: the Republicans were operating on an understanding of the presidency that had simply been unknown at the time the Convention was writing down its rules. Call it the *plebiscitary theory:* Jefferson had become the People's choice for president since his party had put him at the top of their ticket and had won electoral support in the electoral campaigns around the country. Since the Founders had not foreseen the rise of parties, they could hardly conjure with the plebiscitary theory. Little wonder, then, that their constitutional text could generate an outcome so greatly at variance with its dictates—and that the Republicans could question the good faith of men, like Horatius, who aggressively pushed legalism in the Federalist direction.

The *Washington Federalist* was the party's paper in the new capital, and it was voraciously devoured by politicos. Though Jefferson was already writing privately about the threat of a Marshall presidency, the fact that the Federalists had gone public made the prospect far more serious. So far as the Republicans were concerned, Marshall was emerging as a potential leader of a constitutional coup.

Matters reached tragicomic heights later in the month when Adams named Marshall to the Supreme Court, asking him also to stay on as secretary of state. As the Founding system spun out of control, Marshall loomed as acting secretary of state, permanent chief justice of the Supreme Court, and potential interim president of the United States![17]

Who Dunnit?

And we have not yet glimpsed the worst of it. To put the point gently, there is substantial reason to believe that the brilliant author of the Horatius essay was none other than John Marshall himself.

This was the view of Marshall's great biographer of the early twentieth century, Albert Beveridge, though his enthusiasm for his hero blinded him to the damaging implications of his conclusion.[18] More curiously, Beveridge's discovery has almost entirely dropped from view in our more scientific and skeptical age. I have found only one passing mention of it during the past half-century of scholarship,[19] and the Horatius essay is not even mentioned, much less reproduced, in the authoritative edition of John Marshall's papers painstakingly edited by a team of scholars under the general editorship of Herbert A. Johnson and Charles E. Hobson. In response to my inquiry, Professor Hobson explained the omission:

> I am afraid there is nothing in our collection that can confirm Marshall as the author of the "Horatius" essay. I would be skeptical of Beveridge and even more skeptical of the political gossip and rumors of the time that pointed to M. as the author of this piece and of much of what appeared in the *Washington Federalist*. We certainly would have published it as a Marshall document if there was some stronger proof than that collected by Beveridge.[20]

In the five years since I received Professor Hobson's letter, I've been puttering around for "stronger proof," since I very much agree with Beveridge that Horatius's presentation is "so perfectly in Marshall's method of reasoning and peculiar style of expression that his authorship would appear to be reasonably certain."[21]

In contrast to the discoveries about Thomas Jefferson to be presented in Chapter 3, I can't claim to have discovered conclusive proof, but the bits and pieces do add up to something pretty substantial.[22] I have reprinted Horatius's essay at the end of this book to allow you to consider the matter yourself.

I organize my detective report in terms of Marshall's opportunities, interest, and "political gossip and rumors."

Opportunities

Beveridge came upon Horatius in the January 6 issue of the *Washington Federalist,* but the article was actually published first by the *Advertiser* of Alexandria, Virginia, on January 2. This discovery will enter several times in my detective report, but for starters, it suggests that Horatius didn't have much time to write his very polished and sophisticated essay. News of the tie between Jefferson and Burr reached Washington on or about December 18,[23] giving Horatius less than two weeks to dash off his 2,500 words and arrange for publication. But the second of these weeks was Christmas, so it seems realistic to suppose that the essay was finished in a week or so, and that the author was a Washingtonian, or he could not have made the necessary arrangements.

A week is a short time to produce such a polished product, but Marshall was a very fast worker. For example, the only time he entered the newspaper wars as a judge, he managed to write nine essays of Horatian length in about two weeks.[24] There were very, very few people in the Washington area with the Federalist convictions, the constitutional sophistication, the brainpower, and the powerful prose style to carry this off, and almost all would arrive in late November for the opening of Congress. Marshall, in contrast, had been stuck in Washington since June, when President Adams put his secretary of state in charge of handling government business while he himself deserted the swampy capital village for the summer, to return from Massachusetts in early November.[25] So compared with most other potential Horatians, Marshall was relatively well settled by Christmas—he had the priceless luxury of his own office as secretary of state, and he could spend some undistracted hours at work while others were crowding into noisy boarding houses.

There were almost no well-established lawyers in Washington. The Census of November 1800 reports 501 "heads of household" in the "City" (2,500 white residents in all, many illiterate) and among them, only a handful of lawyers.[26] In searching for suspects, we should also consider more established places nearby—Georgetown (containing 3,400 whites) and Alexandria (3,700 whites).

The Federalist attorney general, Charles Lee, was a resident of Alexandria, a personal friend of Marshall, and a man of substantial legal abilities.[27] His sole known entry into popular polemics suggests an un-Horatian sensibility. Writing as "Virginiensis" in 1798, Lee published a 48-page pamphlet defending the constitutionality of the Federalists' Alien and Sedition Acts.[28] In contrast to Horatius's cool and disciplined essay, Lee's pamphlet indulges in many oratorical flourishes as it rambles through its legal arguments. Perhaps Lee performed best under severe time pressure, and his desire to publish quickly as Horatius led him to a newfound clarity. But generally speaking, great haste leads to greater prolixity. In contrast, Marshall had already amply displayed his remarkable capacity to write with both speed and elegance.

I have also investigated other well-established residents of the Washington area, and they all seem less likely candidates than Lee.[29] So if the writer wasn't Marshall, he was probably some Federalist who came to town for the opening of Congress in late November. Yet newcomers would have had trouble arranging for publication—not once, but twice, in rapid succession. Not Marshall: he had intimate connections with the publishers of the papers in Alexandria and Washington, both brand-new operations seeking to take advantage of Washington's new prominence.

Begin with Marshall's links to Samuel Snowden of the *Alexandria Advertiser*. Snowden had initially planned the *Advertiser* as a Washington paper. On July 22, 1800, he announced in the Georgetown *Centinel of Liberty* his intention to establish the *"Washington Advertiser"*; on August 12, 1800, he issued a prospectus. Only after publishing one Washington issue in early November did he move his paper across the Potomac to Alexandria. Between July and November Snowden was the prospective publisher of the only Federalist newspaper in town,[30] and Marshall was the

Federalist actually in charge of the government. Since Washington was a mere village, it's hard to believe that Federalist editor and Federalist statesman didn't cross paths.

By the time most other leading Federalists arrived for Congress, Snowden was setting up shop in Alexandria. Of course, he might well have been bobbing back and forth across the Potomac during the early days of the session; and he might well have been friends with other Federalists. Nevertheless, Marshall had an exceptionally favorable opportunity to get in touch with Snowden and arrange for quick publication.

What is more, there is hard proof that Marshall used Snowden as a publisher when he returned to the newspaper wars to defend his great decision of 1819, McCulloch v. Maryland. Nobody knew about these essays until Gerald Gunther discovered them in the 1960s, but his archival work provides some clues for our own newspaper-hunt. As Gunther tells the story, Marshall asked his colleague Bushrod Washington to use the *Gazette and Daily Advertiser* in Alexandria, Virginia, to publish nine essays that he had prepared under the pseudonym "Friend of the Constitution."[31] While the newspaper had changed its name since 1801, the publisher hadn't: Samuel Snowden was still in charge.[32] And Marshall's instructions to Bushrod Washington are revealing:

> I find myself more stimulated on this subject than on any other because I believe the design to be to injure the Judges & impair the constitution. I have therefore thoughts of answering these essays & sending my pieces to you for publication in the Alexandria paper . . . As the numbers will be marked I hope no mistake will be made by the printer & that the manuscript will be given to the flames. I wish two papers of each number to be directed to T. Marshall, Oak Hill, Fauquier. I do not wish them to come to me lest some suspicion of the author should be created.[33]

Marshall was obviously concerned about maintaining his anonymity, and his mailing instructions may have sufficed to hide his authorship from nosy post-riders, neighbors, and servants. But they wouldn't have hidden it from Snowden: imagine Washington—who is, after all, a Supreme Court justice—coming to the publisher's door and telling him to send a couple of copies of each essay to "T. Marshall." It wouldn't take much imagination on Snowden's part to suspect that Bushrod was acting as a literary agent for the great chief justice. As an experienced diplomat and statesmen, Marshall would have been well aware of such an obvious risk. Alexandria is but a stone's throw from the gossipy capital. If Marshall had not been absolutely confident in Snowden, he would have taken greater care to hide his identity—but perhaps Snowden had already proved his discretion in the Horatius affair.

There is another obvious possibility: perhaps Marshall's confidence in Snowden arose not from the Horatius episode but from covert dealings during the eighteen-year interval between 1801 and 1819. Gunther assures us, however, that Marshall's essays of 1819 are "the only newspaper replies of his judicial career."[34] In contrast, before becoming a judge, Marshall had defended the Washington administration in a Richmond newspaper, writing first as "Aristides" and then as "Gracchus"—classical references that resonate with "Horatius."[35] If he had connected with Snowden in 1801, he was simply continuing his career as a controversialist, and it is perfectly plausible that he retired from the fray when he became a judge—only to return to it in 1819 upon extreme provocation.

So the discovery that Horatius first published in Alexandria, not Washington, is significant. It both suggests that Marshall could more easily arrange for rapid publication than many other leading Federalists and provides evidence of his confidence that Snowden could be trusted with the publication of pseudonymous essays.

Marshall's connections to William Rind, the publisher of the *Washington Federalist,* are even clearer. Rind was working at the *Virginia Federalist* in Richmond in 1799, when Marshall was running a successful race for Congress.[36] By September 1800 he had moved to Georgetown, where he began publishing the *Federalist* before moving his press to Washington—announcing Snowden's departure to Alexandria in the November 25 edition of his newly designated *Washington Federalist.* As a fellow citizen of Richmond, and the new voice of Federalism in the capitol, Rind must have reestablished contact with the secretary of state very quickly—and there is abundant contemporary evidence of Marshall's ongoing connection with the editorial content of the paper, as we shall see later in this chapter.[37]

Marshall stands out from the pack in terms of opportunity. Not only was he in a good position to write the essay, he was in a great position to arrange publication at both papers.

Interest

And Marshall would be the big winner if Horatius's arguments ultimately prevailed. If Horatius had been prudently considering the larger interests of his party, he would have contented himself with a more modest argument, calling upon the Federalists to invoke the Succession Act of 1792 to appoint one of their senators as acting president while a special election took place. This would have allowed the Federalists to maintain control of the presidency in the short term without enraging Republicans by passing a brand-new statute granting the interim presidency to their best candidate for a full term in office.

But Horatius was no sober defender of a well-established statute. His essay uses the Constitution as a sword as well as a shield. He insists that the Constitution won't tolerate the appointment of a senator as interim president, but that only a man like John Marshall, holding a commission as an "officer of the United States," can constitutionally serve as interim president.

Only one person had a special interest in making this high-stakes claim. And even if we move beyond Marshall's obvious interest in the presidency, the particular argument used by Horatius has his fingerprints all over it. Marbury v. Madison—written only two years later, in 1803—is all about the special status of government officials who have commissions signed by the president. Horatius's insistence that interim presidents must have such commissions fits comfortably within Marshall's special fixation on this arcane subject.

My legalistic point adds nuance to the crude picture of Marshall using the Constitution as a weapon to batter his way to the presidency. Even if I'm right in fingering him as the author, Marshall could well have believed that Horatius was telling the truth about the Constitution—while simultaneously noting that, as secretary of state, he himself just happened to be the principal beneficiary of good legal logic. Or perhaps Marshall simply found it impossible to disentangle his love of the Constitution from his lust for power. In any event, these complex motivations certainly distinguish him from any other suspect, and they deserve due weight in the scale.

Political Gossip and Rumors

That's what the editor of the Marshall Papers called it, but it strikes me as more substantial. As Beveridge reports, rumors about Marshall were rife in Republican circles. By mid-January they had already reached Richmond, where they were recycled back to Washington by Governor James Monroe in a letter to Thomas Jefferson:

> It is said here that Marshall has given an opinion in conversation with Stoddard, that in case 9 States shod. not unite in favor of one of the persons chosen, the legislature may appoint a Presidt. till another election is made, & that intrigues are carrying on to place us in that situation. This is stated in a letter from one of our reps. (I think Randolph) & has excited the utmost indignation in the legislature . . . There has been much alarm at the intimation of such a projected usurpation, much consultation, and a spirit fully manifested not to submit to it. My opinion is they shod. take no step founded on the expectation of such an event, as it might produce an ill effect even with our friends.[38]

Benjamin Stoddert was secretary of the navy in Adams's cabinet—and so the first point about this report is that it does not directly attribute the Horatius essay to Marshall. But it is relevant that Marshall was seriously considering the prospect of an interim presidential appointment. To be sure, we are only dealing with hearsay: the likely source of the report is John Randolph, and this Republican congressman certainly would not have been allowed to attend any serious strategy session between Marshall and Stoddert.

Nevertheless, we are dealing with something more significant than a casual rumor. Monroe was the governor of Virginia, and he was writing a confidential letter to his friend and would-be president. This was not an occasion for rumor-mongering, but for intelligence-sharing. Moreover, he was explaining why Marshall's dangerous opinions should *not* provoke an extreme response. Given his cautionary aim, Monroe had an incentive to express doubts about the reliability of Randolph's report and thereby emphasize the imprudence of a rash Republican response. But he expressed no doubts. He treated the report as credible political intelligence in a letter intended to be taken seriously.

Things got more complicated at this point. On February 9 the Republicans went public with the Marshall-Stoddert report. The *Richmond Examiner* published an essay by George Hay—Monroe's son-in-law, who would become Jefferson's attorney general.[39] Adopting the pseudonym "Hortensius," Hay wrote a public letter to John Marshall, warning that the opinion he expressed to Stoddert had "already diffused throughout America," generating "anxiety and alarm": "The appointment will be considered an usurpation, as an act of direct and palpable hostility against the Constitution and the people, and will be instantly, and firmly, repelled." The attack continued under the name "Lucius" in the following issues of the *Examiner:* "I foresee your design General Marshall—You are the Idol of your party, and are well aware of the influence, which your opinions will have, upon their minds."[40]

Hortensius's charges against Marshall were conveyed to Washington with blinding speed. Three days later the *Washington Federalist* was already printing a reply:

> See also the intemperate counsel of a certain would be attorney-general of the United States (George Hay, Esq. of the ancient dominion) contained in the same paper, under the signature of Hortensius, and addressed to General Marshall, in consequence of a lie fabricated against him relative to an opinion said to have been given by him upon the late presidential election which the honorable attorney knew to be a lie, as well as we did, but was fearful of being forgot, and despaired of getting a better opportunity to shew himself!!![41]

The speed of this turnaround suggests, at the very least, that William Rind, the paper's publisher, was remarkably solicitous of Marshall's interests. But doesn't the paragraph itself deny that Marshall is Horatius?

Absolutely not. When the newspaper denounces a "lie fabricated against" Marshall that is "relative to an opinion said to have been given by him upon the late presidential election," it is not talking about "The Presidential Knot"—for the simple reason that George Hay never accused Marshall of writing it, but only of suggesting an interim presidency in a private conversation with Stoddert.

Even this limited denial by the newspaper is worth taking with a grain of salt. Marshall didn't put his own reputation on the line by signing the article, nor did he issue a personal denial on any other occasion. Instead, it is best seen as part of a duel between partisan newspapers indulging in a familiar sort of thrust and parry: he said it, no he didn't. In contrast, the earlier report by Monroe to Jefferson in a private letter looks more credible, though it certainly doesn't deserve a great deal of weight in the overall appraisal.

So: Who Dunnit?

Very few Federalists could have written Horatius's brilliant essay under the best of conditions, and almost all of them were jammed into a few boarding houses. Marshall was sitting quietly in his office, with close connections to the newspapers. He already had a record of pseudonymous polemics, and when he later returned to the newspaper wars he used the very same printer who first published "The Presidential Knot." Horatius's arguments not only furthered Marshall's political interests but invoked constitutional concerns that were central to his jurisprudence. And Marshall's political opponents seriously believed that he was an active advocate for an interim presidency. Ladies and gentlemen of the jury, what say you?

On one level, your answer doesn't really matter. Even if Horatius wasn't Marshall, the fact is that the leading Federalist paper in Washington was seriously proposing to make Marshall interim president. Looking at the big picture, the Constitution was spinning out of control: the Federalists were publicly threatening to rip up the election returns by means of an aggressively legalistic reading of the text. Little wonder, then, that Madison responded by proposing to vindicate "the will of the people" by circulating revolutionary plans to violate the Constitution, albeit "in form only." A fearsome gap was opening between the Republicans' plebiscitary theory of the presidency and the Federalists' legalistic manipulation of the electoral college.

The constitutional crisis did not depend on whether Marshall was pushing himself for president, or whether some other hothead was taking the lead. But from a human point of view, the question looks different. Contemporary biographers cast Marshall as an Olympian demigod, splendidly detached from the fierce struggles going on all round him.[42] To put it mildly, this is an exaggeration. We will see that Marshall was an extreme partisan throughout the month of February. This doesn't mean that he wrote as Horatius in January—only that he was capable of playing the part.

Human, all too human? We will probably never know for sure. In any event, it isn't a crime to blow one's own horn behind the screen of anonymity. Even on Olympus, the gods were pretty pushy folk.

And our story has only just begun.

3

Jefferson Counts Himself In

With Federalists and Republicans preparing themselves for extreme measures, Congress settled down for the formal count of electoral votes on February 11, and it immediately confronted a surprise. When the president of the Senate opened the envelope containing Georgia's four electoral votes, the ballot paper was blatantly irregular.

Nobody expected this. The newspapers had confidently placed Georgia in the Republican column, and nobody had raised the issue in private correspondence. If Georgia's voting papers were disqualified, it would make a big difference in the upcoming House runoff. Under the Constitution's ground rules, Jefferson and Burr could not exclude their Federalist competitors from the runoff unless they each received the support of a majority of the nation's electors. Since there were 138 electors from the 16 states in 1800, the magic number was 70. Without the 4 votes from Georgia, Jefferson and Burr were left with 69, and the Constitution required them to enter a five-man runoff that would include the Federalists John Adams (65 votes), Charles Cotesworth Pinckney (64), and John Jay (1).

This condemned Jefferson to a tough contest. In a two-candidate race, the Federalist members of the House would be stuck with Burr, but in a five-man race, they would have more options. They could begin the balloting by supporting John Adams, but if things bogged down and the March 4 date loomed, the Federalists had a much more attractive compromise candidate than Burr to offer. Their vice-presidential nominee, Charles Pinckney of South Carolina, would appeal to many southerners backing Jefferson once they were persuaded that their hero could not get elected.

The problem with Georgia's ballot was widely reported in the press, and it passed into constitutional lore for a couple of generations. Once again, modern historians have lost sight of the story, and I will be retelling it with the aid of original documents uncovered in the National Archives.[1]

So let us return to February 11, 1801, armed with a copy of the written Constitution: "The President of the Senate shall, in the Presence of the Senate and House of Representatives, open all the Certificates, and the Votes shall then be counted." This provision does not envision problems arising in the vote count, so it fails to provide explicit guidance on their resolution. But it is clear about one thing: the president of the Senate is the person who is supposed to "open" the ballots. This threw yet another monkey-wrench into the machinery. In choosing the Senate president, the Framers had managed to give the job to the worst possible official. Under the Constitution, the Senate presidency is assigned to the sitting vice president—in this case, none other than Thomas Jefferson. Once again, the written Constitution was creating problems instead of solutions: rather than giving the job to a neutral officer, the Framers allowed Jefferson to make a key decision in his own case.

I begin with my punch line: Jefferson used his power as Senate president to his own advantage—counting the four Georgia votes into the Republican column, counting his Federalist rivals out of the runoff. And he acted in a way that made it especially difficult for Congress to overrule.

The facts are startling, and raise obvious questions: How did the Framers manage to place Jefferson in such an awkward constitutional position? Should Jefferson have used his power differently?

Founding Blunders

The vice presidency gave the Framers many problems. They might well have dispensed with the office entirely, but their design of the electoral college made its creation imperative. To check the tendency toward provincialism, the Convention gave electors two ballots but forbade them to cast both votes for residents of their own state. Without the vice presidency, electors might well have left their second ballot blank to maximize the impact of their vote for a native son. But with the vice presidency in existence, the electors would hardly let their second ballot go to waste. Their thoughts might go like this: "Of course George Washington is an out-of-stater, but I might as well vote for the best man since the Constitution requires me to move beyond my local favorites. And in any event, I did get a chance to cast a ballot for our home-town guy, the Honorable John Q. Squire, who might even have a chance to be vice president."

This logic came to the surface at the Convention when Elbridge Gerry (himself a future vice president) questioned the need for the office. Hugh Williamson of North Carolina responded that "such an officer as Vice-President was not wanted. He was introduced only for the sake of a valuable mode of election which required two to be chosen at the same time."[2]

Alas, the Founders were wasting their time on their clever electoral machine. With Federalists and Republicans nominating national candidates for the vice presidency, their two-vote system was itself generating a constitutional crisis as Jefferson and Burr came out in a tie. Worse yet, the Founders' effort to solve a non-problem was now causing real problems in its own right.

Once the Convention created a vice president, it had to figure out what to do with him while the president was alive: How to prevent him from attempting a coup that would oust the chief executive and destroy the Constitution? The Convention did not come up with a compelling answer, but it tried to minimize the danger by channeling the vice president's activities in a harmless direction. For want of anything better, it assigned him the largely ceremonial office of president of the Senate.

But the office was not entirely ceremonial, and the Framers didn't think this matter through. Anticipating that the Senate would generate tie votes from time to time, they expressly granted the president of the Senate a tie-breaking vote.[3] Unfortunately, they did not consider other moments when the president of the Senate might wield real power.

Their most obvious blunder involves impeachment. The Founders recognized the absurdity of allowing the vice president to preside over the Senate when the president was on trial for "high Crimes and Misdemeanors."[4] The vice was inevitably an interested party in this affair, since he would ascend to the presidency if the incumbent was convicted. Given his personal stake, it was inappropriate for him to preside over the president's trial, and so the text explicitly replaces him with the chief justice in this one case.[5]

Unforgivably, the Framers ignored the possibility that the vice president might also be impeached, and failed to designate the chief justice as the presiding officer in this type of trial as well. Read literally, the Constitution authorizes the vice president to preside over his own impeachment![6]

Our present story is rooted in the same Founding failure. The vice president may be a fine ceremonial leader of the Senate, but he is a natural candidate in the next presidential contest. It is a bad mistake to designate him as the presiding officer for the counting of electoral votes.

If the Convention had focused on the matter, the lapse could have been readily remedied. There was an obvious solution: just as the chief justice replaced the Senate president when it came to impeachment trials, he should also replace him when it came to selecting the president.[7] But the Convention never spotted this problem, or its obvious solution, and intellectual inertia propelled the president of the Senate into an unsuitable role.

Everybody makes mistakes—and this one might have been innocuous, except for the transformation of presidential politics during the next decade. Now that political parties had taken the lead in presidential politics, the two-vote rule became a potential booby trap. Whenever the winning side lacked strict party discipline, the losing *presidential* candidate could easily slip into the vice presidency.

This is what happened in 1796, when John Adams won the presidency with 71 electoral votes but 12 Federalist electors chose favorite sons over their party's vice-presidential candidate, Thomas Pinckney, leaving him with only 59.[8] This allowed Thomas Jefferson to squeeze into the vice presidency with 68 votes,[9] and placed him in the Senate chair at vote-counting time in 1801.

This mistake was exacerbated by another blunder. The Constitution doesn't clearly say what should happen once a vote-counting problem arises. To repeat the crucial formula: "The president of the Senate shall, in the Presence of the Senate and House of Representatives, open all the Certificates, and the Votes shall then be counted." Although this clearly assigns the vice president the task of opening the certificates, it does not expressly authorize him to make a final ruling in a controversy. Although the text instructs the two Houses to be "presen[t]," it doesn't expressly grant them decisionmaking authority either. In short, the Founders managed to place a leading partisan in the chair without any clear ground rules to control overreaching. By failing to provide clear guidelines, the Convention deferred the vote-counting problem to the worst possible moment, when partisan passions would be at their most intense.

The point did not go unnoticed in the bitter run-up to the 1800 election. Federalists in Congress sought to fill the constitutional gap with legislation that would allow them to control Jefferson's discretionary authority.[10] But this effort was unsuccessful, and the protagonists were left to explore no-man's-land on their own.

Here is where a final Founding blunder entered. The Republicans had won a strong victory in the congressional elections of 1800, but under the constitutional calendar the new Congress would not convene in Washington until December 1801.[11] Instead, Jefferson would confront the strongly Federalist Congress elected in 1798. If the Senate president gave Congress a clear chance to rule on the Georgia ballot, the Federalists had every incentive to invalidate the state's four votes and force a five-man House runoff that included their own candidates.[12]

If things got to this point, Jefferson might insist that it was he, and not Congress, who had the final say. After all, the Constitution merely authorized the House and Senate to be "presen[t]" at the vote count; it didn't give them any authority to act affirmatively. As a consequence, Jefferson could claim that Congress could do nothing while he made the final decision on Georgia's four votes.

But Jefferson's claim to make final decisions was on equally shaky ground. The text only gave him the express power to "open" the ballots, not to make any final decisions. The truth is that the Framers had utterly failed to resolve the issue, leaving it wrapped in the mystery of the passive voice: "and the Votes shall then be counted."

A very bad mistake.

The Problem with Georgia's Ballot

Whatever its other obscurities, Article II of the Constitution contains some plain instructions for each state's electors: "And they shall make a List of all the Persons voted for, and of the Number of Votes for each; which List they shall sign and certify, and transmit sealed to the Seat of the Government of the United States, directed to the President of the Senate."[13] Call this the *electoral vote,* and it is the document that created legal problems for Georgia in 1800.

A few statutory requirements are also relevant. George Washington's first election preceded the first session of Congress, but in 1792 Congress enacted a framework law for future contests. The statute tells the "executive authority of each state" to create a second document that certifies the names of the electors who have been selected by the state. Call this the *certificate of ascertainment.* The statute instructs the electors to enclose this certificate with their electoral vote. Once they have placed both documents in an envelope for delivery to the president of the Senate, they must also "certify" on the envelope that "a list of the votes . . . for President and Vice President is contained therein."[14]

The Georgia electors fulfilled both of these requirements in 1800, but their electoral vote—the key document required by the Constitution—failed to comply with the requirements of Article II and the norms established by the uniform practice of the states in every early election.[15] To set the stage, Figure 1 shows what Georgia's perfectly proper ballot looked like four years earlier, in 1796. It states that the electors met at a "place directed for the Electors to meet for the election of President and Vice President" and that "We the underwritten Electors do certify the above [four votes for Jefferson and four votes for George Clinton] to be a true" list of their votes.

As the Constitution prescribes, the upper half of the document contains "a List of all the Persons voted for, and of the Number of Votes for each." The bottom half satisfies the command: "which List they shall sign and certify."[16] Georgia's 1796 submission also contains a proper certificate of ascertainment.[17]

In contrast, Georgia's envelope of 1800 contains a single sheet of paper, not the two provided by every other state. On one side of the sheet, there is a legally perfect certificate of ascertainment, signed by Governor James Jackson, identifying the state's four electors. But there is no physically distinct document that reports the state's electoral vote. The only indication of the electors' choices appears on the obverse side of the certificate of ascertainment. It is shown in Figure 2.

This document plainly fails to satisfy the formal requirements set out in the Constitution. The Georgia document contains a "List," but it does not say that it represents a list of "the Persons voted for." The four names appearing below "Jefferson" and "Burr" are those certified by Governor Jackson, but the electors themselves have not "sign[ed] and certif[ied]" that the list actually represents a true statement of their preferences. For all that appears, this paper could be one-half of a sign-up sheet for a debate between partisans of the contending presidential tickets.

These requirements are formal, but they are not trivial. When understood as part of the larger scheme, they seem quite important. Immediately after imposing the formalisms violated by Georgia, the Constitution

Thomas Jefferson.   Aaron Burr.

John Morrison   John Morrison
Dennis Smelt. M. D. Dennis Smelt. M. D.
Hen: Graybill   Hen: Graybill
Ed. Blackshear   Ed. Blackshear

proceeds with a text that should, by now, be familiar: "The President of the Senate shall, in the Presence of the Senate and House of Representatives, open all the Certificates, and the Votes shall then be counted."[18] Given the opacity of this language, a bit of formalism might well help ensure the smooth operation of a potentially contentious process. Perhaps the best way of ensuring an operational vote count is to impose a crisp rule on the electors: if you satisfy the forms, your vote "shall then be counted"; if not, not. Any other approach threatens to involve the president of the Senate in an uncertain proceeding in which he might be an interested party. The formalist's premise of a smoothly functioning machine, moreover, was regularly fulfilled during the early years of the republic: Each state in every prior election had submitted technically perfect electoral votes and certificates of ascertainment.[19]

Yet formalism has the vices of its virtues: the disqualification of an entire state is a very serious matter. In 1800 Georgia was a frontier region without much legal sophistication. If Georgians had merely made a technical error, wouldn't it be wrong to disqualify their choice of Jefferson and Burr? Worse yet, the blunder had decisive national ramifications, transforming a two-man House runoff into a five-man race. Why should the nation's fate hinge on some backwoods lawyering?

But *was* the mistake merely technical?

Viewing the matter from Washington, D.C., it was hard to know for sure. After all, no other frontier state had ever made such a mistake. Tennessee, for example, had a much shorter history than did Georgia, but it had no trouble complying with the law. Figure 3 presents Tennessee's 1800 ballot.[20]

Georgia's ballot stuck out like a sore thumb, and there was something particularly suspicious about it. Its electoral votes are written on the back of the certificate of ascertainment. This anomaly raises a disturbing possibility. Suppose that Georgia's four electors actually did what everybody else did. They prepared a proper ballot, put it into the envelope with the certificate of ascertainment, and signed the outside of the envelope.[21] And suppose that at this point some devious character opened the envelope, removed the standard ballot, and cast four defective votes for Jefferson and Burr on the back of the remaining paper. He then resealed the envelope and sent it on its way.

This scenario casts a more sinister light on the legal deficiencies of the

Pursuant to our duty as Electors for the State of Tennessee, having convened in Knoxville on the first Wednesday of December in the year eighteen hundred, and being legally qualified; We do certify that we voted by ballot for President and Vice President of the United States.— And upon counting the votes they were as follows.—

For Thomas Jefferson of the State of Virginia three votes.— .

For Aaron Burr of the State of New York three votes.—

Given under our hands at Knoxville in the State of Tennessee this third day of December, One thousand eight hundred.

DanSmith
John Cocke
R. Love

state's ballot. Criminals don't spend much time reading the Constitution. If a fraudster had removed the genuine ballot, he might well have created a legal mess when writing up his counterfeit. Pretty suspicious. And Georgia was already notorious for shady dealing. In the recent Yazoo scandals, the state's leading politicians had sold vast tracts of public land at ridiculously low prices: "[O]nly one of the legislators voting for [the Yazoo act] had not been bribed in some way by the land companies."[22] Georgia's voters had recently swept the corrupt politicos out of office,[23] but could Jefferson be confident that their replacements were not playing similar games?

Other bits of evidence pointed in a more reassuring direction. Pursuant to statutory instructions, Georgia's four electors had "certif[ied]" on their envelope to the president of the Senate "that a list of the votes . . . for President and Vice President [was] contained therein." As a comparison of Figure 4 with Figure 2 suggests, these four signatures match quite well with their namesakes on the defective ballot.

The history of humankind is littered with clever forgeries, and even today handwriting analysis is more art than science. Nevertheless, if Jefferson had compared the ballot with the envelope, he would not have detected obvious evidence of fraud.[24] So perhaps the unconstitutional Georgia ballot was the product of legal incompetence, not skullduggery?

Jefferson's Decision

One thing is clear. The Georgia ballot took everybody by surprise. All through January newspapers were reporting that Jefferson and Burr had won Georgia's four electoral votes.[25] I have also inspected much of the correspondence written by leading partisans during the run-up to the run-off. This contains a great deal of strategizing about a two-man contest between Jefferson and Burr, but no mention of a possible five-man race. The silence is deafening—nobody anticipated the Georgia problem.

Jefferson was as surprised as everybody else.[26] Here is an astonishing account, published in 1836:

> On the 11th of February the ballots were opened. During the performance of this ceremony a most extraordinary incident occurred. As it is known to but few now living, and never been publicly spoken of, it has been deemed proper to record it here, as a part of the history of that exciting contest.
>
> The Aurora of the 16th of February, 1801, remarks, that "the tellers declared that there was some informality in the votes of Georgia; but, believing them to be true votes, reported them as such." No ex-

planation of the nature of this informality was given; nor is it known that any has ever been given since.

. . .

. . . Mr. Jefferson was the presiding officer. On opening the package [of] endorsed Georgia votes, it was discovered to be totally irregular. The statement now about to be given is derived from an honourable gentleman, a member of Congress from the state of New-York during the administration of Mr. Jefferson, and yet living in this state. He says that Mr. Wells (a teller on the part of the Senate) informed him that the envelope was blank; that the return of the votes was not authenticated *by the signatures of the electors, or any of them, either on the outside or the inside of the envelope, or in any other manner;* that it merely stated in the inside that the votes of Georgia were, for Thomas Jefferson *four,* and for Aaron Burr *four,* without the *signature of any person* whatsoever. Mr. Wells added, that he was very undecided as to the proper course to be pursued by the tellers. It was, however, suggested by one of them that the paper should be handed to the presiding officer, without any statement from the tellers except that the return was informal; that he consented to this arrangement under the firm conviction that Mr. Jefferson would announce the nature of the informality from the chair; but, to his utmost surprise, he (Mr. Jefferson) rapidly declared that the votes of Georgia were *four* for Thomas Jefferson and *four* for Aaron Burr, without noticing their informality, and in a hurried manner put them aside, and then broke the seals and handed to the tellers the package from the next state. Mr. Wells observed, that as soon as Mr. Jefferson looked at the paper purporting to contain a statement of the electoral vote of the state of Georgia, his countenance changed, but that the decision and promptitude with which he acted on that occasion convinced him of that which he (a federalist) and his party had always doubted, that is to say, Mr. Jefferson's decision of character, at least when his own interest was at hazard.[27]

This remarkable story comes from the *Memoirs of Aaron Burr,* published by Matthew Davis, Burr's literary executor, and there are plenty of reasons to treat it cautiously. At the very best, it comes third hand from the alleged eyewitness, Senator Wells, and like many hearsay reports it contains significant errors.[28] Davis is wrong, for example, in claiming that Georgia's envelope was "blank"—as Figure 4 shows, the envelope bore the signatures of the state's four electors. And both Davis and Wells were Jefferson's avowed political enemies.[29]

Nevertheless, Davis certainly did not create the story out of whole cloth. The *Aurora* says what he says it says, and similar reports may be found in newspapers throughout the country.[30] Most important, the original documents in the National Archives confirm the key fact that the Georgia ballot was formally defective, and blatantly so.[31]

Davis goes beyond the 1801 documents at one important point. The newspapers focus on the tellers' public announcement of Georgia's deficiency, but Davis highlights Jefferson's aggressive action to preempt further consideration by the House and Senate. Davis isn't alone here. Jefferson's involvement was sufficiently memorable to survive as part of the constitutional law surrounding the vote count. As late as 1876, Senator Hannibal Hamlin recalled the event:

> [T]here was no certificate accompanying the return that the Electors met and balloted. It had nothing on its face to show that the votes were given for anybody. Clearly it did not conform to the Constitution, but it was counted as shown by the record.
>
> There was a tradition that the tellers handed it back to Mr. Jefferson, who returned it to them, and decided that it must be counted.[32]

This seems to be the last time Jefferson's decision was publicly acknowledged before my recent discovery. Yet Hamlin speaks as if it were an uncontroversial part of the constitutional "tradition" recognized on Capitol Hill. And Hamlin was free of the anti-Jeffersonian partisanship that impairs Davis's credibility.[33]

The Davis-Hamlin account also accords with common sense. The Constitution makes no mention of the role of tellers from the House and Senate, who merely served by custom as aides of the vice president at the vote count.[34] When they declared that "there was some informality in the votes of Georgia," it was perfectly sensible to hand the voting papers to the Senate president, the only officer designated by the Constitution to play a role in "open[ing]" the ballots. Once the Georgia problem had been called to his attention, surely Jefferson—like any other competent official—would have examined the Georgia ballot carefully before proceeding. The Davis-Hamlin reports merely confirm the obvious.

The key question is raised at the next step. Jefferson was perfectly free to call Congress's attention to the problem before making a ruling from the chair. Or he could have made a clear decision on the Georgia ballot, thereby inviting Congress to overrule him if it disagreed. He did neither of these things. He simply counted the Georgia votes for Jefferson and Burr as part of the running total, and only acted decisively at the end of the count.[35] Here is the account of his formal ruling from the *Annals of Congress:*

> The PRESIDENT of the Senate, in pursuance of the duty enjoined upon him, announced the state of the votes to both Houses, and declared that THOMAS JEFFERSON, of Virginia, and AARON BURR, of New York, having the greatest number, and *a majority of the votes of all the Electors appointed,* and, being equal, it remained for the House of Representatives to determine the choice.[36]

With these words, Jefferson counted out his three Federalist rivals from the House runoff: Adams (65 electoral votes), Pinckney (64), and Jay (1). But without the four votes from Georgia, Jefferson and Burr had only 69 valid ballots, placing them one shy of "a majority of the votes of all the Electors appointed." As a matter of constitutional mathematics, Jefferson's pronouncement required him to take responsibility for upholding the validity of the Georgia ballot—despite its plain violation of the formal requirements imposed by the Constitution, and despite his questionable authority.

To be sure, Jefferson took this dramatic step in the least obvious way, making it as hard as possible for others to challenge his decision. What to make of this fact?

Statesmanship?

Constitutional muckraking isn't much the fashion in these hagiographic times, but it is tough to ignore some embarrassing questions: Surely the Framers should have been clever enough to notice the danger of appointing the fox to superintend the chicken coop? Surely Jefferson should have been more up-front about excluding his Federalist rivals from the House runoff?

Heaping blame on both the Framers and Jefferson has the charm of impartiality, but I will be taking a harder line. The fault lies entirely with the Founders, and it was only Thomas Jefferson's crafty statesmanship that saved the country from a worse crisis.

Place yourself in Jefferson's chair and ponder your choices. Until the Georgia envelope was opened, Jefferson had every reason to believe he had won the state's four votes. That's what the newspapers were reporting, and given the ferocity of partisan combat, the Georgia electors would have complained loudly if their votes had been publicly misrepresented. And there were three representatives from Georgia present at the vote count, two of whom—Benjamin Taliaferro of the House and James Gunn of the Senate—had been elected as Federalists.[37] Surely they would have protested if their Georgia constituents had been telling them that the electors had voted a Federalist ticket?

The Georgians' silence had a plain meaning. No smoke equals no fire. The formal defects in the Georgia ballot were almost surely the product of frontier lawyering, not fraud.

Even if this is conceded, consider the devious way in which Jefferson preempted serious congressional deliberation. Given his overwhelming self-interest in the affair, wasn't it grotesque to count his rivals out without explicitly telling Congress what he was doing?

There is no denying the grotesquerie, but the question is whether Jefferson's evasions avoided an even worse outcome. Begin by considering Jefferson's maneuvers more precisely. His silence didn't actually deprive congressional Federalists of their chance to challenge the Georgia ballot. The three tellers—two from the House, one from the Senate—did announce the existence of the problem loud enough for newspapers to carry the story throughout the land.[38] Two of the tellers were Federalists, and one of them—if Davis is to be believed—was shocked by Jefferson's disposition of the matter. If the Federalists from Georgia, or elsewhere, had raised a protest from the floor, the Federalist tellers were in a position to stop the vote count by refusing to hand the next envelope to Jefferson.

It is wrong, then, to accuse Jefferson of exploiting his position to keep his opponents in the dark. His official silence concealed his ruling from posterity, but the Georgia problem was not a secret to the assembled senators and representatives. His action is best understood as shifting the burden of inquiry onto the Federalists in Congress. He was not going to help them, but they had the tools they needed to precipitate a constitutional confrontation if they really believed the problem was serious.

All things considered, Jefferson's obfuscations provided the best way out of the dark situation left by the Founders. Recall that the constitutional text simply did not specify whether the Senate president or the Congress had the final say. If Jefferson had raised the issue squarely, there would have been no straightforward way to reach an authoritative decision. Federalists would have argued passionately for the powers of Congress, and Republicans would have supported Jefferson, but everybody would have confronted an infinite regress: Could the president of the Senate claim the right to decide whether the president of the Senate possessed the contested power? To which the Federalist majorities in the House and Senate would counter that their constitutionally required "presence" at the vote count authorized them to override the president's rulings from the chair. And so forth.

Without any clear Founding markers to resolve this dispute, the vote count could well have disintegrated amid a cloud of bitter legalisms—the worst possible result. The nation was already in an uproar over the electoral college tie that had thrown the presidency into the House; the threat of mass violence was very real during the week it took to resolve the impasse between Jefferson and Burr. If the proceeding had never reached the House in the first place, violent confrontation might well have been inevitable.

Worse yet, the conflict couldn't be solved by taking a practical course and dispatching a special mission to Georgia find out the facts. It was the dead of winter, and a snowstorm was swirling around the half-built Capitol.[39] Even during calmer weather, it would take a week or two to travel on terrible roads all the way to Augusta, the state capitol.[40] But only three weeks remained before the inauguration of a new president. Time would run out before a delegation could complete its fact-finding mission and return to Washington, D.C.[41]

There is no denying the awkward position in which Jefferson found himself. Nevertheless, his maneuverings did manage to avoid a destructive institutional struggle, and they pushed the count in the direction probably favored by the Georgia electors. It was the Founders, not Jefferson, who failed to discharge the most elementary function of a written constitution. They had not provided clear rules of the game to determine the selection of the most powerful official of the American government. And they chose the worst possible official to exercise discretionary power. Jefferson's evasions managed to compensate for these blunders.

Obviously, his actions were self-interested. And yet they turn out to be more complicated than they first appear. A brief historical detour will be required to do them justice. Jefferson and Adams first struggled for the presidency in 1796, and it happens that the Founders' blunders in regulating presidential selection were already beginning to take their toll. The electoral returns had given Adams a three-vote lead over Jefferson in the electoral college, but newspaper accounts were questioning the validity of the four electoral votes that Vermont had cast in Adams's column.[42]

Madison, serving as Jefferson's campaign manager, wrote to his candidate at Monticello for further instructions: "I can not yet entirely remove the uncertainty in which my last [letter] left the election. Unless the Vermont election of which little has of late been said, should contain some fatal vice, in it, Mr. Adams may be considered as the President elect."[43]

Jefferson categorically refused Madison's invitation to engage in legalistic quibbling:

> I observe doubts are still expressed as to the validity of the Vermont election. Surely in so great a case, substance & not form should prevail. I cannot suppose that the Vermont constitution has been strict in requiring particular forms of expressing the legislative will. As far as my disclaimer may have any effect, I pray you to declare it on every occasion foreseen or not foreseen by me, in favor of the choice of the people substantially expressed, and to prevent the phaenomenon of a Pseudo-president at so early a day.[44]

Jefferson was clear that he had in fact lost Vermont to Adams, and that "substance & not form should prevail." His words were decisive. The Republicans dropped further public agitation on the Vermont matter, and refused to raise a legalistic challenge to the state's four electoral votes when the president of the Senate "open[ed]" the ballots in February 1797. Though Jefferson was on the losing side, he was willing to restrain his own ambitions "in favor of the choice of the people substantially expressed."

The same principle hung in the balance four years later, but this time it favored Jefferson. Thanks to the Founders, he had been placed in a position in which self-interest and principle dictated the same result.

It is sometimes the mark of statesmanship to accept the benefits of principle even under unseemly circumstances. This was one of those times. All things considered, Jefferson did the right thing in acting decisively "to prevent the phaenomenon of a Pseudo-president at so early a day."

I have been reconstructing Jefferson's position at the moment of decision, refusing to indulge in hindsight. While the Founders had put him in an awkward position, he did not have the luxury of time. If he had not acted decisively, the outcome might well have spun out of constitutional control. He deserves to be judged on the basis of what he reasonably believed in Washington, D.C., not on what Georgia's electors actually did in their state capital.

Nevertheless, we have the luxury of time, and it turns out that Jefferson was absolutely right. Documents from the Georgia archives conclusively establish that the electors did indeed vote for Jefferson and Burr, "to the great satisfaction of a large concourse of people assembled on the occasion."[45] It was bad lawyering, not fraud, that accounted for their defective ballots.

This finding further reinforces the wisdom of Jefferson's maneuver. To see my point, suppose that he had responded to his Georgia surprise by taking a very different tack, announcing to his shocked audience: "Given my personal involvement, it would be most unseemly to count this defective ballot in my own column. The honorable course is to give my Federalist opponents the benefit of the doubt and allow them to compete with Burr and me in the House runoff."

As the next chapter suggests, even a two-man runoff presented big challenges for Jefferson, with the Federalists backing Burr for thirty-five ballots before reluctantly capitulating. But Burr was not the Federalists' candidate of choice—they backed him in a last-ditch effort to stop their archenemy Jefferson. With a five-man runoff, they could have thrown their support to real Federalists, and their blocking coalition would have had more staying power. After fifty or sixty ballots, the Federalists' vice-presidential candidate, Charles Cotesworth Pinckney, would have seemed an exceptionally attractive dark horse.[46] Pinckney had a long and distinguished record of public service in the Revolution and the Constitutional

Convention, and he had established a record of moderation during the 1790s—supporting his party when it came to the war with France, but opposing the oppressive Alien and Sedition Acts.[47] And he was a South Carolinian, capable of attracting support from Jefferson's southern base.[48] Once the Federalists had decisively blocked Jefferson, his followers might well have bitterly consented to the selection of another southerner of great distinction.[49]

All this is speculative, but it suggests the dangers lurking in my hypothetical scenario leading to a five-candidate runoff. Consider the uproar when the truth from Georgia emerged a couple of weeks after a Pinckney victory: Jefferson actually had won all four Georgia votes, and it was only his constitutional punctilios as president of the Senate that enabled Federalist partisans to displace him with Charles Cotesworth Pinckney.

The resulting crisis would have been far worse than Hayes-Tilden in 1876 or Bush-Gore in 2000. In these cases the losers could never prove, beyond a reasonable doubt, that they had actually won the underlying electoral votes. But in 1801 it would have been perfectly obvious that Jefferson had been denied the presidency by his own honorable actions in response to a technicality.

If Pinckney had refused to resign his office, the country would have been on the brink of civil war.[50] This was a crisis the infant republic did well to avoid.

Dumb Luck

The speculative scenario also adds an ironic twist to the critique of the Founders that is emerging from our story. To be sure, they had made a bad blunder in consigning the vote count to the tender mercies of the Senate president. But, given Jefferson's statesmanship, it might have turned out worse if the Convention had made a better choice. To see my point, suppose that the Framers had spotted the problem and had tried to solve it: If the sitting vice president was a poor choice to supervise the ballot count, who should be his replacement?

The obvious pick was the chief justice—the only constitutional official possessing the impartiality required for the vote-counting job.[51] But if the Framers had made this decision in 1787, it would have generated bad results in 1801. Jefferson would have been replaced by Chief Justice John Marshall, whom the Federalists had placed in office only the week before. The new chief justice was a confirmed Jefferson-hater,[52] and he would have found himself in the delightful position of making a technically correct ruling against Georgia that favored Federalist interests. Since the Constitution explicitly requires that all the electors "sign and certify" their state's return, and clearly designate the persons they were "vot[ing] for," the formal case was open and shut: "Sorry, Georgia, but you don't count (and, alas, given the execrable postal service southward, your formal deficiency cannot be cured by March 4)." So the chief justice would rule that the vote total stood at sixty-nine for Jefferson and Burr, one short of a majority, and the Federalists would get their men into the runoff.

Marshall was eminently capable of transcending such rigid formalisms when it got in the way of his constitutional vision. But this vision certainly did not include Thomas Jefferson as president of the United States. And not even the most partisan Jeffersonian could reasonably complain if the chief justice, following the express commands of the Constitution, declared that there were only sixty-nine valid votes in favor of Jefferson and Burr. After all, hadn't the Founders put the chief justice in the chair precisely to ensure that vote counting would proceed in strict compliance with the law?

No less important, the Jeffersonians could not have launched an effective challenge to Marshall's decision. The Federalists controlled both houses of Congress, and would have voted down any Republican motion to overrule the chair. So if the Framers had done their homework, the vote count would have provided Marshall with a splendid opportunity to enter history, slightly prematurely, as a great defender of the written Constitution—but with a very different result.

Consider a few scenarios. Suppose first that, despite Marshall's ruling, Jefferson emerged victorious from the five-man runoff. Then Marshall would have been clearly marked out by Jefferson as Public Enemy Number One. With the president threatening reprisals, would the chief justice have had the courage to write Marbury v. Madison? If so, would Jefferson have swept Marshall out of his office through an aggressive use of impeachment?

Even without this added provocation, Jefferson came pretty close to purging the Federalist Supreme Court. Marshall's effort to block the door to the President's House could well have contributed the extra presidential energy needed to push the purge to successful completion.

Marshall's prospects would have been no less grim had his ruling led to the victory of his patron Adams or his friend Pinckney.[53] At best, the chief justice would have tied his judicial reputation to a ruling that would have been reviled by a large portion of the population; at worst, his decision would have helped precipitate a bloody conflict over presidential succession.

As I contemplate these scenarios it is impossible to mistake the contribution of dumb luck to the affair. By "dumb," I mean that the Founders were mistaken in putting the vice president in a constitutional situation marked by an egregious conflict of interest; by "luck," I mean that we are all lucky that they were stupid, since if they had been smarter things would have come out worse, maybe much worse.

Only one thing is clear: in America's first great crisis, the written constitution wasn't going to come to the rescue—to the contrary, it was only making things worse. To achieve a successful transition of power, much more would be required than following the rules laid down by the Founders. Only creative statesmanship had a chance of preventing the constitutional text from unraveling into civil war.

The first act of statesmanship involved Thomas Jefferson counting his rivals out of the runoff. But there were many more to come.

4

On the Brink

Jefferson's decision to count the Georgia ballot eliminated a time bomb, but it didn't resolve the basic problem posed by the Founding misdesign of the electoral college. Despite the expectations of ordinary Americans, Jefferson still wasn't president. He remained in a dead heat with Burr, and it was up to the House to pick the winner. The Constitution optimistically instructed the House to act "immediately,"[1] but it would take six bitter days before Jefferson emerged with the victory.

Conventional accounts focus on the wheeling and dealing that finally led to Jefferson's defeat of Burr on the thirty-sixth ballot. But this narrow focus fails to do justice to the situation. Thanks to poor draftsmanship, the Constitution invited the Federalists to escalate the crisis through the use of an adventurous two-step strategy.

Step 1: Since the text required the runoff to continue until Jefferson or Burr won nine of the Union's sixteen states, the Federalists could create a deadlock in the House by denying both candidates the requisite majority.

Step 2: As the nation confronted the prospect of a vacant presidential chair on March 4, the Federalists could use their political power to pass a new statute naming somebody like John Marshall as interim chief executive. Or they might stretch existing statutory authority to appoint the Federalist president pro tem of the Senate as acting president.

We have already seen James Madison laboring mightily to formulate a Republican response to this Federalist deadlock strategy in early January—just at the moment when Horatius was elaborating a particularly provocative version of the strategy in Federalist newspapers. As the crisis reached a climax in February, both sides refined their plans, laying the legal foundation for aggressive moves in the event of a House impasse.

These moves and countermoves greatly enhanced the danger that the crisis would spin out of control. So long as the contest remained in the House, the Constitution provided clear rules of the game. Once the House deadlocked, each side would be manipulating the constitutional silence to design the next phase of the contest to push its own partisan into the President's House, with military force determining which side would prevail.

It isn't enough, then, to understand why Jefferson beat Burr on the thirty-sixth ballot. The key question is why the Federalists kept playing the game in the House, rather than implementing their deadlock strategy. My answer will emphasize the importance of the balance of military power in resolving the crisis, and ultimately, John Adams's statesmanship in ensuring the peaceful transition of political power.

We are getting ahead of ourselves. This chapter tells the story of the House runoff in a way that underscores the prospect of deadlock, the rival preparations for partisan advantage, and the threats of violence that confronted Federalists tempted by their deadlock strategy. The next chapter explores the basic factors that enabled statesmen to contain the crisis at the very moment it seemed to be lurching out of control.

Partisan Prelude

Two days before the runoff the Federalists set the stage to their advantage. Since this was the first presidential tie in history, the House was obliged to create the rules under which it would proceed. By a party-line vote of 54 to 45, the Federalists established that the "doors of the House shall be closed during the balloting"[2] without any members of the public present; by 53 to 47, they insisted that the House "shall not adjourn until a choice is made."[3]

In other words, if Jefferson failed to win on the first vote, the Republicans couldn't stall further balloting while they rallied their forces in the country to demand that the House comply with the will of the People. They would be obliged to participate in an all-night session without any outsiders witnessing the wheeling and dealing sure to come.

No less ominously, the new House rules created a system that made it hard to learn how individual representatives were voting. Each member simply dropped his secret ballot into a special box reserved for his state's delegation.[4] If the all-night session put Burr into the presidency, it would be tough to figure out who had done what, when, and why.

The Federalists had arranged matters for a fait accompli. After a night's fierce bargaining, they might emerge with Burr as the constitutional choice, and stare down all efforts by the Republicans to protest that it was Jefferson who represented the emergent will of the People, as expressed through the system of party competition.[5]

Once the balloting actually began, the constitutional situation changed to the Federalists' disadvantage. As the procedural votes demonstrated, they had little trouble controlling the House under normal rules. But the Founders had insisted that the president be selected under a special rule granting a single vote to each state delegation, regardless of its size. And by a stroke of good luck, the special rule had relatively happy consequences. Republican congressmen were distributed pretty evenly throughout the South and the Mid-Atlantic states, while Federalists were more concentrated in New England. This made it easier for Republicans to aggregate their individual votes into what really mattered—control over state delegations. In numerical terms, Republicans managed to swing six states into Jefferson's column by the margin of a single congressional vote while the Federalists carried only two states by this margin, wasting many of their votes by dominating the New England states with lopsided majorities. As a consequence, the Republicans came out ahead on the first House ballot—eight states voting for Jefferson, six for Burr, and two delegations (Vermont and Maryland) dividing evenly.

Unfortunately, the rules approved at the Philadelphia Convention required the victor to gain the support of an absolute majority—nine of the sixteen states then in the Union. Jefferson's shortfall by a single state created a fearsome gap between the living Constitution of parties and plebiscitary presidencies and the written Constitution of electoral colleges and House runoffs.

Balloting began at one in the afternoon on February 11, in the midst of a severe snowstorm that made it tough for members to get to the Capitol from nearby rooming houses.[6] Once the initial results were announced, members hunkered down for more balloting—which began ominously for the Republicans. The official results were unchanged, but trouble was brewing beneath the surface. On the first ballot, eleven Federalists recognized that Jefferson had indeed won a mandate from the People, and deserted their party to vote on his behalf. When Jefferson fell short, five returned to their party and cast their second ballot for Burr, giving the latter a two- or three-vote majority in the House as a whole.[7] Momentum was shifting away from the self-described tribune of the People. In the words of Congressman James Bayard, a Federalist leader, "By deceiving one Man (a great blockhead) and tempting two (not incorruptible) [Burr] might have secured a majority of the States."[8]

After a rapid succession of ballots without any change in result, the two sides resolved to vote every hour on the hour, throughout the night and into the morning, until they broke the impasse. But in vain: when the twenty-seventh ballot, cast at one o'clock in the afternoon, revealed no change, they called it quits.[9] In desperate need of sleep, they put off the next vote until the next day, Friday the 13th, despite the fact that the rules had forbidden them to "adjourn until a choice is made."[10]

Friday was no different, and, rather than endure another ordeal, the House postponed further balloting until the next day—when three further ballots merely established that the impasse continued.[11]

We are now up to Saturday, February 14—two and a half weeks to go before March 4, and no president. The protagonists began to take their other options seriously. The Republican leader Albert Gallatin wrote: "We have postponed balloting till Monday, twelve o'clock. That day will, I think, show something more decisive, either yielding on their part or an attempt to put an end to balloting in order to legislate. We will be ready at all points and rest assured that *we* will not yield."[12]

Brinksmanship

Both sides had been preparing for this moment, refining the strategies advanced by Horatius and Madison the month before. The Federalists had begun setting the stage for a legalistic effort to name an interim president; the Republicans were moving beyond Madison's unconventional proposals in ways that emphasized the new plebiscitarian understanding of the presidency.

Gallatin's Plan

Even before the balloting began, Albert Gallatin had prepared "a plan which did meet with the approbation of our party" in the House of Representatives and was then "Communicated to Nicholas and Mr. Jefferson."[13]

This "Balloting Plan" is a powerfully reasoned document which distinguishes three Federalist strategies and defines a Republican response to each. The first scenario involves a Federalist effort to seduce enough Republicans to award the election to Burr, and "may be defeated by our own firmness." The second and third options respond to the Federalists' deadlock strategy.

Under scenario two, the Federalists content themselves with invoking that part of the Presidential Succession Act of 1792 which authorizes the calling of a new election; under scenario three, they not only call an election but also select an interim president to "assume executive power" while the new election takes place. The Republican caucus in the House responded differently to these last two scenarios. They opposed any effort to name a Federalist as interim president, but they were surprisingly supportive of a new election to break the impasse.

Begin with the Republicans' emphatic negative. Gallatin detailed three ways in which the Federalists might push their man into the presidency on an interim basis: "[This] may be effected, 1, by law; 2, by Mr. Adams convening the Senate; or, 3, by the Senate convening themselves . . . If they . . . pass a law, it will be by declaring that in any of the cases of vacancy in the office of President, Vice-President, President pro temp., and Speaker, contemplated by the Constitution, the Chief Justice, or any other officer designated by the law, shall act as President, which law would be constitutional."

Gallatin singles out John Marshall, recently appointed as chief justice, as the likely interim president if the Federalists succeed in passing a new statute. But in sharp contrast to Horatius, Gallatin rejects this option:

> [W]hether the assumption be made by law or without it, the act of the person designated by the law or of the President pro temp. assuming the power is clearly unconstitutional.
>
> For the Constitution has not provided any mode by which the Presidential power can be exercised except in the specific cases of vacancy therein enumerated.
>
> If they shall usurp, for unconstitutional assumption is usurpation, are we to submit or not?[14]

Not on your life, says Gallatin, but let us defer his particular proposal for resisting "the usurper," and consider the caucus's very different reaction to the final option: calling a new election.

Gallatin points out that Jefferson might well lose the special election, which might lead to the "reanimation of the hopes and exertions of the Federal party in some States, and despair of success on the part of the Republicans."[15] Nevertheless, the caucus accepts the legitimacy of this tie-breaking procedure—with one proviso. The previous election had seen party loyalists in many states manipulating the electoral rules to their partisan advantage. As a Pennsylvanian, Gallatin was particularly aware of the bitter conflict in his state between the Republican House and the Federalist Senate, which had almost prevented the state from casting electoral votes for anybody at all in the 1800 contest.[16] Would a rerun lead to another round of manipulation?

Gallatin emphasizes this risk in the Balloting Plan, but explains it more elaborately in a letter to his wife:

[A]s no State has provided for an election in such cases [of a special tie-breaking vote for presidential electors]; as the concurrence of the Legislature of any one State will be necessary to pass a law providing for the same; as in the five New England States, Jersey and Delaware (which give 49 Federal votes), both branches of the Legislature are Federal, whilst in New York, Pennsylvania, Maryland, and South Carolina, where we have a majority, the State Senates are against us; the consequence might be that the Senates of these four last States refusing to act, the 49 votes of New England, Jersey, and Delaware would outweigh the 44 votes of Virginia, North Carolina, Georgia, Kentucky, and Tennessee; and they would thus, by in fact disfranchising four States and annulling the last election, perpetuate themselves in power, whilst they would in appearance violate none of the forms of our Constitution.[17]

Even this danger did not deter the caucus from supporting a new election. After all, says Gallatin, the electoral results would not be final until the electoral votes were recognized by the new Congress when it met in December. Since the Republicans would control the next House, they could take effective steps if the Federalists played fast and loose: "[L]et them [the Federalists] order a new election whenever they please, they cannot count the votes and complete the election without Congress being convened, and then the next House may act either on the new or on the present election."[18]

In other words, if the Federalists used their political power in the states to stifle the popular voice, the next Republican House could throw out the results of the second election, assert the continuing validity of the first election, return to the "one state–one vote" backup procedure, and use its new majority to deliver the nine states Jefferson needs for victory. But if the second election was conducted fairly, and all the states counted, the Republicans were prepared to recognize that they might legitimately lose the presidency.

This point is made more emphatic by the caucus's explicit rejection of a plan that would have guaranteed the presidency for Jefferson. Recall the unconventional proposal made by Madison a month earlier. Under this alternative, Jefferson and Burr would jointly issue a proclamation summoning the next Congress to Washington as soon as possible, and thereby allow the Republican House to vote Jefferson into office quickly. As Madison had pointed out, since Jefferson or Burr was entitled to the presidency, wouldn't a joint proclamation by both cure any constitutional deficiency?

No, says Gallatin:

[Madison's proposal] is predicated on an assumption of executive power on our part, which is liable to two formidable objections:

1. Danger of dissolution of Union, should the Eastern States support the measures which might be adopted by the present Congress.

2. Even in case of complete success on our part, the immense danger which must result to our republican institutions generally from the principle of an assumption of power not strictly warranted by the forms and substance of our constitutions being adopted, and adopted by us in any one case.

The remedy is so dangerous that, unless the plan of a new election should be connected with usurpation of power during the interregnum, submission, with all its inconveniences, may, on cool reflection, be thought preferable.[19]

Gallatin's objection no. 1 contemplates the "dissolution of the Union," leaving it to his fellow pols to fill in the details. But given the passage of two centuries, it is worth spinning out the story in more detail.

It begins with the Federalists calling for new elections under the Succession Statute before they leave Washington on March 4. As the states consider their next step, Jefferson and Burr assume executive powers and jointly summon the new Congress to Washington, and the Republican House quickly installs Jefferson as president and Burr as vice president. While all this is going on, the Federalist states of New England (the "Eastern states") respond to the Federalist call for new elections, and predictably register electoral college victories for Marshall or some such candidate. Under this scenario, it would be the Federalists who would be linking the presidency more firmly to its new basis in democratic party competition, while the Republicans would be using some very questionable constitutional maneuvers to stifle the People's will as manifested through elections.

Could the Republicans sustain this position in the court of public opinion? Facing the threat of "dissolution" of the Union, wouldn't they be obliged to back down and hold new elections in the other states? If so, wouldn't Jefferson's premature lunge for presidential power cast a pall over the Republicans' prospects during the next round of electioneering?

Madison's unconventional proposal, in short, made very little political sense: even if civil war or dissolution could be avoided, it would result in the Jeffersonians transforming their close victory in 1800 into a disastrous electoral defeat in 1801 or 1802. Gallatin's objection no. 1 seems compelling.

But not objection no. 2, which cites the illegality of Madison's proposal as a reason for preferring new elections. If it is "clearly unconstitutional" for Madison to call on Jefferson and Burr jointly to usurp presidential power by summoning the next Congress to Washington, why isn't it equally unconstitutional for Gallatin to call for new elections?

Gallatin doesn't answer this question because it is unanswerable. Our earlier discussion of the Horatius essay has already surveyed the crucial issue: Article II of the Constitution authorizes Congress to legislate for the cases involving an "inability" of the president and vice president to continue in office. It is unclear whether the language limits Congress to cases of death or other physical inability, or whether it also gives Congress the power to fill vacancies after March 4. If it does, Congress has the power to provide for both an interim presidency and new elections; if not, Gallatin's election proposal is as unconstitutional as Madison's suggestion of the joint exercise of presidential prerogatives by Jefferson and Burr.

Once this is recognized, the most important thing about the Balloting Plan is not its decision to play fast and loose with the text but its self-conscious recognition of the new constitutional principle that had displaced the Founding idea: that the presidency properly belongs to the candidate whose party has won an electoral mandate from the People.

I have called this the plebiscitarian principle, and the Balloting Plan's expression of support is especially significant since it did not serve the Republican's partisan interest. Gallatin and his associates might have taken cheap and easy recourse to the new principle in protesting against Federalist efforts to deadlock the House. After all, Jefferson could only gain through a plebiscitarian protest against Federalist manipulation of the Founding rules. In supporting Gallatin over Madison in the Balloting Plan, the members of the Republican caucus knew they were taking a serious political risk: that a new election might well lead to Jefferson's defeat. Nonetheless, they were prepared to resolve the crisis generated by the rise of party competition by holding another round of party competition. Despite the partisan risks, the Republicans were remaining steadfast to the principle that it was up to the people to pick the president. They were confronting the choice between constitutional statesmanship and mere opportunism—and they were choosing to take the higher road.

But they weren't fools. We can also appreciate why they balked at the appointment of an interim president. It was one thing to seek a plebiscitarian way out of the constitutional impasse by calling on the People once again to make a choice. It was quite another to give their opponents an electoral advantage by handing over the interim presidency to a Federalist, who could then campaign for a full term from the President's House. Better for some ministerial underling to preside over the special elections—even if the underling turned out to be holdover Secretary of State John Marshall.

To sum up: the House Republican position—"Interim President No, Special Elections Yes"—made no sense as a matter of constitutional interpretation. But it made perfect sense when viewed as an unconventional adaptation to the Founding failure to anticipate the rise of the plebiscitarian presidency.

John Adams's Legalist Response

As the House Republicans were salvaging a new notion of the presidency from the wreckage, John Adams remained the incumbent president with lots of influence on the course of events. In his view, the old Constitution was plenty good enough, providing ample authority for the sitting Federalists to resolve the succession crisis in the case of a House deadlock. As he explained to Elbridge Gerry in a letter dispatched four days before the balloting began in the House: "I know no more danger of a political convulsion if a President, pro tempore, of the Senate, or a Secretary of State, or Speaker of the House, should be made President by Congress than if Mr. Jefferson or Mr. Burr is declared such. The President would be as legal in one case as in either of the others, and the people as well satisfied."[20] Adams was notorious for his irascibility, but the letter reveals a striking coolness under pressure—and just at the wrong time?

Danger lurks in these lines. The president is not merely contemplating the prospect of the Senate's selection of a Federalist as interim president of the United States; he might even follow Horatius's advice and sign a statute that placed John Marshall, then secretary of state, in the President's House.

This is in a private letter, but Adams's public conduct was hardly less provocative. On January 30 he issued a public invitation to the Senate to meet in special session on March 4.[21] Washington had extended similar invitations at previous inaugurations,[22] but Adams's message took on a different meaning when there might not be a president around to inaugurate.

This was well understood by the other side. Here is Gallatin's Balloting Plan setting out the Republican's strategic priorities:

> Outlines of our conduct.
>   1. Persevere in voting for Mr. J.
>   2. Use every endeavor to defeat any law on the subject.
>   3. Try to prevail on Mr. A. to refuse his assent to any such law, and
>   not to call the Senate on any account if there shall be no choice by
>   the House.
>   4. The Republican Senators to secede from any illegal meeting of
>   the Senate . . .[23]

More publicly, the *Philadelphia Aurora,* the Republican standby, sounded the alarm: "By what clause in the constitution he is authorized to call together that body over whom he cannot preside, or with whom he cannot even communicate after the 3d, we know not."[24]

Thomas Jefferson was in a particularly good position to make his displeasure known. Vice presidents had previously left the Senate chamber during its closing days to allow the senators to select a president pro tem for the next session. This time Jefferson broke with this custom, stuck to his Senate chair, and did all within his power to prevent the appointment—much to the delight of his party's newspapers.[25]

Constitutionally speaking, Jefferson's gesture would not prove decisive at the critical moment. Since the Senate is a continuing body, it was perfectly capable of meeting on March 4 after Jefferson's term as vice president had expired. As Congressman Elizur Goodrich explained in a private letter: "The House of Reps. indeed expires, by a succession of individuals, with new Commissions, but the Senate is a permanent Body with perpetual succession and have the same Secretary &c. without reappointment. Of course in case of no Elections by the Reps. a President of the Senate will exist to administer the Government."[26] With the Senate's secretary temporarily in the chair, the Federalist majority would be perfectly free to choose its new president pro tem, who could then immediately claim possession of the President's House under a broad reading of the statute of 1792 and the Constitution.

Gallatin's Balloting Plan suggests that the Republicans would respond by boycotting the Senate in protest.[27] But there were too few of them to deprive the Senate of a quorum,[28] so they could not launch a serious constitutional objection to the Senate meeting—though, as the Balloting Plan suggested, a popular insurrection was quite another matter.[29]

When Worlds Collide

As the House runoff continued indecisively, Thomas Jefferson began confidential dealings with John Adams:

> I called on Mr. Adams. We conversed on the state of things. I observed to him, that a very dangerous experiment was then in contemplation, to defeat the Presidential election by an act of Congress declaring the right of the Senate to name a President of the Senate, to devolve on him the government during any interregnum; that such a measure would probably produce resistance by force, and incalculable consequences, which it would be in his power to prevent by negativing such an act. He seemed to think such an act justifiable, and

observed, it was in my power to fix the election by a word in an instant, by declaring I would not turn out the federal officers, nor put down the navy, nor spunge the national debt. Finding his mind made up as to the usurpation of the government by the President of the Senate, I urged it no further . . . and turned the conversation to something else.[30]

Hear the sound of two worlds colliding. So far as Jefferson was concerned, it was Adams's constitutional responsibility to veto any statute that aimed "to defeat the Presidential election." The Republicans' election victory made Jefferson the choice of the People, and that was that. So far as Adams was concerned, this was sheer poppycock—the Constitution had not created a plebiscitarian presidency, and it was up to Jefferson to reassure his opponents on basic matters of policy and personnel before expecting them to hand over power. And if the man of the People refused to deal, his opponents were well within their constitutional rights to appoint an interim president and appeal to the People for a final judgment at a new election.

The problem, of course, is that both of them had a point. Worse yet, neither side could resolve the dispute by pointing to an authoritative provision of the written constitution. Unforgivably, the Founders had simply forgotten to say what should happen if the House failed to select a president by March 4. Rather than supplying clear rules of the game, the constitutional text was exacerbating the conflict. It is hardly surprising that Federalists like Adams and Marshall should want to retain control of the presidency on an interim basis. But the ambiguity of the text made it easy for them to convert this desire into perfectly plausible constitutional arguments—and to proceed full speed ahead with a clear conscience.

And the same was true for the Jeffersonians. They too could support their view of the text with plausible arguments. And they too could denounce, in perfectly good faith, the Federalists' effort to cling to presidential power as "plainly unconstitutional."

What is more, the Republicans had emerging constitutional principles on their side—the pervasive sense that the presidential office belonged to the candidate who won the support of the People, and not merely the electors. As a consequence, they might not only denounce any Federalist effort but call upon their supporters to rise up against "usurpation."

But the Federalists, on their side, had power: until March 4, they were in control of the House, the Senate, and the presidency. And power is no small thing.

A Fateful Weekend

As congressional Republicans braced themselves, a new factor entered into the calculations: a mob had descended on Washington, D.C. Here is an eyewitness account transmitted to the French embassy: "Persons whom curiosity had brought to Washington, more than a hundred thousand of them, began to get impatient and to mutter at the obstinacy of the Federalists, saying that the representatives of that party were voting for Burr only to throw the country into confusion."[31] More than a "hundred thousand of them"? I don't know whether the French took this seriously, but I don't.[32] Yet it is clear that the throng was big enough to overwhelm the primitive village that was then Washington, D.C. According to a letter from "a gentleman in Washington to the editor of the Baltimore *American*": "[V]ast numbers have crowded hither from all parts of the Union . . . The hotels and lodging houses have been so much crowded that in the house where I lodge fifty have slept on the floors, with no other covering than their great coats—no other underlay than their blanket."[33]

Federalists charged that a *"Parisian Game is to be attempted,"*[34] and surprisingly, this charge is substantiated by the sober Gallatin—albeit many years later when it was safe to make the concession. As he recalled the scene: "the threatened attempt to make a President by law . . . produced an excitement out-of-doors *in which some of our members participated.* It was threatened that if any man should be thus appointed President by law and accept the office, he would instantaneously be put to death."[35]

What a difference a few days make. When the balloting began on Wednesday, February 11, Washington was isolated by a snowstorm and ripe for the constitutional fait accompli envisioned by the Federalist rules. But now that the Federalists' all-nighter had failed to produce the presidency for Burr, their effort to shift constitutional gears, and appoint somebody like John Marshall interim president, was provoking death threats.

The mob in Washington was an augury of worse to come. Newspapers were full of threats of military intervention, and this wasn't idle talk on the Republican side.[36] Republicans controlled the governorships in the two states that could most easily organize a march on Washington—and James Monroe of Virginia and Thomas McKean of Pennsylvania were already taking steps to prepare their state militias for effective action. As balloting proceeded in the House, both governors were in daily contact with the Jeffersonians in the capital.

As matters built toward a crisis over the weekend, McKean was sent a dispatch that, in Gallatin's later recollection, "submit[ted] to him the propriety of having in readiness a body of militia who might, if necessary, be in Washington on the 3d of March."[37] McKean had already issued a proclamation commanding all citizens to turn in weapons belonging to the militia,[38] and had drafted a letter to Jefferson assuring him that Pennsylvania's Republicans would not "submit[] to an appointment of any other person than one of the two elected by the Electors." He reported that "arms for upwards of twenty thousand were secured, brass pieces etc. etc. and an order would have been issued for the arresting and bringing to justice every Member of Congress and other persons found in Pennsylvania who should have been concerned in the treason."[39]

Monroe had established "a chain of expresses" between Richmond and Washington with riders traveling "day and night with the dispatches entrusted to their care." He had also made secret plans to seize four thousand guns at the federal armory, and had obtained the authority to convene the state legislature "without delay" should "any plan of usurpation be attempted at the federal town."[40]

Within this setting, we have every reason to credit Jefferson's account of his negotiations with the Federalists, provided in a letter written to Monroe on Sunday, February 15:

> If they [the Federalists] could have been permitted to pass a law for putting the government into the hands of an officer, they would certainly have prevented an election. But we thought it best to declare openly and firmly, once for all, that the day such an act passed, the Middle States would arm, and that no such usurpation, even for a single day, should be submitted to. This first shook them; and they were completely alarmed at the resource for which we declared to

wit, a convention to reorganize the government and to amend it. The very word 'convention' gives them horrors; as in the present democratical spirit of America, they fear they should lose some of the favourite morsels of the constitution. Many attempts have been made to obtain terms from me. I have declared to them unequivocally, that I would not receive the government on capitulation, that I would not go into it with my hands tied.[41]

We shouldn't be surprised by Jefferson's favored remedy—an uprising of Republican militias leading to a new convention.[42] He famously denied that constitutions were forever.[43] He was in Paris at the time of the 1787 Convention, and only the emphatic efforts of his intimate friend Madison convinced him to become a reluctant supporter. If push had come to shove, he would have loved to follow the great Washington's example and serve at the head of a new convention devoted to codifying "the present democratical spirit of America." As to the prospect of violence, he was notorious for his musings on the need to "refresh the tree of liberty with the blood of tyrants."[44] And what would be more tyrannical than the prospect of John Marshall at the helm?

So far as the Federalists were concerned, such threats only confirmed their long-standing view of Jefferson as a fanatical Jacobin hell-bent on turmoil and bloodshed.

Violence is not always the product of evil men bent on nefarious deeds. It often comes from sincere, if conflicting, understandings of the nature of political reality—and a partisan readiness to follow principles to their logical conclusion. All the ingredients were there for disaster: America was very close to the brink.

And yet, on February 17, the Federalists yielded to Jefferson on the thirty-sixth ballot. After a series of bitter caucuses, a few Federalists decided to cast blank ballots and thereby deliver some additional states to Jefferson.

Rather than jubilating in his triumph, Jefferson wrote these outraged lines to Madison a day after the Federalist capitulation:

The minority in the H. of R. after seeing the impossibility of electing B. the certainty that a legislative usurpation would be resisted by arms, and a recourse to a Convention to reorganize and amend the government, held a consultation on this dilemma, whether it would be better for them to come over in a body and go with the tide of the times, or by a negative conduct suffer the election to be made by a bare majority, keeping their body entire & unbroken, to act in phalanx on such ground of opposition as circumstances shall offer; and I know their determination on this question only by their vote of yesterday . . . [T]here were ten states for one candidate [Jefferson], four for another [Burr], and two blanks. We consider this therefore as a declaration of war, on the part of this band.[45]

Apparently it was not enough for his opponents to give him the presidency; they should have done so by affirmatively joining in a universal acclamation of his merits. To do less was to declare war.

The passage of two centuries should allow a more detached view. The challenge is to understand why the Federalists chose, at the last moment, to yield the formidable legal weapons the written Constitution had placed at their command, without precipitating a civil war or a second constitutional convention.

5

What Went Right?

The constitutional miracle, if there was one, did not happen in the Philadelphia of 1787 but in the Washington of 1801. It is one thing to write a Constitution; quite another for it to survive; and still another for it to survive in a world for which it was not designed. And yet on March 4, 1801, John Marshall swore in Thomas Jefferson as the third president of the United States. The Federalists weren't particularly good sports: Marshall turned his back on Jefferson during the inaugural ceremony, and Adams refused to attend, riding out of town at four o'clock in the morning to avoid a face-to-face encounter.[1] And yet the deed was done.

It would have seemed less miraculous if the protagonists had accepted modern norms of party competition. But they did not. They persisted in viewing each other as malignant factionalists intent on destroying the republic. The transition had occurred despite their views of party competition, not because of them.

Worse yet, the Founders' Constitution was a technical mess, making the transition far more difficult than it should have been. The Philadelphia Convention had failed to think through essential details on a host of matters: the treatment of defective electoral ballots, the authority of the Senate president, the dangers of a lame-duck Congress and president, the voting rules for the House runoff. To top it off, it had created a legal vacuum if a president wasn't selected by March 4, encouraging problematic constitutional maneuverings, and threats of violence, in anticipation of an impasse.

Given these obstacles, it was surprising that the protagonists managed to fill the president's chair with anybody at all. They accomplished far more. They had successfully adapted the maladroit legalisms of the text to the living constitutional meanings of the new century. Despite the intentions of the Framers, the presidency had become the focus of an intense partisan struggle over the country's future; and despite the mechanics of the electoral college, Jefferson was on firm ground in insisting that his party had won the election and had thereby gained a mandate from the People.

If the House had selected Burr or Adams or Pinckney, or if the lame ducks in Congress and the presidency had placed Marshall in the President's House, the constitutional damage would have been severe. While the country managed to absorb electoral college disasters in 1824, 1876, and 2000, it could cushion those shocks with decades or centuries of democratic experience. But in 1800 the Constitution had not yet become an icon.

As Thomas Jefferson put the point when deferring to John Adams's electoral victory in 1796, it was imperative "to prevent the phaenomenon of a Pseudo-president at so early a day."[2] Now that the People had awarded Jefferson victory in 1800, he was acting consistently with his principles in refusing to submit, "even for a single day," to a Federalist effort to transform John Marshall, or some other party leader, into an interim president. Jefferson was in earnest in threatening to "arm" the "Middle States" and convene a new constitutional convention to redeem the "present democratical spirit of America."[3]

Suppose he had been bluffing. Even then, a Federalist presidency would have mocked the Constitution's claim to speak for We the People. The Founding text of 1787 would have been revealed as a legalistic brake on popular sovereignty, not as a creative structure for its vindication. By adapting the obsolete textual machine to the living constitutional understanding, the protagonists did the country a great service. How precisely did they carry it off?

Truth to tell, I don't think I've gotten to the bottom of this one. At the very least, I will be avoiding an obvious mistake: I won't be searching for a single act of triumphant statesmanship that saved the day. As I return once more to our story, I will be trying to show how a series of decisions made by different statesmen created a whole that was larger than the sum of its parts. I begin with John Adams and his crucial role in creating a military balance of power conducive to a peaceful transition. This requires me to turn back the clock three years to 1798, and begin at a very different moment in the political cycle: Federalists were up, Republicans were down, and Adams was anticipating a decisive triumph over his foes in the 1800 election. But he passed up his easy path to victory, and in a way that turned out to be highly significant for the peaceful resolution of the electoral crisis. I then return to February 1801, to explore how classical republican ideals mixed with new ideas about the presidency, how sincere efforts to avoid civil war mixed with crass political patronage, to yield a constructive result.

Lots of luck was required as well—but luck is what you make of it, and there is much political artistry to admire.

John Adams and the Military Temptation

The country was facing tough times in 1798, but for Adams and his party there was a brighter side. If they played their cards right, they could look forward to a long period of political ascendancy.

Foreign affairs was their trump. Jefferson and his friends had placed their bets on the French Revolution. During the early 1790s this had won them great popularity. Most Americans had seen the French as continuing their own revolutionary struggle against the despots of Europe. When war broke out between France and England, Americans began to have second thoughts. President Washington issued a proclamation declaring U.S. neutrality, which the French denounced as a betrayal of the great struggle for republican principles in the West. A succession of French governments refused to take American neutrality seriously. By June 1797 three hundred American ships had been seized under color of French authority.[4] When Adams sent a special diplomatic mission—including the rising star John Marshall along with seasoned veterans Charles Cotesworth Pinckney and Elbridge Gerry—to Paris to negotiate for an accommodation, it arrived at just the wrong time. Napoleon's armies were sweeping the field, and the French Directory cared little about the weak-kneed Americans who had attempted to remain "neutral" in the great ideological struggle they themselves had begun in 1776.

Talleyrand had just succeeded to power as foreign minister, and was intent upon using the office to enrich himself. He told the Americans that the Directory would not begin negotiations unless they came up with a hefty bribe. Such demands were hardly unprecedented, and Americans had paid up in the past. But this time the diplomats held firm, with Marshall reporting the sordid details in secret dispatches back to Washington. A deeply humiliated country responded with outrage as President Adams discreetly presented Congress with a description of the efforts by Frenchmen "X, Y, and Z" to feed at the American trough.

The Federalists rode the wave of public opinion as far as it would carry them. They enacted a Sedition Act to serve as a potent weapon against the opposition press during the upcoming election campaign. Their success at whipping up war fever promised further political dividends. The American navy was engaged in armed combat with the French, and the Federalists prepared the country for much worse to come: "Millions for defense, not one cent for tribute." Congress ordered the immediate enlistment of 12,000 recruits to quadruple the standing army of 3,500 officers and men. And it went further to create, on paper at least, another army of 50,000 more.[5]

Adams called George Washington out of retirement to serve as titular commander. Washington accepted, but on condition that Alexander Hamilton be placed in effective command of the troops. Though Adams resisted the appointment of his rival, he didn't have much choice but to go along, and the result was a great political success. Both the nation and the Federalists—was there a difference?—breathed a collective sigh of relief. Washington and Hamilton had been a fine team during the Revolution, and their reunion on the symbolic battlefield was political dynamite. Let the Jeffersonian Francophiles rage: there was nothing like a splendid little war to unite the country behind its president.

Then, and for this the republic must be eternally grateful, John Adams began to have second thoughts. Despite the war hysteria, he concluded that the French were more open to peaceful resolution than he had been led to suppose by his High Federalist advisers. In February 1799 Adams announced a total change in course: peace, not war, would be the order of the day. He dispatched William Vans Murray on another mission to France, and he dissolved Hamilton's expanded army, with the last regiment retiring from the field in June 1800.

This turnaround is crucial for an understanding of the resolution of the electoral crisis.[6] If Hamilton's army had remained in the field, Jefferson's threat to call out the militia would have lost its menace. Republicans would no longer have been able to threaten to move on Washington from their strongholds in Pennsylvania and Virginia while the Federalist militias of New England remained far from the scene. Hamilton's standing army would have had the upper hand in defense of the capital, putting the Federalists in a far stronger position to execute their deadlock strategy. With the troops behind them, it would have seemed entirely realistic to pass a statute placing Marshall at the helm, and they might have republished Horatius's brilliant essay explaining why this step was in perfect conformity with the Constitution.

Adams's policy reversal altered the political equation as well. His pacific overtures to France completely alienated Hamilton and many other leading Federalists, who were bewildered by his sudden change in course both as a matter of principle and as a matter of politics. Since Adams had inherited his cabinet from Washington, he could not even count on the loyalty of most of its members, who took their cue from Hamilton and resisted the peace policy as best they could.[7] By the spring of 1800 Adams was thoroughly sick of this foot-dragging and sabotage. But he was well aware that purging his cabinet for disloyalty might lead to an all-out conflict with Hamilton at a crucial electoral moment.

This was a time when the presidential campaign was conducted over many months, with each state holding its own election on its own schedule. New York was among the first, with its electoral results known by April,[8] and when Burr and his Republicans beat Adams in Hamilton's home state, Adams reacted with rage. Without New York's electoral vote, his future looked bleak. Suspecting Hamilton of sabotaging the election, he fired two Hamiltonians from his cabinet—replacing one with John Marshall as secretary of state. Hamilton reacted in kind: by the fall, he was publishing a pamphlet proclaiming Adams emotionally unfit for a second term.[9]

This stab in the back did grievous damage to the Federalist cause. Public backbiting is never a good thing, but it had particularly toxic effects in the political world of 1800. As we have seen, the national parties lacked the organizational resources we take for granted today. Politics was emphatically local, with a thin national political elite serving as a crucial network for coordinating activity. If the members of the elite didn't trust one another, why should their more locally rooted friends and political connections work together as part of a national team? Given the declaration of war between Adams and Hamilton, could local Federalists be confident that like-minded elites in other states would be making a major effort for the Adams-Pinckney ticket? The resulting demoralization was palpable.[10]

The disintegration of party unity also had a profound impact on John Adams. Never a man to pander for popularity, he was deeply uncomfortable about the rise of party politics. He much preferred to think of himself as a worthy successor to the great Washington—a revolutionary of the pen, not the sword, but no less distinguished. It was his service as a legislator, diplomat, and thinker that qualified him for the presidency, not petty partisan manipulation. Within this framework, Adams's courageous reversal on the war with France was further evidence of his patriotic willingness to put the nation first. If Hamilton and the others refused to follow his lead, so much the worse for them. They were nothing better than "a British faction," he repeatedly declared, adopting an older vocabulary.[11]

Adams was no political naïf. He recognized the new realities, and he desperately wanted to win in 1800—but on his own terms.[12] A scene reported by Jefferson beautifully captures these psychological complexities and suggests how they contributed to the peaceful solution of the constitutional crisis. The moment must have been excruciatingly delicate. On the same day Adams learned of his electoral defeat in New York, Jefferson spoke with the president in his capacity as vice president:

> I called on Mr. Adams on some official business. He was very sensibly affected, and accosted me with these words: "Well I understand that you are to beat me in this contest, and I will only say that I will be as faithful a subject as any you will have." "Mr. Adams," said I, "this is no personal contest between you & me. Two systems of principles on the subject of government divide our fellow-citizens into two parties. With one of these you concur, and I with the other. As we have been longer on the public stage than most of those now living, our names happen to be more generally known. One of these parties therefore has put your name at it's head, the other mine. Were we both to die to-day, tomorrow two other names would be in the place of ours, without any change in the motion of the machine. Its motion is from its principle, not from you or myself." "I believe you are right," said he, "that we are but passive instruments, and should not suffer this matter to affect our personal dispositions."[13]

Jefferson is inviting Adams to see the two of them as sharing a common fate, as fellow revolutionaries caught up by the forces of party politics, but connected by bonds of service to the republic that nothing can erase. It is this recollection of the past, not some nonexistent commitment to a two-party system, that helps explain Adams's performance during the crisis.

We don't know whether Jefferson is accurately reporting Adams's remarks, but if he is, Adams wasn't true to his word. He was a sore loser who refused to attend his successor's inauguration and cut off all personal communication for a more than a decade, despite Jefferson's efforts to renew contact. Nonetheless, Adams's distinctive form of self-understanding contributed to the peaceful resolution of the crisis. As the House of Representatives repeatedly failed to elect a president in the days after February 11, he did nothing dramatic to break the impasse in favor of his own party—for the simple reason that he did not understand himself as a party man first and foremost.

To be sure, he did call a special session of the Senate for inauguration day, thereby creating the legal basis for the appointment of a Federalist interim president. But at the moment of maximum crisis, he was content to sit back in the President's House and allow the Constitution to take care of itself, as befitted a nonpartisan successor to the great Washington.

Alexander Hamilton also made a paradoxical contribution. His disastrous attack on Adams had done him grievous damage in the eyes of other party leaders, but he was a dominating character and skillful tactician, and if he had set his mind to it he might have greatly enhanced the Federalists' capacity to exploit the crisis for short-term partisan advantage. Happily he did not do so, if for serendipitous reasons.

The crucial contingency: Hamilton and Burr both came from New York and were bitter political rivals. For Federalists from all other states Burr's election promised a continuing partnership with executive power; but for Hamilton it meant renewed struggle with his archrival from a vastly inferior position. If Federalists in New York wished to maintain good relations with the new president, Hamilton would lose standing as their leading spokesman—especially after his egregious blunders during the election campaign.

Little wonder, then, that Hamilton began an enthusiastic campaign against Burr. Writing to Congressman James Bayard (who, as we will see, played a crucial role in the outcome), Hamilton condemned Burr as an unscrupulous adventurer who "almost certain[ly] will attempt usurpation," a charge with special power at a moment when Napoleon was destroying Americans' great hopes in the future of the French Republic. Hamilton closed his lengthy exercise in character assassination with a final "point . . . which seems to me decisive":

> If the Antifoederalists [the Republicans] who prevailed in the election are left to take their own man, they remain responsible, and the Foederalists remain *free united* and without *stain*, in a situation to resist with effect pernicious measures. If the Foederalists substitute Burr, they adopt him and become answerable for him . . . Mr. Burr will become *in fact* the man of our party. And if he act ill, we must share in the blame and disgrace. By adopting him we do all we can to reconcile the minds of the Foederalists to him, and prepare them for the effectual operation of his arts. He will doubtless gain many of them, & the Foederalists will become a disorganized and contemptible party.[14]

The last lines suggest Hamilton's anxieties over his political future, but the earlier passage suggests something different and more interesting. The real-world struggle between Federalists and Republicans was prompting Hamilton to rethink the role of political parties. He was no longer condemning them in the manner of George Washington's Farewell Address (which Hamilton had largely written). He now saw them as part of the ordinary operation of government. His remarks supposed that a two-party system was here to stay—and that the Federalists would be in a better position to *return* to power if they voluntarily *gave it up* in the immediate future. There is a germ here of the modern view that considers party rotation an essential aspect of American democracy.

Yet this was not the dominant opinion in 1801. If we are to understand why the Federalists reluctantly ceded power, pride of place must go to the older forms of anti-party consciousness exhibited by John Adams during his presidency. It was precisely Adams's refusal to put his party first that led him to make peace with France and deprive the Federalists of a large standing army that could be used with decisive effect during the electoral college crisis.

Even with the military option off the table, the fate of the Constitution wasn't secure. If the Federalist leadership had played the constitutional game with unity and decision, depriving Jefferson of the presidency would have been well within its power. Worse yet, the reigning anti-party ideology could have readily justified the exclusion of Jefferson as a praise-worthy effort to contain the disease of faction before it destroyed the Commonwealth.

Paradoxically, it was precisely Adams's anti-party consciousness that played a stabilizing role. Once again, the root of the matter goes back to his decision to pursue peace with France at the cost of Federalist unity. By February 1801 this had made it impossible for Adams and Hamilton to unite behind a coordinated strategy. Instead of cooperating with each other to sustain Federalist power at the national level, they left the Federalist caucus in the House of Representatives to make its own strategic decisions without strong leadership from above.

This still did not guarantee a peaceful transition to a Jefferson presidency. There were many hotheads in the Federalist caucus, hell-bent on using the Constitution as their final defense against Jefferson and his "atheistical and Jacobinical" program.

But it didn't turn out that way. Before returning to the microdrama in the House of Representatives, consider the way in which the Republican leadership was preparing itself for the struggle.

Jefferson and Burr

For Thomas Jefferson, the stakes were clear enough. The Republicans' victory at the polls was simply another triumphal event in the saga of the American Revolution. Just as Jefferson had stood at the head of the revolutionary movement in 1776, he was now taking a stand against the Federalists' slouch toward monarchy. And once again, his appeal to the People had struck a resonating chord. The Republicans' electoral victory was not merely an occasion for a quadrennial transfer of power. It was a decisive effort by the People to reclaim their government from the corruptions of Federalism.

As a consequence, Jefferson saw the electoral college crisis in suitably apocalyptic terms. For Adams, the Constitution allowed for any number of legal resolutions to the crisis—ranging from the selection of Jefferson to the selection of Burr to the selection of Marshall. For Jefferson, there was only one legitimate answer: despite the elaborate contraption built at Philadelphia, the presidency had become a plebiscitary office, and he was the People's choice. If the Constitution failed to support this judgment, it stood revealed as illegitimate.[15]

Given the natural megalomania of political men, Jefferson's view of his victory is unremarkable. Far more revealing is the fact that his running mate, Aaron Burr, agreed with this diagnosis. Burr was skilled in the rationalizing arts of self-justification—it would have been child's play for him to adopt Adams's legalistic views and declare himself a legitimate candidate in the House runoff. This is precisely what Burr did not say in his December letter to Representative Samuel Smith, which swept through the nation's newspapers at the end of the year:

> It is highly improbable that I shall have an equal number of Votes with Mr. Jefferson; but if such should be the result every Man who knows me ought to know that I should utterly disclaim all competition—Be assured that the federal party can entertain no wish for such an exchange. As to my friends—they would dishonor my Views and insult my feelings by harbouring a suspicion that I could submit to be instrumental in Counteracting the Wishes & expectations of the U.S.—And I now constitute you my proxy to declare these sentiments if the occasion shall require.[16]

For Burr no less than Jefferson, the presidency had become a plebiscitary office. But did he really mean it? Burr had written that letter before he knew the final tally. Now that he was officially in the running, would he still "disclaim all competition"?

No, said anxious letters rushing toward Jefferson. And there seems to have been substance to the rumors. While Burr never changed his public stance, he privately refused to say he would decline the presidency if it were offered—rejecting such requests as "unnecessary, unreasonable and impertinent."[17] Two centuries onward, it's hard to say how actively Burr schemed on his own behalf, and how much he merely allowed others to scheme for him.

One thing is clear: Burr blinked at the critical moment. As the balloting began in Washington, Burr was celebrating his daughter's wedding in Albany and pondering his next step. Here is how Peter Townsend, one of the leading New York Republicans, described the scene:

> When the election by the House was about to come on Col. Burr sent for him (Mr. T.) and Genl. Swartwout to his room at Albany

(where they then all were) and laid before them a letter from Albert Gallatin, informing Burr, what was going on—telling him that the election was in the hands of Genl. Smith of Maryland—Lynn of NJersey & Edward Livingston of NY who held the balance of those three states, that they were friendly to Burr—but to secure them he must be on the spot himself, and urging him by all means to hasten to Washington without an instants delay—Burr submitted to them this letter and asked them what he should do—They replied—get into the first Conveyance you can procure—lose not a moment—hasten to Washington and secure the prize—He agreed to do so—they left him—went to the legislature—Burr did not come—they supposed he was preparing—After the House adjourned, they called at his lodgings—found his baggage packed and he ready—but at the critical moment his heart failed him—he remained at Albany and wrote letters.[18]

This story was recorded thirty-three years after the event, but it seems basically accurate.[19] And we will soon be encountering more evidence corroborating the main point: Burr's presence *was* urgently requested by his partisans in Washington, who believed that his personal engagement in the wheeling and dealing was needed to obtain the key swing votes.

What accounts for Burr's reticence? Undoubtedly, the sentiments expressed in his public letter played an important part. He recognized that the presidency had been transformed into a plebiscitary office, and that his active and public conniving would deeply compromise him if he succeeded in gaining the office in defiance of "the Wishes and expectations" of the American people. In contrast, if the House gave him the gift of the presidency while he sat passively in Albany, he might more readily weather the initial storm of public outrage and redeem himself by his conduct in office.

The strategy of public passivity also made sense within a more old-fashioned set of conventions. Under the classical republican view, it was utterly wrong for a would-be Washington to launch an aggressive campaign for office. Instead of scrambling for the job, candidates left this dirty business to friends and connections while they simply waited for the electors to appreciate their past service to the republic. By rushing down to Washington to engage in the wheeling and dealing, Burr would have violated both the old and the new understandings of the presidency at the same time.[20]

Jefferson found himself in much happier circumstances. As vice president under Adams, he could *legitimately* place himself in the nation's capital to preside over the Senate. We have already seen him using this position to his advantage, counting out his Federalist rivals from the House runoff. His constitutional role had also given him a geographic advantage over his remaining rival. While Burr paced restlessly in Albany, Jefferson was in Washington, perfectly placed to make the covert threats and secret deals necessary to emerge victorious.

Although the Founders had made an obvious blunder in assigning the Senate president a central role in the presidential vote count, this mistake had the happy consequence, in this case, of giving the right candidate a systematic strategic advantage. But it is one thing to be in the right place at the right time; quite another, to close the deal.

The Emergence of James Bayard

The House was deadlocked for thirty-five ballots: eight states for Jefferson, six for Burr, and two not voting because of ties in their state delegations. To win the presidency, Jefferson needed to induce only one state to change its vote.

All states weren't equally good bargaining partners. The easiest deals could be struck with states like Delaware, which had only a single representative in the House.[21] Delaware's congressman, the Federalist James A. Bayard, might have had less bargaining power if his party's leaders outside the House had been making a coordinated effort to control the Federalist caucus. But with Adams and Hamilton at loggerheads, the Federalist members of the House were largely thrown back on their own resources, as structured by a Constitution written in blithe ignorance of their plight.

If Delaware had sent a fool or a hothead to Congress, the nation's history might well have taken a different turn. America was lucky in Delaware's choice: although Bayard was only thirty-three years of age, he was not overwhelmed by the crisis. He explained to the Federalist caucus that

> unless Burr made his appearance here, there was no prospect of our prevailing in the present contest; that the opposite party, he was well assured, would persevere to the 4th of March before they would re-

nounce their candidate, undismayed by whatever disasters might result from leaving the nation without a president, and, consequently without a government, an event which, so far from exciting any fearful apprehensions on their part, would rather accord with their disorganizing principles; that he would continue to vote as he had done until some one of the gentlemen present of Burr's personal acquaintance would address a letter to him on the point at issue, and wait a reasonable time to receive an answer; but that, holding, as he did the vote of a state, he could not consent that the 4th of March should arrive without a chief magistrate.[22]

Dumb luck: the Founders should never have allowed the fate of the presidency to hang upon the identity of the sole representative of a tiny state, but in the circumstances, the nation could have done much worse than rely on Bayard.

Luck goes only so far in accounting for the micropolitics of the outcome. Notwithstanding Jefferson's decision to bar his Federalist competitors from the House runoff, and notwithstanding Bayard's statesmanly reluctance to push the country over the precipice, crucial decisions remained to be made—most notably by Aaron Burr.

Bayard wasn't bluffing when he told the Federalist caucus that it was up to Burr to make the next move. As he explained in a letter to Hamilton:

In one case I was willing to take Burr . . . If by his conduct he had completely forfeited the confidence and friendship of his Party and left himself no resort but the support of the federalists, there are many considerations which would have induced me to prefer him to Jefferson. But I was enabled soon to discover that he was determined not to shackle himself with federal principles . . .

The means existed of electing Burr, but they required his cooperation. By deceiving one Man (a great blockhead) and tempting two (not incorruptible) he might have secured a majority of the States. He will never have another chance of being President of the U.states and the little use he has made of the one which has occurred gives me but a humble opinion of the talents of an unprincipled man.[23]

Bayard's condemnation of Burr was shared by Jefferson, who was filling his diary with his anxieties about Burr's intentions.[24]

Burr has gotten a bum rap. His refusal to break with traditional and emerging constitutional norms saved the republic from a violent lurch in the Latin American direction. I reckon his restraint as the second most important single factor in accounting for the peaceful transition of power— only John Adams's decision to disband Hamilton's army was more important.[25]

Once Burr refused to take an express coach from Albany to Washington, a space had been cleared for James Bayard to play the part of statesman. The revolutionary scenes playing out in the capital city were particularly troubling to a man from Delaware, a border state which might readily become a battleground if hostilities between Federalist New England and the Republican South began in earnest. As Bayard wrote to John Adams shortly after the crisis, "representing the smallest State in the Union, without resources which could furnish the means of self protection, I was compelled by the obligation of a sacred duty so to act as not to hazard the constitution upon which the political existence of the State depends."[26]

But if anxieties about "self protection" helped propel the man from Delaware into action, Bayard quickly moved beyond them as he considered his next step. Having condemned Burr as "unprincipled," he could now indulge in some wheeling and dealing of his own. Following classical Republican norms, Bayard did not approach Jefferson directly but dealt through an intermediary, Representative Samuel Smith of Maryland.[27] As in the later electoral college crises of 1825 and 1877, things get cloudy at this point. Smith reported to Bayard that Jefferson would go along with his demands—which mixed matters of high policy with very concrete efforts to keep control over the customs houses of Wilmington and Philadelphia. But Jefferson later denied that he had stooped to such sordid dealings.[28]

Two centuries later, it is hard to say what really happened. In his eagerness to induce Bayard to end the crisis, perhaps Smith misrepresented Jefferson's intentions, or perhaps Jefferson misremembered later, or was simply lying.[29] There is no doubt, however, that Bayard thought he had a deal. He immediately wrote to Allen McLane, the incumbent Federalist in charge of the customs house in Wilmington: "I have taken good care of you."[30]

I hardly wish to blame Jefferson for bargaining his way into the presidency. If Paris was worth a Mass, surely the Constitution was worth the

Collectorship of the Port of Wilmington. While future generations of scholars might have been fascinated by the proceedings of a second Constitutional Convention chaired by Thomas Jefferson, there can be no doubt that Jefferson made the wise decision: if Bayard was willing to give him the presidency, there was no need to push the nation over the constitutional brink.

On February 17, 1801, the House awarded the presidency to Jefferson on its thirty-sixth ballot, with the Republicans' leading newspaper, the *Philadelphia Aurora,* trumpeting the significance of the event: "[T]he Revolution of 1776, is now, and for the *first* time arrived at its completion . . . On Tuesday last . . . the question . . . on the issue of which rested the Liberty, Constitution, and happiness of America, was terminated as every republican and honest man wished . . .—and on that day the sun of aristocracy set, to rise no more."[31]

The *Aurora*'s shout of triumph was distinctly premature. Jefferson and his new Republican majority in Congress would seek to realize their "revolution of 1800," but their failure to call a constitutional convention proved consequential. Time and again, the structures of the Constitution of 1787 would throw the system into crisis as Federalists counterattacked and Republicans tried to consolidate their victory.

The Synergies of Statesmanship

It was no small thing for the country to survive its first great constitutional crisis, and it is well to reflect on the mixture of statesmanship and luck that made it possible. John Adams's courageous decision to seek peace with France and disband Hamilton's army created a geomilitary space that made a peaceful transition more likely. If the Federalists had engaged in desperate legalistic maneuvers in Washington, D.C., the Republicans could have called out the militias of nearby Pennsylvania and Virginia, while the Federalists would have had to appeal to forces in far-off New England. If Hamilton's army had still been in existence, the balance of forces would have been very different. Adams also acted with restraint during the critical week when the presidency was up in the air—refraining from a strategy of bitter-end opposition, and leaving the Federalist caucus in the House to its own devices.

A second unsung hero was Aaron Burr. Despite his notorious reputation, he displayed a good deal of statesmanship at his moment of truth. To be sure, he mixed his statesmanship with self-interest. If he had wished to be a Republican saint, he could have categorically told his allies, in private meetings, that he would decline the presidency under any circumstances. But Burr was no more a saint than Jefferson or Marshall. He allowed his allies to scheme on his behalf, but he refused to take the fateful step that might have won him the presidency at the cost of shattering the republic's fragile legitimacy. At the critical juncture, he kept his distance from Washington, D.C., making it very tough for him to compete with Jefferson, who was on the scene, wheeling and dealing. This was a key decision, and Burr knew it. Nevertheless, he stayed in Albany, in deference to both traditional notions of republican honor and the rising idea of popular sovereignty.

With Burr absent and Adams passive, Jefferson made the most of his opportunities in Washington as sitting vice president. Through dumb luck, he was given the chance to prevent his rivals from entering the House runoff. He then played his strategic cards well. While he threatened force in private, he never issued military pronunciamentos in public; and while he almost certainly cut a deal with Bayard, he did it with an indirection that permitted deniability. There were no obvious signs of military coup or corrupt bargain. So far as the broader public could see, the House of Representatives had, after strenuous deliberation, selected the People's choice as president through constitutional means.

And finally, James Bayard made a signal contribution. The geomilitary context was important: Delaware might have become a battlefield if the Pennsylvania militia had started its march on Washington. But this bloody prospect might not have deterred a hothead from joining a bitter-end effort to block Jefferson. The country was lucky that the tiny state of Delaware had chosen a large statesman to discharge the grave responsibilities that the Framers of the Constitution, in a fit of inadvertence, had assigned to him.

Adams and Jefferson, Bayard and Burr: each of them had a chance to throw a monkey wrench or two into the machinery of government. Somehow or other, they managed to restrain themselves. With the help of an awful lot of luck, they cranked up the creaking constitutional machine to generate a grand new principle: that the president should be the *choice of the People,* as revealed through democratic party competition.

PART TWO

The People and the Court

Constitutional Brinksmanship

After taking his oath of office, Thomas Jefferson used his Inaugural Address to reflect upon the remarkable character of his victory: "During the contest of opinion through which we have passed, the animation of discussions and of exertions has sometimes worn an aspect which might impose on strangers unused to think freely and to speak and to write what they think; but this being now decided by the voice of the nation, announced according to the rules of the Constitution, all will, of course, arrange themselves under the will of the law, and unite in common efforts for the common good."[1]

The new president chose his words carefully. According to Jefferson, it was the "voice of the nation" that had selected him, with the Constitution merely providing "the rules" through which this judgment was "announced."

All in all, an accurate diagnosis—or so I suggested in Part One of this book. And yet it contained the germ of grave difficulties for the future. What if the "voice of the nation," as expressed by its living representatives, conflicted with the will of the People, as expressed by the Constitution?

Jefferson's Inaugural Address rejects this possibility: now that the election is past, Americans would, "of course," unite for the common good. The Republicans were a party that would end all parties.[2] Their victory would restore the party-free politics that the Founders had envisaged. There would always be factions—but their multiplicity and special interests would enable large-souled statesman like Jefferson, Madison, and Monroe to transcend their narrow demands as they searched for the public good. "We are all Republicans, we are all Federalists," his famous words assured the multitude.

These anti-party convictions may seem naive to us, but Jefferson turned out to be right in the middle run. By a paradoxical twist, the Feder-

alists' demise was brought about by the incompetence of Republican foreign policy—which led the country into a disastrous war with England for
which it was utterly unprepared. Just as the Republicans' cumulating military blunders drove the New England Federalists to consider secession at
the Hartford Convention, the wheel of fortune turned: Napoleon went
down to defeat in Europe, the war with Britain became pointless, peace
was restored, Andrew Jackson won his famous victory at New Orleans,
and the Federalists suddenly became discredited as seditious factionalists—thereby redeeming Jefferson's view of them. While the great man
was forever fearful of a Federalist renaissance, he went to his grave on July
4, 1826, without witnessing the rebirth of party politics under the Democrats Andrew Jackson and Martin Van Buren—and without learning that
the sun would never again set on the two-party system in America.

But in 1801 these twists and turns were for the trackless future. During the next decade the Federalists remained a significant political force—
waning and waxing and regularly contesting the Republican vision of the
common good.[3] Since they were always a minority in Congress, the Republicans could readily contain them there—but the courts were another
matter.

Jefferson and his party confronted a solidly Federalist judiciary with
John Marshall at its head, ready to use the written Constitution of 1787 to
disparage the "voice of the nation" expressed by repeated Jeffersonian victories at the polls. As Republicans returned to Washington to take control
of Congress in December 1801, Jefferson was already clear about the
present danger: "[The Federalists] have retired into the judiciary as a
stronghold. There the remains of federalism are to be preserved and fed
from the treasury and from that battery all the works of republicanism are
to be beaten down and erased. By a fraudulent use of the Constitution,
which has made judges irremoveable, they have multiplied useless judges
merely to strengthen their phalanx."[4]

The stage had been set for a fierce struggle over the meaning of the
revolution of 1800 and its relationship to the constitution of 1787. Jefferson and Marshall repeatedly went to the brink to gain the upper hand, and
each man repeatedly overreached himself. My story ends with them glar-
ing at each other across the institutional barricades, each hoping to upset
the constitutional balance and attain a decisive advantage at the next opportunity.

Yet despite their intentions, their exercises in brinksmanship proved remarkably productive. As Americans began their second war with England in 1812, their Constitution was emerging as a creative synthesis of 1787 and 1800, incorporating both Federalist and Republican values into reigning doctrine.

I view this creative synthesis as the great achievement of the Founding era. If either side had won decisively, the other would have been alienated from the ongoing constitutional project. If both came away with something, it made sense to continue arguing about what that something amounted to. By creating a constitutional law of partial victories, the two sides constructed a world of constitutional meaning that was larger than the sum of its Republican/Federalist parts. The next generation would be invited to view the Constitution as a resource transcending partisanship, permitting a distinctive language for a never-ending dispute over fundamental values.

The standard story fails to appreciate this point. It recalls this period principally to celebrate the Marshall Court's defense of the Constitution of 1787 in Marbury v. Madison—as if the Republican revolution of 1800 were an historical detail of middling importance.

This distorts *Marbury*'s significance. Marshall's arguments for judicial review were not particularly new.[5] But he adapted them in *Marbury* to confront a genuinely new challenge—the shattering rise of the plebiscitary presidency to constitutional prominence. My aim is to locate *Marbury* within the process of creative confrontation, brinksmanship, and adaptation precipitated by Jefferson's victory in 1800. Chapter 6 returns to 1800 and presents a fuller account of the Federalist reaction to the presidential election returns. I have been emphasizing Adams's remarkable restraint in allowing his rival to win the presidency in the House runoff. He was a different man when it came to the judiciary, refusing to allow the new president and Congress to determine the future of the federal courts. The Federalists used their last days in power to appoint Marshall as chief justice and to create a new cadre of Federalist circuit judges to dispense their version of justice throughout the land.

Federalist brinksmanship generated a massive Republican reaction when the rising party came to town in December. Chapter 7 describes how Congress, under Jefferson's leadership, destroyed the new Federalist courts and ordered the Supreme Court justices to cooperate in their colleagues' destruction.

This judicial purge forced the Marshall Court to engage in some brinksmanship of its own. Chapter 8 follows the justices as they considered whether to respond to the Republican assault on judicial independence by going on strike. After contemplating the dangers of dramatic resistance, the justices retreated from the edge of the abyss. They reluctantly chose to cooperate with Jefferson's purge of the Federalist courts.

Their final surrender was announced in Stuart v. Laird. The Marshall Court issued this decision one week after *Marbury*, and once it is taken seriously, it requires a fundamental reinterpretation of that famous case. Once *Marbury* is read together with *Stuart*, it no longer seems a definitive effort by the Marshall Court to lay down the law to the Jeffersonian presidency. *Marbury* and *Stuart* together appear as a very preliminary effort at judicial synthesis—seeking to integrate the meaning of the revolution of 1800 into the Court's interpretation of the Constitution of 1787.

Jefferson wanted total victory. Chapter 9 explores the Republican campaign to sweep the Supreme Court clear of Federalist obstructionists, reaching its climax with the impeachment trial of Justice Chase. Chase's narrow acquittal in the Senate marked the limits of the presidentialist transformation. Despite the destruction of the Federalist lower courts, the Federalist Supreme Court managed to maintain its independence—a crucial victory, at least as crucial as Marbury v. Madison.

Chapter 10 then considers how the Court used its institutional victory to develop a more complex message about the relationship between 1787 and 1800. By the time the nation confronted its second war with England, the Court began to weave major themes from 1800 into the living law of the Constitution. There is no mystery behind its growing appreciation of Republican values—by this point the Court was composed of a majority of justices appointed by Republicans, who could hardly be expected to ignore entirely the political movement that had placed them on the Court.

Most parts of this story are familiar, at least to a few specialists. Unfortunately, they treat each episode separately, and often with the zeal of latter-day partisans. Many leading legal historians have written in tones of Federalist outrage as they describe the Republican assault,[6] while political historians have often looked upon Marshall as engineering a Federalist coup.[7]

With the distance of two centuries, we should be trying for a more sympathetic form of understanding. I will not be writing as if I were an appellate judge of the Supreme Court of history, pronouncing the last word on the constitutional merits of each side's brief. My aim will be to show how the Constitution provided both Republicans and Federalists with a language for their heated debates about the meaning of 1787 and 1800— resulting in a constitutional synthesis that would have bitterly disappointed both sides at the moment of Jefferson's First Inaugural.

And a good thing too.

6

Federalist Counterattack

Return to the 1800 election one last time, but from a different constitutional angle. We have been observing the Federalists in Washington flirting with a strategy that would deadlock the House, and transform John Marshall into the next president, without focusing on a rather obvious question: Why would the Constitution give the folks who had lost the election the right to stay in power for three months to make so much mischief?

Modern constitutions don't make this mistake. Once the powers that be lose an election, they are quickly sent packing, so that the repudiated incumbents can't do any serious damage. How could the Framers have missed such an obvious point?

I raise the question now because it provides the indispensable entry into the next phase of the crisis. While the lame-duck Federalists finally allowed Jefferson to gain the presidency, they exploited their position for everything it was worth when it came to the judiciary. Not only did they refuse to allow the incoming president to fill the vacant chief justiceship; they created an entirely new tier of federal courts and packed them with Federalist judges before Adams's term ran out on March 4.

This exercise in brinksmanship generated a powerful backlash when the Republican Congress finally arrived in Washington in December 1801 —setting up a crisis that grievously damaged the principle of judicial independence and threatened to sweep away the Supreme Court. And yet, for all the Sturm und Drang, and the genuine danger, this Federalist overreaching proved remarkably creative. Without it there would have been no chief justiceship for John Marshall, no Marbury v. Madison.

At the same time, Federalist overreaching also created the first great precedent in the history of the plebiscitary presidency—establishing its power to sweep away a power-hungry establishment of officeholders when they set themselves against the will of the American people.

Before telling this story, I will consider how it could have happened in the first place. Why did the Constitution allow lame ducks to exploit their political power without regard to a negative judgment by the People at the polls?

The Dangers of Muddling Through

Amazingly enough, nobody at the Convention ever asked this question. It was resolved by default, and in a disastrous way.[1]

Begin with the single constitutional provision that speaks to the issue: "Congress shall assemble at least once in every Year, and such Meeting shall be on the first Monday in December, unless they shall by law appoint a different Day."[2] If the First Congress had started in December as provided, the lame-duck problem might have been minimized. The states could have organized congressional elections in the early fall, just a few months before the new Congress assembled "on the first Monday in December."

Historical accident intervened. The Philadelphia Convention went public with its proposal in September 1787, and it took about a year before nine states ratified, giving life to the document.[3] On September 13, 1788, the old Continental Congress passed a resolution specifying the terms for transition to the new regime. This is when a mismatch emerged between the Constitution's December starting date and mundane political realities. It was already too late for the new government to begin in December 1788. It was simply impossible for the states to hold congressional elections, choose senators, and select presidential electors within ten short weeks. At the same time, December 1789 seemed a long way in the future—apparently too long for the Continental Congress.

This is, at any rate, the best I can do to explain the Congress's decision to set Wednesday, March 4, 1789, as the day "for commencing proceedings."[4] This ordinance pushed the states into electoral gear, but a majority of Congress did not get to New York City in time to start up the government. Only on April 1 did a majority of House members straggle into town, thereby constituting a quorum, and it took the Senate until

April 6 to meet this hurdle—at which time the electoral votes were counted, and George Washington and John Adams were sworn in as president and vice president.[5] Despite these facts, the Continental Congress's resolution, setting the start-up date for March 4, was—for no obvious reason—taken as determinative. Congress not only treated it as the official beginning of its own term; it also supposed that Washington's term began then as well, setting March 4 as the date on which future presidents would begin their service in office.[6]

This ill-considered decision had terrible consequences. The fiat of the Continental Congress engaged the text of the Constitution in unanticipated but unfortunate ways. The crucial bits of text decree that representatives shall serve for two years, presidents for four, and senators for six. Since the government's birthday was established as March 4, the text required the terms of all incumbents to end on that date for the next 150 years—until the Twentieth Amendment, passed in 1933, changed the rules.

The March 4 date did not mesh well with the constitutional provision instructing Congress to meet each year on "the first Monday in December." If Congress held to this schedule, the December starting date would generate a constitutional anomaly every other year. Consider, for example, how the calendar unfolded for the First Congress, elected during the winter of 1788. Although their successors were selected in 1790, the terms of the members of the First Congress did not end until March 4, 1791. Despite their repudiation by the voters, these lame ducks possessed full lawmaking power during a "short session" beginning on the first Monday in December and ending at noon on March 4. In contrast, congressmen elected in 1790 would wait more than a year before taking over on the "first Monday in December" in 1791.

No sane member of the Convention would have authorized this silly schedule. It was merely a remote possibility in 1787, springing into reality only when the Continental Congress breathed life into the new Constitution later on.

But wait, all hope was not lost. The Constitution did grant Congress the express authority "to appoint a different day" for its opening session, and this gave the First Congress a chance to deal responsibly with the lame-duck problem.

A rough-and-ready solution was at hand. Congress might have passed a general statute setting March 4, say, as the normal starting date for its annual sessions. Under this schedule, the First Congress would have met in March 1789 and March 1790, completing its election-year session before the 1790 campaigns began in earnest. Congressmen elected in 1790 would then have been able to convene on March 4, 1791, and there would have been no need for a lame-duck session of the First Congress.

Nobody paused to consider this possibility.[7] At its second session, the First Congress simply voted a resolution convening a third session in December 1790, even though its members would be lame ducks by that point.[8] This non-decision set a precedent that later Congresses mindlessly carried forward.[9]

Until the Twentieth Amendment was enacted in 1933, Congress met on this silly schedule. Each new Congress began its first session more than a year after members were elected, on "the first Monday of December." This was called the "long session" since it could go on indefinitely. The next December, the lame-duck Congress would meet for its "short session," limited in duration because the terms of all members of the House, and one-third of the Senate, automatically expired on March 4.

Why did the First Congress make such a fateful decision with so little thought? To some degree, it was a product of parliamentary procedure. The constitutional text required Congress to act affirmatively and pass a statute to change the December starting date, which operated automatically otherwise. So there was no pressing need for Congress to debate whether to meet for a third session after the elections—inertia sufficed to bring a lame-duck meeting into existence. Shortsightedness also intervened: members of the First Congress thought they still had work to do, and wanted to do it, even though newly elected representatives were waiting in the wings.

Self-interest also played a part. America was an agricultural country, and winter sessions of Congress were most convenient, since nothing much was happening on the farm. If they had decided to begin annual sessions in March, many congressmen would have been pulled away from their plantations at planting season, the worst possible moment.

Finally, the First Congress did not expect regular party competition to become a fixture of national political life. It recognized that the recent campaign for the Constitution had split the country, but it didn't expect this split to continue. While there were many disagreements during the First Congress, these had not hardened into partisan patterns.[10]

In a world without parties, the pathological potential of the lame-duck schedule was not so obvious. Each election would bring new men to Congress, but the newcomers would not encounter two coherent groupings on the floor, eager to integrate them into their ongoing struggle for power. Instead, they would enter a more diffuse environment, with congeries of local notables representing the dominant opinions of their communities in more mediated ways. Within this political setting, the problem posed by lame-duck authority might not have seemed big enough to warrant disruption of the planting season. In any event, the early Congresses muddled along on the December schedule, making temporary changes in the calendar from time to time,[11] but never confronting the underlying lame-duck problem—until it exploded into public view in December 1801.

As the Sixth Congress returned to Washington for its "short" lame-duck session, the Federalist majorities in both houses found themselves in a condition of overwhelming temptation. Thanks to inadvertence at the Founding and the serendipitous decision of the Continental Congress to begin matters in March, the constitutional machine was giving them a golden opportunity to abuse their political power before handing it over to their rivals.[12] If anybody at the Philadelphia Convention or the early Congresses had focused on this prospect, nobody would have allowed it to take place.

That is just the point. Federalists and Republicans would have to work out the consequences of the Founders' blunders on their own—manipulating the institutions and texts of 1789 in ways never anticipated a decade earlier.

We have already explored one big consequence of the lame-duck blunder. If it had been up to the newly elected House to resolve the standoff between Burr and Jefferson, the electoral college crisis would have been easily resolved. The newly elected House, with its strong Republican majority, would have picked Jefferson on the first ballot. Jefferson experienced such heavy sledding only because he had to convince the lame-duck Federalist House of his merits—and he succeeded only because of the Constitution's curious voting rules that prevented the Federalists from using their House majority to select Burr.

But as to all other matters, the Federalists were not encumbered by these special voting rules. Adams and the lame-duck Congress could pass any law, and make any appointment, on the basis of a simple majority vote. Looking back from the twenty-first century, it is pretty clear how the Federalists should have handled themselves. Party leaders should not be spoilsports: once they have lost the election, they should not squeeze the last drop of short-term gain out of their waning power. They should cooperate with the winners to ensure a smooth transition. In the long run, everybody will be better off.

The Federalists and the Republicans viewed this matter differently. They were perfectly aware that the two-party division was tearing the constitutional fabric apart. But they had a very hard time integrating this insight into the *anti-party* framework that still dominated so much of their thinking.

Begin with Adams, who saw himself as following in Washington's footsteps of nonpartisan loyalty to the Constitution and its vision of strong central government. He understood the Federalists' efforts at party organization strictly in defensive terms: the Jeffersonians had been mobilizing in a seditious effort to push the Republic down the disastrous path marked by the atheistic French, and Washington's followers had no choice but to organize their own political forces in self-defense. Rather than seeing himself as a party leader, Adams believed—with a good deal of justice—that he had lost the election by placing the public good above partisan advantage in seeking peace with France.

There was nothing wrong, then, in struggling onward for the public good during the lame-duck period. If there was any doubt, it was resolved by the precedent set by the great Washington at the end of his administration. With Adams preparing for his inauguration, Washington had continued making appointments and proposing legislation.[13] Why not continue in the same spirit?

This is not, to put it mildly, the way Jefferson and his fellow Republicans saw the situation. On their view, the People had spoken in the last election—revealing the Federalists for the factionalists they were. Now that their fellow Americans had repudiated this small band of Anglomen and monocrats, it was utterly wrong for them to push onward as if nothing had happened. Yet this is precisely what Adams and his Federalists insisted on doing—with results both predictable and paradoxical.

Predictably, the Federalists' unfettered exercise of lame-duck power threw the system into renewed crisis. Though the Constitution had stupidly given the Federalists an opportunity to exploit their last moments in power, it did not allow them to postpone the day of reckoning indefinitely. When the newly elected Republican Congress finally arrived in Washington in December 1801, the new majority immediately began to reverse the decisions of the lame-duck Federalist Congress they considered illegitimate. The resulting struggle once again shook the system to its foundations.

At the end of the day, a curious paradox emerged. Generally speaking, abuses of power lead to further abuses which yield a corrosive decline in overall institutional legitimacy. But in this case the Federalists' abuse of lame-duck authority ultimately yielded some very constructive outcomes. John Adams would have never appointed John Marshall, and Marbury v. Madison would have never been written, were it not for the ridiculous lame-duck schedule that had been foisted upon the American people through a collective fit of inadvertence. Centuries later, the modern institution of judicial review continues to be shaped by its serendipitous origins.

For the moment I am more interested in seeing how things stood in December 1800, as John Adams began to confront news of his defeat and the prospect of three more months in office as president of the United States.

Marshall's Appointment

Adams's moment of electoral truth came just when Oliver Ellsworth's letter of resignation as chief justice arrived in Washington, D.C., in mid-December. If the president was going to fill this office, he would have to act fast.

Adams did not hesitate, refusing to do the gentlemanly thing and allow the next administration to fill the office. He was a bitter man. While he harbored no love for the Jeffersonians, he was no less estranged from many members of his own party, led by Hamilton, who had betrayed him during the recent election. As a consequence, he did not consult with the Federalist members of the Senate who had it within their power to reject his nominee. He took the posture of the heroic Washington, rising above party and using his final appointments to serve the public good that was so deeply threatened by the oncoming Republican ascendancy. And yet, while Adams conceived himself in the heroic mode, he was very alert to the micropolitical dimensions of the situation. John Marshall would never have made it to the Court had it not been for John Adams's grim determination to squeeze every bit of advantage out of his waning days of power.

Marshall was not Adams's first, or even second, choice. The president nominated John Jay for the job within four days of receiving Ellsworth's resignation—and the Senate moved with equal speed in confirming the nomination on December 19.[14] The logic of the choice expressed Adams's view of himself as a nonpartisan leader in the tradition of the great Washington. Indeed, Washington himself had selected Jay as the nation's first chief justice—and Jay had served until 1795, when he resigned from the bench to become New York's governor. Now that his term was ending, perhaps he might be willing to return to the Court?[15]

Jay had ostentatiously refused to collaborate with Hamilton's scheming during the last election. This made him the perfect choice. He was a strong Federalist, untainted by Hamiltonian faction. And his past service to the republic would insulate his selection from predictable complaints from the Jeffersonians: surely the most virulent partisan would not dare to challenge the nomination of a man found worthy of the chief justiceship by Washington himself?

There was only one problem: Would Jay accept? After all, he had quit the Court in 1795.

With the clock ticking, Adams didn't take the time to find out. His nominated Jay without asking him, and once the Senate approved, Secretary of State Marshall dispatched the commission to the governor's mansion in Albany. Meanwhile, Adams was busy preparing Plan B for the possibility—indeed probability—that Jay would reject the appointment. His backup strategy had two parts: first, promote one of the senior sitting justices, most probably Paterson, to the chief justiceship; next, fill the vacancy created by Paterson's promotion with a leading Federalist from Pennsylvania—a large state which had been unrepresented on the Court since James Wilson's death.

Adams's choice was Jared Ingersoll, then United States district attorney in Philadelphia and a leading Federalist. On December 23, one day after he sent the commission off to Jay, Adams wrote to his son Thomas, a young lawyer in Philadelphia: "I have appointed Mr. Jay chief Justice. He may refuse, if he should I shall follow the line of judges [sitting on the Supreme Court] most probably & then there will be a vacancy I wish to know if Mr. Ingersoll would accept an appointment as one of the assistant justices of the superior court."[16] Ingersoll proved noncommittal, though the younger Adams was confident that, in the end, he would accept: "He has a stake in the common weal, and cannot be indifferent as to its protection from wild theories, and no less extravagant practise. I hope he may come in."[17] Not much more could be done about Plan B until the fate of Plan A was determined.

Certainly Adams minced no words in pleading with Jay:

> I have nominated you to your old station. This is as independent of the inconstancy of the people, as it is of the will of a President. In the future administration of our country, the firmest security we can have against the effects of visionary schemes or fluctuating theories, will be in a solid judiciary; and nothing will cheer the hopes of the best men so much as your acceptance of this appointment . . . I had no permission from you to take this step, but it appeared to me that Providence had thrown in my way an opportunity, not only of marking to the public where, in my opinion, the greatest mass of worth remained collected in one individual, but of furnishing my country with the best security its inhabitants afforded against the increasing dissolution of morals.[18]

To put it gently, Adams did not view the Republican victory in the modern way—as a standard feature of a democratic system based on the regular alternation of power. He saw his defeat as an indicator of "the increasing dissolution of morals," and called upon Jay, his fellow statesman and revolutionary comrade, to stand as a heroic bulwark against "visionary schemes or fluctuating theories."

Many times before, Jay had responded to the call. This time he turned Adams down flat. His problem was more physical than spiritual. He well remembered that Supreme Court justices did not spend much time hearing appeals in the nation's capital. Instead, they spent most of their professional lives riding circuit in one or another region of the country, holding trials in collaboration with the resident district judge on matters of federal importance. The result was physical exhaustion, which the fifty-five-year-old Jay was not willing to endure: "independent of other considerations, the state of my health removes every doubt, it being clearly and decidedly incompetent to the fatigues incident to the office."[19] He had hoped that Congress would attend to the repeated complaints of the justices and make the Supreme Court into a strictly appellate panel, assigning the task of conducting trials to a special cadre of circuit judges. But, he wrote to Adams,

> those expectations have not been realized, nor have we hitherto seen convincing indications of a disposition in Congress to realize them. On the contrary, the efforts repeatedly made to place the judicial department on a proper footing have proved fruitless.
>
> . . . I am induced to doubt both the propriety and the expediency of my returning to the bench under the present system; especially as it would give some countenance to the neglect and indifference with which the opinions and remonstrances of the judges on this important subject have been treated.[20]

When Jay posted this letter from Albany on January 2, he had no reason to suspect that the lame-duck Congress was going to respond to his complaints with unexampled energy. But it took more than two weeks for Jay's letter to wend its way from Albany to Washington—and politics can change a lot in two weeks.

On January 5 the Federalists brought a sweeping judicial reform to the floor of the House which proposed a decisive end to the justices' circuit-riding labors. If the Federalists got their way, the Supreme Court would stay in Washington, and trials would be conducted by a new corps of federal circuit judges. Apart from the merits of this initiative, the expansion of the judiciary had one obvious partisan advantage: it would provide a home for Federalist loyalists who might gain the favor of the lame-duck president and Senate by March 4.

When Jay's letter of rejection finally reached Secretary of State John Marshall on January 19, the House was already on the verge of passing the bill and sending it to the Senate for expeditious approval. We shall shortly consider the bill more carefully, but for now the important aspect has to do with the size of the Supreme Court. During the first decade of the republic there were six justices riding circuit throughout the country. Now that the Court was going to function principally in an appellate capacity, six seemed an awkward, and excessive, number. It too easily allowed for deadlock when the Court divided three to three. The annual number of appeals was also modest. Five justices were more than enough. The Federalist bill cut the Court's membership from six to five.[21]

This reform was sensible enough, but it also had a partisan implication. The existing vacancy on the Court would vanish the moment the new statute was signed into law, but if Adams acted quickly, six justices would continue to sit until one decided to retire.

Since Adams was holding himself aloof from his fellow party members on the appointment, Federalist congressmen used Secretary of the Navy Benjamin Stoddert to impress him with the urgency of the situation. Bad weather prevented Stoddert from making the case in person—or perhaps Stoddert used the weather as an excuse for avoiding an interview with the notoriously irascible Adams. In any event, Stoddert's written message of January 19 has come down to us, leaving a trace of the strategic dynamics.

He tells Adams of the House's plan to pass the measure on to the Senate on the very next day, and he concludes with a cautionary note: "As the bill proposes a reduction of the Judges to five—and as there are already five Judges in commission, it is suggested that there might be more difficulty in appointing a chief Justice without taking him from the present Judges, after the passage of this bill *even by one branch of the Legislature,* than before."[22] Stoddert wasn't telling Adams anything he didn't already know: the lame-duck rush by Congress to appoint a new group of Federalist circuit judges was threatening his lame-duck rush to appoint a sixth Supreme Court justice.

Or more precisely, the congressional dynamic had increased the stakes involved in Adams's appointment. If the president was going to fill the vacancy, he would have to act *very* quickly. If he succeeded, however, he would reap even greater gains in his campaign against "the increasing dissolution of morals." Once he filled the sixth slot with a right-thinking Federalist, the subsequent enactment of the Court-shrinking statute would deprive Adams's successor of his first Supreme Court appointment—since the next vacancy would merely reduce the six-man Court down to its newly specified size of five. The game was now double or nothing: either Adams would lose his own chance to make an appointment or he would deprive his "dissolut[e]" opponents of their chance to fill a vacancy.

One thing was clear. If Adams hoped to win, he would have to abandon Plan B. Less than a month had passed since he had been preparing the way for a promotion of Paterson to the chief justiceship and the nomination of Ingersoll to fill Paterson's seat on the Court. Now this two-step strategy verged on unseemliness—once he announced Paterson's nomination as chief justice, it would be yet more egregious to rush to fill the resulting vacancy during the few short days before the new statute extinguished it. Worse yet, Adams could not be sure that Ingersoll would accept the appointment. If he was to win his race against time, he would have to pick somebody who (1) was not serving currently on the Court, (2) could credibly be nominated as chief justice, (3) could say yes *immediately*, which implied (4) that he was already in Washington, D.C., then a tiny village.

The president might well have been pondering the dilemma posed by Stoddert's letter when his secretary of state, John Marshall, arrived with bad news: John Jay's letter rejecting the chief justiceship had finally arrived. Marshall later described the scene: "When I waited on the President with Mr. Jays letter declining the appointment he said, 'Who shall I nominate now?' I replied that I could not tell, as I supposed that his objection to Judge Patteson remained. He said in a decided tone 'I shall not nominate him.' After a moments hesitation he said 'I believe I must nominate you.' I had never before heard myself named for the office and had not even thought of it. I was pleased as well as surprized, and bowed in silence. Next day I was nominated."[23] Shortly thereafter, the Federalist House passed the new judiciary bill by a party-line vote of 51 to 43.[24]

The lame-duck dynamic not only explains Marshall's nomination but also accounts for the president's success in persuading the Senate to go along. The nomination went over like a lead balloon for many Federalist senators, who had much closer ties to Paterson than to Marshall, and who perhaps failed to appreciate the rapidly changing strategic situation. In any event, the pro-Paterson group tried to block the appointment and to force Adams to reconsider. Adams held firm, knowing that time was on his side. Paterson's allies in the Senate buckled within a week, allowing the nomination to go through on January 27—just a couple of days before the Senate took up judicial reform in earnest.[25]

The evidence is overwhelming: Marshall's nomination and confirmation owe everything to lame-duck dynamics.[26] It was also an important factor in Marshall's decision to accept. He had been offered a place on the Court by Adams in 1798, but had turned it down without great soul-searching.[27] Thanks to the Federalist reform speeding through Congress, the office was looking much more attractive. No longer would Marshall be condemning himself to an endless round of exhausting circuit-riding duties. Instead, the appointment seemed to offer a very cushy job—involving about six weeks' work a year and paying a handsome salary of $4,000 per annum.[28]

The prospect of a sinecure would be rudely shattered by Thomas Jefferson once he took power. But at the moment of his appointment, Marshall did not appreciate the level of outrage the Federalists' lame-duck activities would generate. It appears, then, that the lame-duck dynamic was a crucial factor not only in procuring Marshall's nomination and the Senate's confirmation but also in inducing him to accept the job. Indeed, if John Jay had known of the impending lame-duck transformation of the Court into an appellate tribunal, he might well have preempted Marshall by taking the job himself—recall that he declined largely because he was unwilling to endure "the fatigues incident to the office."

The Federalist Judiciary Act

When viewed from one angle, the Federalist Judiciary Act of 1801 was a thoughtful solution to a long-standing problem. The original Judiciary Act of 1789 did not grant district judges authority to try most federal cases on their own but required them to wait for a Supreme Court justice to travel to their circuit to try them jointly.[29] If transportation or ill health prevented a justice from showing up, nothing could happen—except the demoralization of lawyers, parties, and witnesses primed for the event. When a circuit justice was seriously indisposed, Congress sometimes passed a special statute to allow a particular district judge to hold a circuit court by himself, but this was a Band-Aid.[30]

Even when circuit justice and district judge arrived on time, there were problems. When the two disagreed, the case was held over until the next term; and if disagreement continued, the judgment of the district judge—not the Supreme Court justice—prevailed.[31] A further embarrassment occurred on appeal to the Supreme Court—since the justice who had sat on circuit would find himself on the reviewing panel .

Unsurprisingly, this system generated lots of complaints. Within a year, the justices were protesting against the physical demands of circuit riding and the impropriety of reviewing the errors of colleagues on appeal, and the Washington administration was proposing fundamental reform. But this, and subsequent appeals, fell on deaf ears in Congress.[32]

So there was nothing especially partisan about John Adams's call for renewed consideration in his State of the Union Address of December 1799. The Federalist majority then established a special House committee to prepare a serious reform initiative. Alas, the committee's initial proposal was so sweeping that Republicans derailed it when it came up for consideration on the House floor in March 1800. When the lame-duck Congress returned in the fall of 1800, the Federalists slimmed down their plan a bit, dividing the country into six new circuits and creating three new circuit judges in each.[33] These judges would sit in panels and relieve the Supreme Court justices of their circuit-riding duties. The initiative enabled the federal courts to dispense justice in more places, and much more reliably. It also permitted the Supreme Court to overrule decisions on appeal without damaging the pride of the circuit justice who had conducted the trial.

All this seemed sensible enough, but for a single overwhelming fact—the elections of 1800 had transformed Congress into an assembly of lame ducks. The political provocation was heightened by a constitutional point: the president and the Senate may appoint judges for life, provided only that the appointees maintain "good behavior." If the new bill became law, Adams and the Federalist Senate might pack the courts in a way that the next administration could not readily reverse. As Jefferson explained to Madison, "I dread [the judiciary bill] above all the measures meditated, because appointments in the nature of freehold render it difficult to undo what is done."[34]

Two centuries onward, it is easy to say that the Federalists should have resisted temptation. It is hard to imagine modern-day politicians succumbing under similar circumstances. Like Federalists and Republicans of yore, they sometimes reach great heights of ideological fervor. But they wouldn't stoop to this particular dirty trick: returning to Washington after a sweeping electoral defeat to expand the judiciary and pack it with their henchmen. The ethic of the two-party system has become so ingrained as to make such a step unthinkable.[35]

It is curious, then, to see Adams and his fellow Federalists prate on about "the increasing dissolution of morals" while rushing to create splendid new jobs for their friends. This juxtaposition only helps prove my point—which is not that the Federalists were immoral, but that their political morality had not embraced the ethic of a two-party system.

The Race against the Clock

Even after discounting for anachronism, the behavior of Adams and his associates was remarkably injudicious—provoking another round of crisis that could have been avoided by more moderate behavior. The Federalists' failure of common sense was partly a consequence of the genuine novelty of the situation: losers hadn't transferred power to winners before, and it isn't surprising, I suppose, that they blundered on the first experiment. But in part the problem was the silly constitutional calendar left behind by the Framers. With every passing day, the Federalists got closer to the inauguration of a new president on March 4, and the closer they got, the more they rushed to consolidate their power; and the more they rushed, the more morally obtuse, and politically provocative, they became.

This race against the clock was already taking its toll as the judiciary bill passed from the House to the Senate on January 21. Though leading Federalists believed that the bill was "rough" and could use some perfecting amendments, they rejected any change since this would require a conference with the House, causing further delay and possible defeat.[36] Instead, they pushed the bill through on a party-line vote of 16 to 11 on February 7, provoking the Senate's presiding officer, Thomas Jefferson, to visible annoyance as he signed the bill and sent it on to the lame-duck president.[37]

Jefferson's humiliation took place only two days before House Federalists passed special rules requiring an all-night session to resolve the presidential runoff, and four days before the all-nighter occurred. The message couldn't be clearer: the Federalist party was grimly determined to take all steps within its power to preserve the republic from the Jeffersonian *faction* that threatened to destroy its foundations. President Adams then signed the judiciary bill into law on Friday the 13th—about the same time that Republican crowds were massing around the Capitol in an effort to break the House impasse.

Adams would not actually proceed with judicial nominations until the identity of his successor was settled, but he was already hard at work behind the scenes. As the judiciary act was speeding through the House and Senate, jobseekers were in lobbying mode ("There is something awkward in applying . . . for an office before it is created,"[38] wrote one, who nevertheless applied), and partly in reaction, Adams was searching for more worthy candidates. When Richard Stockton, New Jersey's leading Federalist lawyer,[39] wrote a letter of January 17 suggesting nominees from his state for the new judgeships, Adams wrote back on January 27 offering Stockton a job. By the time the Senate passed the bill on February 7, Stockton's reply was already in Adams's hands. He was much honored by the offer, but the job looked too temporary for serious consideration: "It is true a Judge cannot be removed from office by a new President but the law under which he is appointed may be repealed by a predominant party—and his life may be embittered by unmerited censure and slander."[40]

At the moment he received this rejection, Adams could still hope that the next president of the United States might be Burr or even Marshall, and that men like Stockton would think again about the permanency of the jobs on offer. When the House chose Jefferson on February 17, Adams found himself in a very tough spot. With two weeks to go, he would be hawking damaged goods to men who were agonizingly slow to reach by mail. While Adams might tell himself he was aiming for distinguished statesmen of the highest standing, his race against the clock was threatening moral and political disaster. He would no longer have the time to cajole his preferred candidates to accept. The critical question would be a nominee's availability: if a trusted associate could guarantee Adams an acceptance, even for an otherwise questionable candidate, the temptation to move forward might prove irresistible.[41]

But the more questionable the candidates, the more their appointment would provoke the Republicans; and the greater the provocation, the more likely it would be that Jefferson would retaliate in just the way Stockton predicted—by purging the "midnight judges" of their offices and threatening the very future of an independent judiciary.

This is, at least, the cautionary advice that a sober adviser might have offered a bitter and harried president. After all, was it all *that* important to fill all sixteen jobs? Wouldn't it be wiser to stick with men of unquestioned distinction, and if they refused, simply leave some openings for the new president to fill? Shouldn't Adams avoid a patronage extravaganza that might discredit the very idea of a strong system of federal courts?

Such good counsel was beyond the ken of Adams's principal confidant in the affair. This was none other than John Marshall—confirmed unanimously by the Senate as chief justice on January 27, but continuing as secretary of state at the president's request. Whatever else one might say of this dual role, it should have alerted Marshall to the dangers of rushed appointments. President Adams might be leaving town on March 4, but Chief Justice Marshall was not. If the Jeffersonians responded to provocative appointments by retaliating against the judiciary, the chief justice would inevitably find himself in the middle of the ensuing ruckus, at grave risk to his future career.[42]

Marshall was entirely oblivious to this danger. Rather than cautioning the president, or detaching himself from Adams's hunt for nominees, he became the president's principal collaborator in the short-sighted rush to consolidate Federalist power before March 4. Consider the nomination of Oliver Wolcott, who had recently been forced to resign as secretary of the treasury amid charges of fraud after a suspicious fire in the treasury building. Here was a man who had never practiced law in his life (though he had been admitted to the Connecticut bar in 1781). But he was out of job, and in straitened economic circumstances—which made his acceptance certain. At the last minute, Adams chose him over a more qualified candidate.[43]

Adams was also most unwise to succumb to the pleas of Maryland congressmen for Philip Barton Key—a good Federalist, and recently defeated in a race for the state legislature, but earlier in life the captain of a regiment that fought for the king during the Revolution.[44]

And then there was the matter of nepotism. If a leading politician obtained a judgeship for one of his relatives, he could both help a family member and credibly guarantee Adams that his offer would be accepted. Nevertheless, such appointments did not precisely suggest a single-minded search for the public good.

Consider the ever-resourceful James Bayard of Delaware. On February 10 he was already writing to his father-in-law, Richard Bassett: "If it is good news I can assure you of a seat upon the Bench of the Circuit Court. 2,000 dollars are better than anything Delaware can give you, and not an unpleasant provision for life." On February 12, as the House all-nighter was grinding to an impasse, Bayard found time to dash off a note telling Bassett that his job was "secure"; as the electoral college crisis escalated over the weekend, he visited the president and wrote that Adams was now promising Bassett the *chief* judgeship of the circuit—a remarkable prize for tiny Delaware, since the chief judgeship would ordinarily go to the nominee from Pennsylvania, the biggest state in the circuit.[45]

The meeting with Adams occurred on Sunday, February 15; Bayard defied the Federalist caucus and announced for Jefferson on Monday the 16th; Jefferson was elected on the 17th; and Adams submitted a list of twelve judicial nominees on the 18th.[46] The list reveals that Bassett had been demoted in the meantime from chief to associate judge of the circuit—perhaps Adams was not pleased by Bayard's decision to give Jefferson the presidency?[47]

In any event, the appointment of Bayard's father-in-law testified to the congressman's continuing influence, but it didn't contribute much to the sense that the Federalists were on a mission of principle. To be sure, Bassett should not be confused with an obvious incompetent like Wolcott: Bassett was then serving as governor of Delaware, had some previous judicial experience, and, as we shall see, possessed a powerful legal mind. Despite his merits, surely it would have been better if Adams had selected someone whose appointment was less enmeshed in the conspiratorial goings-on in Washington?[48]

The prize for nepotism went to John Marshall, who managed to secure judgeships for *two* of his brothers-in-law, James Keith Taylor of Virginia and William McClung of Kentucky. The latter appointment was particularly egregious since it represented the only circuit judgeship assigned to the overwhelmingly Republican frontier districts of Kentucky, Tennessee, and Ohio. Republican congressmen from the region were backing a candidate who, as Kentucky Senator John Brown assured Adams, was a moderate man of no party.[49] But Adams was more impressed by the urgings of his secretary of state, operating in tandem with Kentucky's other senator, the Federalist Humphrey Marshall. Humphrey was John Marshall's cousin as well as his brother-in-law—and was also brother-in-law to the nominee McClung.[50] His bid for reelection had just been defeated, and he was serving his last days as a lame-duck senator. And yet, as his rival Senator Brown complained in the *Kentucky Gazette:* "Mr. Adams was deaf to every argument in opposition to the recommendation made by Messrs. J & H Marshall."[51]

By Monday, February 23, Adams had tendered all his nominations to the Senate,[52] generating a certain queasiness in the ranks. Here is Federalist Senator Gouverneur Morris defending the affair to his fellow New Yorker Robert Livingston:

> I have agreed heartily and cordially to the new judiciary bill which may have and probably has many little faults but it answers the double Purpose of bringing justice near to men's doors and of giving additional fibres to the root of government . . . That some improper appointments may take place under this law I can readily suppose but in what country on earth are all appointments good? That the leaders of the federal party may use this opportunity to provide for friends and adherents is I think probable; and if they were my enemies I should condemn them for it. Whether I should do the same thing myself, is another question. I believe that I should not. They are about to experience a heavy gale of adverse wind can they be blamed for casting many anchors to hold their ship through the storm? The measure is doubtless very disagreeable to their adversaries and therefore it is I believe the more adviseable in them.[53]

Morris agrees "heartily and cordially" with the merits of the new measure, but his letter betrays an anxious recognition that lame-duck conditions have cast a pall. Since the senator was justly renowned as a fire-eating Federalist, his disturbing portrayal of the headlong rush "to provide for friends and adherents" is more remarkable than his palliative remarks in its defense.

Not all of Adams's appointments were questionable. But there were enough to taint the entire effort, and matters got worse as the constitutional clock ticked on. Consider Adams's effort to find a proper nominee from Pennsylvania. At first the president's mind naturally turned to the Philadelphian Jared Ingersoll. Only a couple of months before he had tapped Ingersoll for the Supreme Court, and it was only the slow mails that had led him to push Marshall into Ingersoll's spot, lest it disappear entirely in the Federalist rush to pass the judiciary act.

Ingersoll traveled to Washington to talk to Adams in early February, but we do not know what was said. On February 18 Adams submitted the Philadelphian's name to the Senate as his nominee for the chief judgeship of the Third Circuit—only to receive a letter from Ingersoll declining on February 23. This news set the Federalist senator from Pennsylvania, William Bingham, into action: "Why is not Some Person designated to Supply the Place of Mr. Ingersoll . . . is it intended to place the feature nomination within the power of the new administration?"[54] Three days later Adams proposed a leading Philadelphia lawyer, Edward Tilghman, but Bingham immediately told him that Tilghman wouldn't take the job. So the next day the president nominated Tilghman's cousin in a brief note requesting that "William" be inserted in the nominating papers previously prepared for "Edward."[55]

In case William should mistake the point, Bingham takes great pains to explain the deal: "I assured the President (& I was authorized in So doing, for the Tenor of Letters I had received) that you would accept the appointment–Another Consideration of primary Importance, is that it will be too late, to make any other Change, under the present administration."[56] The Senate confirmed this last-minute appointment on March 2,[57] William took the job, and the race was won—but not in a way that did him, or the president, credit.

Things went from bad to worse on February 27, when President Adams signed a statute creating a three-judge court for the District of Columbia, possessing all the powers that circuit courts exercised in the rest of the nation. With four days to go, he appointed his thirty-two-year-old nephew, William Cranch, and John Marshall's brother James to the lucrative positions.[58] The third job as chief judge was offered to Thomas Johnson, who declined, leaving the job open for Thomas Jefferson to fill.

Here is John Marshall's reaction to the news of this last-minute turndown in a letter to his brother James: "I am excessively mortified at the circumstances relative to the appointment of the Chief Judge of the district. There was a negligence in that business arising from a confidence that Mr. Johnson woud accept which I lament excessively. When Mr. Swan parted with us at your house I thought he went to send an express the next morning."[59] The letter reveals that the rush of events had overwhelmed

Marshall's good judgment: the only feature of the story that makes for "excessive[] mortifi[cation]" is his associate's failure to guarantee, by an express rider, that Johnson would accept.

While all this was going on, Marshall was also point man for a second enterprise in patronage in the District of Columbia. The Federalists' last-minute creation of a DC circuit court was part of a larger project organizing the government of the new federal district, involving the appointment of a host of positions as marshal, register of wills, and justice of the peace. Acting at the behest of local Federalists, Adams responded with a series of rapid-fire nominations, which were confirmed by the Senate on March 2—including forty-two justices of the peace, an extraordinarily large number for such a sparsely settled district.[60] With the hours dwindling to a precious few, Marshall proved weak on follow-through, leaving at least four JP commissions undelivered by midnight of March 3. One of these was addressed to William Marbury, whose later effort to obtain it led to the great case of Marbury v. Madison.

At the time Marbury's appointment was a minor matter—which is why Marshall gave it a low priority as compared, for example, with his urgent efforts to deliver a circuit court commission to Thomas Johnson. We shall return to *Marbury* in due course, but can already remark one aspect of the case, namely Marshall's effrontery in choosing to participate in the decision of the case at all. *Marbury* not only required the new chief justice to assess the constitutional implications of his own negligence in failing, as secretary of state, to deliver the commission to the hapless JP. His involvement would ineluctably lead the larger public to remember his unseemly participation in the larger Federalist patronage project. And yet Marshall not only failed to recuse himself but assigned himself the opinion in *Marbury,* so that he might better flaunt his involvement in the face of his Jeffersonian opponents.

If there is another case in the annals of the Supreme Court that reveals such grotesque forms of judicial impropriety, I have yet to come across it.[61]

The Loss of the Senate

I do not wish to portray Adams or Marshall as utterly obtuse to considerations of political morality or entirely unconcerned with the quality of their appointments. My point is a bit more subtle: lacking a two-party ethic, and acting under intense time pressures, they suspended their better judgment in pursuit of the greater good of depriving the Jeffersonians of as much power as possible.

To do Adams justice, it is only fair to note his frequent use of an appointments strategy that promised to put his project on a nobler foundation. As he looked around the country, there was one obvious way of beating the constitutional clock and nominating men of high quality whose acceptance was virtually guaranteed. And that was to offer the existing district judges a promotion to the new circuit court.

So far as these judges were concerned, the new judiciary act would greatly reduce their position in the world. Although they formally retained their positions, and their salaries, they were a shadow of their former selves. Even under the old regime, they had limited jurisdiction to preside over federal cases on their own; but their powers were greatly enhanced when they joined with their visiting colleague from the Supreme Court to conduct trials as a two-judge circuit court. The new federal statute stripped the district judges of this very substantial power: thenceforth, the expansive trial jurisdiction of the circuit courts would be superintended by the new circuit judges sitting in panels of three, and the old judges would be obliged to retreat to the narrow jurisdictional boundaries of the district courts, which had been narrowed yet further by the new statute.[62] Formerly the preeminent permanent representatives of federal power in their regions, the district judges had suddenly become marginal presences.

The notables of the early republic were especially sensitive to such blows to their social standing, and Adams could confidently expect that they would happily accept his offer of a circuit appointment, which also carried a raise in salary.[63] And so it is not surprising that he filled six of his sixteen jobs with district judges—a course that promised to provide him with both highly qualified nominees and likely acceptances. Indeed, Adams went so far down this path that he even nominated two district judges—John Sitgreaves of North Carolina and Joseph Clay of Pennsylvania—who were Republicans.[64]

This high-minded strategy rapidly led to another round of embarrassment. The promotions generated a chain reaction of vacant district judgeships, and these provided another promising field for patronage—to be sure, the office was less powerful than before, but it was a lifetime job, and it did pay well enough. What is more, it was a job that sitting members of

Congress could obtain for themselves, and not only for their friends and relations. While the Constitution barred the president from nominating senators and representatives to any office created during the terms for which they were elected, it permitted their appointment to long-established offices. This meant that district court, but not circuit court, slots were available for congressional incumbents, and three Federalist members of Congress quickly took advantage of the opportunity to obtain life tenure for themselves.[65]

Two of them were senators—Ray Greene of Rhode Island and Elijah Paine of Vermont—and their success in winning nominations from Adams had nothing less than epochal consequences. Quite simply, if the two men had stayed in their places, the Federalist party would have maintained control of the Senate for the first two years of Jefferson's administration, putting them in a wonderful position to block, or water down, all major Republican initiatives, and especially the threatened repeal of the judiciary act.

The Federalists had already lost some ground in the Senate in the 1800 elections, which, in the aggregate, had cost them three seats. Extrapolating from these returns in a letter to Alexander Hamilton, Federalist Senator James Gunn lamented: "Within two years the Senate will be Democratick." Nonetheless he confidently predicted that "at the commencement of Jeffersons administration the Senators will Stand 17 Federal and 15 Anti-Fedl."[66]

Gunn's prognostications proved accurate. When the Senate convened on March 4 to witness the inauguration of Jefferson and Burr, the body was composed of 18 Federalists and 14 Republicans,[67] but one of the Federalists was representing Maryland on an interim basis.[68] Even though Maryland chose a Republican successor by December, the Federalists would have been in control by a margin of 17 to 15—but for the fact that Greene and Paine were replaced by Republicans.[69]

How could Adams and Marshall have made such a blunder? Surely they could add as well as Gunn? Could they not see that these two patronage appointments were placing their entire enterprise in the gravest danger?

Nowadays, no competent politician would make a similar attack. The two-party system has become second nature, and nobody would ever hand over control of the Senate in a fit of inadvertence. In a sense this proves my point: we are seeing the birth of proto-modern parties, but not yet the stabilization of a two-party *system*. The protagonists were still stumbling in their effort to assimilate the strategic, as well as the moral, implications of life in an unfamiliar and uncongenial party-ridden world.

And within this context, the constitutional clock may well have played a decisive role. Time was moving so fast, Adams and Marshall were trying to do so much, that it was easy to lose sight of the big strategic picture. Consider how the president announced his choice of Rhode Island Senator Greene for the district court. He did not devote a special message to this single nomination. He made it a small part of a larger package resolving all major appointments matters in the First Circuit containing New England—beginning with the nomination of the three circuit judges, and including the nomination of United States attorneys for Massachusetts and Rhode Island, as well as a second district judge to another vacancy created by a promotion to the circuit court. This context suggests that Adams was focusing more on the dynamics of politics and patronage in New England than on the future balance of political power in the United States Senate.[70] If the proposals had remained on the table for a substantial period, Senator Gunn or somebody else would have forcefully brought the political arithmetic to Adams's attention. But all these nominations raced through the Senate on Friday, February 20—just forty-eight hours after they had been submitted on Wednesday, February 18.[71]

Marshall also seems to have been asleep at the switch. Once the Senate approved, it was up to him to send Greene his commission. Marshall botched the job: the document he prepared designated Greene as a circuit judge, not a district judge. Greene, alas, did not notice Marshall's mistake until he had resigned his Senate seat and was preparing to take up his new position. By this point, Jefferson had come to power, and Madison, the new secretary of state, resolutely refused to correct the error. Thanks to Marshall's incompetence, poor Greene had resigned his Senate seat for a worthless piece of paper, and never served as a district judge.

Marshall's negligent handling of Greene's commission suggests a larger failure to appreciate the strategic importance of the appointment. He may well have been so distracted by the swirling politics of circuit court judgeships that he was treating nominations to the district court as if they were secondary issues.

Matters were more rushed by Tuesday, February 24, when Adams submitted the nomination of Federalist Senator Paine as district judge.[72] This time the Federalists in the Senate whisked the appointment through the chamber in a single day[73]—and in the blink of an eye, the party lost control over the Senate, leaving itself at the mercy of the Jeffersonians once Congress returned in December.

As we marvel at the political incompetence of the Adams-Marshall team, keep in mind that the Republicans had revealed a similar ineptitude a few months earlier, when they allowed all 73 of their electors to cast ballots for Burr as well as for Jefferson—thereby inadvertently throwing the election into a House of Representatives dominated by Federalists. At this earlier stage it had been the Federalists who had displayed superior political savvy, carefully assuring that John Adams would win one more electoral vote than his vice-presidential candidate, Charles Pinckney.[74] Political coordination of the electoral vote was particularly tricky, since presidential electors met separately in each state and could easily get their signals crossed. If the Federalist leadership was capable of mastering this strategic problem, it *is* surprising that they so casually handed control of the Senate to their rivals.

Nonetheless, this is what happened. The outcome serves as a cautionary tale for those who wish to reduce the mysteries of politics to rational strategic calculation. The Federalist blunder, like the previous Republican mistake, plunged the system into crisis, as the newly ascendant Jeffersonians sought to use their control over the presidency and both houses of Congress to purge the judiciary and consolidate their "revolution of 1800."

Once again, America was on the brink.

Writing to James Monroe amidst the Federalists' feeding frenzy, James Madison reflected on the meaning of it all: "Instead of smoothing the path for his successor, he [Adams] plays into the hands of those who are endeavoring to strew it with as many difficulties as possible; and with this view does not manifest a very squeamish regard to the Constn."[75] This letter is dated February 28, only days after the judicial appointments of Senators Greene and Paine—perhaps Madison had them in mind in expressing his "squeamish[ness]" about Adams. Surely Adams was violating the spirit, if not the letter, of the Constitution when he offered senators jobs that would not have been vacant except for their own decision, earlier in the month, to enact the new judiciary act. And once they received their judicial commissions from Adams, the two senators violated the express terms of the Constitution by continuing to hold their Senate seats for a time rather than resigning immediately. As we shall see, the president would have done his party, and the constitution, a favor if he had steered clear of this gray zone and allowed Greene and Paine to stay in the Senate.

But if Madison was passing judgment on the larger scene, he failed to assess his own part in the affair. After all, John Adams had not attended the Constitutional Convention. It was not he, but Madison, who had contributed to a document that allowed presidential elections to end in constitutional crisis; it was not he, but Madison, who had made it possible for the losers in national elections to wield legislative and executive power in such an irresponsible fashion.

While nothing in the Constitution required Adams to end his term with a staggering series of moral and strategic blunders, we should not forget the mistakes of the constitutional architects who made this miserable performance possible. Nor should we forget that it was John Adams's earlier decision to make peace with France, and disband Hamilton's army, that predisposed the participants to a peaceful resolution of the presidential crisis.

As for that blinkered partisan John Marshall, his moment of truth was yet to come.

7

Republican Triumph

The Founders did not anticipate a two-party system, but they did expect noisy and selfish factions to arise in the popular House of Representatives. Their remedy was the separation of powers: with presidents and senators selected indirectly, and for more extended terms, the demagogic tendencies of the House would be checked and balanced by cooler heads elsewhere.

This Founding aspiration had failed its first great test. The Republicans' triumph had been especially impressive in the newly elected House, where they would outnumber their rivals by 69 to 36. But as a result of Bayard's statesmanship and Adams's political blunders, both the presidency and the Senate had also fallen under the Republicans' sway. So far as Jefferson and his allies were concerned, this triple victory did not signify the triumph of faction, but presented a precious opportunity to redeem their promise to the People, cleanse the Augean stable of Federalism, and place government on a new and more solidly Republican foundation. True, the constitutional calendar required the Republicans to wait until December 1801 before they could convene the Seventh Congress. Yet the day of party victory could only be delayed, not denied, by the Founders' Constitution.

The Republican Congress opened with a calculated contrast to the Federalist past. Washington and Adams had begun each session in British style: just as the king might deliver a speech from the throne to Parliament, the president presented his State of the Union Address to the assembled houses of Congress with regal dignity. Jefferson refused to go to Congress in mock-imperial mode, and instead submitted a simple written statement. Behold, the dawning of a new age of Republican simplicity.

Nobody was taken in by these appearances. Jefferson was in fact the undisputed leader of a triumphant party—and this gave him more effective control over Congress than any exercise in presidential pomp and circumstance. The first session of the Seventh Congress was among the most productive in American history, inaugurating a recurrent pattern in which a newly ascendant political party tries to redeem its revolutionary promises quickly before deadlock emerges between rival leaders in Congress and the presidency. Before recounting the great constitutional dramas of Jefferson's first term, I want to turn to the deeper structural factors that would shape, if not determine, the ultimate outcome.

Resources of Presidential Leadership

It was one thing for Jefferson to organize a political party to serve as a springboard into the executive mansion; quite another for him to use it as a reliable instrument of government. While he had narrowly triumphed over the anti-party design of the electoral college, the congressionalist structures of 1787 presented him with another set of obstacles as soon as he took his oath of office.

At its most fundamental, the legacy of 1787 can be reduced to a single line: the Constitution requires congressmen and senators to run for office independently of the president. Americans may take this point for granted, but it represents a structural decision of the first importance. Consider, for example, the different design of the modern British system of parliamentary democracy, and how radically it restructures the incentives of members of Parliament. When British voters cast their ballots on election day, they cannot vote for prime minister directly. The only way they can affect the choice of prime minister is by voting for the local MP associated with the PM's party. This means that local constituents do not take it kindly if their local MP subsequently deserts his PM and votes with the opposition in parliament on a measure of major importance. In sending their man to Westminster, the locals are not primarily interested in the particular MP's character or positions; they are doing their part to gain control of the government for the party of their choice. Except in the rarest of circumstances, local MPs who ignore this basic point, and stab their PM in the back by voting against him, can expect their "vote of conscience" to win them repudiation at the polls the next time around—which is why such behavior is so rare in the British system.[1]

The separation of powers gives American senators and congressmen much greater political freedom. They do not serve as local proxies for a national contest for chief executive, since the president's tenure does not depend on the continuing support of a parliamentary majority. As a consequence, constituents will not remorselessly punish congressmen who refuse to support the major initiatives of presidents of their own party—indeed voters will often think better of a congressman if he stands up for local interests, or tries to push the president in an ideological direction he might not otherwise travel.

This does not mean that the president is a weakling in his dealings with Congress. To be effective, however, he cannot pretend he is a prime minister who can take his majority for granted. He must work constantly to overcome the centrifugal forces generated by the separation of powers and induce his party-mates in the House and Senate to conclude that loyalty to the president is the best policy.

Many presidents fail to solve this constitutional puzzle, and even Jefferson did not succeed perfectly. But by any reckoning he ranks very high—and a canvass of his underlying resources is important if we hope to understand the dynamics that permitted him to succeed in his plans for judicial reorganization and yet fall short of total victory.

Jefferson's success is all the more surprising since he lacked so many of the resources of more modern presidents. Most obviously, there was little patronage in a government whose nonmilitary personnel totaled 2,700 in 1802.[2] Congressional turnover was very substantial, with about one-third of the members leaving the House after the elections of 1802, 1804, and 1806.[3] This meant that presidential deals would be constantly undone by the election returns.

The presidential office also lacked the plebiscitarian symbolism it has since acquired. Nowadays, it is no big news when each president publicly claims a "mandate" from the People and urges Congress to pass legislation that will redeem his promises to the voters. This rhetorical development was only at its beginning in 1800.

Not that Jefferson failed to grasp the symbolic potential of a plebiscitarian presidency. His Inaugural Address claimed that "the voice of the nation" demanded his election, which was merely "announced according to the rules of the Constitution."[4]

The Republican party took its plebiscitarianism seriously. As Gallatin's Balloting Plan made plain, the House caucus was prepared to risk Jefferson's claim to the presidency on the outcome of a special election. Nevertheless, and in sharp contrast to later presidents,[5] Jefferson did not make public appeals to the People an integral part of his governing strategy. Rather than calling upon Congress to redeem his "mandate," he exercised his power behind the scenes—giving marching orders to his lieutenants in Congress, who took up the partisan cudgels on his behalf. This allowed him to play a public part that was virtually indistinguishable from those played by Washington and Adams, while effectively pushing his program through Congress in ways they had never deployed.[6]

The president found this public posture personally congenial. He was a terrible public speaker. The very prospect of a bully pulpit would have struck terror into his heart. And as with most gentlemen of his generation, his classical education had taught him the dangers of populist demagogy. So he was predisposed to a Whiggish belief that Congress, not the presidency, should be at the center of public life—but at the same time he placed himself at the center of effective leadership.

It is easy to underestimate the significance of Jefferson's rhetorical restraint in accounting for the system's success in reaching a rough and ready equilibrium. As broadly contemporaneous developments in Latin America suggest, presidents of other infant republics found it easy to reorganize republican ideology to make plebiscitarian appeals a standard technique of government. Simon Bolivar provides an instructive example.[7]

Suppose that Jefferson had anticipated Bolivar, and had refused to leave the rhetorical struggle against the Federalist judiciary to his congressional lieutenants. Taking center stage, he publicly and persistently insisted that Congress impeach leading Federalists, including Marshall, from the Supreme Court in the name of the "revolution of 1800." Would this rhetorical thrust have succeeded in ousting his antagonists from power?

There is reason to think so—though we can only reach an informed judgment at the end of our story. For now, the question usefully refines my basic thesis. It emphasizes that the American Constitution would begin the struggle to domesticate presidentialism under quite favorable conditions. Without the rhetorical resources that future presidents would develop, and with very little patronage at his disposal, Jefferson does not appear exceptionally formidable to modern eyes.

To some extent the new president could compensate for these weaknesses by exploiting the underdeveloped condition of competing power centers. Especially during the early years of his term, most important congressional business was conducted directly on the floor, without prior reference to standing committees. If the president could control the floor, he could win without the need to propitiate committee chairmen intent on preserving their institutional prerogatives. Moreover, congressional Republicans did not seek to elect their own party leaders, so Jefferson had the immense advantage of shaping his own leadership cadre. While the president varied his choice of administration spokesmen from issue to issue, he relied heavily on a chosen few, especially John Randolph in the House.[8] Reliance on Randolph proved to be a mistake in the end, but in the beginning Jefferson could expect a kind of responsiveness from congressional leaders that would astound future presidents. Similarly, he did not have to contend with the interest-group organizations that proliferated during later periods—these simply did not exist, nor did cabinet officers strike their own separate deals with congressional supporters.[9]

There is more to Jefferson's success than the institutional underdevelopment of potential competitors. His immediate successors operated in roughly similar environments, but they were far less successful in dealing with their congressional party. Several more affirmative aspects of Jefferson's situation deserve attention. First, "Jefferson had the advantage of riding the crest of a public reaction against the Federalists. He came to power with a congressional party fresh from victory, still having momentum from the organizing effort which helped produce that victory, and still rallied around a distinctive political creed."[10] To mark this point, I have called the Republicans a *movement-party*, full of men who were genuinely committed to political ideals, and not merely victory in the next election. And they entered Congress with enormous force: fully 52 percent of House members were new to the Seventh Congress.[11] Thomas Jefferson's enormous stature within the Republican movement—as the drafter of the Declaration of Independence[12] and the unchallenged leader of the party since its inception—is another crucial explanatory variable. Up to a certain point, there was no need for him to use plebiscitarian rhetoric as an integral part of his ongoing governmental technique. Jefferson *personified* the "revolution of 1800," and it wasn't necessary for him to trumpet the obvious.

Instead of overwhelming his fellow Republicans with public rhetoric, Jefferson worked endlessly to charm them. Both before and after his term in office, presidents restricted their socializing to stiff weekly levees and holiday receptions. But "Jefferson abolished the levee immediately upon assuming office and substituted small dinners held almost nightly when Congress was in session, with legislators predominating among the guests." He did not mix Republicans with Federalists on his invitation list; nor did he usually ask Cabinet members to his soirees. Night after night, year after year, the "field was reserved for the Chief Executive and legislators."[13]

This unique combination of moral authority and unremitting face-to-face political work will help explain both Jefferson's remarkable success in repealing the Federalists' judiciary act and his ultimate failure to sweep Marshall from the Supreme Court. To complete the picture, though, we must turn to the public side of the drama and examine its own distinctive dynamics and complexities.

Marbury as Provocation

As soon as Jefferson took office, he was privately denouncing the last-minute appointments by Adams and Marshall. As he explained to a close associate, "all appointments to *civil* offices *during pleasure,* made after the event of the election was certainly known to Mr. Adams, are considered nullities. I do not view the persons appointed even as candidates for the office, but make others without noticing or notifying them."[14]

But judicial appointments were not made during the president's "pleasure." They were lifetime jobs conditioned on "good behavior," and so Jefferson could not simply ignore the judicial appointments Adams had made after December. Nevertheless, the case of Ray Greene gave him an early opportunity to reveal his true views. Greene was the senator from Rhode Island whom Adams appointed as a district judge to fill a last-minute vacancy caused by a promotion to the new circuit courts. During the rush, Marshall blundered in executing Greene's commission: rather than filling out a paper naming Greene to the district court, he filled one out naming him to the circuit court. When Greene discovered the clerical error, he returned the paper for correction, only to find that the new secretary of state, James Madison, blandly pocketed the commission and refused to return it. Treating Greene's appointment as a legal nullity, Jefferson nominated the Republican David Barnes to fill Greene's place. Though this move predictably scandalized Federalist New England,[15] Jefferson was unrepentant—if John Marshall's commission as chief justice had contained careless clerical errors, the president would doubtless have considered it a legal nullity as well.

While the Federalist press kept up a drumbeat of criticism condemning Jefferson's lawlessness in the Greene affair, a similar dispute involving William Marbury pushed the matter into the courts.[16] Marbury's complaint was a miniaturized version of Greene's. Rather than gaining a district court appointment from President Adams, he was one of the forty-two men who had been confirmed by the Federalist Senate on March 2 as justices of the peace for the District of Columbia.[17] With one day left to go, Marshall blundered again, failing to deliver a commission to Marbury (and several others) before time ran out on the Adams administration.[18] Predictably, Jefferson denounced Marbury's appointment as a legal nullity and told Madison to withhold the commission.[19]

As a constitutional matter, Marbury's case raised similar but smaller issues than Greene's. The office of JP was not a job for life, specially protected by Article III, the judiciary article of the Constitution. It was only a five-year position, created under Congress's general authority to govern the District of Columbia. Despite its air of tempest-in-a-teapot, the lawsuit did raise fundamental issues—though, at the time, these seemed to involve the status of the presidency more than the power of the Court to invalidate congressional statutes. In particular: Did Jefferson have the authority to reverse Adams's grant of a commission merely because he found it inconsistent with the principles of his revolution of 1800? Or was he bound by the Constitution of 1787 to follow meekly in his predecessor's footsteps and make good on the appointment? No less fundamentally, was it up to the president or the Court to answer these questions?

With the new Republican Congress coming to town in early December, this was neither the best moment nor the most auspicious vehicle for the Federalists to rattle sabers from the Supreme Court, their remaining redoubt. Yet this is what happened on December 16, 1801, when Madison received notice demanding that he appear the next day to defend against a motion for a mandamus ordering him to hand over Marbury's commission. Republican reaction was predictable. The *Philadelphia Au-*

rora reported an (unidentified) congressman as denouncing this "high-handed exertion of Judiciary power" whose "true intention . . . is to stigmatize the executive."[20] Jefferson responded to Marshall's summons by instructing his secretary of state to boycott the entire proceeding.

The threads of civility were beginning to unravel. At no point in the litigation did Jefferson or Madison deign to send an attorney to argue their side of *Marbury* before the Court. While this suggests the ease with which the two sides could indulge in mutual excommunication, I do not want to overemphasize *Marbury*'s importance in fueling passions at this moment.[21] As events in Washington were already proving, the president had no need of further provocation to launch his own campaign against the Federalist judiciary. And it was the debate over this initiative, not the one over *Marbury,* that took the center of the constitutional stage.

The Rhetoric of Repeal

Two weeks before Marshall had vainly summoned Madison to the bar of the Supreme Court, the Republicans finally assembled for their first session of the Seventh Congress. The president presented them with a State of the Union Address that marked out a comprehensive and revolutionary rejection of the Federalist status quo. So far as Jefferson was concerned, a large military force was neither "needful [n]or safe." The president also condemned the Federalist vision of a large executive establishment as a violation of the principle "that this Government is charged with . . . external and mutual relations only . . .; that the States themselves have principal care of our persons, our property, and our reputation." Within this spare Republican framework, the bloated judiciary presented an obvious target:

> The judicial system of the United States, and especially that portion
> of it recently erected, will of course present itself to the contempla-
> tion of Congress, and, that they may be able to judge of the propor-
> tion which the institution bears to the business it has to perform, I
> have caused to be procured from the several States and now lay be-
> fore Congress an exact statement of all the causes decided since the
> first establishment of the courts, and of those which were depending
> when additional courts and judges were brought in to their aid.[22]

Jefferson produced data showing that dockets were in decline, and would decline further now that the Federalists' sedition act had lapsed and federal judges were no longer in the business of political repression. All in all, an odd time to be expanding the courts.

The president made repeal of the Federalist judiciary act the first order of congressional business. In its opening months, the new Congress considered only one other major initiative—and that was taxes. These, needless to say, had reached oppressive levels thanks to the Federalists' free-spending ways, and the Republicans proposed some radical relief. They would repeal all internal duties and require the government to live off the revenue gained from customs duties, land sales, and the like.

The Republicans could take such a popular step only if they aggressively pruned the federal government of Federalist pretensions, as exemplified by the "army" of thirty-eight national judges permanently ensconced throughout the nation to dispense federal "common law" in competition with state courts. Jefferson's technocratic complaints about declining dockets, in short, could be readily linked to deeper constitutional values. Here is John Breckenridge making the link as he inaugurated the debate in the Senate:

> Could it be necessary then to *increase* courts when suits were *decreasing?* . . . I am inclined to think, that so far from there having been a
> necessity at this time for an increase of courts and judges, that the
> time never will arrive when America will stand in need of thirty-eight
> federal judges. Look, sir, at your Constitution, and see the judicial
> power there consigned to federal courts, and seriously ask yourself,
> can there be fairly extracted from those powers subjects of litigation
> sufficient for six supreme and thirty-two inferior court judges? To me
> it appears impossible.[23]

The distinctive mix of technocratic and constitutional argument is quite remarkable for its time and provided the Republicans with rhetorical advantages in their struggle for repeal. It allowed Jefferson to appear the nonpartisan Chief Magistrate he hoped to become. Though he repeatedly denounced Adams's "fraudulent use of the Constitution" in his private correspondence,[24] he remained officially above the fray. Having submitted the relevant data, and his comprehensive critique of Federalist pretensions, in his report on the State of the Union, he delegated the task of unleashing a steady stream of partisan denunciation to his congressional lieutenants.

They energetically complied, but they also found the presidential number-crunching rhetorically useful. It gave them a neutral rationale that served them well in the constitutional debate: Wouldn't it be counterproductive to deny that Congress had the power to pursue efficiency in the organization of the federal courts?[25] Here is the leading Republican John Randolph:

> I am free to declare, that if the intent of this bill is to get rid of the judges, it is a perversion of your power to a base purpose; it is an unconstitutional act. If, on the contrary, it aims not at the displacing one set of men, from whom you differ in political opinion, with a view to introduce others, but at the general good by abolishing useless offices, it is a Constitutional act. The *quo animo* determines the nature of this act, as it determines the innocence or guilt of other acts.[26]

The Federalists refused to be impressed by such bland professions of technocratic innocence. They regularly tried to demonstrate that Jefferson's numbers were defective and his policy implications spurious. On their view, the decline in federal dockets was caused by litigants' aversion to the inconveniences and delays generated by circuit riding,[27] America's burgeoning population would predictably increase judicial business over time,[28] and in any event, the cost savings were meager—perhaps no more than $30,000.[29] In contrast, the constitutional integrity of Article III was at stake: "The judicial Power of the United States, shall be vested in one supreme Court, and in such inferior Courts as the Congress may from time to time establish. The Judges, both of the supreme and inferior Courts, shall hold their Offices during good Behaviour, and shall, at stated Times, receive for their Services, a Compensation, which shall not be diminished during their Continuance in Office." The Federalists read the first sentence to mean that their act of 1801 had *vested* judicial power in the new circuit courts; and the second, that these judges *shall*—implying an imperative—hold their offices, and receive their salaries, unless they were impeached.[30]

These words had a different meaning for the Republicans. The first sentence, they emphasized, authorized Congress to establish inferior courts "from time to time," suggesting the legitimacy of recurrent judicial reorganization when public needs required.[31] They conceded that the second sentence guaranteed the judges their offices—but only so long as these offices existed. If they were abolished in a judicial reorganization, surely it was a bit much for the judges to demand lifetime pay for no work?[32]

These conflicting textual readings propelled the debate into basic principles. For the Federalists, the Republicans were destroying a central pillar of the Union, depriving the courts of their capacity to dispense federal justice in a cheap and accessible fashion.[33] Worse yet, they were assaulting the very idea of an independent judiciary:

> But another criticism, which, but for its serious effects, I would call pleasant, has been made: the amount of which is, you shall not take the man from the office, but you may take the office from the man; you shall not drown him, but you may sink his boat under him; you shall not put him to death, but you may take away his life. The Constitution secures to a judge his office, says he shall hold it, that is, it shall not be taken from him during good behaviour; the Legislature shall not diminish, though their bounty may increase, his salary; the Constitution provides perfectly for the inviolability of his tenure; but yet we may destroy the office which we cannot take away, as if the destruction of the office would not as effectually deprive him of it as the grant to another person. It is admitted that no power derived from the Constitution can deprive him of the office, and yet it is contended that by repeal of the law that office may be destroyed. Is not this absurd?[34]

There was something more absurd, countered the Republicans—a constitutional interpretation that authorized a partisan Congress to expand the judiciary without limit and without any hope of subsequent legislative correction.

To make the point concrete, William Branch Giles recalled the political conditions under which President Adams had signed the Judiciary Act on February 13. It was a day when the House had just cast its twenty-ninth vote for the presidency:

> [N]eed I remind the gentlemen, now present, who were agents in the exciting scenes, of the extraordinary situation of Congress at that

moment? When in the House of Representatives the ordinary business of legislation was suspended, a permanent session decreed; when
lodging and subsistence were furnished the members within the walls
of the Chamber; when even a sick bed was introduced to enable its
patient to discharge a sacred duty. Need I awaken the recollection of
our fellow-citizens, who were looking with indignant anxiety on the
awful scene; beholding their representatives, urged by the most tem-
pestuous passions, and pushing forward to immolate the Constitution of their country? No, sir, the awful scene is freshly remembered!
And what was its object? To prevent the fair and known expression of
the public will in the highest function it has to perform—in the
choice of the Chief Magistrate of the nation. In this state of things,
when all confidence amongst the members of this House was lost, in
the highest paroxysm of party rage, was this law ushered into existence. And now its advocates gravely tell us to be calm—to guard
against the danger of our passions. They tell us, at the same time,
that the law they have passed is sacred! inviolable! irrepealable![35]

When Senator George Mason presented a cooler analysis of the same
events, he managed to go deeper into their theoretical and institutional
implications:

> The revolution in public opinion had taken place before the intro-
> duction of this project [to expand the judiciary]; the people of the
> United States had determined to commit their affairs to new agents;
> already had the confidence of the people been transferred from their
> then rulers into other hands. After this exposition of the national
> will, and this new deposit of the national confidence, the gentlemen
> should have left untouched this important and delicate subject . . .
> This would have been more dignified than to seize the critical mo-
> ment when power was passing from them, to pass such a law as this.[36]

Mason was confronting the problem of lame-duck authority with critical
self-consciousness. During the first decade of the republic, it might have
seemed a minor failing of the Philadelphia Convention, and the early Congresses, to allow the rise of lame-duck sessions out of a casual unconcern
with the nuts-and-bolts of the electoral calendar. Now, quite suddenly, the
activities of the lame-duck Federalist president and Congress began to appear as an outrageous abuse of power—involving a disdain for the "known

expression of the public will." It followed, in the words of Mason, that the responsibility for the repeal rested squarely with the Federalists, "who, in defiance of public opinion, passed this law, after that public opinion had been decisively expressed."[37]

For the Federalist response, I turn to James Bayard, who had now become the undisputed leader of his party in the House:

> It has been stated as the reproach, sir, of the bill of the last session, that it was made by a party at the moment when they were sensible that their power was expiring and passing into other hands. It is enough for me, that the full and legitimate power existed. The remnant was plenary and efficient. And it was our duty to employ it according to our judgment and conscience of the country. We thought the bill a salutary measure, and there was no obligation upon us to leave it as a work for our successors. Nay, sir, I have no hesitation in avowing, that I had no confidence in the persons who were to follow us. And I was the more anxious while we had the means to accomplish a work which I believed they would not do, and which I sincerely thought would contribute to the safety of the nation, by giving strength and support to the Constitution through the storm to which it was likely to be exposed . . . We are told, that our law was against the sense of the nation. Let me tell those gentlemen, they are deceived, when they call themselves the nation. They are only a dominant party, and though the sun of Federalism should never rise again, they will shortly find men better or worse than themselves thrusting them out of their places.[38]

Like his Republican antagonists, Bayard continued to associate "party" with faction, and differed only in his identification of the bad guys. The real factionalists, for him, were the Republicans. Their victory in the last election did not entitle them to "call themselves the nation." All factions engage in this conceit, only to find themselves displaced by the remorseless electoral cycle. For him, only the vision expressed by the Constitution deserved to be associated with the People. In seizing their last opportunity to create a strong federal judicial system, the Federalists were not betraying the People but protecting them—taking advantage of the chance to provide more "strength . . . to the Constitution through the storm to which it was likely to be exposed."

For the Republicans, Bayard had gotten things precisely backward: "Is not an abuse of power more to be dreaded from those who have lost the public confidence than from those whose interest it will be to cultivate and retain it?" asked John Randolph.[39]

The question, in short, was the constitutional meaning of the election of 1800. For the Republicans, the Federalists had betrayed Founding values during the 1790s, and the election of 1800 had authorized a great cleansing in the name of the People. For the Federalists, the election had marked the passing triumph of a faction, and they had been completely justified in making a last desperate effort to batten down the hatches of the ship of state.[40]

Bayard's defense of lame-duck authority rang hollow to most Americans at the time.[41] When he turned from defense to offense, his institutional diagnosis resonated more broadly. On his view, the elections of 1800 had revealed a very different institutional danger—not the abuse of lame-duck authority but the rise of the plebiscitarian presidency:

> Do not say, that you render the judges dependent only on the people. You make them dependent on your President. This is his measure. The same tide of public opinion which changes a President, will change the majorities in the branches of the Legislature. The Legislature will be the instrument of his ambition, and he will have the courts as the instrument of his vengeance. He uses the Legislature to remove the judges, that he may appoint creatures of his own. In effect, the powers of the Government will be concentrated in the hands of one man, who will dare to act with more boldness, because he will be sheltered from responsibility . . . The first moments of power, gained by a struggle, are the most vindictive and intemperate. Raised above the storm, it was the Judiciary which was to control the fiery zeal, and to quell the fierce passions of a victorious faction.[42]

Bayard had hit a sore point. Both the original Constitution and rising Republican ideology looked upon the prospect of an aggrandizing executive branch with undisguised anxiety. Indeed, as we have seen, Jefferson was taking pains to preserve a public appearance of nonpartisanship.

And yet, was it not all a sham? Didn't everybody recognize the invisible hand controlling his puppets on the congressional stage? Wasn't this a predictable consequence of the Republicans' incessant talk of a mandate from the People? If the election of 1800 marked a new stage in the American Revolution, wasn't the People's chosen instrument the writer of the Declaration of Independence? In short, weren't the Republicans inaugurating a new era dominated by the plebiscitarian presidency?[43]

While Republicans repeatedly invoked the authority of the president in justifying their own support of repeal,[44] they sidestepped Bayard's deeper questions, which would ricochet through generations of American history. For the present, I have said enough to suggest the complexity and profundity of the constitutional debate—as well as its danger.[45] After two months of intense engagement, it was clear that neither side viewed the regular transfer of power from one party to the other as a normal part of democratic life. Both continued to understand their rivals as mere factionalists, not as good-faith participants in a two-party system.[46]

And therein lies the danger. Quite simply, this premodern framework could easily justify all-out war against the losing side. Just as the Federalists, when they were in power, had struck blows against the seditious Republicans, would the Republicans repress the Federalist faction now that they had gained the upper hand?

This was the ultimate question, and for a time the result teetered uncertainly in the Senate. As we have seen, it was only John Adams's political incompetence that gave the Republicans a razor-thin margin in the upper house. But a couple of Republicans had not arrived in Washington, and one had defected—reflecting a more general Republican unease with the constitutional proprieties.[47] Seizing the moment, the Federalists moved to recommit the judiciary bill to a special committee for a compromise: "Mr. Dayton concluded by saying, that it could not come to good, if measures, admitted by some to be bold and violent, and believed by many others to be unconstitutional, should be carried by a bare majority, and he trusted, therefore, that this proposition would now succeed."[48] The motion gained a 15–15 tie, allowing the new vice president, Aaron Burr, to demonstrate his future political availability by casting his vote with the Federalists, sealing his fate forever in Jeffersonian circles.[49] As soon as another Republican arrived in Washington,[50] the party wasted no time gaining retribution—forcing the measure back onto the floor, and ramming it through to final passage, on a vote of 16 to 15. The result in the House was more open-and-shut. After a vigorous debate, passage came on a strong party vote of 59 to 32.[51]

All in all, a distinctive performance. On the one hand, the constitutional argument was of very high quality, and was extensively reported to the newspaper-reading public.[52] Discursively, at least, the participants had succeeded in linking 1800 to 1787 in the public mind. Despite their belief that the Federalists had abused their authority in ignoring the "revolution in public opinion" revealed in the elections, the Republicans did not ignore their rivals' cries of unconstitutionality, and sought—however uneasily—to square the constitutional revolution of 1800 with the prior constitutional achievements of 1787.

Yet the Founders would have been horrified by the way the debate ended—with disciplined battalions of Republicans and Federalists marching to the beat of party, without much pretense at independent judgment of the constitutional merits. The spirit of party had propelled repeal through Congress with blinding speed, the president signing the bill into law on March 8, 1802.[53]

Toward Confrontation?

The repeal of the judiciary act left the Federalists in a state of shock. Representative Charles Matoon wrote from "Congress hall a few minutes after the death of the Constitution. I confess my feelings were very much moved at this wanton assassination . . . I anticipate all the horrors of a French revolution."[54] The Federalist press was no less combative. The circuit judges, declared the *Washington Federalist,* should

> continue to hold their courts as if the bill had not passed. 'Tis their solemn duty to do it; their country, all that is dear and valuable, call on them to do it. By the judges this bill will be declared null and void; the country will then be divided into two sects only, those who hold to the independency of the judges and to the constitution, and those who hold to the sovereignty of Virginia, and the uselessness of any general constitution. We say *the sovereignty of Virginia* because that state now wields the rod of Empire.[55]

Behind the scenes, leading Federalists were plotting their next steps.[56] Acting at the behest of Senator James Ross, Congressman John Rutledge visited John Marshall in Richmond to sound out the new chief justice's intentions. By March 26 he was reporting Marshall's assurance "that the firmness of the Supreme Court may be depended on should the business be brought before 'em."[57] Roger Griswold of Connecticut was corresponding with Oliver Wolcott, the "midnight" circuit judge from his home state, who quickly came up with a very concrete proposal:

> The Judges of the *Supreme Court* . . . can indeed, if they think
> proper, refuse to perform the duty of *Circuit* Judges, and if it could
> be known that they would so *refuse*, it might perhaps be proper, for
> the *Circuit Judges* to inform the Gentlemen of the Bar, that they will
> attend at the usual times & places, when they will expect to hear the
> arguments of Council, upon the great question whether the Courts,
> are or are not abolished . . .—a basis may thus be laid, for obtaining
> the final decision of the Supreme Court, in a regular form.[58]

A Supreme Court strike would not have been unprecedented. This was precisely the response of the justices in 1792, when they were called upon to administer a popular law providing pensions to revolutionary war veterans. They refused to comply on the ground that their decisions would be reviewed by the secretary of war—or so wrote Justices Wilson and Blair (together with District Judge Peters) to President Washington: "[S]uch revision and controul we deem radically inconsistent with the independence of that judicial power which is vested in the courts; and consequently, with that important principle which is so strictly observed by the Constitution." Justices Jay and Cushing had reached the same conclusion when riding circuit with District Judge Duane, but they opted for a different course. Rather than going on strike, they adjourned their court from time to time so that they could "proceed as commissioners to execute the business of this act in the same court room, or chamber." By moving beyond their commissions as judges,[59] Jay and Cushing expressed their "desire to manifest, on all proper occasions, and in every proper manner, their high respect for the National Legislature." And so the matter stood for a couple of months, until Justice Iredell, sitting with a district judge on the southern circuit, had his chance to devise a different straddle: on the one hand, he would accept applications for pensions under the act; but on the other, "this Circuit court cannot be justified in the execution of that part of the act which requires it to examine and report an opinion."[60]

These acts of judicial disobedience—reprinted verbatim in the United

States Reports—had ended happily for all concerned. After hearing an appeal that raised the issue, the justices held off final decision until the next term of court, during which time "the Legislature, at an intermediate session, provided, in another way, for the relief of the pensioners."[61] In its first constitutional clash with the judiciary, Congress had blinked. Might not history repeat itself?

The justices would shortly be in a perfect position to consider the matter more deliberately. Under the old judicial calendar, reinstated by the repeal, the Supreme Court was scheduled to meet in Washington for a regular session in June 1802—just days before the July 1 date set for the dissolution of the Federalists' new courts and the resumption of the old circuit-riding system. If some justices favored a strike, the Washington meeting would give them a precious face-to-face opportunity to persuade their more cautious brethren. And if they were successful, they would have the ideal forum to put their case to the nation. Rather than justices issuing a scattershot of opinions while riding on circuit, the Washington meeting might serve as the site for a joint statement explaining why the Court could not cooperate with the Jeffersonians' unconstitutional assault on the Federalists' court system.

As the Federalists were conspiring and propagandizing, the Republicans in Washington moved quickly to fashion a statutory weapon to deflect the emerging threat. By April 5 the Senate passed a second judiciary act—which, among other things, canceled the Court's June session. To put the best face on this measure, Congress made it part of a more general scheme altering the court's calendar. Thenceforth, the Court would meet in plenary session only once a year in February, rather than continue its custom of twice-yearly sessions in December and June.[62]

Nobody was taken in by this. "Are gentlemen afraid of the judges? Are they afraid that they will pronounce the repealing law void?"—asked the omnipresent Bayard.[63] Rather than answering, the Republicans swept the bill through the House on a party-line vote on April 23.

Republicans outside the capital were less impressed by their colleagues' strong-arm tactics. Here is James Monroe, then governor of Virginia, weighing in with a letter to Jefferson:

I heard with concern on my return that a bill before Congress proposes a postponement of the meeting of the court of appeals, to some later period than the existing law provides for. I fear that such a measure wo.d produce a bad effect. I am persuaded it wo.d inspire a doubt among the people of the propriety of the late appeal . . . If the repeal was right we sho.d not shrink from the discussion in any course which the constitution authorises, or take any step which argues a distrust of what is done or apprehension of the consequences. A postponement by law of the meeting of the court is also liable to other objections. It may be considered as an unconstitutional oppression of the judiciary by the legislature, adopted to carry a preceding measure which was also unconstitutional. Suppose the judges were to meet according to the former law notwithstanding the postponement, and make a solemn protestation against the repeal, and this postponement, denouncing the whole proceedings as unconstitutional and the motive as impure. It might be said and truly that they had no right to meet by the law; yet as they wo.d claim to meet under the constitution, to remonstrate against the law as having violated the constitution, it is probable that that objection wo.d not be attended to. If they attack the law, I mean the act of repeal, and are resolved to avail themselves of the occasion it furnishes, to measure their strength with the other departments of gov.t, I am of opinion that this postponement wo.d give their party new colour to their pretensions, new spirits to their party, and a better prospect of success. It will perhaps not be possible to avoid the collision and the crisis growing out of it. A measure of the kind referr'd to invites it. The best way to prevent one is to take a bold attitude and apparently invite it. The court has a right to take its part, and ought not to be deprived of any pre'existing means. I am not apprehensive of any danger from such a collision, & am inclined to think the stronger ground taken by the court especially if it looks toward anarchy, the better the effect will be with the publick. The people will then have a simple, tho' important question before them. They will have to decide whether they will support the court, or in other words embark again under the auspices of the federal party, or cling to an adm.n in two of the departments of gov.t which lessens their burdens & cherishes their liberty. It is even probable that such a collision may produce in many respects a beneficial effect. The mild republican course of your admn. has tended to put at repose the republicans & relieve from further apprehension the federalists. In such a state of things the former have little motive for exertion. Having overthrown their adversaries they think it beneath their character to pursue them further. Many from the habit of activity they have acquired, from independence of spirit, rivalry or other cause, begin to separate from each other & even criticise the measure of reform that are proposed. But shod the federalists rally under the judiciary, and threaten anything serious, it is presumable that the republicans will revive from their lethargy and resume their former tone.[64]

Monroe's letter, dated April 25, arrived in Washington too late to influence Jefferson—who undoubtedly had made up his mind to sign the bill much earlier than April 29, the day he put his pen to paper.[65]

Nevertheless, it usefully frames a deeper analysis. Modern historians tend to view the Federalists' threat of a strike as wildly revolutionary, but this is not Monroe's view: "The court has a right to take its part, and ought not to be deprived of any pre'existing means." Any statutory move against the upcoming June meeting would prove counterproductive—allowing the Court to portray itself as a victim of "unconstitutional oppression," and giving the Federalists "new colour to their pretensions, new spirits to their party, and a better prospect of success." The best course would be "to take a bold attitude and apparently invite" judicial confrontation. If the Court took the bait and went on strike, "[t]he people will then have a simple, tho' important question before them. They will have to decide whether they will support the court, or in other words embark again under the auspices of the federal party, or cling to an adm.n in two of the departments of govt. which lessens their burdens & cherishes their liberty."

Monroe's view is very close to those of Federalists like Wolcott: the two men merely disagreed about the public's likely response to a judicial strike. Wolcott hoped it would provoke a popular mobilization against the Republicans' unconstitutional purge; Monroe, that it would halt the Republicans' decline into petty politics, and mobilize popular support for the Jeffersonian vision. Yet this disagreement should not obscure a shared understanding of the evolving process. Neither man supposed that the great constitutional questions raised by the Jeffersonian assault on the Federalist judiciary had been settled by the simple passage of the repeal act. Both saw the prospect of judicial resistance as a legitimate, if unconventional, option in the larger process of engaging the popular will.

But there was only so much that interested outsiders like Wolcott and Monroe could accomplish. Now that Jefferson and Congress had raised the stakes by canceling the June meeting, the next move was up to the justices. Would they confirm Monroe's prophecy and hold a defiant session? Or would they crumble? Or would some third strategy emerge in the ensuing give-and-take?

8

Marbury v. *Stuart*

"Mr. Ross calls to tell me he is advised that the Chief Justice is disposed to go quite as far as we could wish," Gouverneur Morris confided to his diary on April 5, 1802[1]—the very day the Republicans were ramming their second judiciary bill, abolishing the Court's June session, through the Senate over the opposition of Federalists like Ross and Morris.[2] Morris's diary confirms Congressman Rutledge's letter, two weeks earlier, reporting Marshall's assurance "that the firmness of the Supreme Court may be depended on."[3]

Marshall is giving every sign of reenacting his familiar role as Federalist partisan. Just as he threw himself imprudently into the appointment of the midnight judges, he seems to be assuring his friends that he will defend the cause, once again, against the Jeffersonian onslaught.

On the same day Morris is voicing confidence, Marshall is preparing for the next act in the drama. In a letter written from Richmond, he thanks Wolcott for sending a copy of the Republicans' proposal for a second judiciary act: "I regret that the next June term will be put down, but I have no doubt the immediate operation of the bill will be insisted on."[4] Whatever Monroe may think, Marshall has no doubt that Jefferson will move decisively to prevent the justices from getting together in Washington to plot their next move. Despite his regrets, Marshall is not prepared to meekly accept Jefferson's fait accompli. Instead, he tries to rally his colleagues by epistolary means.

Only four of Marshall's letters remain in the archives, but all take the same position. If the justices consulted first principles, the Constitution gives them no choice—they must defy the new statutory command and refuse to go circuit riding. For Marshall, a simple point was decisive: when he and his colleagues obtained their appointments, they received commissions to serve as justices of the Supreme Court, and not as all-purpose providers of judicial services. The jurisdiction of Supreme Court justices is defined in Article III of the Constitution, and it does not include a grant to ride around the country holding trials with district judges. Before Marshall and the others could be required to engage in extensive trial work, the president and Senate would have to appoint them to a second, distinct office. In the words of his letter to Justice Cushing on April 19: "For myself I more than doubt the constitutionality of this measure & of performing circuit duty without a commission as a circuit Judge."[5]

The Switch in Time

To the end of his days, Marshall would maintain the profound conviction that resumption of circuit riding had been unconstitutional.[6] But as the moment of decision approached, two other factors intervened. First, Marshall could hardly deny that all the justices had in fact gone circuit riding throughout the 1790s without expressing any constitutional qualms. If circuit riding had been acceptable earlier, why not now?

Then there were some brute facts of politics—judicial and otherwise. Marshall couldn't make this decision on his own. He would have to cajole all five of his colleagues to take a unified stand. If a single Federalist justice returned to the circuits, this would gravely undermine the political force of the others' appeal to the People. We see Marshall struggling with this and other questions in the most elaborate letter that remains in the archives, the one to Justice William Paterson on April 19:

> Dear Sir
>
> It having now become apparent that there will be no session of the supreme court of the United States holden in June next & that we shall be directed to ride the circuits, before we can consult on course proper to be taken by us, it appears to me proper that the Judges should communicate their sentiments on this subject to each that they may act understandingly & in the same manner.
>
> I hope I need not say that no man in existence respects more than I do, those who passd the original law concerning the courts of the United States, & those who first acted under it. So highly do I re-

spect their opinions that I had not examind them & shoud have proceeded without a doubt on the subject, to perform the duties assignd
to me if the late discussions [surrounding the repeal of the judiciary
act] had not unavoidably producd an investigation of the subject
which from it would not otherwise have receivd. The result of this
investigation has been an opinion which I cannot conquer that the
constitution requires distinct appointments & commissions for the
Judges of the inferior courts from those of the supreme court. It is
however my duty & my inclination in this as in all other cases to be
bound by the opinion of the majority of the Judges & I should
therefore have proceeded to execute the law so far as that task may
be assignd to me; had I not supposd it possible that the Judges might
be inclind to distinguish between the original case of being appointed to duties markd out before their appointments & of having
the duties of administering justice in new courts imposd after their
appointments. I do not myself state this because I am myself satisfied
that the distinction ought to have weight, for I am not—but as there
may be something in it I am induced to write to the Judges requesting the favor of them to give me their opinions which opinions I will
afterwards communicate to each Judge. My own conduct shall certainly be regulated by them.

This is a subject not to be lightly resolvd on. The consequences of
refusing to carry the law into effect may be very serious. For myself
personally I disregard them, & so I am persuaded does every other
Gentleman on the bench when put in competition with what he
thinks his duty, but the conviction of duty ought to be very strong
before the measure is resolvd on. The law having been once executed
will detract very much in the public estimation from the merit or
opinion of the sincerity of a determination, not now to act under it.

Not knowing how to direct to Judge Cushing I inclose my letter
to him in this & ask the favor of you to forward it.

I shall be happy to hear from you in Richmond where I shall be in
a few days.[7]

Marshall is on an especially sensitive mission. His addressee, Paterson,
would have been Adams's choice for chief justice had not the pressures of
time forced the president to pick Marshall. Paterson was also present, as

Marshall was not, at the Philadelphia Convention, and so could speak with special authority. His decision to join the strike not only is important in itself but will affect the decisions of the others.

Marshall takes on his task with all the rhetorical resources at his command. As a newcomer to the Court, he is implicitly rebuking the old-timers for thoughtlessly accepting an unconstitutional practice throughout the 1790s. He discharges this mission with Mandarin politeness. Only the great debate over repeal has induced him to take the question seriously, and, by implication, it is equally appropriate for the others to do so.

His next move is gently to offer his new colleagues a legal characterization that might enable them to detach themselves from their previous blunder. When originally appointed to the Court by President Washington in 1793, perhaps Paterson might have understood his commission as implicitly authorizing circuit riding, since this was a basic part of the job as the statutes then defined it. Now that the Federalists' judiciary act of 1801 has released Paterson from circuit riding, he is confronted with a different legal question: Does his *old* commission as a Supreme Court judge authorize him to take on *new* duties in the trial courts?

Marshall does not push the point too strongly; since he himself never rode circuit in the 1790s, he is in a distinctly different position from his colleagues. It is up to Paterson to decide whether he can dig himself out of the hole he dug for himself in the 1790s. All that Marshall can do is offer a shovel.

Then there is the artful paragraph emphasizing the dangers of a strike. Marshall does not deny the obvious: the consequences of challenging Jefferson may "be very serious," and so the "conviction of duty ought to be very strong" before throwing down the gauntlet. But read as a whole, the letter suggests that the battle is well worth fighting. Marshall confides that he cannot "conquer" his conviction that circuit riding is unconstitutional—and if a conviction is "[un]conquer[able]," it would seem to be "very strong" indeed. The operational question to Paterson is clear enough: Is he brave enough to "disregard" the dangers and follow the demanding path of pure "duty"?

I have belabored Marshall's text because most recent commentators have read it, rather flat-footedly, as an argument against war with the Jeffersonians.[8] If Marshall wanted to retreat from the precipice, there was an easy way to do it: he could simply write a letter unequivocally announcing his intention to obey the Republicans' statutory commands. With the chief justice committed to circuit riding, the others were sure to follow.

The only point of Marshall's letter to Paterson was to keep the path open for all-out confrontation. He did not call directly for a strike, but doing so would have been counterproductive. If others followed up on his gesture toward the lofty but perilous path of judicial duty, it would be time enough to consider what should happen next.[9]

Justice Samuel Chase did not need to be asked twice. Like Paterson, he was favored by Marshall with a letter of April 19,[10] and by April 24 he responded with a 3,000-word memorandum attacking the constitutionality of the repeal: "The distinction of taking the office from the Judge, and not the Judge from the office, I consider as puerile and nonsensical." After a powerful analysis of the constitutional issues, Chase turns to consider the appropriate judicial response:

I have three objections to the Judges of the Supreme Court holding the Circuit Courts. First. If the repealing law has not abolished the Circuit Courts, which it certainly has not done, . . . and if the repealing Act has not destroyed the office of the Judges appointed, commissioned, and qualified under the Law repealed; it follows that the offices of these Judges are now full; and consequently no Judge of the Supreme Court . . . can exercise the office of a Judge of such Courts, without violating the Constitution.—Secondly. If the repealing Act be void so far, as it intends to destroy the office of the Judges under the Law repealed, and a Judge of the Supreme Court . . . should hold the Circuit Court, I think he would thereby, be instrumental to carry into effect an unconstitutional Law . . . If one person exercises an office, to which another has legal title, he is a wrongdoer, and ought to be removed; and the wrongdoer ought to be restored to his office. Shall a Judge be a wrong-doer? . . . [Thirdly.][11] I think (as at present advised) that a Judge of the Supreme Court cannot accept, and act under a Commission, as Judge of a Circuit Court. The Constitution . . . gives the Supreme Court original Jurisdiction in causes of Ambassadors etc. etc.; & appellate Jurisdiction of the cases enumerated. It appears to me, that Congress cannot, by Law, give the Judges of the Supreme Court original Jurisdiction of the same Cases, of which it expressly gives them appellate Jurisdiction. If a cause originates in the Circuit Court, and is tried there, the Judge of the Supreme Court may, alone, (or with the District Judge) hear & decide a case, of which the Constitution expressly gives him appellate Jurisdiction. The Constitution intended that the Judges of the Supreme Court should not have original Jurisdiction, but only in the few cases enumerated. The inference is just that, as the Constitution only gave the Supreme Court original Jurisdiction in a few specified cases, it intended to exclude them from original Jurisdiction in all other Cases . . . I think it is in the power of the Judges to meet at Washington in July, or August next; and I wish you would urge it . . .

The burthen of deciding so momentous a question, and under the present circumstances of our Country, would be very great on all the Judges assembled; but an individual Judge, declining to take a Circuit, must sink under it.[12]

Chase's arguments go far beyond those advanced previously by the chief justice. For Marshall, it is enough to insist on Chase's third point—that Supreme Court justices cannot go circuit riding without obtaining a second commission as circuit judges. Chase also assaults the constitutionality of the repeal itself, while Marshall's judicial correspondence is silent on this important matter.[13]

If the justices had gone on strike, Marshall would have been obliged to break his silence. Unless the Court declared repeal unconstitutional, the result would be a jurisdictional vacuum under which no federal trials of any sort could occur. On the one hand, the Supreme Court justices could not hold trials since this was beyond their commissions; on the other hand, the midnight judges couldn't either, since their statute had been constitutionally repealed. Of course, such a vacuum would have been temporary—supposing that the Republicans had won the battle for public opinion, Congress would have undoubtedly created another set of circuit courts, manned by Jeffersonian loyalists, to take the place of the justices.

However this vacuum might have been filled, it is a serious mistake for modern historians to treat Marshall's narrow focus as suggestive of a compromising disposition. To the contrary, if he wished to build support for a strike, it was only sensible to focus his colleagues' attention on the narrowest legal ground that justified this result, isolating it from all the collateral issues raised by Chase's wide-ranging critique.

Most important, the legal differences between Marshall and Chase should not blind us to the main point: both were in favor of a strike. Their different approaches were more complementary than competitive—Chase ventilating the larger issues, and Marshall focusing on the decisive question. This combination gave the other judges a good sense of the territory, but did they want to go there?

Bushrod Washington was the first to say no, and so quickly that Chase's memorandum could not possibly have reached him. Here is how Marshall describes the situation to Paterson on May 3:

> Mr. Washington also states it as his opinion that the question respecting the constitutional right of the Judges of the supreme court to sit as circuit Judges ought to be considerd as settled & should not again be movd. I have no doubt myself but that policy dictates this decision to us all. Judges however are of all men those who have least right to obey her dictates. I own I shall be privately gratified if such shoud be the opinion of the majority & I shall with much pleasure acquiesce in it; tho, if the subject has never been discussd, I shoud feel greatly embarassd about it myself.
>
> I have also receivd a letter from Judge Chase whose opinion is directly opposite to that of Judge Washington but he expresses an earnest desire, which he has requested me to communicate to every member of the bench, that we shoud meet in Washington for the purpose of determining on the course of conduct to be pursued, in that place. I shall communicate to Judge Moore & will thank you to correspond with Judge Cushing on the subject & let me know the result.
>
> If we determine certainly to proceed to do circuit duty it will I presume be entirely unnecessary to meet in August. If we incline to the contrary opinion, or are undecided we ought to meet & communicate verbally our difficulties to each other.[14]

Once again, the big surprise is that Marshall is still keeping a judicial strike open as a live option. As Chase's letter emphasized, a strike couldn't possibly succeed without a united front, and Washington has already said he isn't interested. Nonetheless, Marshall responds by subtly disparaging Washington's position: a no vote is pragmatically sound, but mere "policy" is unworthy of judges. While the chief justice might be gratified "privately" if the majority went along with Washington, he would be much "embarrassd" if the subject had "never been discussd." Rather than accepting Washington's veto as decisive, Marshall is still suggesting the need for a face-to-face meeting if "we incline to the contrary opinion or are undecided"—without mentioning that this meeting would defy the new schedule enacted into law the week before.[15] He doesn't give up on the project of resistance, but asks Paterson's help in polling the remaining justices,[16] and Paterson cooperates by sending his report on Chase and Washington to Cushing on May 25.[17]

At one level, the Republican effort to disrupt the Court's deliberative processes has plainly failed. Under the leadership of Marshall and Chase, the Court is refusing to accept congressional repeal as a fait accompli. Each of the justices is squarely confronting the great constitutional issues raised by the resumption of circuit riding. But on another level, the Republican effort has succeeded—as is suggested by Paterson's reply of late May:

> On the constitutional right of the Judges of the supreme court to sit as circuit judges, my opin[i]on coincides with Judge Washington's. Practic[e] has fixed construction, which it is too late to disturb. If open for discussion, it would merit serious consideration; but the practical exposition is too old and strong & obstinate to be shaken or controled. The question is at rest. If this should be the prevailing opinion, & their be nothing more in the case, our meeting would be of no use.[18]

Note the caveat: "If open to discussion, it would merit serious consideration." Cushing's response contains a similar hesitation: he admits that "doubts would have arisen" if the question of circuit riding had been raised originally, but concludes that, given the sustained practice of the 1790s, "to be consistent . . . we must abide by the old practice . . . [and] leave brother Chase to exercise his Singular Jurisdiction in August."[19]

These lines suggest that the Republicans' second statute, disrupting the Court's deliberative processes, may have succeeded in its basic strategic objective. If the justices had come together for their customary face-to-face deliberations in June, the dynamics might well have been different. After Chase presented his forceful brief in person, Marshall could have subtly steered his weaker colleagues toward a stronger stand—as he managed to do on many future occasions. But given the pieces of paper before him, the chief justice had no choice but to call it quits and instruct Chase to recommence his circuit-riding duties without further ado.

However fascinating such might-have-beens, they should not distract us from the events that indisputably did occur. These are important not only in themselves but because they initiated constitutional patterns that have recurred repeatedly at great turning points in American history. The Republicans were the first, but not the last, political movement to gain sweeping control over the political branches on the basis of (what they were pleased to call) an electoral mandate from the People; nor were they the last to confront a Supreme Court full of holdovers from a bygone era; nor the last to respond by seeking to disrupt the Court's efforts to rule upon the constitutionality of the new movement's transformative initiatives.

To be sure, the precise nature of the Republicans' threat was obscure. If the Court had held a defiant meeting culminating in a judicial strike, the justices' appeal to the People might have proved persuasive in the court of public opinion; but if not, the future standing of the Court would have been at risk. By passing their follow-up statute of April 29, the Republicans put the Federalist justices on notice that they should not treat their problem as part of the normal give-and-take generated by the separation of powers—as had occurred in response to the judicial strike on veterans' pensions in 1792. Instead, the Republicans were telling the Court that further resistance to the congressional initiative threatened its continuing standing as an independent actor in the emerging system of separation of powers. If you can forgive the jargon, I shall say that the disruptive Republican statute launched an *unconventional threat*.[20]

The justices didn't have any trouble decoding the message—talk of "grave consequences" and "sinking" abounds. And yet they did not simply crumple before the Republican juggernaut. Under Marshall's leadership, they conducted themselves like a court, soberly considering the pros and cons of further resistance.

But in a distinctive manner—while the majority appreciated the points of principle advanced by Marshall and Chase, they were more persuaded, in the end, by their assessment of likely public reaction. Having obeyed the Federalist command to ride circuit throughout the 1790s, how would it look if they suddenly announced constitutional scruples now that the

Republicans were doing the commanding? Would public opinion accept this new constitutional construction when the Republicans denounced it as the crowning example of Federalist factionalism?

This is the nerve of the objection entered by Cushing and Paterson: "Practic[e] has fixed construction, which it is too late to disturb." And as our story unfolds, we will see that these voices for accommodation were entirely correct—a judicial strike would have ended in disaster for the Supreme Court. For now, let the record show that, at this first great turning point in constitutional history, the justices looked squarely at the unconventional threat hurled at them by Thomas Jefferson and his Republican Congress, soberly considered whether they could win the ensuing battle in the court of public opinion, and chose to accommodate the presidentialist initiative at the cost of their constitutional convictions.

Call this a switch in time.

Public Meanings

While all this was going on in private, the public drama began with the formal repeal of the Federalist judiciary act on July 1, 1802. From outward appearances, the prospects for a shattering confrontation still seemed high. The justices had previously served as a bulwark of the Federalist order, assisting the Washington and Adams administrations in countless delicate tasks.[21] And they had gone to great lengths to support the regime during the last election. When they went on circuit in 1800, they had campaigned vigorously for Adams and Pinckney, transforming their grand jury charges into partisan stump speeches.[22] They had aggressively prosecuted Republican editors under the Sedition Act, weakening opposition voices at a crucial moment. To make matters more ominous, the Court had now been reinforced by the last-minute appointment of a chief justice whose recent conduct as secretary of state did not—to put it mildly—promise moderation.

Nor were the recently appointed circuit judges prepared to accept defeat without a fight. After much correspondence and a private meeting,[23] circuit judge Richard Bassett began circulating a lengthy public protest in the name of his "*associates* in office."[24] Bassett's protest reads like a judicial opinion—and one that sounds all the themes that Marshall would make familiar in Marbury v. Madison. Like Marshall, Basset calls for the judicial invalidation of the repeal based "upon the words and expressions of the *People,* contained in the constitution, as it came from their hands." And he develops a Marshallian understanding of the nature of judicial commissions as vested rights:

> With this commission and grant in his hand; with the *law* of Congress, *creating his office* and fixing the *compensation,* to authorize it; and with the *constitution* of the United States before his eyes, positively assuring him, that *the office* and *salary* shall be holden by him *during* his *good behaviour,* he accepts it upon the terms offered. And shall he be deprived of *both office and salary* the next month or year? Or whenever the legislature, who is but *one* out of *three* parties to the solemn covenant, shall be pleased to say, "you are no longer *necessary* or *agreeable,* we can find *judges* to exercise your offices cheaper, or who will be more subservient to our wishes!"

I have reprinted Bassett's protest in the Documents section at the end of this book, since it is unavailable elsewhere and provides a sense of how easy it would have been for the Marshall Court to write a *Marbury*-like opinion in defense of the circuit judges' commissions. For now, it is enough to note that the Protest concludes by calling upon the Supreme Court justices to go on strike—"to refuse any *cooperation,* which would effectuate, or *tend* to effectuate . . . the prohibited act of the Legislature."

When it became clear that the justices were declining this invitation, Federalist lawyers opened a second front. As the justices began once more to ride circuit, they quickly confronted objections from the bar. When cases were called up from the spring term's docket, leading Federalist lawyers challenged the jurisdiction of the new courts. These cases, they argued, were still properly before the panel of three circuit judges who had heard them in the spring. They could not be heard in any other courts, for the simple reason that the repeal statute was unconstitutional.

The Federalist justices initially responded by dancing around the question. They did not issue an opinion rejecting the challenge on its merits. Instead, they adjourned their court overnight, allowing time for some frank talk between judges and counsel. And on the next day the Federalist lawyers dropped their motions without further argument.

The official silence hardly concealed the momentous questions at stake. Here is the Republican *Independent Chronicle* describing the scene as Justice William Cushing and District Judge John Davis opened their circuit court for business in Boston on October 11, 1802:

> When the judges assemble, impanel the jury, and the crier announces the organization of the court, it is taken for granted that the jurisdiction is authorized by the constitution. At this period, if an individual should arrest the proceedings, by a plea which strikes at its existence, it is an act of assumption which demands the highest authority for his conduct . . . As citizens, we have a right to inquire, by what authority any part of the business of the present court was suspended by your interference? . . . It is understood, sir, that your plea involved in it, not merely the jurisdiction of the court on a particular action, but struck at the foundation on which the judiciary superstructure was raised. The judges, with the utmost condescension, referred your question to be argued at 10 o'clock on the next day. In the interim the court was adjourned, and certain actions were suspended till you had offered the arguments in support of your allegations.
>
> During this intermission, the public mind was agitated; the courts of law were considered as palsied; the actions depending were hung up as doubtful in their issue; the jury were retarded in the accomplishment of their business; in short, the laws of the country, for twenty-four hours, if not annihilated, were judged by many as progressing to a dissolution.
>
> The hour arrived, sir, in which this interesting question was to be argued. The court assembled, and sat in solemn suspense, whether they were, or were not a constitutional jurisdiction, competent to the purposes of trying all causes which were presented on the docket. At this awful crisis, it was announced, that you had waived the consideration of the question, which the day before you had pledged yourself to urge—or, in plain English, that Theophilus Parsons, Esquire, had permitted the court of justice to proceed on business without any further interruption!
>
> An individual thus to trifle with a court of justice, is an indecency, in my opinion, of the greatest magnitude.[25]

Theophilus Parsons was no mere Esquire, but a giant among Massachusetts Federalists—indeed, John Adams had found time to nominate him as attorney general during the last desperate days of his presidency. The appointment was purely honorific: Parsons hardly had the time to execute his official duties, except perhaps when he undertook the activities reported by the *Independent Chronicle.*

By this point, Parsons was very much the ex–attorney general, but his actions were colored by his former office. Perhaps we can best appreciate his subtlety by contrasting it with more straightforward alternatives. On the one hand, Parsons and his fellow grandees could have taken a position of total intransigence—boycotting all court proceedings and leading Federalist New England on a campaign of civil resistance to the judicial usurpers. On the other, Parsons might have vigorously pressed his constitutional objections, demanding that judges Chase and Davis justify themselves in official language. In contrast, his pattern of challenge and submission signifies something distinctive: an undying Federalist constitutional objection to the legitimacy of the status quo, but a bitter recognition that further debate was pointless.

This ritual of submission was repeated by Federalist notables farther south. Congressman Roger Griswold had been at the very center of Federalist opposition to repeal, but he now bent the knee before the Second Circuit in Connecticut, as did Robert Goodloe Harper and Luther Martin before the Third Circuit in New Jersey.[26] And then, just when the meaning of this dance seemed unmistakable, it took a different turn when John Marshall opened his circuit court in Virginia in December.

Once again, the dramatis personae could not have been more distinguished. Adams's attorney general, Charles Lee, came forward, in his capacity as a private lawyer, to challenge the jurisdiction of Adams's chief justice, John Marshall. The plot thickens: Adams had nominated Lee as chief judge of the newly established three-judge court for the Fourth Circuit (thereby creating the opening for the appointment of Parsons).[27] In the rush by Adams and Marshall to create midnight judges, they seem to have misread Lee's intentions. As soon as Lee learned of the nomination he turned it down, requiring Adams to name a replacement a week later.[28]

Now Lee emerged from the shadows to serve as the champion of the court whose chief judgeship he disdained. This time there was no ritual of submission. Marshall reached the merits of Lee's plea in a case styled Stuart v. Laird. No opinion survives, but Senator William Plumer, a generally reliable source, wrote that "Chief Justice Marshall has over-ruled a plea to the jurisdiction of the Circuit Court in Virginia, without deciding whether the repeal of the Judiciary law was constitutional."[29]

Marshall's precise reasoning was less important than the bare fact of his decision. It gave Lee the chance to appeal directly to the Supreme Court—at which time the chief justice would be free to change his mind, if he so chose. Lee jumped at the chance, and the Court immediately set down Stuart v. Laird for plenary consideration at its next session along with Marbury v. Madison. By taking this decision, the justices were making a large shift in the jurisprudential quality of their response to the Jeffersonian assault. They were no longer engaging in a silent ritual of submission; they were setting themselves up to write an opinion on *the* great questions of the day: Was it unconstitutional for them to serve as trial judges when they only had commissions as Supreme Court justices? On what basis could they constitutionally displace circuit court judges who had been confirmed by the Senate to undertake this precise function?

To be sure, the rituals of submission shaped the answers the justices could plausibly give to this great question. Having obeyed Congress by resuming their circuit riding, they would find it much harder to convince the public that this practice was unconstitutional. Nonetheless, modern historians are wrong to treat *Stuart* as if it were a minor matter compared to *Marbury*. To the contrary, it provided the justices with the vehicle for confronting the great issue of the day, and in a way that could never be reached by the complaints of minor officials like Marbury and his fellow justices of the peace. At the very least, the Court's decision to take up both cases invited its immediate audience, and posterity, to construct a larger pattern of constitutional meaning out of the *Stuart-Marbury* complex. In case this point was missed, Charles Lee could be counted on to make it loud and clear. As we shall see, he was the lawyer in *Marbury* as well as in *Stuart,* and he emphasized their relationships when making his arguments to the Marshall Court. If we don't choose to hear him, we only have ourselves to blame.

But before the Court would confront its moment of constitutional truth, the voters would have a chance to have their say.

The Election of 1802 and Its Aftermath

The Jeffersonian assault on the circuit judges was a great point of controversy during the elections of 1802. Bassett's protest was broadly circulated by the Federalist press,[30] while Republican papers such as Boston's *Independent Chronicle* denounced it as election-year propaganda: "Why Judge Bassett should presume to appeal to the people, at this moment, is very evident. His son-in-law, Bayard, is a candidate for a place in Congress, and if a very few weak people could be shaken, why then his labours would not be in vain—for his son would be chosen representative of Delaware."[31] In the end the voters were not impressed by the Federalist defense of judicial independence. It was buried in an overwhelming Republican landslide, magnified by the redistricting required under the 1800 census. The old House contained 69 Republicans and 36 Federalists, but the new one had 102 Republicans and 39 Federalists; and only 9 Federalists remained in the Senate.[32]

This crushing victory immediately reshaped the debate over the circuit judges, who had not given up their campaign for vindication. This time it was Oliver Wolcott from Connecticut who took the laboring oar, gaining general support from the circuit judges for a formal memorial submitted to Congress on January 27, 1802:[33]

> In virtue of appointments made under the constitution of the United States, the undersigned became vested with the offices so created, and received commissions authorizing them to hold the same, with the emoluments thereunto appertaining, during their good behavior . . .
>
> [I]nfluenced by a sense of public duty, they most respectfully request of Congress to . . . define the duties to be performed by the undersigned . . .
>
> The right of the undersigned to their compensations they sincerely believe to be secured by the constitution notwithstanding any modification of the judicial department which, in the opinion of Congress, public convenience may recommend. This right, however, involving a personal interest, will cheerfully be submitted to judicial examination and decision, in such manner as the wisdom and impartiality of Congress may prescribe.[34]

Acting with remarkable speed, the House of Representatives, sitting as a committee of the whole, took up the matter on the same day it was submitted. The Republican leader, John Randolph, rejected the appointment of a select committee on the ground that "the subject, in all its bearings, had undergone the maturest investigation, not only of every member on that floor, but of every thinking man in the United States."[35]

A fascinating colloquy followed, with Congressman Nicholson rejecting the Federalist claim that an appeal to the judiciary was the right way to resolve the dispute:

> In his opinion, Mr. N. said the best method of trying the right of Congress to repeal the judiciary act had been for some time, and was yet in operation. The people constituted the great tribunal before whom the constitutionality of laws of Congress should be brought, and by them this question will be decided. Some of them have decided, and the remainder will decide by their elections. It is an impartial tribunal, to whom we may all appeal, and their judgment will bind us. To their decision it is already referred, and with them he was willing to leave it rather than to any court of justice.

On the same day it took up the judges' memorial, the House rejected it on a party-line vote.[36]

The Senate was more deliberate, sending the matter to a select committee, which returned to the floor on February 3: "*Resolved*. That the President of the United States be requested to cause an information, in the nature of a *quo warranto*, to be filed by the Attorney General against Richard Bassett, one of the said petitioners, for the purposes of deciding judicially on their claims."[37] During the discussion of the motion, Senator Wright echoed Nicholson: "As to the law of the last session, by which these judges had been deprived of their offices, Mr. W. had no fear that the Supreme Court, or anybody else would attempt to set it aside. The whole nation has approved the measure, as many of those who opposed it have fatally experienced." Once again, the judges' memorial was rejected on a strict party-line vote: 15 to 13.[38]

To grasp the significance of this poorly understood episode, imagine a different scenario. Rather than "fatally experienc[ing]" the wrath of the voters, suppose that the Federalists had returned from the elections in triumph. Would this have changed the outcome of the debate?

During the earlier debate on repeal, the Republicans themselves had been of two minds on the question of compensation, and their uncertainty was repeatedly recalled by the Federalists during the discussion.[39] Consider how the appeal of Gouverneur Morris, the chairman of the Senate's select committee, might have resonated if his Federalist party had won the election:

[I]s it not the duty of every good citizen to heal, as far as possible, the wounds of society? To calm those irritations which disturb its repose? To remove all things which may alarm, torment, or exacerbate?

We have heard from those who are more in the confidence of our Cabinet than we are . . . that there is reason to believe that this country is on the eve of war. I hope not. I hope we shall not be visited by so great a calamity. But if this be our doom, let us prepare to meet it like men, with boldness, with unanimity. Let us banish, let us destroy every circumstance that can excite or keep alive a spirit of party.[40]

If his party had been victorious, Morris predictably would have claimed that the voters supported his views, and that the cause of national unity would best be served by making a request to the president "to cause an information, in the nature of a *quo warranto,* to be filed by the Attorney General against Richard Bassett, one of the said petitioners, for the purposes of deciding judicially on their claims."[41] And the party-line vote would have gone Morris's way.

If Congress had heeded Morris's plea, American constitutional law would have taken a very different path. United States v. Bassett, not Marbury v. Madison, would have been the great case establishing the Court's authority to review acts of Congress. Marshall's pronouncements would have been occasioned by a *public* lawsuit, initiated by the attorney general, with the support of the Congress, in an effort to sustain the rule of law. Our founding case, in short, would have more closely resembled the type of constitutional review now familiar on the European Continent, where courts regularly resolve fundamental issues at the request of parliament or the president, without any hint of private involvement.[42]

But the Senate's party-line rejection of the judges' memorial meant that the Court would consider the problem of judicial review in a very different posture. *Marbury* and *Stuart* came to the Court without any show of congressional or presidential support for the justices' constitutional pretensions. They took the form of ordinary lawsuits brought by private parties seeking private advantage, not public lawsuits by the attorney general seeking the public good.

Worse yet, the accidents of the common law conspired to present a particularly unattractive set of facts for judicial resolution. Consider, for example, how a little-known case might have clarified the issues coming before the Court. According to newspaper accounts, one of the deposed circuit judges, Joseph Reed, did indeed bring an action challenging the constitutionality of repeal to federal court.[43] Reed dropped his lawsuit, but suppose that he had pushed his complaint all the way to the Supreme Court. It is easy to see that his case would have allowed the justices to frame a more nuanced response to the Jeffersonian revolution.

In contrast to Marbury, Reed was not merely a justice of the peace, appointed for five years under a humdrum statute governing the District of Columbia. He was a real judge appointed for life so long as he stayed clear of impeachment. In further contrast to Marbury, Reed was already in possession of his judicial commission. To grant him relief, the Court had no need to engage in a high-stakes confrontation with the secretary of state, commanding him to hand over a piece of paper granting Marbury his office. It could simply order a clerk in the treasury to keep paying Reed his judicial salary.

By the same token, *Reed* would have been a much easier case to handle than *Stuart*. *Stuart* did not invite the Court to issue a narrow order to the treasury, but to go on strike, and thereby invite severe retribution from the Jeffersonians in Congress. In contrast, Reed's case offered a much more tenable legal position—as is suggested by Joseph Story's classic treatment of the problem in his constitutional commentary:

> The result of this act [of repeal], therefore, is . . . that, notwithstanding the constitutional tenure of offices of the judges of the inferior courts is during good behaviour, congress may, at any time, by a mere act of legislation, deprive them of their offices at pleasure, and with it take away their whole title to their salaries. How this can be reconciled with the terms, or the intent of the constitution, is more, than any ingenuity of argument has ever, as yet, been able to demonstrate . . . The act may be asserted, without fear of contradiction, to have been against the opinion of a great majority of all the ablest lawyers at the time; and probably now, when the passions of the day have subsided, few lawyers will be found to maintain the constitutionality of the act. *No one can doubt the perfect authority of congress to remodel their courts, or to confer, or withdraw their jurisdiction at their pleasure. But the question is, Whether they can deprive them of the tenure of their office, and their salaries, after they have once become constitutionally vested in them.*[44]

Story bisects his constitutional problem, conceding the power of Congress to reorganize the lower courts but denying that it can deprive sitting judges of their vested rights to their salaries and commissions. Note the confidence of Story's judgment—he treats his point as if "few lawyers" would seriously dispute it.

Story published his *Commentaries* in 1833, and he was appointed to the Supreme Court in 1811. Nonetheless, his treatise is a summa of Federalist jurisprudence, and its identification of an "easy case" serves as a reliable marker of the dominant opinion held by John Marshall and his fellow Federalists on the bench. Story is on firm ground in suggesting that the consensus on this narrow point extended far beyond Federalist circles.[45]

This leads to an obvious question: Why *didn't* Reed and his fellow judges push their lawsuit all the way to the Supreme Court? How could they have failed to see that their case provided a better vehicle for the Court than either *Marbury* or *Stuart*?

I don't know. The question suggests that the vagaries of common law case selection deprived the justices of a suitably modulated vehicle for addressing the challenges of the Jeffersonian revolution. They were stuck with *Stuart* and *Marbury*—the former requiring them to go on strike to raise a constitutional challenge, the latter raising issues that were tangential to the Jeffersonian purge of the judiciary.

Indeed, if different lawyers had argued the two cases, the Court might have entirely ignored their doctrinal interrelationships. But in this respect at least, *Marbury* and *Stuart* departed from the common law norm. With a bit of poetic license, they appear as early examples of the coordinated "public interest" litigation familiar to modern lawyers. The former attorney general Charles Lee was counsel in both cases, and he did a masterly job transforming *Marbury* and *Stuart* into a doctrinal package that was larger than the sum of its parts.

Spinning the Doctrinal Web

Less than a week after the Senate rejected Wolcott's petition, the Supreme Court finally got its chance to return to the field of action. After fourteen months without a plenary session, it began its term on February 10, 1802, with Charles Lee's argument for Marbury, which was answered by ominous silence from the administration. Upon taking office, Jefferson had found Marbury's commissions "on the table of the department of State," and he had personally "countermanded" their delivery.[46] He had then instructed his secretary of state, James Madison, to boycott all judicial proceedings. Marshall knew he was skating on thin ice.

Nevertheless, it took Marshall precisely two weeks to hand down his opinion—at a moment when Charles Lee was back in the courtroom arguing *Stuart*.[47] Lee responded to Marshall's opinion in *Marbury* with a bravura performance as an advocate, immediately integrating its reasoning into his legal brief. Now that *Marbury* was on the books, Lee showed that, as a matter of doctrinal logic, it virtually compelled a judicial strike in cases like *Stuart*.

The justices were unmoved by Lee's splendid exercise in legal geometry. They caved in before the Jeffersonians' commands to return to circuit riding—and wrote a feeble opinion implicitly acknowledging the problematic character of their decision. In one sense, their capitulation was no surprise—they had already returned to circuit riding over the objections of Chase and Marshall, and *Stuart* merely served as the formal flag of surrender. But in another sense, Lee's triumph in advocacy greatly enhances our reading of the *Stuart-Marbury* cases—it establishes, as a matter of public record, that the justices were perfectly aware of what they were doing when they abandoned their defense of the Constitution of 1787 and allowed the Jeffersonians to purge the judiciary in the name of the People of 1801.

To appreciate Lee's achievement as an advocate in *Stuart*, a barebones summary of *Marbury* will suffice. As we have seen, the would-be JP was suing to obtain his commission from Secretary Madison, and this prompted the chief justice to reflect broadly on the nature of judicial commissions. These documents, he emphasizes, create a species of "vested rights,"[48] whose legal protection goes to "[t]he very essence of civil liberty."[49] Marshall denies that America could be a nation governed by the rule of law if it "furnish[es] no remedy for the violation of a vested legal right."[50] To sum up this large portion of Marshall's opinion, it treats judicial commissions as *legally determinate and protected grants of power*.

The chief justice's opinion then executes a famous swerve: he declares that the Court cannot order the secretary (and the president) to hand over Marbury's commission. Although justice and legality imperatively require it, the Court lacks the jurisdiction to issue the order. While Marshall's concerns may seem technical, he assures us that the integrity of the Constitution is at stake.

Significantly for present purposes, Marshall's problem centers on the power of justices to hold trials. As he reads the constitutional text, it requires the Supreme Court to discharge a largely appellate function, permitting them to hold trials in only two classes of very sensitive cases.[51] Since Marbury's complaint falls in neither category, the Court doesn't have jurisdiction to hold a trial in his case, and so is constitutionally barred from ordering Madison (and Jefferson) to do the right thing and hand over his commission.

There is much to be said about this legal analysis. For now it is enough to note that it pivots on Marshall's claim that *expanding the Supreme Court's original jurisdiction is unconstitutional.*

We are now in a position to appreciate how brilliantly Lee responded to Marshall's pronouncements as soon as he heard them in open court. Recall that *Stuart,* no less than *Marbury,* deals with the status of judicial commissions—but this time, the relevant commissions weren't held by lowly JPs but by the justices themselves. In particular, these commissions only authorized the justices to conduct business appropriate to the Supreme Court, which *Marbury* asserts is largely appellate. Given this fact, was it within the power of the justices to follow the Jeffersonians' command and hold countless trials while riding circuit throughout the land?

With *Marbury* on the books, it was easy to see that the correct doctrinal answer is no. Consider the following constitutional syllogism:

1. The commissions of Supreme Court justices are not to be treated as mere verbiage on a piece of paper. They instead define *legally determinate and protected grants of power.*

2. These commissions, moreover, cannot authorize the justices to conduct the full range of trials demanded in the circuit courts. The original jurisdiction of the Supreme Court is narrowly limited by the constitutional text and *expanding the Supreme Court's original jurisdiction is unconstitutional.*

3. It follows that no Supreme Court justice can hold trials in circuit court unless and until he is given a distinct commission as a circuit

judge. But before this can occur, Marshall and his colleagues must first be nominated to circuit judgeships by the president and confirmed by the Senate.

4. This hasn't happened. Instead, Jefferson and the Congress have simply passed a statute ordering the justices to hold trials as circuit judges.

5. It follows that the lower court decision in *Stuart* should be overruled on the basis of *Marbury*. Since the justices don't have commissions to preside over Stuart's case, it would be unlawful for them to conduct his trial. Q.E.D.

Observe how closely Lee tracks this legal syllogism in his own argument, as summarized by the Court's Reporter:

> [T]he laws are . . . unconstitutional, because they . . . are a legislative instead of an executive appointment of judges to certain courts. By the constitution all civil officers of the United States, including judges, are to be nominated and appointed by the president, by and with the advice and consent of the senate, and are to be commissioned by the president.
>
> The act of 29th April, 1802, appoints the *"present Chief Justice of the supreme court"* a judge of the [circuit] court thereby established. He might as well have been appointed a judge of the circuit court of the district of Columbia, or the Mississippi territory. Besides, *as judge of the supreme court,* he could not exercise the duties or jurisdiction assigned to the court of the fifth circuit, because, by the constitution of the United States, the supreme court has *only appellate* jurisdiction; except in the two cases where a state or a foreign minister shall be a party. The jurisdiction of the supreme court, therefore, being *appellate only,* no judge of that court, *as such,* is authorized to hold a court of *original* jurisdiction. No act of congress can extend the original jurisdiction of the supreme court beyond the bounds limited by the constitution.[52]

The Reporter's summary shows how forcefully Lee presented the syllogism. Having elaborated *Marbury*'s constitutional geometry, Lee stared down the contrary precedent established by the justices' years of circuit riding during the 1790s:

If it be said that the practice from the year 1789 to 1801 is against us; we answer that the practice was wrong, that it crept in unawares, without consideration and without opposition; congress at last saw the error, and in 1801 they corrected it, and placed the judicial system on that ground upon which it ought always to have stood. By the act of February 13, 1801, the precedent was broken, so that now precedents are both ways. If there are twelve years' practice against us, there is one year for us.[53]

All this must have been very familiar to the Court—it is no different from what Marshall wrote to his colleagues when encouraging them to go on strike.

But Paterson and the others had been unpersuaded then, and they were unpersuaded now. And they were even less impressed by Lee's more ambitious efforts to convince them to declare the entire purge of the Federalist judiciary null and void, in the manner advocated by Chase in his earlier memorandum.[54] After barely a week's consideration, Paterson handed down an opinion for the Court rejecting all of Lee's contentions and reaffirming its collective determination to return to circuit riding.

The opinion begins by making short work of Lee's all-out assault on the repeal statute. Despite the emphatic argument that repeal had unconstitutionally destroyed the judges' offices, Paterson blandly asserts that the only question raised by the case was whether Congress could shift cases from one to another inferior court as "from time to time [it] may think proper." The implication was clear enough: If the circuit judges wished to protest about their treatment under the statute, they would have to bring a different lawsuit.

In contrast to his dismissive attitude toward Lee's (and Chase's) attack on the statute, Paterson concedes the relevance of Lee's constitutional syllogism to the case at bar:

Another reason for reversal is, that the judges of the supreme court have no right to sit as circuit judges, not being appointed as such, or, in other words, that they ought to have distinct commissions for that purpose. To this objection, which is of recent date, it is sufficient to observe, that practice and acquiescence under it for a period of several years, commencing with the organization of the judicial system, affords an irresistible answer, and has indeed fixed the construction.

It is a contemporary interpretation of the most forcible nature. This practical exposition is too strong and obstinate to be shaken or controlled, and ought not now to be disturbed.[55]

Note that Paterson does not say that the justices could *rightfully* ride circuit, any more than he says that Congress could *rightfully* strip the circuit judges of their commissions, any more than he makes mention of *Marbury*. He merely says that the "practical exposition is too strong and obstinate to be shaken or controlled"—and turns a blind eye to the plain doctrinal implications of the majestic opinion handed down by the chief justice. *Marbury* was yesterday, and today is today.[56]

Throughout this solemn ceremony of capitulation, Marshall remains silent, which, to put it mildly, was not his custom. Between 1801 and 1804, Marshall wrote all of the other twenty-three opinions for the Court, with his colleagues contributing zero dissents and only one concurrence.[57] Marshall's monopoly was in sharp contrast with prior practice, when each justice wrote his own separate opinion in most important cases.[58] Why, then, his remarkable silence?

The Court Reporter explains: "The *Chief Justice,* having tried the cause in the court below, declined giving an opinion."[59] But this was only a fig leaf. Although the justices often recused themselves on appeals from their own decisions as circuit judges, "there was no fixed rule,"[60] and it is easy to find justices making exceptions without incurring censure.[61] Two years later, Marshall himself wrote an opinion for the Court in a case from his own circuit.[62] And in 1808 the entire Court expressly repudiated the entire idea of recusal.[63]

If Marshall had been truly motivated by considerations of judicial propriety, he would have chosen a very different case for recusal. Rather than absenting himself from *Stuart,* he should have remained silent in *Marbury.* It was his conduct as secretary of state that was the cause of Marbury's problem. It was Marshall, and nobody else, who had forgotten to give the JP his commission. In failing to recuse himself, Marshall was breaching the most fundamental principle of all—if you caused the problem, let somebody else decide the lawsuit.[64]

Apart from the obvious breach of propriety, Marshall's participation undermined the operation of the judicial process. Madison refused to confirm that Marbury's commission had ever existed,[65] and the Republican-controlled Senate denied access to records establishing that he had been confirmed as JP. There was one obvious way to establish that Marbury had a right to his office: call the man who signed his commission to the stand, and have him assert that the document had remained in the office of the secretary of state.

But Marshall was sitting on the bench, leaving Lee in an embarrassing position. After thrashing about, Lee finally established the existence of Marbury's commission by producing a mysterious affidavit from one of the circuit judges of the district. This judge asserted that the threat of riots in Alexandria had led him "to call at the office of the secretary of state, for the commissions of the justices of the peace," so that he could recruit them to help suppress the unrest. Finding it impossible to deliver several of them, including Marbury's, he had returned them to the office.[66]

All very well, you might say, until I tell you that the judge who wrote the affidavit was none other than Marshall's brother, James, whom Marshall had pushed into the post as one of the midnight judges.

The scene might have come straight from *The Mikado:* the new chief justice, the former secretary of state, relies on the testimony of his brother, another last-minute judge, to proclaim that the republic will crumble unless the new secretary of state delivers yet another last-minute commission that the chief justice had neglected in his desperate race against the clock.[67] As if this weren't sufficiently ridiculous, Madison's boycott of the proceedings put yet another tragicomic turn on the affair: Was Marshall seriously proposing to write an opinion of the Court in his own case, on the basis of his brother's testimony, *without even hearing the opposing arguments?*[68] Wouldn't it have been oh-so-much-better for Marshall to have appeared as a witness, and allowed another justice to write an opinion for the Court? If there ever was a time for a sober judge to recuse himself, surely this was Marshall's moment?

Instead, Marshall recused himself in *Stuart* and blundered forward in *Marbury*. It wasn't a sudden attack of judicial ethics that caused this curious inversion. Marshall withdrew in *Stuart* because he didn't want to write an opinion explaining why the commissions of Supreme Court justices were not as sacrosanct as the commissions of lowly justices of the peace. He didn't want to write an opinion explaining why it was unconstitutional for Congress to expand the original jurisdiction of the Supreme Court, but it was perfectly okay for Congress to force the justices to hold

trials throughout the United States. And he certainly didn't want to announce an opinion ignoring *Marbury* entirely, and thereby suggest that
the Court didn't take its own pretensions seriously. Let Paterson do it.

And he didn't want to dissent either. He hated dissents, filing only
eight in thirty-four years on the bench, and only one on a constitutional
question.[69] He certainly wasn't going to contribute to judicial disarray at a
moment when the court was reeling from an onslaught by the Jeffersonians. So he grasped at any decent excuse to disassociate himself from an
opinion announcing *Marbury*'s eclipse. If he ignored Paterson's failure to
take *Marbury* seriously, perhaps history would turn a blind eye as well.

A similar logic seems to have inspired Samuel Chase, even though he
could not hide behind Marshall's fig leaf: *Stuart* had not arisen in his circuit, so he had to stay on the bench. Self-restraint must have been difficult,
since Chase had written separate opinions often during the 1790s, and his
private correspondence with Marshall had made clear his emphatic agree-
ment with Lee's arguments. Nevertheless, he squirmed silently as his colleague Paterson presented the "opinion of the Court" as if there were no
objections.

Washington insiders weren't fooled. Upon hearing that *Stuart* was
coming before the Court, Senator William Plumer wrote home to New
Hampshire that "it is said that the Supreme Court will, *with two dissenting
voices,* confirm the decision" below.[70]

Nor did Chase have much success holding his tongue over the longer
run. Within a couple of months he went on a public campaign against the
Republicans' assault on the judiciary act of 1801—provoking the president to escalate his attack on the Federalist judiciary by procuring Chase's
impeachment by the House of Representatives.

I am getting ahead of myself. Before turning to the next great Jeffersonian purge campaign against the judiciary, we should reflect further on
the *Marbury-Stuart* story.

The Sounds of Silence

Marshall's decision to hold his tongue in *Stuart* was one of the wisest in
his career. If he and Chase had made a big fuss in a formal dissent, later
generations would have framed *Marbury*'s grand pronouncements against

Marshall's bitter protest at the Court's failure to live up to them in *Stuart*. By keeping quiet, Marshall let Paterson's bland capitulation sink gradually into the sands of time—to the point where *Stuart's* significance is entirely ignored in the leading texts on constitutional law. Standard authors present Marshall's ringing defense of judicial review as if it were the only significant outcome of the Jeffersonian revolution.[71]

This wasn't the view held by the Jeffersonians. The most widely published analysis coupled *Marbury* with *Stuart*—denouncing the former as "grotesque," praising the latter for "calming the tumult of faction."[72]

In viewing the two cases as part of a larger whole, I hardly wish to disparage *Marbury's* continuing importance. To the contrary, Marshall's opinion should be read with greater care than is customary. *Marbury* is understood as the *locus classicus* for a theory of judicial review based on a written constitution.[73] But Marshall builds his case on a deeper foundation. Consider his opening paragraphs:

> The question, whether an act, repugnant to the constitution, can become the law of the land, is a question deeply interesting to the United States; but, happily, not of the intricacy proportioned to its interest. It seems only necessary to recognise certain principles, supposed to have been long and well established, to decide it.
>
> That the people have an original right to establish, for their future government, such principles as, in their opinion, shall most conduce to their own happiness is the basis on which the whole American fabric has been erected. The exercise of this original right is a very great exertion; nor can it, nor ought it, to be frequently repeated. The principles, therefore, so established, are deemed fundamental. And as the authority from which they proceed is supreme, and can seldom act, they are designed to be permanent.[74]

Marshall's defense of judicial authority begins not with the written Constitution but with a claim about constitutional politics as something very special, requiring "a very great exertion." Only then does he present the Court as defending the principles hammered out by the People after great exertion during previous exercises of constitutional politics.[75]

Before the chief justice can reach his desired conclusion, he requires one more premise. It is not enough for him to glorify the work of the Philadelphia Convention of 1787; he must also denigrate the quality of the politics practiced by the Republicans of 1800. His own logic requires him to claim that Jefferson and his party had *not* successfully engaged in one of those "great exertions" of popular sovereignty that entitled them to speak for the People. Yet Marshall does not explicitly defend this premise. His opinion merely presupposes it.

The Republicans disagreed. On their view, the chief justice was simply perverse in refusing to recognize them as worthy inheritors of the tradition of popular sovereignty. Just as Jefferson had raised his voice against the king in his great Declaration of 1776, he had raised his voice against the Federalist oppression in the 1790s. And just as an aroused citizenry had heard Jefferson's call to throw out the British, the People were on the march again. While civil war had been narrowly avoided, the elections of 1800 made it plain that the People would no longer tolerate Federalist efforts to deflect their will. And when Adams pushed his crony Marbury into office, he was trying to do just that.

We have already seen Jefferson justifying his refusal to hand over Marbury's commission on precisely these grounds. We should try, however, to place this decision within the larger framework of Republican self-understanding. Here is Jefferson's description of the meaning of his electoral victory in a letter to John Dickinson two days after his entry into the presidency:

> No pleasure can exceed that which I received from reading your letter of the 21 ult [responding to Jefferson's election by the House]. It was like the joy we expect in the mansions of the blessed, when received with the embraces of our fathers, we shall be welcomed with their blessing as having done our part not unworthily of them. The storm through which we have passed, has been tremendous indeed. The tough sides of our Argosie have been thoroughly tried. Her strength has stood the waves into which she was steered, with a view to sink her. We shall put her on her republican tack, & she will now show by the beauty of her motion the skill of her builders. Figure apart, our fellow citizens have been hood-winked from their principles, by a most extraordinary combination of circumstances. But the band is removed, and they now see for themselves. I hope to see shortly a perfect consolidation, to effect which, nothing shall be spared on my part, short of the abandonment of the principles of our revolution.[76]

No less than Marshall, Jefferson is placing himself within a narrative framed by the great revolutionary decade from 1776 to 1787. He has simply changed the identity of the factionalists: it is now Adams and Marshall and their ilk who steered the ship of state "with a view to sink her," while it is he and his fellow Republicans who have "removed the band" imposed by factionalists and have earned the right to speak for a citizenry who "now see for themselves." In promising fidelity to "the principles of our revolution," Jefferson certainly does not suggest that he wishes to betray the Constitution of 1787, "our Argosie." His point is subtler—that any interpretation of the Constitution which is not mindful of the People's repudiation of Federalist distortions is illegitimate.

There is a certain logic, then, to Jefferson's refusal to defend his administration's conduct before the Court in *Marbury*. He viewed Marshall's appointment, after the election results were already known, as paradigmatic of the rear-guard Federalist conspiracy to defy and deny the voice of the People. The very idea that a midnight judge like John Marshall should preside over the petition of another midnight appointment like William Marbury was enough, in Jefferson's eyes, to condemn the entire proceeding as a factional distortion of constitutional meaning—and surely it didn't help to learn that the lawyer for the petitioner was Adams's attorney general.

Rather than dignify such factional shenanigans with his participation, Jefferson chose to press his side of the argument in more congenial places, most notably the Republican Congress. As we shall see, his boycott of *Marbury* was part of a larger campaign to convince the Senate to cleanse the Supreme Court by impeaching its most notorious Federalist members. This strategy might have seemed sensible at the time, but Jefferson's boycott turned out to be a mistake in the long run. We can never know what Madison would have said in court if Jefferson hadn't muzzled him. But there is every reason to expect that he would have transformed Marshall's monologue in *Marbury* into one of the great dialogues of our tradition.

In great debates, the protagonists don't shout past one another, but give voice to profound disagreements while sustaining mutual intelligibility. If this is the recipe for greatness, Madison v. Marshall had all the makings. The two men shared the same basic constitutional understandings. Both placed popular sovereignty at the center of constitutional thought, both believed that constitutional politics required "great exertion," and both believed that such exertion should not be "frequently repeated."[77]

These common understandings would have led both to a common question: After the Jeffersonians' struggle to mobilize popular opinion against Federalist repression in the late 1790s, should the Jeffersonian electoral victories of 1800 and 1802 be understood as a popular mandate to repudiate the Federalist interpretation of the Constitution?

There were many different ways Madison might have asked and answered this question. My principal complaint about modern legal scholarship is its failure to compensate for Madison's silence. Some recent work usefully emphasizes the continuing importance of popular constitutionalism in the early republic. Even these scholars don't focus on the ways in which the plebiscitary transformation of the presidency served as the institutional vehicle for the expression of popular sovereignty, enabling the Republicans to mount a sustained assault on the pretensions of the Marshall Court.[78] And the main line of constitutional thought continues to treat Marshall's monologue as if it were the only enduring statement defining the constitutional meaning of the Jeffersonian revolution. By failing to penetrate Madison's silence, we enable Marshall's monologue to displace the living dialogue of constitutionalism that in fact prevailed in the early republic.

I don't suggest that the standard treatment of *Marbury* is overtly celebratory. When American law students are introduced to *Marbury*'s mysteries, the rite of passage is transformed into a demonstration of the opinion's technical inadequacy. Law teachers throughout the land demonstrate that the chief justice's pronouncements about judicial review were utterly unnecessary: it is child's play to construe the suspect statute in ways that avoid all constitutional doubt. Almost as embarrassing is the Court's lengthy disquisition on the limits of presidential power. If Marshall had no jurisdiction over Marbury's application for relief, he had no business mouthing off on the merits of Marbury's dispute with Madison and Madison's boss, Jefferson. No jurisdiction means just that—no power to say what the law is. So why didn't Marshall simply dismiss the case without entertaining us with his dicta on presidential power?[79]

This technical critique may create the illusion of legal mastery in the minds of anxious students, but it does nothing to help them grasp *Marbury*'s relationship to the larger struggle over constitutional legitimacy. A generation ago, Robert McCloskey broke new ground. He refused to view Marshall's discussions of presidential and congressional power within the narrow framework of the particular facts of Marbury's case. He urged us to see the chief justice's opinion as a brilliant institutional response to the rise of the Republicans in the presidency and Congress:

> If [the Court] upheld Marbury and ordered delivery of the commission, the order would surely be ignored by Madison, the Court would be exposed as impotent . . . If, on the other hand, they did not uphold Marbury, they would give aid and comfort to Jefferson and might seem to support his denunciation of the "midnight appointments."
>
> But Marshall was equal to the occasion. Marbury's commission, he said, is being illegally withheld from him by the Jeffersonian administration and a writ can appropriately be directed to a cabinet official when he fails his duty. However, the Supreme Court is not the proper tribunal to supply Marbury with a remedy in this case . . . For the Court's original jurisdiction is defined in the Constitution, and a congressional act [expanding it by granting the Court the writ of mandamus] is therefore unconstitutional . . .
>
> A more adroit series of parries and ripostes would be difficult to imagine. The danger of a head-on clash with the Jeffersonians was averted by the denial of jurisdiction; but, at the same time, the declaration that the commission was illegally withheld scotched any impression that the Court condoned the administration's behavior . . . [T]he Court was in the delightful position, so common in its history but so confusing to its critics, of rejecting and assuming power in a single breath.[80]

McCloskey is half right. Once the case is reframed in institutional terms, Marshall's non sequiturs about congressional and presidential power take on a different appearance—as exquisitely crafted to make it impossible for the president and Congress effectively to respond to the Court's pretensions.

But he is half wrong. The problem comes in his claim that, in writing *Marbury*, Marshall "scotched any impression that the Court condoned the administration's behavior." Once we bring *Stuart* into the picture, McCloskey's suggestion is flatly untenable. In contrast to *Marbury*, *Stuart* is placing its imprimatur on the Jeffersonian purge, and in the most dramatic possible way—by making the justices themselves serve as Jefferson's willing collaborators in ousting the midnight judges and dispensing federal justice on Jefferson's terms.

By returning to circuit riding, the justices were degrading their own judicial commissions in ways that Marshall had declared constitutionally intolerable in *Marbury*.[81] Despite Marshall's proud declaration that Congress could not expand the Court's original jurisdiction, the justices were preparing themselves for a lifetime of trials; despite Marshall's declaration that the terms of judicial commissions granted vested legal rights, the justices would continue to hold circuit court without any appropriate legal commission, and in defiance of the judicial commissions held by the Federalist circuit judges appointed by Adams (with the aid of Marshall).

Nor would this utter capitulation in *Stuart* be a passing moment in the history of the Court. John Marshall would be obliged to savor his ironical relationship to Marbury v. Madison with every lousy meal, lumpy bed, and bumpy road he encountered on the endless ride around his circuit. Each daily indignity could only impress upon him the triumph of Thomas Jefferson's Constitution, as codified by his own Court in Stuart v. Laird. And each time the great chief justice began a new trial, he was once again establishing that it was the Constitution of 1801, not that of 1787, which served as the foundation of justice in the country.

Marshall would not live to redeem *Marbury's* promise of judicial review of federal legislation. The next case to invoke this power was the infamous *Dred Scott* decision, which helped precipitate the Civil War. It would be a long, long time before the Supreme Court would begin to stabilize its relationship to the presidency and Congress, especially during periods when mass movements were seeking to transform traditional constitutional understandings.

Two centuries onward, we have yet to reach anything resembling a stable equilibrium.

The Complexities of Synthesis

I do not want to be too hard on McCloskey, since his pathbreaking work prepared the way for my discussion. Both of us are trying to understand the Marshall Court in terms of political realities that the Founders had never anticipated: the rise of national party politics and the consequent transformation of the presidency. McCloskey goes wrong only in failing to see that *Marbury* was only one-half of the story.

The *Marbury* half should be viewed as a *moment of conservative resistance*—the point when the Court, full of members appointed by prior presidents, presents itself as an embattled defender of the ancien regime, struggling to preserve the hard-fought principles of the past against the brash transformations proposed in the name of the People of the present. But after *Marbury* comes *Stuart,* and the *moment of judicial accommodation*. Notwithstanding *Marbury*'s protestations of fidelity to the "great exertions" of the constitutional past, the *Stuart* Court executes a switch in time, and participates—however reluctantly—in the legitimation of the new constitutional order.

Of course, Paterson's opinion seeks to obscure the extent of his doctrinal betrayal. Yet its real-world implications are plain. Thanks to *Stuart,* the Federalist effort to create a strong system for the administration of federal justice had come crashing down, permitting the state courts to dominate the scene for a very long time to come. For all their brave talk about the sanctity of judicial commissions, the justices of the Supreme Court had become Jefferson's collaborators. It was they, and nobody else, who would transform the Republican vision of a weak federal government into an operational reality in the courtrooms of the United States.

All this happens with blinding speed in *Marbury-Stuart*. It took only one week for the Court to attack and to retreat, to declare itself the privileged representative of the great constitutional past and to capitulate before the People's representatives of the constitutional present.

McCloskey helps explain how the Court could maintain at least a semblance of credibility despite this bewildering turnaround. He rightly emphasizes that *Marbury* is carefully designed to have no real-world effect. By denying the JP any relief, Marshall's opinion carves out a constitutional realm of purely powerless discourse: declaring that Jefferson has done a great constitutional wrong, but declaring that the Constitution prevents the court from doing anything about it. Having created this airy domain, Marshall brilliantly takes advantage of two great silences—Madison's in *Marbury,* his own in *Stuart*—to create the appearance of an enduring and uncontested monument to judicial review.

This rhetorical achievement was inherently unstable. Marshall's silence in *Stuart* could not conceal the facts on the ground. In their first real-world confrontation with the ascendant Republicans in the presidency and Congress, the Federalist Court had capitulated, failing to follow the dictates of *Marbury* in an "easy" case involving the integrity of their very own commissions as justices. If they continued to retreat before the triumphant tribunes of the People in future cases, Marshall's effort to present the Court as the defender of the Federalist Constitution of 1787 would vanish into thin air. Whatever the Court said, or failed to say, it would become increasingly evident that, on all contestable matters, it was the Jeffersonian vision affirmed by the People in 1800, and not the Marshallian interpretation of the Federalist principles of 1787, that would serve as the motivating force of the living constitution.

To put the matter more affirmatively, the Court's bewildering performance set the stage for its continuing struggle with a distinctive interpretive problem: how to reconcile Marshall's interpretation of 1787 with the Jeffersonian vision of 1800. Call this the question of *intertemporal synthesis,* and it is easy to see why the *Marbury-Stuart* combination could not possibly serve as a final answer. On the one hand, *Marbury* suggested that *everything* from 1787 survived, including the right of a lowly justice of the peace to demand his commission from the president of the United States. On the other hand, *Stuart* suggested that *nothing* had survived—not even the justices' authority to defend the constitutional integrity of their own commissions as justices. It was almost as if the Court were repealing Aristotle's law of the excluded middle, proclaiming both A and not-A simultaneously true.

Marbury-Stuart was more a statement of a problem than a solution—only time would tell which case would be more important. Under one scenario, the Supreme Court might ultimately win the authority to declare that *Marbury* stated the general rule and *Stuart* the narrow exception: "*Stuart* involved a single issue—circuit riding. And it simply held that we would not seriously confront a new constitutional challenge to its legitimacy, given our previous acceptance of circuit riding during the 1790s. Beyond this narrow holding, *Stuart* augurs nothing for the future of our constitutional development."

But in 1803 only a fool would have bet on this resolution. It was far more likely that *Stuart* would provide the key to the future—that whenever the Marshall Court announced a Federalist interpretation of the principles of 1787, its constitutional initiative would collapse under the weight of Jeffersonian opposition. With every judicial retreat, *Marbury*'s promise would become more hollow. After repeated failures, would the Court finally abandon the attempt to reassert (some) Federalist principles of 1787 in the hostile constitutional world created by Thomas Jefferson in the name of the People?

This daunting prospect permits an insight into a more puzzling feature of our story. As we have seen, one of the displaced circuit judges, Reed, did bring a lawsuit challenging the repeal, but then did not pursue the matter. What accounts for his surprising diffidence?

The circuit judgeships carried an annual salary of $2,000—a hefty sum. And we have seen that Reed's complaint would have been far easier than Stuart's for the Supreme Court to satisfy: it would merely have had to order the treasury to continue paying Reed his salary.

Given all this, it is hard to see why Reed and his fellow judges didn't insist that the justices redeem the promise of *Marbury*. After all, the chief justice himself had declared judicial commissions to be a species of "vested right," requiring judicial protection in any nation committed to the rule of law. How could Reed's commission be rendered worthless without demonstrating that *Marbury* was a puff of hot air?

If the Court had vindicated Reed's claim, the judge might not have gotten his money. Marshall and his colleagues could issue as many judicial orders as they liked, but it was up to the treasury to decide whether to pay. Since Secretary of State Madison had boycotted *Marbury*, perhaps Treasury Secretary Gallatin would have refused to cooperate in *Reed*. Behind both secretaries loomed the figure of Thomas Jefferson, and his opinion of the factionalists on the Court was plain enough.

Nevertheless, if Reed had been interested only in dollars and cents, the prospect of Jeffersonian resistance would not have deterred his lawsuit. Even if the present administration had refused to pay, Reed's judicial victory would still have had substantial cash value. Once he had obtained a final judgment from the courts, he would have been able to collect on it, with interest, any time a more friendly administration came to power. Recall that one of the circuit judges, Oliver Wolcott, wrote a petition to Congress, signed by eleven circuit judges, demanding payment of their salaries. If these worthies were sufficiently organized to go to Congress, why didn't they join in Reed's lawsuit?

Perhaps because they were more interested in the future of the Federalist Supreme Court than in their private bank balances? A contemptuous refusal by Gallatin to honor the judiciary's order in *Reed* would have been one more sign that the Marshall Court was a paper tiger within the new constitutional order created by Thomas Jefferson.[82] Far better for far-sighted Federalists to drop the entire controversy and defer further judicial challenges to the Republicans to a more propitious political juncture.[83]

For the moment, the meaning of *Marbury* would remain mysterious. *Stuart* had made it painfully clear that the Court would not carry its commitment to *Marbury* to the point of challenging the central planks of the Republican program endorsed by the president and Congress. But *Marbury*'s proud pronunciamento put the Republicans on notice that the Court might well try later to defend the principles of 1787 despite the revolution of 1800.

The Marshall Court had not yet explained which fragments of 1787 it hoped to preserve, and which elements of 1800 it was willing to accept. And even when it sought to draw this line, would it be able to defend its understanding of 1787 against further attack?

Nobody knew, but at least the *Marbury-Stuart* combination opened up a synergistic possibility. Notwithstanding their implacable hostility, Marshall and Jefferson might build a constitutional whole that was larger than the sum of its parts—synthesizing the principles of 1787 and 1800 in a way that neither Federalists nor Republicans could endorse, but both could live with.

Then again, they might not.

9

Presidential Purge

As John Marshall was building up *Marbury's* meaning on a mountain of judicial silences, Thomas Jefferson was dominating the constitutional stage.

Even before *Stuart* had sealed the fate of the circuit judges, Jefferson opened up a new campaign against the Federalist judges who remained on the bench.[1] The campaign reached its climax with the impeachment of Justice Samuel Chase by the House and his narrow acquittal by the Senate. If a few votes had gone the other way, the next man on the firing line would have been John Marshall, the greatest of the midnight judges. Chase's acquittal marked a turning point. It pushed Jefferson in the direction of reluctant accommodation with Marshall—and yet, even after the Senate's vote for acquittal, the president would continue to search for a propitious moment to renew his attack.

The Impeachment of Pickering

From the start, the Federalists had been predicting the worst. As the Republican purge of the circuit judges cleared Congress, the *Washington Federalist* was already looking to the future:

> Should Mr. Breckenridge [the Republican leader in the Senate] now
> bring forward a resolution to repeal the law establishing the Supreme
> court of the United States, we should only consider it a part of the
> system intended to be pursued. It can as well be done, as consistently
> with the constitution, as what has been done. It may seem too bold
> for this session, but the democrats having established the principle

that there is no such thing as breaking the constitution, do what you will, we sincerely expect it will be done next session, should we have another session under the present remnant of our constitution. They can then repeal the law establishing that court, having caution not to have the *repeal* operate till the *new law* commences: then the old judges cease of course with the old law, the executive appoints new judges for the new law; & still they will comply with the constitution which says there shall be one supreme court.[2]

The next session redeemed the *Federalist*'s prophecy, but not quite in the way predicted. Rather than substituting one Supreme Court for another, leading Republicans attempted to establish impeachment as an all-purpose tool for the removal of politically unacceptable judges.

On February 4, 1803—the day after the Senate rejected the circuit judges' memorial, but before the Court had heard argument in either *Marbury* or *Stuart*—the president began his second great campaign against the judiciary. He called on the House to consider the impeachment of District Judge John Pickering.[3] The old man had declined into senility and alcoholism, and was plainly "insane" under the standards of the day, so his impeachment raised a larger legal question. An insane man lacks culpable intent: if Pickering could be impeached despite his lack of culpability, so could other judges.

The House upheld the impeachment on a party-line vote, and when the matter came before the Senate, the key issue was framed in constitutional terms:[4] Should the Senate determine whether the judge was "guilty of high crimes and misdemeanors," suggesting culpable intent, or should it simply ask whether he was "guilty as charged"?[5] The Senate adopted the weaker formulation, with Senator White protesting: "[G]ood behaviour, he observed, would be no longer the tenure of office; every officer of the Government must be at the mercy of a majority of Congress, and it will not hereafter be necessary that a man should be guilty of high crimes and misdemeanors in order to render him liable to removal from office by impeachment; but a conviction upon any facts stated in articles exhibited against him will be sufficient."[6]

The same message was implied by the Senate's rush to judgment. This famously deliberative assembly refused to delay the proceedings, despite the absence of Pickering or his lawyer, and despite his son's petition for time to allow his father to come to Washington to give "further testimony in his behalf, which will enable the Court to judge for themselves as to the insanity of the said John Pickering."[7] Instead, it went along with the House managers' claim that it was enough to provide affidavits attesting to the judge's senile and drunken behavior. When the majority pressed for a final vote on whether the judge should "be removed from office," five senators walked out, with Dayton and White protesting that the question was "an unfair one, and calculated to preclude them from giving any distinct and explicit opinion upon the true and most important point in the cause, viz.: as to the insanity of Judge Pickering, and whether the charges contained in the articles of impeachment, if true, amounted in him to high crimes and misdemeanors or not."[8] Heedless, the Republicans pushed onward and removed the judge by a two-thirds vote on March 12, 1804.

Here is a leading Federalist senator, William Plumer, reflecting on the meaning of it all in a Boston newspaper: "How far these proceedings will form a precedent to establish the doctrine, That when requested by a majority of the House, two thirds of the Senate can remove a Judge from office without a formal conviction of high crimes and misdemeanors, time alone can develop."[9]

The Impeachment of Chase

Plumer did not have long to wait. John Randolph, a manager of Pickering's impeachment and a principal spokesman for the administration, immediately turned to bigger game. Within an hour[10] of his success in persuading the Senate to "remove" Pickering, Randolph gained the support of the overwhelming Republican majority in the House to impeach Samuel Chase of the Supreme Court.[11]

Jefferson did not comment in public, but he played an organizing role behind the scenes. The president had been especially provoked by Chase's recent charge to a Baltimore grand jury in which, according to the custom of the time,[12] he took "the liberty to make a few observations which I hope you will receive as flowing only from my regard to the welfare and prosperity of our common country."

Chase's prognosis was dire:

You know, gentlemen, that our State and national institutions were framed to secure to every member of the society equal liberty and equal rights; but the late alteration of the Federal Judiciary by the abolition of the office of the sixteen circuit judges, and the recent change in our State constitution by the establishing of universal suffrage, and the further alteration that is contemplated in our State judiciary (if adopted) will, in my judgment, take away all security for property and personal liberty. The independence of the national Judiciary is already shaken to its foundation, and the virtue of the people alone can restore it.[13]

Outraged, Jefferson wrote to Joseph Nicholson, one of the Republican leaders of the House: "You must have heard of the extraordinary charge of Chase to the grand jury at Baltimore. Ought this seditious & official attack on the principles of our constitution, and on the proceedings of a state, to go unpunished? And to whom so pointedly as yourself will the public look for the necessary measures? I ask these questions for your consideration. As for myself, it is better that I should not interfere."[14] Given Chase's blatantly political provocations, the president's equally political motivations, and the precedent of the Pickering case, Randolph rushed the House to judgment. He offered a summary motion that "Samuel Chase . . . be impeached of high crimes and misdemeanors," together with an unanalyzed pile of documents in support of the charge.[15] After a brief debate about the informality of this procedure, his impeachment motion won on a party-line vote of 73 to 32.[16] The impeachment managers came up with a set of formal charges three weeks later, on the next-to-last day of the session—but the House itself did not get a chance to debate or approve these particulars, and, as we shall see, they would be modified later.

Mr. Justice Chase was not amused. Fearing that the managers would allow the House to rise without making any formal charges, he prepared an elaborate memorial denouncing the procedures by which he was impeached and demanding a set of articles: "It is in vain that he [Chase] has looked . . . for a statement or even a hint of the offenses of which he stands charged." Then, when the managers came forward at the last moment, Chase circulated his memorial together with a letter of protest: "[The articles of impeachment] contain the most aggravated and inflamed construction which it was possible for passion and party spirit to put on the ex parte evidence, whereon the vote of impeachment was founded, they will become a very powerful engine in the hands of calumniators and party zealots."[17]

The questions all this raised were clear: What was the nature of impeachment? If the Senate could remove the mad Pickering without a serious trial, what was wrong with doing the same for the impetuously partisan Chase?

Before the Senate got its chance, the voters would get into the act. Between March and December Americans would return to the polls to determine the future of Thomas Jefferson and the Republican Congress. The impeachment would have inevitably entered into the electoral debate, but Chase's request "to the editors of all the newspapers in the United States" that they publish his letter and memorial, as well as the articles of impeachment, helped dramatize the issue in the partisan struggle that followed.

The Twelfth Amendment

In returning to the polls, Americans were not returning to the same Constitution that had almost been shattered by the election of 1800. While the constitutional status of the judiciary was still up for grabs in 1804, the Republicans had already reconstructed the presidency by enacting the Twelfth Amendment. The constitutional amendment, in turn, only demonstrated further the extent to which the *Stuart-Marbury* compromise was essential to the Court's survival as an independent actor in the new presidentialist world.

Republican Samuel Smith vividly recalled to the Senate the scenes that had required decisive constitutional action:

> Two candidates before the House—party spirit high; the one determined to support the candidate upon whom public affection and confidence had unequivocally centered; the other seeking to place in the Executive Chair, not a candidate of their original choice, but a candidate through whom they wished to retain at least a share of power; unsuccessful in that effort, bringing forward a proposition to create a President; and how? By a law to be passed for the purpose; and in which the person was to be named, leaving the votes and

choice of the people out of consideration altogether. Had this been effected, what other result would follow but civil war? Without pretending to be in the counsels of either party on that occasion, he [Smith] believed that civil war was seriously apprehended, and so much so, that he felt perfectly convinced, that had a choice been made in the way proposed, and a person could be found to accept it, that his head would not have remained on his shoulders for twenty-four hours afterward. Dangers of this kind he was solicitous to avoid.[18]

With the head of John Marshall rolling down the aisle,[19] as it were, the senators got down to business. The Republican goal was clear: "[T]he election of the Executive should be in the people, or as nearly as was possible, consistent with the public order and security to the right of suffrage. The provision admitting the choice by the House of Representatives was intended only for an extreme case, where great inconvenience might result from sending a defective election back to the people, as is customary in Massachusetts, where, if the majority is deficient, a new election is required."[20]

But the Republicans pursued their goal in an uninspired way. They did not seriously consider Massachusetts-style innovations, but merely tried to prevent a rerun of 1800. That debacle had been caused by the Framers' decision to allow each elector to cast two votes for president, with the runner-up obtaining the vice presidency as a consolation prize. To prevent a replay, the Republicans proposed to change the Constitution so that each elector must thenceforth cast two distinct ballots—one for the presidency, the other for the vice presidency. Under their proposed constitutional amendment, the two candidates of the winning party could now obtain the same number of electoral votes without throwing the election into the House.

This narrow provision didn't solve other problems raised by the 1800 experience, but it did give the Republicans short-term strategic advantage. They were expecting to win the presidency in 1804, but they weren't sure by how much, and they were determined to save the vice presidency for their party. By requiring the electors to vote separately for the two offices, they would prevent the Federalists from slipping their man into second place.[21] And by giving their amendment a narrow focus, they might convince three-fourths of the states to ratify it in time for the 1804 election. Anything more ambitious would take too long.

The Federalists pretended to be scandalized that "the ruling party of the day, ha[s] brought forward this amendment, for the purpose of preventing the choice of a Federal Vice President at the next election."[22] They opposed this "despoti[c]"[23] scheme by seeking to revive the anti-party rhetoric of the Founding. "Great good may come from the present mode; men of each of the parties may hold the two principal offices . . . Would not one of a different party . . . tend to check . . . the overheated zeal of party?"[24]

Absolutely not, replied the Republicans, and in explaining why, they elaborated further on the rising plebiscitarian conception of the presidency:

> It has been urged, sir, by the gentlemen in opposition, in a mode, as if they supposed we wished to conceal or deny it, that one object of this amendment is to bestow upon the majority a power to elect a Vice President. Sir, I avow it to be so. This is one object of the amendment; and the other . . . is to enable the Electors, by perfecting the election of a President, to keep it out of the House of Representatives. Are not both obviously correct, if . . . the Constitution, in all cases where it refers elections to the popular principle, intended that principle to act by majorities?[25]

In contrast to 1787, the electoral college was no longer viewed as a clever mechanism for selecting a nonpartisan statesman capable of transcending faction. It was now perfectly appropriate to describe presidential elections as contests by rival parties for majority support; and once the winning side had gained a mandate from the People, it was wrong to deprive the victorious party of executive power merely because the president suffered some personal calamity. The amendment, in short, neatly operated to transform the executive into a reliable instrument of party rule.

Given the Republicans' landslide victory in the elections of 1802, and their partisan interest in securing the executive, the result of the congressional debate was foreordained. Good party men had little difficulty joining together to give the Twelfth Amendment the necessary two-thirds in both Houses; and their colleagues in the state legislatures rapidly pushed the amendment through in time for 1804. Though scholars typically pass over the Twelfth Amendment in silence, it marked an early—if painfully inadequate—attempt to domesticate the plebiscitarian presidency into our standing constitutional arrangements.[26]

But, as always, the consolidation of a presidentialist structure only raised new questions about its relationship to the evolving whole. As was all too clear, Jefferson and his party were on a constitutional campaign to reorganize the judiciary as well as the presidency. The Marshall Court had already acquiesced in the Republican assault on the circuit courts, but the status of the Supreme Court was still an open question—as the pending impeachment of Chase dramatically demonstrated.

With the voters returning to the polls in 1804 to encounter a transformed process of presidential selection, the future of the *Stuart-Marbury* compromise was very much in doubt.

The Election Campaign

What a difference four years makes. In 1800 Republicans were on a rhetorical rampage against a Federalist administration with overweening monarchical ambitions. In 1804 it was the Federalists' turn to mount the same attack in a newspaper war waged on three fronts. First and foremost there was the matter of the Louisiana Purchase. In the Federalists' view, Jefferson had unconstitutionally acquired this dominion, and was now mocking his libertarian reputation by lording it over the territory's inhabitants like a potentate.[27]

But for present purposes, the continuing campaign against the judiciary is of greater interest. Here is a typical comment from the most widely publicized Federalist broadside: "As soon as [the Republican] party shall acquire new strength in Congress, the Supreme court will be swept away, as obstructing the schemes of interest and ambition. The repeal of the inferior courts will be pled as a precedent for that of the Supreme court. Nothing will remain free from the rapacious grasp of faction."[28]

The Republicans did not take these charges lying down. They not only defended the elimination of the circuit judges but also threatened the existing Supreme Court with the same fate. Consider John Taylor's *Defense,* published widely in Republican papers:

We all know that the judges have assumed the power of pronouncing laws unconstitutional; and of refusing to execute them. Such laws may be of vast importance . . . Opinion may be divided on them. A great majority of congress, the president, and the people may consider them constitutional; the judges alone may pronounce them unconstitutional. It is as probable, nay more probable that the judges should err on this point, than the legislature, elected for the special purpose of passing laws . . . Still the judiciary put their veto upon the laws, and thereby jeopardise life and property, and the peace of the country. Are the legislature, in this case, to submit? Are they to give an absolute control over the laws to the judiciary? For it is apparent that the power of impeachment may be futile, as any number over a third of the senators may frustrate a conviction, and as this number may be found among those senators who do not represent quite one ninth of the people of the United States. If this absolute control is not given, then the power of abolishing the office is the only effectual remedy.[29]

What is more, according to Taylor, the Republicans' original decision to abolish the offices of the circuit judges had now gained authoritative approval:

[T]here is one criterion of the constitutionality of the repealing act, which ought, in our government, to be conclusive; one which could not be urged when the law passed. A lively appeal has been made to public opinion; and the people have been called upon to displace those who supported the measure. In every instance, except one, they have re-elected those who supported it; and in numerous instances they have ejected its opponents. In the congress that passed this act the republicans in the House of Representatives were sixty-eight, and the federalists thirty-eight; and in the Senate the republicans were eighteen, and the federalists fourteen. In the present Congress the republicans in the House are ninety-six, and the federalists thirty-eight; and in the Senate the republicans are twenty-five; and the federalists nine. The increase of republican members in the House is twenty-eight; and in the Senate seven; while the federalists have lost five senators, and have not gained a single representative, notwithstanding the increased representation. More than two thirds of both branches, and three fourths of the states are likewise republican. Public opinion, therefore, the highest and the only competent tribunal, in litigated cases, has decided this question, with a strength adequate to effecting, if necessary, a correspondent alteration in the constitution, had that been necessary.[30]

These words took on a new weight as the election returns came in.[31] In contrast to 1800, Jefferson won by a landslide, and the Republicans carried Congress with even bigger majorities. The new House would contain 116 Republicans and only 25 Federalists; and the new Senate would see 27 Republicans dominate 7 Federalists. If, as Taylor argued, and as the *Stuart* court had recognized, the People had given their decisive support to the removal of the Federalist circuit judges, how would the participants in Washington interpret the meaning of this most recent mandate?

The Turning Point

As the lame-duck Senate reconvened in December, it began deliberating on the rules by which Chase would be tried. John Quincy Adams, then a Federalist senator from Massachusetts, provided this scandalized report to his father:

> We were seriously told in long and studied speeches that impeachment, so far from being a criminal prosecution, was *no prosecution at all.* That the Senate, sitting for the purpose of trying impeachment, was *not a court,* and that it ought not to derive its forms or rules of proceeding, either from courts of impeachment in other countries, or from any of the judicial courts in our own. It was even intimated that *not much* pleading ought to be allowed, and a hint sufficiently explicit was given, that a general issue, a mere declaration of "not guilty," was the only answer which ought to be received to the articles charged by the House of Representatives. Conformably to these opinions the word "court" was, in two instances at least, struck out of the rules for proceeding in cases of impeachment, reported by a committee at an early period of the session.[32]

These procedural views expressed a larger vision. For Randolph and some other House managers, impeachment was a vehicle for the expression of the popular will, sweeping out officers who had lost the confidence of the nation.[33] This plebiscitarian view resonated with some leading Republicans in the Senate,[34] but others took a more legalistic approach.

The nature of impeachment was very much up for decision: legalistic trial or political forum? The answer was resolved, in large measure, by Randolph's need to win a two-thirds majority for conviction. With the Senate containing 25 Republicans and 9 Federalists, the House managers could lose only two Republicans if they hoped to oust Chase. The legalistic resistance of a few sufficed to push the proceedings in a trial-like direction. Trial-like procedures reinforced, in turn, the incipient legalism of the substantive discussion.

The Trial

Formal proceedings began on January 2, 1805, with Chase appearing at the bar of the Senate to request a three-month extension. Vice President Burr responded with hostility, repeatedly interrupting the defendant, leaving him "to sink in weakness and despair."[35] The Senate denied his request, giving him only one more month to prepare his defense.

But by the time trial began in earnest, the specter of a Pickering-style proceeding had dissipated, and business proceeded in a more deliberate fashion—with Chase and his outstanding legal team given ample opportunity to rebut the charges against them, and Vice President Burr presiding over the Senate with great impartiality. This placed Randolph at a serious disadvantage, since he was not a lawyer and his biting but disjointed rhetoric seemed out of place in a court-like setting.[36]

The articles of impeachment focused on Chase's rulings at two notorious trials that he had conducted while riding circuit.[37] When John Fries organized a small band of farmers in a violent tax protest, President Adams issued a proclamation calling it "treason," and Chase presided over the ensuing trial in a heavy-handed fashion to the point where the defendants' lawyers quit the case. Fries was convicted and Chase then sentenced him to death "without having been heard by counsel . . . to the disgrace of the character of the American bench."[38] While Chase defended the legality of his rulings, his actions had so embarrassed President Adams that he had pardoned the man whom Chase would have sent to the gallows.[39]

Chase's treatment of James Callender was no less injudicious. When he received a hot-headed pamphlet by Callender accusing Adams of despotism, he set out to make the Republican pamphleteer pay for his libel. Arriving in Richmond in his ride around his circuit, he summoned Callender to court on a warrant generally used for felons, and forced the trial to begin during the presidential election season, despite the absence of material witnesses.[40] He then refused to allow an important witness for Callender to testify, and placed many restrictions on his counsel's ability to conduct an effective defense. Once again, the House was hardly frivolous in charging Chase with actions "unbecoming even a public prosecutor, but highly disgraceful to the character of a judge."[41]

The final article of impeachment focused on the recent political diatribe that had provoked Jefferson to bring the constitutional battering-ram into play:

> [T]he said Samuel Chase, disregarding the duties and dignity of his judicial character, did, at circuit court for the district of Maryland, held at Baltimore, in the month of May, 1803, pervert his official right and duty to address the grand jury then and there assembled . . . for the purpose of delivering to the said grand jury an intemperate and inflammatory political harangue, with intent to excite the fears and resentments of the said grand jury, and of the good people of Maryland, against their State government and constitution—a conduct highly censurable in any, but peculiarly indecent and unbecoming in a judge of the Supreme Court of the United States; and, moreover, that the said Samuel Chase, then and there, under pretence of exercising his judicial right to address the said grand jury . . . deliver[ed] opinions, which, even if the judicial authority were competent to their expression, on a suitable occasion and in a proper manner, were at that time, and as delivered by him, highly indecent, extra judicial, and tending to prostrate the high judicial character with which he was invested, to the low purpose of an electioneering partisan.

To all of this, Chase had a straightforward reply: none of the articles alleged that he had committed a crime, and without an indictable offense, the Senate was obliged to render a verdict of not guilty.[42] Once Chase left the Senate chamber, his skilled defense team was not prepared unequivocally to endorse his legal view of the matter. They reluctantly conceded that some impeachable offenses might not be indictable, but they tried to keep this concession from destroying their case.[43]

The Republican managers countered with a mix of themes. Although the Constitution guarantees judges tenure during "good behavior," it was up to the House and Senate to interpret this vague term: "[I]t therefore becomes the duty of the representatives of the people, as the grand inquest of the nation vested with the general power of impeachment, when they know . . . that acts of misbehavior have been committed, to present the delinquent to this high tribunal."[44] But the Republicans did not rest their case on this broad appeal to popular sovereignty. They also fought on more legalistic terrain, denying that the criminal law provided the key to "high crimes and misdemeanors." They insisted that "high misdemeanors" had traditionally been understood to include "abuse or violation of some public trust,"[45] and that Chase's conduct fell squarely within the traditional understanding of this term.[46] On this view, the particular offenses added up to a more pervasive abuse. Chase had transformed "the judicial power into an engine of political oppression." His course of conduct revealed "a mind inflamed by party spirit and political intolerance."[47]

For his defenders, the Republicans had made a mountain out of molehill. Perhaps Chase had made some mistakes of legal judgment, but his general course of conduct was well within the judicial mores of his time. It was the Republicans, not Chase, who were engaged in a political vendetta.[48]

The Senate responded in a complex fashion. The nine Federalist members paradoxically redeemed the Republicans' charge of partisanship by acquitting Chase on all counts in a party-line vote. The twenty-five Republicans were a much more complicated bunch. Almost none voted to convict Chase under the two articles that accused him of making legal errors in the Callender case. They required something more substantial. A strong Republican majority—making up a slim majority of the Senate as a whole—voted for conviction when they turned to the more abusive aspects of Chase's conduct at the Fries trial. The condemnation of Chase reached its apogee with his political denunciations of the Republicans before the Baltimore grand jury. On this matter, the vote was 19 to 15, only four votes short of conviction.

Since this slender margin had profound consequences for the future, it should be interrogated with care. Republican resistance would be readily explicable if Chase had been a man of spotless reputation, innocent of all wrongdoing. But Randolph was right in pointing to a series of serious improprieties, and conviction did not require extreme theories of popular sovereignty that would have placed all future judges in permanent jeopardy. Senators generally give their party leaders the benefit of the doubt—especially when dealing with one of their party's most notorious and obnoxious enemies. The resistance of some Republican senators—admittedly a small number—should be viewed as quite surprising. After rushing forward to convict the mad Pickering, why did they hesitate when confronting somebody who had, with sound mind and provocative intent, acted in such a partisan fashion? Especially when the Republican revolution had just been reinforced by a landslide victory at the polls?

The Dog That Didn't Bark

On one level, the answer is simple enough: the surprising resistance in the Senate was due to John Randolph's remarkable ability to alienate his fellow Republicans. During the Pickering trial, Randolph addressed the Senate as a leading member of the House, speaking with the full authority of Jefferson.[49] By the time of the Chase trial, his position had been gravely weakened by his break with the president on an entirely unrelated matter.

This involved a great scandal of the early republic, in which speculators obtained a vast tract of land from the state of Georgia 1795 after an "orgy of corruption." When the Yazoo land grant was later revoked by the newly elected legislature, the speculators—and those who had bought land from them in good faith (?)—launched a campaign to gain compensation. During the first Jefferson administration, they attempted to organize a raid on the federal treasury, only to encounter ferocious opposition from Randolph. The dispute had a regional aspect, with the disappointed speculators overwhelmingly from New England and Randolph speaking for an outraged South. When Jefferson supported a compromise, Randolph loudly denounced him for betraying true Republican principles, and repeatedly defeated administration measures by means of a largely southern vote.[50] "It would be difficult," says Richard Ellis, "to overemphasize the disruptive effect this had upon the party . . . As a consequence many Republicans who at first favored the Judge's removal later changed their minds because they did not want to increase Randolph's prestige and influence."[51]

Faced with Randolph's political collapse, the president sought to fill the leadership vacuum by working behind the scenes. Consider his treatment of Aaron Burr. He had distrusted his vice president ever since the electoral college crisis—freezing him out of patronage, replacing him with George Clinton as his running mate in 1804, and otherwise treating him as a nonentity. Burr's position had sunk further after he killed Alexander Hamilton in a duel in July 1804. Under indictment in New Jersey for murder,[52] Burr was terribly vulnerable as he presided over the impeachment trial as a lame-duck vice president.

And the president exploited this fact with his usual finesse. After four years in the wilderness, Burr suddenly found himself enjoying the fruits of presidential favor. In the weeks before Chase's trial, Jefferson appointed three of Burr's friends and relatives to high positions in Louisiana, the territory purchased from the French the previous year. He also conveniently arranged for congressional Republicans to intercede on Burr's behalf in an effort to quash the New Jersey indictment.[53] In case the larger point was missed, the president rewarded the three principal witnesses against Pickering with federal patronage.[54] The message was clear enough to the attentive band of politicians in the Senate—vote the right way on Chase, and you will reap your reward.

Yet these blandishments did not quite save the day. They may well have accounted for Burr's severe treatment of Chase at his preliminary hearing before the Senate. But during the month before the trial began, the Republicans gave up on their effort to make the proceeding a replay of the Pickering affair, and Burr presided over the trial with exemplary impartiality. When push came to shove on the final vote, the president did not gain the victory.

Not that he wasn't trying. His subterranean influence is suggested by a curious juxtaposition. On the floor of the Senate, the focus of debate was on Chase's conduct of the Callender and Fries trials. When the time came for voting, it was the article singling out Chase's political speech before the Baltimore grand jury that got the most votes. Since nothing on the surface of the debate accounts for this inexplicable surge, it seems fair to detect the effect of the president's hidden hand. Recall that this speech had provoked Jefferson's decision to lobby for impeachment in the first place.

We know, moreover, that the president was following the proceedings with intense interest. His papers reveal him keeping score on each senator's vote with his own personal tally sheet.[55] As we imagine him scrutinizing the tally in the hope of finding a few more votes for conviction, we come to a moment of truth. During the perfervid days of the electoral college crisis, Jefferson had been willing to threaten the use of force, or to demand another constitutional convention, if his opponents manipulated the legal rules to ignore his claim to office as the choice of the People. Yet now he chose to accept defeat in silence rather than to proclaim something like this: "Americans cannot tolerate a judge who abuses his office by making political stump speeches while denying a fair trial to citizens who have simply sought to exercise their freedom of speech. In the name of the People, I demand that we purify the judiciary, and thereby inoculate it against further outbreaks of gross partisanship."

Such thoughts surely crossed the president's mind, but he never gave them public voice—and this despite his inaugural claim to serve as "the voice of the nation." While he indulged in private maneuverings, he avoided the bully pulpit. In keeping public silence in the case of Chase, Jefferson was not doing anything out of the ordinary. Rhetorical self-restraint was characteristic of his presidency as a whole.[56]

Nevertheless, our story owes a great deal to this particular dog that didn't bark. After his triumphant purchase of Louisiana and his sweeping reelection victory in 1804, Jefferson was at the very height of his political authority. Speaking out publicly against Chase might well have been enough to compensate for Randolph's political collapse. After all, the margin for acquittal was only four votes, and the Senate Republicans would have been under intense pressure to save their preeminent leader from embarrassing defeat.[57]

Once Chase had been dispatched, the stage would have been set for the grand climax: the impeachment and conviction of John Marshall. By deciding Marbury v. Madison, the chief justice had abused his judicial office in a fashion that might have made Chase blush. Whatever his deficiencies, Chase had never tried to judge a lawsuit caused by his own negligence. This was precisely what Marshall had done in *Marbury*, even insisting on writing the opinion. Only a blind partisan would go this far in abusing his judicial power—or so the bill of impeachment might, very plausibly, have alleged. If Chase's misconduct amounted to an impeachable offense, how could Marshall be allowed to escape condemnation?

Surely Jefferson would have pursued the point with even greater vigor. At least Chase had a perfect right to his commission as Supreme Court justice. But so far as the president was concerned, Adams had acted illegitimately in making any judicial appointments—let alone one to the chief justiceship—after the election results had come in. What is more, Jefferson detested Marshall with a rare passion. Forcing his despised rival from the Court would have given him exquisite satisfaction.

So Jefferson's rhetorical restraint in Chase's case was consequential. If he had publicly put his presidency on the line in the struggle against Chase, our story might well have had a different ending. Looking backward, modern constitutionalists would remember impeachment as the decisive tool through which the Republicans gained control of all three branches of the federal government. Marshall would never have gotten a chance to write the nationalizing opinions that serve today as the great constitutional landmarks of the early republic. A Supreme Court packed with Jeffersonians would have left us a formidable "states' rights" jurisprudence, emphasizing strong limitations on federal power. Marbury v. Madison, in contrast, would principally be remembered as an example of the absurd judicial misbehavior of a discredited chief justice, not as an epic vindication of the Federalist Constitution of 1787.

The Race against Time

We tell ourselves a different story. With the plebiscitarian president remaining silent, six Republican senators chose to join all nine Federalists in acquitting Chase on the eighth article condemning his Baltimore stump speech.

This act of desertion had a devastating impact on Randolph's career.[58] He had invested himself utterly in the prosecution, and if he had won, he would have vastly increased his stature as the man who had cleansed the Augean stables of the Federalist judiciary. He returned to the House a diminished leader. Though he would remain a thorn in Jefferson's side, the defeat pushed this brilliant and charismatic but erratic man into a descending arc of political effectiveness.[59]

It could have been otherwise. Before the Yazoo controversy, Randolph had frequently confronted other administration decisions that offended his principles, and yet he had managed to swallow his pride and maintain his loyalty to the president.[60] For example, he was deeply troubled by the constitutional implications of the Louisiana Purchase, but gave it solid support as leader of the House.[61] If he deferred to his president on such great matters, there was nothing preordained about his break with the administration on the relatively minor Yazoo affair. If Randolph had labored loyally for another year, he would have been in a commanding political position at the Chase trial. Rather than inviting Republican senators to cut him down to size, he could have presented himself as part of a smoothly functioning team, declaiming against the egregious Chase in public while Jefferson plied his fellow Republicans with smiles and favors in private.

On one level, then, the acquittal of Chase is a lesson in the importance of interbranch coordination, and the ease with which congressional barons of the president's party can disrupt a key initiative by means of ideological hair-splitting or sheer prima donnishness. Beyond this, it provides a deeper structural lesson.

To see my point, suppose that the Chase drama had arisen within a British-style parliamentary system that did not separate power between the executive and legislative branches. Under this scenario, Jefferson would be serving as a popular prime minister, recently returned to office by a landslide. If a rising young politician like Randolph publicly voiced opposition to the PM's policies, he would be dispatched instantly to the back benches of the House of Commons. When the time came to impeach Chase before the Republican-controlled upper house, the prime minister would never give Randolph the job of managing the impeachment, but would hand the task to a trusted loyalist. As a consequence, the Republicans in the upper house would not be tempted to cut Randolph down to size, but would focus single-mindedly on the main question: Did the partisan and overbearing Chase deserve to stay in office?

Within this framework, Chase's questionable behavior would have appeared in a uniformly darker light. My thought-experiment suggests that the split between Jefferson and Randolph should not be treated merely as an accidental concatenation of personal factors—though it was that too.[62] We should see it as a surface manifestation of a fundamental decision of 1787 that made congressmen electorally independent of the president's political fortunes. Randolph's renegade activities were possible only because the constitutional separation of powers made it possible for him to win reelection even if he broke with the president.

The impeachment of Chase reveals a fundamental tension generated by the rise of presidentialism in a world still profoundly shaped by the congressionalist structures of 1787. Following in the footsteps of Jefferson, future presidents would claim popular mandates on the basis of party victories at the polls, and they would become much more willing to make public appeals to the People on behalf of their initiatives. Nevertheless, they would frequently find themselves in a Jeffersonian predicament—seeing nominal congressional allies defecting from presidential initiatives on behalf of their own personal or political agendas.

The Founders did not "intend" this outcome: since they had no inkling of a national party system, they did not consider how such a system would interact with the separation of powers. Nonetheless, the conjunction of the congressionalist legacy of 1787 with the new presidentialism of 1801 provides an introduction to a distinctive dynamic that would recur throughout the next two centuries of American history.

Call it *the presidential race against time*. Under this scenario, a plebiscitarian president seeks to make the most of the moral and political authority he has won at the polls before the party leaders in Congress desert him—either on ideological grounds or simply because their local political interests are better served by an oppositional stance. The longer a plebiscitarian president can sustain congressional cooperation, the more profound the ensuing constitutional revolution.

As the president sets out in his race against time, he is far more likely to gain the support of the House than the Senate. Since representatives are elected every two years, they are more likely to express the same ideological currents that swept the president into power. As a consequence, the rise of a plebiscitarian presidency will characteristically generate a distinctive institutional struggle. The Senate will appear as a forum for resistance, and a combination of the president and House will seek to overwhelm senatorial opposition through an institutional pincers movement.

Part of this pattern was anticipated by the men of 1787, who did indeed consider that the luxury of six-year terms would allow senators to serve as a buffer against the populist enthusiasms of the House.[63] But they did not expect the president to join in these popular crusades, and they failed to consider how the Senate might respond to the combined onslaught.

The Chase trial also suggests the importance of legalistic framing in establishing a credible form of senatorial resistance. When the Constitution of 1787 authorized removal for "high crimes and misdemeanors," it provided senators with a distinctive form of political insulation in responding to the pincers movement. The textual formula allows them to insist that they should view impeachment not as party loyalists but as impartial judges. The more legalistic the debate, the more plausible this claim and the easier for senators to insulate themselves from political retribution if they vote against their party.

This legalization strategy is optional, not mandatory, as the juxtaposition of the Pickering and Chase cases suggests. Though the rush to convict Pickering generated legalistic protests from some senators, these did not slow the process sufficiently to provide a compelling legalistic frame for the impeachment proceeding; recall that the Senate simply voted that Pickering should be "removed from office" without explicitly finding him guilty of "high crimes or misdemeanors." In contrast, the trial-type evolution of the Chase impeachment provided a more compelling context for senatorial independence. Within the legalistic setting, the House managers' demand for Chase's removal in the name of the People was only one element in a chorus of disputation—with a sharp legalistic counterpoint provided by Chase's insistence on proof of an indictable crime. The extreme claims made by Chase and some of the Republican managers set the stage for the development of a host of complex arguments that encouraged the Senate to function as a forum for autonomous constitutional assessment.

Chase's activities had undoubtedly raised a fundamental issue. By energetically suppressing the Republican campaign of 1800, and by continuing with public protests after the Republican victory, he had dramatically called into question whether Federalist judges could be trusted to accommodate themselves to the emerging constitutional regime.

The answer was no, according to the president and the House, but the Senate managed to gain the authority to exercise an independent judgment. Thanks to the strong trial-type presentation, Republican senators could use the textual formulas of 1787 to insulate themselves from devastating political retribution if they chose to offer an olive branch to the Marshall Court and wait to see whether Chase and his colleagues would respond in kind.

The Senate's decision was hardly foreordained. Even within a strictly legalistic framework, it was an open question whether Chase should be acquitted or convicted. And when viewed politically, a vote for acquittal carried obvious risks. No senator could be sure how well his posturing as a constitutional statesman would defuse the anger of Republican loyalists back home—or how much it would count against his future patronage requests from a president with a very long memory.

The Court's Role

As the pendulum swung uncertainly, a final factor loomed large. This was the behavior of the Supreme Court. Quite simply: the more confrontational the Court, the easier for the president and House to overwhelm the Senate's legalistic resistance.

To appreciate this point, recall Chase's role at an earlier stage in the drama. When the Republicans repealed the Federalist judiciary act, Chase was emphatic in his opposition. He urged his brethren to go on strike and refuse to cooperate with the Republican effort to sweep away the circuit judges. If the justices had accepted this proposal, how would this have affected the course of the impeachment trial?

For starters, impeachment would have come much sooner, with a trial in 1803 or 1804, before the split between Randolph and Jefferson. And Chase's conduct would have been more egregious: the articles of impeachment would have cited not only his partisan speeches to the grand jury but also his contemptuous refusal to obey the congressional command to return to circuit riding. Chase was on firm ground in concluding his memo to Marshall urging a judicial strike with a grim prophecy: "The burthen of deciding so momentous a question, and under the present circumstances of our Country, would be very great on all the Judges assembled; but an individual Judge, declining to take a Circuit, must sink under it" (see Chapter 8). Recall that John Marshall was also sorely tempted by the strike option—we owe the Supreme Court's survival to moderates like Paterson and Washington.

By 1805 Marshall was taking a more moderate course. When called as a witness at Chase's trial in the Senate, he angered Federalist die-hards by refusing to defend his colleague's conduct.[64] He had also written a remarkable letter to Chase on the eve of the trial in which he was already steeling himself for the worst.[65] On one level, the letter bucked up Chase's spirits by protesting against one of the articles of impeachment. On another level, it shows Marshall reflecting on the day after tomorrow, when Chase's likely conviction would require the embattled chief justice to consider the need for a change in course:

> Admitting it to be true that on legal principles Colo. Taylor's testimony was admissible, it certainly constitutes a very extraordinary ground for an impeachment. According to the ancient doctrine a jury finding a verdict against the law of the case was liable to an attaint; & the account of the present doctrine seems to be that a Judge giving a legal opinion contrary to the opinion of the legislature is liable to impeachment. As, for convenience & humanity the old doctrine of attaint has yielded to the silent, moderate but not less operative influence of new trials, I think the modern doctrine of impeachment shoud yield to an appellate jurisdiction in the legislature. A reversal of those legal opinions deemd unsound by the legislature woud certainly better comport with the mildness of our character than a removal of the Judge who has renderd them unknowing of his fault.[66]

In plainer language, Marshall was prepared to allow Congress to overrule the Court's constitutional interpretations in exchange for immunity from politicized impeachments. Since Chase escaped conviction,[67] the chief justice was not obliged to publicly retreat from *Marbury*. But if it had been otherwise, his proposal for a legislative override of "legal opinions deemd unsound by the legislature" might well have served as the basis of a constitutional compromise—supposing that Marshall had somehow avoided impeachment himself.[68]

For now, it is enough to emphasize the importance of the conciliatory strategies adopted by the Marshall Court in defending itself against the presidential race against time. If Chase had refused to obey the congressional command to return to circuit riding in 1802, nothing could have saved him from impeachment. The Court's accommodationist approach in upholding circuit riding in Stuart v. Laird began to bear fruit when conflicts among congressional barons weakened the president's political grip.

To put the point in a formula: it was an *accommodating* style of judicial statesmanship, together with a *fractionating* style of leadership in the political branches, that enabled the Court to emerge from the presidentialist revolution of 1800 without sacrificing its claim as a privileged interpreter of the enduring meaning of the Constitution of 1787. The character of this judicial claim cannot be grasped by a narrow focus on *Marbury,* as is the present custom among constitutionalists. It is the *Stuart-Marbury* conjunction that opens our eyes to a larger truth: the Court (barely) managed to maintain its claim to judicial review *(Marbury)* only by accepting the president's claim of a popular mandate to repudiate certain fundamental aspects of the Federalist regime *(Stuart).*

The *Stuart-Marbury* conjunction is only part of the dynamic that allowed judicial review to survive the rise of presidentialist government. We must add the Senate's acquittal of Chase into the constitutional equation. As Marshall's anguished letter to Chase reveals, the future of *Marbury* remained very much in doubt on the eve of the impeachment trial. If we are to do justice to the genesis of judicial review, we must reflect further on the deeper links between the *Stuart-Marbury* conjunction of 1803 and the Senate's decision to preserve judicial independence in 1805.

My point here is deflationary: the judicial retreat in *Stuart* lowered the political pressure on the Senate when dealing with Chase's defiant conduct. By returning to its circuit-riding duties, the *Stuart* Court had reduced Chase's defiant speech to the Baltimore grand jury to mere puffery; though the justice might thunder against "the abolition of the office of the sixteen circuit judges," his actions belied the ferocity of his words. Whatever he might say, he was in fact cooperating with the new Republican regime by holding trial court in place of the midnight judges. Given this background, a small but decisive minority of Senate Republicans could afford the luxury of finding that Chase's public diatribe had not quite reached the level of "high crime and misdemeanor." If the *Stuart* Court hadn't lowered the stakes in 1803, the legalistic frame would not have been strong enough to save Chase (or Marshall) from conviction in 1805.

The Five-Body Problem

From the Jeffersonian campaign against the midnight judges in 1801 to the acquittal of Chase in 1805—this escalating confrontation has generated passionate disagreements over two centuries of historical commentary. Many legalists, deeply committed to judicial independence, look upon the scene with undisguised horror. To them the president appears to be nothing less than an evil genius behind a relentless conspiracy against the rule of law.[69] Democratic critics of Marshall, in contrast, describe *Marbury* as "a political coup of the first magnitude," to invoke Edward Corwin's enormously influential phrase.[70]

I have been trying to move beyond these conflicting accounts of mutual antagonism. The traditional stories rightly emphasize the ferocity of the encounter, but they ignore crucial acts of institutional restraint—and yet it is these acts of restraint that account for the survival of judicial review within the evolving balance of power.

To see this clearly, let's summarize our long and complicated story by reducing it to a pseudomathematical "five body" problem. On one side of the constitutional equation, place all the institutional forces representing the revolution of 1800: the presidency, the House, and the voters who repeatedly strengthened the Republican claim to speak for the People by handing the party consecutive victories in the elections of 1800, 1802, and 1804. On the other side, consider the position of the Court and the Senate, these more conservative actors who managed to constrain the revolutionaries on the basis of the constitutional tradition of 1787.

The decisive moment came in 1805, when the Republicans' third consecutive electoral victory gave renewed resonance to Randolph's claim to speak for the People as he demanded the conviction of Chase before the Senate. Given this plebiscitary dynamic, the ensuing acquittal comes as quite a surprise and suggests the importance of restraining hands on both sides of the equation.

On the side of the revolution of 1800, the key actor was Jefferson himself. Although he was grimly determined to purge the judiciary of its

Federalist virus, he wasn't prepared to do everything imaginable to accomplish this aim. In particular, he refused to go public and *explicitly* put his enormous prestige on the line behind Randolph's claims.

A comparable act of restraint occurred on the other side of the equation. The key actor was the Supreme Court, but neither Marshall nor Chase played the decisive role. Instead, it was the more moderate wing led by Paterson that voted decisively for restraint in the events culminating in Stuart v. Laird.

Without these parallel exhibitions of restraint, Chase would have shared Pickering's fate before the Senate. But the combined decisions by the president and the Court to pull their punches enabled the Senate to function as a legalistic preserver of the Constitution of 1787—if only barely. By acquitting Chase, the Senate gave a primacy to the claim of the text of 1787, and its demand for "high crimes and misdemeanors," over the claims of Randolph and his fellows to speak for the People of 1804. Call this an act of *textual preservation*. And by allowing Chase to remain on the Court, the Senate also sustained the claim of the Court to institutional independence. Call this an act of *institutional preservation*.

The Senate's complex role is worth remarking: it would recur, in other guises, at later turning points in American history.[71] For now it is more important to recognize that Chase's acquittal by no means put the Supreme Court beyond the reach of Jefferson and his party. It only delayed the day of reckoning to the moment of mortality, when new Republican justices would be appointed to replace the old Federalists.

As we are coming to appreciate, time is of the essence in the American system: a decision delayed may turn out very differently when finally confronted in the fullness of time.

10

Synthesis

The Chase acquittal was a turning point but by no means the ending point of the Jeffersonian revolution in constitutional law. The *Stuart-Marbury* synthesis threatened to unravel as congressional Republicans made serious, if unsuccessful, efforts to overturn it by constitutional amendment. And Jefferson was sorely tempted to return to the impeachment wars, but never found a propitious moment.

Jefferson was having greater success with a subtler strategy, and one he forcefully urged upon his successor, James Madison. Both men tried to deprive Marshall of his majority on the Court by appointing solid Republicans when vacancies opened up. They sometimes faltered, but their efforts yielded important results over time. By 1812 Marshall had lost control of his Court. While he stayed silent, Justice William Johnson, Jefferson's strongest choice, wrote the opinion of the Court in a key decision that decisively repudiated basic Federalist principles.

In the longer run, Marshall managed to contain Republican incursions into his Federalist brand of constitutionalism—in part because no vacancies opened for a twelve-year period beginning in 1812, in part because the Jefferson-Madison effort at transformative judicial appointment wavered at critical moments. Nevertheless, it is a mistake to view the Marshall Court as unremittingly hostile to the Jeffersonian vision of the Constitution. Instead, it is best seen as embarking on a project of *intertemporal synthesis*—weaving doctrinal strands emerging from 1800 into the constitutional fabric of 1787.

Formal Amendment or Judicial Adaptation?

Immediately upon hearing the Senate's judgment acquitting Chase, John Randolph returned to the House floor to offer this constitutional amendment: "The judges of the Supreme and all other Courts of the United States, shall be removed by the President, on the joint address of both Houses of Congress, requesting the same, anything in the Constitution of the United States to the contrary notwithstanding."[1] Since the lame-duck House was scheduled to expire in a couple of days, Randolph could do little more than place the amendment on the agenda for the next Congress.

The initiative was taken very seriously by knowledgeable participants. Here is John Quincy Adams assessing its prospects in a letter to his father:

> [Randolph's amendment will be] pursued with persevering ardor. As there is much to be said in its favor as a proper provision, independent of all application to present circumstances; as it is recommended, not only by the example of Great Britain, but by some of the best among our state constitutions; and as it must be in every point of view a desirable alteration to the ruling majority, there is the strongest probability that it will not readily be abandoned. Its success in the Senate, however, will be very problematical, at least until another election shall have intervened.[2]

And Randolph's proposal had something more going for it: Thomas Jefferson was supporting it, behind the scenes, as the party's best response to the failure of impeachment as a tool for consolidating the Republicans' popular mandate.[3]

But when the amendment came up for debate in the next Congress, the political steam had gone out of it. New questions—most notably the dangers of European war—were now dominating the scene. And Randolph was widening his split with the administration, championing a "third party" movement of Republican purists to challenge both Jeffersonians and old-time Federalists for political ascendancy.[4] Since Randolph had made the campaign against the judiciary his signature issue, mainline Republicans were understandably reluctant to go along. Randolph himself recognized this in a spirited speech pressing for a vote on his amendment:

> So far, then, from wishing to postpone this measure, I believe that delay will only serve to enhance the difficulty of obtaining it. It is a maxim laid down by every man that has written on national policy, that those abuses which are left untouched in the period of a revolution, are sanctified by time . . .; and those corruptions and abuses, not reformed at the first session of the seventh Congress, what has

become of them? Have they been suffered to sleep? If they have, is it not to be apprehended that they will rise refreshed from their slumbers with gigantic strength? Fortunate it was that, at the first session of the seventh Congress the midnight Judiciary and the internal taxes were done away; and it would likewise have been fortunate if another measure had been attended to at the same time . . . If the great culprit, whose judicial crimes or incapacity had been called for legislative punishment under the Constitution, and which have given rise to the motion now before us, had been accused at the first session of the seventh Congress, that accusation would have had a very different issue.[5]

Randolph was right about the timing, but he failed to note the Supreme Court's role in deferring the matter beyond the early burst of enthusiasm for the revolution of 1800. After all, the Court could have helped Randolph by provoking a crisis in 1802: it could have followed Chase's advice to go on strike in support of the circuit judges. Instead, it meekly returned to circuit riding, and thereby induced the Republicans to delay their purge campaign against the Supreme Court.

As matters stood in 1806, the House gave Randolph a mixed reception. On the one hand, a strong majority followed him in defeating a motion to postpone consideration of his amendment; but when the appointed time arrived, the promised debate did not take place.[6] The Supreme Court was on probation, as it were—would it take further steps that would reignite Republican demands for sweeping judicial reorganization?

Aaron Burr provided the critical test case. When he left the vice presidency, he was facing criminal indictments in both New York and New Jersey for his duel with Hamilton. Rather than returning to face these charges, he traveled to the western frontier and played with wild plans to revive his political fortunes: perhaps he might lead a military expedition to seize Mexico, perhaps he might separate Louisiana from the United States?

His conspiratorial activities never got very far, but they sufficed to compound Jefferson's view of him as a diabolical schemer. The president ordered his arrest as a traitor, and a military guard forced Burr to return to the East to face these new charges. Jefferson's grim determination to prosecute contrasted with the more forgiving attitude of Burr's enemies in New York and New Jersey, who let the dueling indictments die quietly.[7] When Burr arrived in Richmond, Virginia, to face his trial for treason, the president was in for a rude shock. Thanks to the accidents of jurisdiction, the presiding circuit justice would be none other than John Marshall.

The prospect surely made Jefferson's blood boil. It was unclear which man he detested more. In contrast to Burr, Marshall remained a power in the land, whose very survival on the Court was a continuing provocation. And yet the president would be obliged to remain passive while Public Enemy No.2 presided over the treason trial of Public Enemy No. 1—or was it the other way around? This wasn't precisely what Jefferson had had in mind when he forced Supreme Court justices back to circuit riding in 1802.

Marshall conducted the proceedings aggressively. He not only requested the president to hand over crucial documents to Burr's lawyers. He issued a direct order, commanding compliance—something he had artfully managed to avoid in Marbury v. Madison. Despite this direct challenge, Jefferson obeyed, merely reserving his presidential right, "independently of all other authority," to be the final judge on such matters.[8] Marshall followed up with a series of contestable legal rulings that contributed greatly to Burr's acquittal.[9] He then rubbed salt in the wound by attending a victory dinner given in Burr's honor by his chief defense counsel. This was a terrible gaffe. It's hard to disagree with the Richmond *Enquirer*, which described his attendance at a "treason rejoicing dinner" as "grossly indecent."[10]

Thomas Jefferson's judgment was no less severe. He told one of his congressional confidantes, William Giles, "[I]mpeachment is a farce which will not be tried again." He called instead for another effort "to amend the error in our Constitution which makes any branch independent of the nation . . . If their [the judges'] protection of Burr produces this amendment, it will do more good than his condemnation would have done."[11]

When Congress returned to work, Jefferson formally transmitted the record of the Burr proceedings with the dark remark: "[Y]ou will be enabled to judge whether the defect was in the testimony, or in the laws, or whether there is not a radical defect in the administration of the law? And wherever it shall be found the Legislature alone can apply or originate the remedy."[12] All this led to the reemergence of proposals for a constitutional amendment along the lines proposed earlier by Randolph—but by that point Jefferson's embargo had made the administration deeply unpopular, and brave constitutional initiatives were out of the question.[13]

The *Stuart-Marbury* strategy was paying off. By recognizing the legitimacy of a central plank of the Jeffersonian revolution early on, the Court had bought precious time for itself. Rather than allowing itself to be crushed by the Jeffersonian bulldozer at its moment of maximum vulnerability, the Court could reorient itself for more peaceful coexistence with the new regime.

As Marshall's attendance at Burr's victory dinner suggested, this would not be easy. If the chief justice persisted in political shenanigans, the Court would have continued to serve as a lightning rod. But Marshall's provocations proved to be the last gasp of an older era. However reluctantly, the Federalist justices were using their probationary period to carve out a new, and more stable, role for themselves.

During the 1790s they had actively participated in national politics— providing advisory opinions, sitting on executive boards, and taking leave from the Court to serve on important diplomatic missions.[14] When riding circuit, they saw themselves as "republican schoolmasters" lecturing the grand jury (and the crowd of interested bystanders) on their new obligations as citizens of a federal republic. As leading notables of the national community, it was only natural for them to range widely in these discourses—providing the crowd of provincials with guidance on the leading issues of the day.[15] As we have seen, the rise of party politics had transformed their lectures on political morality into partisan diatribes and their prosecutions of sedition into persecution of political opponents.

The impeachment of Chase prompted an anxious reappraisal. Chase himself never engaged in political provocation again. And despite Marshall's lapse after the Burr trial, his standard course of conduct evidenced a sober recognition of the new realities: "The federal Court commenced its session in this city, on Saturday last. The charge of *Chief Justice Marshall* was, *as it should be, pertinent,* strictly *judicial,* & perfectly free from all extraneous political matter. Strangely altered *indeed* are the times, since the present administration came into power; since Judge Iredell used to deliver his political sermons from the bench of justice, and a federal Grand Jury presented a member of Congress for writing *independent* circular letters to his constituents."[16] The Republicans' failure to achieve a formal amendment does not imply that their larger campaign against the Federalist judiciary was a total failure. The impeachment trial operated as an informal signal to the judiciary, prodding a profound reorientation. The justices could no longer view themselves as political notables playing their part to shore up the Federalist cause. They could only successfully coexist with the new regime by behaving as legal professionals, seeking to create a higher law frame for ongoing political developments.

This narrowing of the judicial role would express itself not only in the behavior of the judges but also in their jurisprudence. As many scholars have rightly emphasized, the Marshall Court was particularly concerned about distinguishing between law and politics and made an effort to convince itself—and its many publics—that its emerging doctrines fell on the legal side of the line. This recurring methodological anxiety is another aspect of the Marshall Court's response to the Jeffersonian revolution.[17]

I want to emphasize another, and less remarked, aspect of the adaptive process. As time marched on, Presidents Jefferson and Madison began to use their power of appointment to reshape the Court's personnel, and this eventually led to a more decisive doctrinal breakthrough. Midway through the Madison administration, a reconstituted Court began reworking substantive doctrine to express the deeper constitutional meanings of the Jeffersonian revolution.

Transformative Appointments

Though a formal amendment was going nowhere, the mortality tables began to provide Jefferson a new opening for his constitutional ambitions. First to go was Alfred Moore, whose declining health was soon overwhelmed by the return to circuit riding. He called it quits in February 1804, giving Jefferson his first chance to change the Court's direction.

The president was obliged to balance four factors in filling the vacancy. The first was sheer physical stamina; the rigors of constant travel eliminated many from the judicial sweepstakes. The second, also made more important by circuit riding, was regional balance—since Moore rode in South Carolina and Georgia, both the local bar and congressional delegations would protest loudly if his replacement did not come from the same region. The third and fourth factors emphasized national politics.

Would Jefferson appoint a man with strong Republican convictions? Would the candidate have the judicial experience and character to stare Marshall down and serve as an eloquent exponent of the Republican vision of the Union?

The ideal candidate would fulfill all four criteria, but the deep South was not rich in such people.[18] Worse yet, the Court did not have much prestige, and was even less attractive now that it had been saddled, once again, with onerous circuit-riding responsibilities.

Before making his choice Jefferson solicited the advice of two trusted congressional Republicans from South Carolina, who produced a memo that evinced a concern with all four criteria and singled out William Johnson for commendation: "a state judge. an excellent lawyer, prompt eloquent, of irreproachable character, Republican connections, and of good nerves in his political principles about 35 years old. was speaker some years."[19] Similar assessments were available from Federalists: "a zealous democrat but . . . honest & capable," according to Senator William Plumer.[20] Both Republicans and Federalists understood Johnson's nomination to be the first shot in a long war to shift the course of constitutional law.

The same can be said of Jefferson's second appointment, in 1806, of Brockholst Livingston. Even in 1804 some had considered Livingston to be the best choice,[21] but he had been passed over on regional grounds. With the death of William Paterson (from New Jersey), the New Yorker now seemed the obvious choice. A strong force in Republican politics since the beginning, he had also proved himself a strong state judge since his appointment in 1802, writing 149 opinions in four years.[22]

But with his third and last appointment, Jefferson stumbled. Opportunity beckoned in 1807, when Congress created a seventh seat on the Court to accommodate a new circuit for Kentucky, Ohio, and Tennessee. In contrast to his prior conduct, this time Jefferson didn't keep his cards close to his chest. Instead, he officially requested each member of Congress to suggest two names, with first- and second-place rankings. Delighted by the invitation, Congress caucused repeatedly, finally coming up with a recommendation of a sitting congressman, George Campbell, for the job. Jefferson was appalled both by Campbell's meager legal qualifications[23] and by Congress's disdain for the constitutional prohibition against the appointment of any "Senator or Representative" to "any civil office . . .

which shall have been created . . . during the time for which he has been elected."[24] Rejecting Campbell, he nominated Thomas Todd, the only name that appeared as either a first or a second choice on all ten of the lists submitted by congressmen and senators from the three states in the new circuit.

Jefferson ended up with a new justice who was a legal mediocrity. What is to account for his sudden, and unprecedented, deference to the predictable cronyism of congressional barons? The answer, I suspect but cannot prove, is his new need for support on matters that had suddenly become more important—in particular, enactment of his disastrous Embargo Act of 1807.[25] Driven by his paramount need to gain legislative support for this bitterly contested and sure-to-be-unpopular initiative, did the president let other long-range priorities slip?

Only one thing is clear: when the next vacancy opened up with the death of William Cushing, Jefferson returned to his transformative objectives with a vengeance—and left a far more elaborate paper trail, since the opening arose in 1810 and he was obliged to bombard his successor and long-time political lieutenant, James Madison, with ceaseless letters of instruction. "[A]nother circumstance of congratulation is the death of Cushing," Jefferson coolly wrote to Madison of the opportunity to give Republicans a majority on the seven-man court.[26] His letter to his postmaster general, Gideon Granger, one of his candidates for the post, sums up the ex-president's hopes: "[T]he substituting in the place of Cushing, a firm and unequivocal republican, whose principles are born with him, and not an occasional ingraftment, [is] necessary to compleat that great reformation in our government to which the Nation gave its fiat ten years ago."[27]

But Jefferson did not hand down to Madison the commanding presidential position he had occupied during the glory days of the revolution of 1800. During his first term, Jefferson had been the unchallenged leader of a broadly popular movement, in confident possession of a "fiat" from the "People" to make good on revolutionary principles as yet untarnished by the corrosive realities of power. A decade later, Madison was reaping the whirlwind from Jefferson's politically disastrous embargo policy, which had seriously damaged his party's popular support, encouraged intra-party squabbling, and gravely injured the leadership position of the presidency.[28] As we saw in Chapter 7, early presidents did not have much in the way of patronage or other practical tools to use in dealing with Congress. Jefferson had compensated by skillfully exploiting his moral authority as leader of a national movement, although his influence had waned sharply in his second term when congressmen ran for political cover as his foreign policy met increasing resistance.

Where Jefferson stumbled, Madison was simply overwhelmed. Lacking his mentor's political savvy, he faced a Congress that had become more institutionally resistant to presidential leadership: a committee system had now assumed substantial form in Congress, and committee chairmen were reaching out to form alliances with heads of departments in ways that eluded presidential control.[29] The prospect of war with England fractionated Congress further.

Within this context, the death of Justice Cushing in 1810 added one more tricky political problem to Madison's over-full plate. On the one hand, Madison had to deal with his Jeffersonian superego, which pushed him forward in a transformative direction. On the other hand, Cushing vacated the New England seat, so the president had to contend with the political implications of a recent Federalist resurgence in the region. How to respond?

Madison did not hesitate. His first instinct was to accept Jefferson's advice and nominate Levi Lincoln, his predecessor's attorney general and a tried-and-true Republican. But the sixty-two-year-old Lincoln was going blind, and he was understandably reluctant to take on the task of circuit riding. Despite a clear rejection of his offer in private communications, the politically inept Madison sent Lincoln's name to the Senate, which confirmed him enthusiastically, only to find Lincoln resolute in his refusal.[30]

The president then turned to another New England stalwart, Alexander Wolcott, a man of fierce Republican allegiance in a region where this was rare. Wolcott's zealous efforts to enforce the embargo as collector of the customs had so outraged the New England Federalists that they launched a barrage of character assassination and disparagement of his (admittedly modest) legal attainments—leading the Senate to reject his nomination by a vote of 9 to 24.[31]

Madison was mortified, but not enough to allow the New Englanders to succeed in their lobbying campaign for Jeremiah Smith, a distinguished chief justice of New Hampshire but a strong Federalist. Still searching for a politically acceptable Republican, Madison turned to John Quincy Adams—a recent convert to the party of Jefferson but a bipartisan choice as the son of the last Federalist president.[32] While the nomination sailed through the Senate, it met with a chilly reception from the young Adams, then minister to Russia. Pleading legal incapacity, and candidly avowing larger political ambition, he left Madison, once again, in an embarrassing and exposed position.[33]

This time Madison did nothing for seven months—though, behind the scenes, Jefferson was relentless on behalf of his old postmaster general, Connecticut's Gideon Granger, another energetic Republican partisan in that traditionally Federalist region. This time Madison resisted his long-time mentor, fearing another Wolcott-style fiasco.[34] After a lengthy delay, the president turned to the nephew of his old friend Isaac Story, asking the thirty-two-year-old Joseph Story to fill the position.[35]

Jefferson, outraged at the news, denounced Isaac's nephew as a "pseudo-Republican," a "political chameleon," and an "independent political schemer."[36] There was also grumbling in the Senate, but not enough to induce the Republicans to prolong their embarrassment. The young Story promptly accepted the job—a lifetime of circuit riding was an entirely acceptable price to pay for the chance of redeeming Jefferson's prophecy of Federalist apostasy.

As Madison was staggering through this political ordeal in 1811, Justice Chase of Maryland also died, leaving him with an easier problem. In New England the president had been caught between the need to propitiate his Jeffersonian superego and the need to name somebody who could run the gauntlet of Federalist opposition in the Senate. But Chase's Maryland was part of the Republican heartland, and Madison found it pretty easy to come up with a name of a solid Republican loyalist, Gabriel Duvall, long-time chief justice of the general court of Maryland.[37] This meant that he could send the names of both Story and Duvall to the Senate when it returned to Washington in November 1811. With their rapid confirmation, the Supreme Court would for the first time have a majority of Republican appointees—with only Marshall and Washington remaining as holdovers from the Federalist era.

The stage had now been set for the next act in the judicial drama.

A Transformative Opinion

Even before the Republicans gained their majority on the Court, Marshall had begun uneasily to adapt to their increasing presence. Before the first

Republican justice arrived, he had completely dominated the writing of opinions—deferring only to let Justice Paterson do the dirty work in Stuart v. Laird.[38] Marshall's extraordinary domination was a tribute to his charm and intelligence, without which the Court could have easily fractionated in response to fierce Jeffersonian opposition. It was also a mark of the weakness of the other justices. As William Johnson, the first Republican justice, recalled the scene upon his arrival in 1805:

> While I was on our state-bench I was accustomed to delivering seriatim opinions in our appellate court, and was not a little surprised to find our Chief Justice in the Supreme Court delivering all the opinions in cases in which he sat, even in some instances when contrary to his own judgment and vote. But I remonstrated in vain; the answer was, he is willing to take the trouble, and it is a mark of respect to him. I soon however found out the real cause. Cushing was incompetent. Chase could not be got to think or write—Patterson was a slow man and willingly declined the trouble, and the other two judges you know are commonly estimated as one judge.[39]

This retrospective assessment comes from a letter of 1822 to Jefferson, and should be discounted as a bit harsh—but only a bit. In any event, Johnson immediately began to nibble away at Marshall's monopoly, filing a separate concurrence in his first term, and publicly dissenting by his third. These performances encouraged others to make occasional shows of independence. But Marshall continued to write nearly all opinions for the Court for the rest of the decade, relaxing his iron grip on only four occasions in 1809 and 1810.[40]

In 1812, all this changed with the arrival of Duvall and Story and the creation of a Republican majority. Marshall suddenly lost his monopoly, writing nineteen of thirty opinions that term.[41] And it was the senior Republican justice, William Johnson, who wrote for the Court in its most important case, United States v. Hudson and Goodwin.

The dispute involved the early republic's ongoing struggle over the legitimacy of criminal prosecutions for seditious libel. After their victory in 1800 the Republicans allowed the Federalists' Sedition Act of 1798 to expire, but the struggle continued in the states, and most notably in Federalist Connecticut, which enacted a sedition act modeled on the expired national statute and began prosecuting Republican papers in the state courts.

   This put the beleaguered Republicans on the defensive until 1806, when the Federalists lost control of the Connecticut federal court with the death of the incumbent district judge. Jefferson appointed the Republican Pierpont Edwards as his replacement, and Edwards quickly moved onto the legal offensive. Opportunity knocked at the very next session of the circuit court, when the Federalist circuit justice, William Cushing, failed to show up because of illness. This gave Edwards the chance to preside alone, and he took full advantage of his moment. When the marshal of the court provided him with a grand jury packed with Republicans, Edwards encouraged them to present five indictments against leading Federalists for seditious libel under the common law. With Republican editors under Federalist attack in the state courts, why not return the barrage?[42]

   So far as the embattled Republicans of Connecticut were concerned, this hammer-and-tongs counterattack might have seemed crude but rough justice. But it had a very different appearance to the Republicans of Washington, D.C. The case, United States v. Hudson and Goodwin, which came before the Court in February 1812, almost magically returned the Republican judicial majority to the heroic struggles of their youth, when the Jeffersonians, still in opposition, had confronted Federalist prosecutions for seditious libel. Only now the shoe was on the other foot: it was the Federalist *Hartford Courant* that stood accused of the "crime" of reporting that Congress had secretly appropriated, at Jefferson's request, two million dollars to bribe Napoleon.

   The case presented by the prosecution conveyed an even more ironical twist. To grasp the sting, return to the days of the Adams administration and consider the broad outlines of the Federalists' defense of their sedition act. So far as Adams and his friends were concerned, the Republicans were way off-base in their critique.[43] Rather than a retrograde measure, their sedition act was a great advance over the common law, for one simple reason. Under the Federalist statute, truth was an absolute defense to a prosecution for libel; in contrast, the British precedents allowed common law courts to punish seditious speech regardless of truth. Thus, for those in the Adams administration, the Federalist Congress deserved praise, not abuse, for enacting such an enlightened statute on sedition.

   The Jeffersonians were not impressed. To make good on their critique they had to do more than oppose the statute; they were obliged to attack the very idea that the federal courts had the constitutional power to prosecute for common law crimes. And this they did with relish, since it fit comfortably within their overarching constitutional emphasis on states' rights and limited federal government.[44]

Indeed, for Jefferson himself, the common law aspiration of the judiciary was the single most obnoxious feature of the Federalist program. Writing to John Randolph in 1799, he declared that even diabolical Federalist enterprises like the alien and sedition acts, or the Bank of the United States, or Jay's treaty were but "solitary, unconsequential timid things, in comparison with the audacious, barefaced and sweeping pretension to a system of law for the U S, without the adoption of their legislature, and so infinitely beyond their [the federal courts'] power to adopt."[45] These ringing Jeffersonian denunciations of a federal common law had an ironic ring as news of the Connecticut common law prosecutions against the Federalists began to circulate throughout the nation.

When Jefferson heard of the indictments in the declining days of his presidency in 1809, he ordered the dismissal of the charges[46]—but not before a scandalized John Randolph moved the House to appoint a special investigatory committee. So far as this Republican purist was concerned, the Jeffersonian revolution of 1800 had made an "end . . . of these prosecutions at common law, as much as of the sedition law." The problem with the sedition law, he emphasized, was not its substance, which was "as good as any," but "the having a federal libel law at all." While such a law might well be appropriate to "a single integral government," it was altogether improper in a "Federal Government, exercising only certain specified powers." In contrast to other moves by Randolph, the House unanimously supported his motion for a special investigation.[47] But neither this initiative nor Jefferson's order had much of an impact on the implacable Republicans of Connecticut, who continued with their plans for prosecution.

When *Hudson and Goodwin* finally reached the Court in 1812, President Madison proved no more cooperative than his predecessor. In the run-up to the campaign of 1800, Madison had written a report to the Virginia legislature in which he sought to destroy the constitutional foundations of a federal common law,[48] and he was of no mind to change his opinion twelve years later. His attorney general, William Pinkney, flatly refused to defend the Connecticut indictment before the Court. Since Pinkney was on record repeatedly as favoring a federal common law of crime, his silence was particularly eloquent.[49] In short, the case brought home to the justices, as perhaps no other could, the constitutional status of the Jeffersonian revolution of 1800. If the Court upheld the Connecticut prosecutions, it would be saying that all the Jeffersonians' grand talk was the sheerest puffery, and that the Federalists had the final claim to constitutional truth.

The senior Republican justice, William Johnson, proved equal to the challenge. It was he, not Marshall, who spoke for the Court in an opinion couched in the broadest possible terms. Johnson repudiated not merely the judicial power to prosecute seditious libel, but the entire notion that the federal courts had jurisdiction over common law crime. And he did so in a way that was calculated to raise hackles:

> The course of reasoning which leads to this conclusion is simple, obvious, and admits of but little illustration. The powers of the general Government are made up of concessions from the several states— what is not expressly given to the former, the latter expressly reserve. The judicial power of the United States is a constituent part of those concessions—that power is to be exercised by Courts organized for the purpose, and brought into existence by an effort of the legislative power of the Union.
>
> . . . [T]he power which congress possess to create Courts of inferior jurisdiction, necessarily implies the power to limit the jurisdiction of those Courts to particular objects; and when a Court is created, and its operations confined to certain specific objects, with what propriety can it assume to itself a jurisdiction—much more extended—in its nature very indefinite—applicable to a great variety of subjects— varying in every state in the Union . . . ?[50]

The prose is positively Marshallian in its magisterial derivation of concrete conclusions from constitutional first principles. But Johnson's first principles were anathema to his chief: instead of a Federalist effort to expand the penumbras of national power, he plumbs the great Jeffersonian truth of 1800, recalled by Randolph in 1809: "The powers of the general Government are made up of concessions from the several states—what is not expressly given to the former, the latter expressly reserve."

Johnson ascribed his reasoning only to a "majority of this Court"— leaving us to imagine how the dissenting brethren were writhing as they heard this ringing herald of a new age in constitutional law.[51] Why did they remain silent? After all, only two years earlier Johnson had written his own special and limited concurrence to Marshall's nationalizing opinion for the Court striking down a state statute in Fletcher v. Peck.[52] Why didn't the chief justice break ranks when the majority was moving the other way?

The moment stands as a tribute to Marshall's fanatical opposition to separate opinions.[53] This commitment must have been severely tested at a time when he was losing control of the Court—especially given that Johnson framed the opinion to heighten its transformative character:[54] "Although this question is brought up now for the first time to be decided by this Court, we consider it as having been long since settled in public opinion. In no other case for many years has this jurisdiction been asserted; and the general acquiescence of legal men shews the prevalence of opinion in favor of the negative of the proposition."[55]

With these peremptory lines, Johnson repudiated a formidable array of legal opinion in support of a federal common law of crime. In the words of the best modern essay on the subject, Johnson had dismissed "at least eight circuit court cases, brushed off the views of all but one Justice who sat on the Court prior to 1804, and departed from what was arguably the original understanding."[56]

That was just the point. To any contemporary reader, Johnson's meaning was clear: the Federalist understanding had been rendered irrelevant by a fundamental transformation of "public opinion" wrought by the Republican success in sustaining their revolution over the last decade. Rather than testing the revolution of 1800 by the preexisting understandings of 1787, Jefferson's new Court conceived its task as elaborating the constitutional meaning of what had "long since [been] settled"—where "long" meant the day before yesterday, and not longer.

It was one thing for the Republicans to "settle" the question in *Hudson;* it was quite another for the matter to stay settled. Although the dissenters were silent for the moment, Marshall's new recruit, Story, immediately launched a public campaign for *Hudson's* reversal. Riding circuit in 1813, Story quickly encountered a case that dramatized, in his eyes, the disastrous consequences of the Jeffersonian revolution in constitutional law. This was easy to do, since the war with Britain, begun three months after *Hudson,* served to reveal the case's devastating impact on the federal administration of criminal law in an era when statutory prohibitions were few and far between.

United States v. Coolidge explored one such gap. It involved the crime of "forcible rescue," which arises when the owners of a lawfully captured ship reassert physical control over the vessel on the high seas. Admiralty law requires the owners to return the ship to shore so that a court can determine the legality of their reassertion of control. If they fail to comply, courts have traditionally treated the seizure as a crime similar to piracy. Despite this well-established principle, Congress had not gotten around to codifying it into a statute, and so *Hudson* seemed to bar prosecution.

In Story's view, this only demonstrated the absurdity of the decision. Whereas the prosecution of the *Hartford Courant* in *Hudson* invited a judicial return to the principles of 1800, the New England prosecution of *Coolidge* seemed to cry out for reappraisal—who could applaud a decision that freed pirates in the midst of war?

Story wrote a blistering circuit opinion. He could have taken a modest course, carving out a limited exception for cases arising on the high seas, but the young man disdained such lawyerly devices. He called for the express repudiation of *Hudson,* saying that since it had been "made without argument, and by a majority only of the court, I hope that it is not an improper course to bring the subject again in review for a more solemn decision." His elaborate opinion claimed that the Constitution presupposed the common law, and that "nothing is more clear" than federal common law crime. He conceived this jurisdiction in the grandest of terms: "Without pretending to enumerate them in detail, I will venture to assert generally, that all offences against the sovereignty, the public rights, the public justice, the public peace, the public trade and the public police of the United States, are crimes and offences against the United States."[57]

When the case came up to the Court in 1816, Story encountered continued resistance from the Madison administration. The attorney general was now Richard Rush, a confirmed opponent of common law crime.[58] Despite Story's eloquence, Rush refused to defend the lower-court opinion, remaining steadfast in his Republican principles:

> COUNSEL: The Attorney-General stated that he had given to this case an anxious attention; as much so, he hoped, as his public duty, under whatever view of it, rendered necessary. That he had also examined the opinion of the court, delivered at February term, 1813 [*sic*], in the case of the United States v. Hudson and Goodwin. That considering the point as decided in that case,

whether with, or without, argument, on the part of those who had
preceded him as the representative of the government in this
court, he desired respectfully to state, without saying more, that it
was not his intention to argue it now.

STORY, J.: I do not take the question to be settled by that case.

JOHNSON, J.: I consider it to be settled by the authority of that case.

WASHINGTON, J.: Whenever counsel can be found ready to argue it, I
shall divest myself of all prejudice arising from that case.

LIVINGSTON, J.: I am disposed to hear an argument on the point.
This case was brought up for that purpose, but until the question
is re-argued, the case of the United States v. Hudson and
Goodwin must be taken as law.[59]

After this anxious colloquy, Justice Johnson delivered an opinion of the
court containing a single paragraph:

> [A] difference of opinion has existed, and still exists, among the
> members of the court. We should, therefore, have been willing to
> have heard the question discussed upon solemn argument. But the
> attorney-general has declined to argue the cause; and no counsel ap-
> pears for the defendant. Under these circumstances the court would
> not choose to review their former decision in the case of the United
> States v. Hudson and Goodwin, or draw it into doubt.[60]

With Attorney General Rush sticking to his guns, the Madison administration saved *Hudson*. So long as Rush refused to argue the case, Justice
Johnson refused to abandon his great statement of Jeffersonian jurisprudence.

Once *Hudson* had survived its moment of agonizing reappraisal, it
would never again be seriously questioned. Almost two centuries later, it
continues to stand as a permanent legacy of the first presidentialist revolution in constitutional law.

An Unasked Question

I have been writing against the grain of the standard story about the Marshall Court, which consigns cases like *Stuart* and *Hudson* to the periphery

and concentrates on the chief justice's struggle to vindicate the Court's authority over its formidable antagonists on both state and national levels.[61] I hardly wish to deny the truth of this account—only to insist that it is a partial one.

To make my point, try to rid yourself of the benefits and burdens of hindsight, and view the Marshall Court as it appeared on the eve of the War of 1812. At that moment, the Court was promising some large synthesis between Federalist and Republican themes. On the one hand, Marshall had handed down the first of his great assertions of national authority in Fletcher v. Peck, decided in 1810.[62] But on the other hand, William Johnson had displaced Marshall as the spokesman for the Court in 1812, proclaiming in *Hudson* that "[t]he powers of the general Government are made up of concessions from the several states—what is not expressly given to the former, the latter expressly reserve." The future, it appeared, belonged neither to the Federalists nor to the Republicans, but to an ongoing judicial effort to weave elements of both visions into a larger whole.

The same complexity can be seen in the Court's relationship to the other branches of government. On the one hand, Marbury v. Madison asserted the justices' authority to treat the Congress and the president as mere creatures of the Federalist constitution of 1787. But on the other, Stuart v. Laird accepted the authority of the Republicans, led by their president, to sweep away large chunks of the Federalist judicial establishment. As they returned to their onerous circuit-riding duties, the justices would have abundant occasion to reflect on the enormous gap between *Marbury*'s claims and existential realities. Their endless travels along the miserable roads of the early republic would cause them to remember the very different life promised by the Federalist judiciary act—in which they would have lived comfortably in Washington D.C., pondering appeals from a well-organized set of federal courts throughout the nation. Instead of standing proudly at the head of a Federalist establishment, they were now reduced to a small and harried band of itinerant judges, institutionally incapable of displacing the state courts as the primary dispensers of justice in the land.

These realities reflected a deeper truth: the Court had failed to gain uncontested standing as the authoritative interpreter of the Constitution. Throughout our story, we have seen the Jeffersonians repeatedly contesting the Marshall Court's pretensions by pointing to the contrary judgment of the people expressed at decisive elections. This expressive use of election returns was only one aspect of a complex practice of popular constitutionalism based on more local exercises in particular communities. The Court's decisions repeatedly generated popular resistance—marches, meetings, and acts of civil disobedience.[63] These popular activities gave deeper meaning to more formal challenges by state governors and judges. When they challenged particular decisions, or the very principle of judicial review, perhaps they were voicing some more profound sentiment of We the People condemning the connivances of a nationalizing legal elite?

Perhaps not. While the Court's many critics managed to sustain a drumbeat of resistance, they failed to win decisive support for their campaign to purge Justice Chase, let alone the great chief justice. The Court had managed to sustain itself, but only by promising a creative synthesis of Republican and Federalist themes in the Constitution it would pass down to the next generation.

*   *   *

When did the Founding end?

With the end of the passions and movements that created the new republic. Speaking broadly, there were three great phases: Revolutionaries against Tories during the War for Independence, then Federalists against Anti-Federalists during the struggle over the Constitution, then Republicans against Federalists over the future of constitutional development.

The War of 1812 brought this great generational cycle to an end. Once Madison negotiated a peace treaty with the British, the Republicans proved remarkably successful in casting Federalist opposition to the war as a treasonous betrayal of America. With the final disintegration of the Federalist party, the Republicans lost their ideological edge. Without the semblance of an opposing party, Republicans in Congress splintered into a host of competing factions which blurred the lines of constitutional conflict. And presidential elections no longer forced Americans to choose between rival constitutional visions. When even John Adams's son—a strong nationalist—could gain election as a nominal member of Jefferson's party, things had gotten very confused indeed.

It is an exaggeration to call this postwar period by its traditional name, "the era of good feeling." Yet for all its partisanship, it was qualitatively different from the previous decade. At the turn of the century, leading politicians supposed that they stood at the head of vast popular movements that supported competing constitutional principles. But after the War of 1812, the leading statesmen harbored no similar pretensions. There were great men among them, who sometimes undertook great acts of statesmanship and compromise. Yet they lived during a period of "normal politics," as I have called it, when their disputes did not divide the nation into great ideological struggles between competing parties.[64] Within this framework, the Supreme Court was relatively free to elaborate its constitutional understandings without the kind of existential threats that had surrounded it in the days of Stuart v. Laird and the impeachment of Samuel Chase.

While some famous figures from the past continued to preside over the government—Madison and Monroe in the presidency, Marshall on the Court—the popular movements that had initially inspired them were now distant memories. It was only in 1828, with the election of Andrew Jackson, that a new popular movement would begin to make itself felt in the nation's capital, confronting the aging Marshall and his fellow justices with new and fundamental challenges to their constitutional premises.

I leave these events for another time. My aim here has been to revise the conventional understanding of the last great phase of the Founding, beginning with the revolution of 1800. The current story is court-centered: Marbury v. Madison is the great event, casting almost everything else into shadow. My story is centered on the rise of new forms of popular sovereignty, not the rise of judicial review. The key point has been to show that the mobilized politics of two-party competition transformed the presidency into a plebiscitarian office in ways that could well have destroyed the system created by the Framers in 1787, which was saved only by many acts of statesmanship, as well as plain old good luck.

Marbury remains important in this new story, but as part of a complex pattern of judicial accommodation to unanticipated forms of popular sovereignty. On this account, the genius of *Marbury* and *Stuart* was their promise of a distinctive judicial function: thenceforth, it would be the great task of the Supreme Court to weave recurring popular mandates, claimed by victorious presidents and their political parties, into the preexisting constitutional traditions of the American people.

It could have been otherwise. American history could have resembled the tragedy of nineteenth-century Mexican constitutionalism, with repeated failed efforts to establish constitutional equilibrium, yielding ever-increasing cynicism about the very possibility of legitimate order. Or America could have looked more like France, with every great political movement generating an entirely new version of constitutional order. On this scenario, Thomas Jefferson might have presided over the Constitutional Convention of 1802, and John Marshall might have returned to Virginia a defeated man, bitterly contemplating redemption by some future generation.

It didn't happen that way. Almost despite themselves, Jefferson and Marshall, and many others, created a new kind of presidency and a new kind of Court: a plebiscitarian presidency speaking for the People, and a Court of professional judges seeking to mediate the popular mandates of the present with the constitutional achievements of the past. This Founding dialectic left a distinctive legacy, promising the continuing construction and reconstruction of constitutional order, from generation to generation.

Until the republic comes to an end.

11

Reverberations

America has two Constitutions, both with roots in the early republic. The history of one begins in 1787; the history of the other, in 1800. The first Constitution emphasizes the place of Congress in our political life; the second, the place of the president. The first gives center stage to congressional notables, politically responsive to their local communities; the second, to presidents claiming a popular mandate on the basis of their party's nationwide victory. The first relies on Congress to enact constitutional amendments when the original design needs correcting; the second relies on the Supreme Court to weave the mandate of the president's party into the fabric of our higher law.

The first constitution was the product of speculation; the second, of experience. In this book I have described the experience.

And there have been many similar experiences over the past two centuries. Generation after generation, the plebiscitarian claims of the presidency have operated like time bombs exploding the antique machinery for presidential selection whenever it fails clearly to select the popular choice. And they have operated as a battering ram when a plebiscitarian president threatens the Supreme Court with dire consequences if it blocks the program that he and his party have swept through Congress in the name of the People.

These recurring crises are symptomatic of a deeper dis-ease: the written Constitution was not designed for the movement party or the plebiscitarian presidency. To compensate for this deficiency, fancy footwork—along with good luck—is regularly required. Statesmanship and fortune were in abundant display during the early republic, and yet they were barely sufficient to avoid disaster. Brinksmanship is a dangerous game.

I have been spinning a cautionary tale. After two hundred years, the

American constitutional system still relies on brinksmanship to control the plebiscitarian presidency. This is a grievous weakness. We ignore it at our peril.

And yet we do ignore it. If anything, constitutionalists seem increasingly determined to blind themselves to the most obvious realities. Worship at the shrine of the Philadelphia Convention has become more fervent of late. Legal scholars have been flooding the journals with competing versions of the "original understanding" of the presidency, barely noticing that the American people repudiated these understandings after a brief decade of democratic experience.

The transformation of the presidency into a plebiscitarian office is not a minor detail. It is a dominating fact of constitutional life. The Philadelphia Convention did not have the answers to our problems. Its members didn't even ask the right questions: Given his recurrent tendency to claim a mandate from the People, how should the president be selected, what powers should he have, and how should his plebiscitarian claims be controlled? Constitutional philosophies stressing the "original intent" are not helpful when it comes to the presidency and the court's reaction to its claims of a mandate.

My story also raises a red flag for the study of comparative government. Countless scholars contrast the "presidential system" exemplified by the United States with the "parliamentary systems" of leading European countries. Talk of an American "system" is misleading if it suggests that the Founders, or anybody else, actually made a systematic effort to integrate a party-driven presidency, claiming a mandate from the People, into the overall machinery of government.

America doesn't have a presidential "system." All it has is a long history in which presidential claims of a mandate from the People have been repeatedly resisted and reshaped by the other branches. We have something to learn from each generation's struggle with the plebiscitarian presidency: What went right, what went wrong, and how should the past guide us in confronting future perplexities?

This is not the place to attempt a definitive answer. It is enough to suggest how the precedents established during the birth agony of presidentialism in the early 1800s continue to reverberate through history.[1]

I begin by reflecting on the paradoxes of success. Adams and Jefferson and Burr and Bayard deserve great praise for adapting the Constitution of 1787 to enable the People's choice to emerge triumphant in February 1801. But success, no less than failure, casts a shadow.

Consider the alternative: If the February crisis had exploded, it would have been a political disaster, perhaps leading to armed conflict, perhaps to disunion. If the tragedy had somehow been overcome at a new Constitutional Convention chaired by Jefferson, one thing is clear: these new Founders would have thrown the 1787 system of presidential selection onto the junk heap. With the country reeling from the cascading failures of the original design, the Jeffersonian Convention would have made the creation of a new system its highest priority.

The successful resolution of the crisis in 1801 took the heat off. Instead of urgently rethinking presidential selection from the ground up, the Republicans dithered until the election of 1804 was staring them in the face, and then applied a makeshift solution that merely eliminated a rerun of the 1800 fiasco.

The Twelfth Amendment is the very opposite of a serious attempt to think the problem through. It even failed to correct many of the most obvious Founding blunders, which haunt us to the present day. In 2000, for example, the Constitution assigned Al Gore, serving as president of the Senate, the job of counting the electoral votes in his hotly disputed presidential contest with George W. Bush. Gore's chance came on January 6, 2001, three weeks after the Supreme Court's decision in December had reduced the vote count to an empty ritual. But when the next electoral college crisis strikes, the Court may not be so interventionist, and it will be up to the president of the Senate, in collaboration with the Congress, to make a final decision on a disputed election.

At that point, Thomas Jefferson's actions as president of the Senate in 1801 will serve as a crucial precedent. How should that precedent be interpreted?

After considering this question, I turn to a different aspect of the early republican legacy. While the successful resolution of the February crisis led to a feeble effort at rewriting the Constitution, it had an energizing effect on the relationship between the political branches and the Supreme Court. The real conflict over the meaning of the "revolution of 1800" took place in a decade-long struggle between the political branches and the Court, not through an elaborate effort at rewriting the Constitution.

The traditional fixation on Marbury v. Madison has consigned this great story to the margins of collective memory, but our historical reconstruction allows us to raise a larger question: To what extent do the institutional dynamics of the early republic cast new light on similar encounters between the Court and the political branches over the next two centuries of American history?

The Republicans of the 1790s were the first of many political movements to rise up in protest against the status quo. Generation after generation, Americans have mobilized for mass political action—sometimes founding new parties, sometimes seizing control of established ones. And rising movements have regularly transformed presidential campaigns into occasions for making their case to the nation—sometimes encountering crushing defeat, sometimes gaining sweeping victory, and sometimes generating a political impasse.

It is at moments of decisive triumph that the struggle between the Republicans and their Federalist antagonists on the Supreme Court becomes most relevant. As in the case of the Marshall Court, the sitting justices will generally be holdovers from the preceding regime, and they will look upon the victors' claims of a mandate from the People with profound skepticism. As the president and Congress enact their mandate into law, the justices will be forced to ask themselves a tough question: Should they aggressively strike down the freshly minted legislation or should they try to reach an accommodation with the rising political order?

This question has been asked and answered in different ways at different times, generating many variations on Founding themes. For the present, I will focus on the historical variation that displays the most striking parallels to the Founding. Like the Republicans in 1800, the New Deal Democrats of 1932 initiated a sweeping constitutional challenge that catalyzed a decade-long confrontation with the Supreme Court. This conflict went through a series of stages—from brinksmanship through judicial retreat through judicial synthesis—eerily similar to those articulated during the early republic. Comparing the two episodes will allow us to gain a better sense of the changing dynamics of presidential leadership and judicial response over the course of American history.

Waiting for the Next Crisis

We have never recovered from the early republic's failure to undertake a thoroughgoing redesign of presidential selection. Just as the Founding generation patched up the system with the Twelfth Amendment, later generations have applied makeshift remedies to particularly painful sore spots. None has attempted the fundamental reconstruction that is so obviously required.[2]

From this vantage point, the election of 2000 represents a lost opportunity. An electoral college crisis is never exactly fun, but 2000 was the perfect year for it to happen. The country was enjoying an unparalleled period of peace and prosperity. The presidential contenders made every effort to blur their underlying disagreements. Nobody supposed that there was much at stake in the choice between Bush and Gore.

If the Supreme Court had not intervened, Congress would have solved the succession problem one way or another, with a tolerable amount of moaning and groaning from the losing side. And whatever the therapeutic value of the screaming headlines, they would have accomplished something of great constitutional significance. They would have confronted ordinary Americans with the grotesque absurdities of the current system. As the television cameras panned to the image of Vice-President Al Gore presiding over his own contest with George Bush, everybody would have agreed on at least one thing: Never again should we tolerate such silliness!

Whoever became president would have had a clear mandate for fundamental constitutional reform. This is not the place to debate the many plausible alternatives to our anachronistic system. Almost all of them are much better than what we have, and 2000 was the perfect year for the newly selected president to propose a constitutional amendment that would lead the country from the eighteenth century to the twenty-first in a sensible fashion.

The Supreme Court's intervention permitted the public to avoid a face-to-face confrontation with the ticking time bomb that is our present Constitution. By awarding George Bush the presidency through judicial decree, the Court allowed him to take office without any felt need to propose a sensible constitutional amendment. Indeed, it would have been something of an embarrassment for President Bush to take this course. Constitutional amendment requires lengthy deliberation in Congress and the states, and these recurring debates would have served as an ongoing reminder of the Florida fiasco. After September 11, 2001, our constitutional problems with presidential selection were pushed aside by more pressing matters. And they will undoubtedly remain on the back burner until the next electoral crisis hits.

When that moment comes, the country may pay a heavy price for its failure to rebuild the electoral system in 2000. When the ancient machine misfires once again, we may be living in times far different from the halcyon days of peace, prosperity, and Monica Lewinsky. We may be in the midst of a foreign war or a domestic crisis, or a time when ideologically polarized parties are engaged in a bitter struggle for the White House.

The election of 2004 should serve as an augury. The electoral college threatened a breakdown, but under far more bitter conditions. As the close-fought race between Bush and Kerry came to an end, the prospect of a rerun of 2000 generated a wave of anxiety. Now that the country has narrowly avoided the danger, it will predictably put this particular skeleton back into the closet until it returns to haunt us at a time of its choosing, perhaps when we are even more bitterly divided than we were in 2004. It may be a moment when even the extraordinary statesmanship—and dumb luck—displayed in 1801 will not suffice to pull us back from the brink.

Our story does provide at least a bit of help for the next crisis. Statutes passed since Jefferson's day have trimmed the discretion of the Senate president when he presides over the counting of electoral votes. Nevertheless, he still has room to act decisively in the toughest cases, and the next time around, Thomas Jefferson's precedent may well become a hotly contested matter.

Begin by defining the hard cases in which Jefferson's precedent remains relevant. They involve a state submitting two sets of electoral returns, each for a different candidate, to the president of the Senate. Under existing law, the Senate president must count the return chosen by both houses of Congress,[3] and when the chambers disagree, the Senate president is told to count the ballot certified by "the executive" of the state.[4] But what if "the executive" signs both sets of returns, or what if different members of the executive branch sign different returns?

At this point, the protagonists have nowhere to look for guidance but at the cryptic terms of the Constitution—"The President of the Senate shall, in the Presence of the Senate and House of Representatives, open all the Certificates, and the Votes shall then be counted"[5]—and the historical gloss provided by Jefferson's decision, in February 1801, to count the Georgia ballot. That is the only time in American history when the Senate president has used his vote-counting power in a consequential fashion,[6] and so the precedent from 1801 will inevitably be recalled at the worst possible moment, when the country is in the midst of a grave crisis and partisans on both sides are invoking Jefferson's actions as part of their desperate efforts to push their candidate into the White House.

At first glance, it isn't obvious that Jefferson's decision should count as a precedent at all. After all, he refused to call the defects of the Georgia ballot to the express attention of the House and Senate. Doesn't Jefferson's silence suggest that he knew he was doing something devious? Doesn't it undermine the precedential value of his ruling?

The objection would be compelling if the House and Senate had really been kept in the dark. The newspapers make it perfectly clear, however, that the tellers appointed by Congress had publicly "declared that there was some informality . . . but believing them to be the true votes, reported them as such."[7] Within this context, Jefferson was not acting deviously in using his power as Senate president to resolve the controversy. He was simply shifting the burden onto the Federalists to raise objections. If a senator or representative had taken the floor to complain, it would have been up to Jefferson to take the next step and make a fully explicit ruling. Since this action might have further destabilized the proceedings, he was acting like a statesman in forcing his opponents to decide whether they really wanted to make his exercise of power into a major issue.[8]

Moreover, Jefferson did take public responsibility for the entire vote count. "[I]n pursuance of the duty enjoined upon him," he declared that he and Burr had won "a majority of the votes of all the Electors appointed"—or so says the *Annals of Congress*.[9] Without the four Georgia votes, neither Republican had a majority, and Jefferson could not have made this declaration. While he certainly could have been more explicit, this public statement does amount to a formal assertion of authority, in his capacity as Senate president, to make a decision on the validity of the Georgia ballot. And despite the bitter partisanship of the time, nobody seems to have protested Jefferson's decision. In short, Jefferson's actions as Senate president managed to resolve a potentially explosive problem in a manner that gained public consent. What more can we ask of a legal precedent?

The Jefferson story dropped from sight during the twentieth century. Nevertheless, it remains the only consequential ruling by a Senate president, and it deserves respectful attention. The fact that it was *Jefferson* in the chair also matters. Putting hagiography to one side, the man had devoted his four years as president of the Senate to drafting that body's first set of rules for procedure—rules which continue to influence the practice of both Senate and House today.[10] If Jefferson's words and actions count on anything, they should count on matters of parliamentary procedure. So it seems pretty clear that the decision of 1801 should serve as a precedent, if only we can figure out what it means.

The meaning, says the cynic, is brutally obvious. You can do anything you like if you're president of the Senate. You can even count your rivals out on the basis of a blatantly invalid ballot.

But this is too quick. Jefferson's actions in 1801 reflect the same principles that had guided him during the previous presidential election, when they had operated to his disadvantage. Recall that his campaign manager, James Madison, offered him a chance to quibble his way to the presidency by challenging the four Vermont votes that gave Adams his edge in the electoral college. Jefferson turned down Madison flat: "I pray you to declare it on every occasion foreseen or not foreseen by me, in favor of the choice of the people substantially expressed, and to prevent the phaenomenon of a Pseudo-president at so early a day."[11]

So Jefferson wasn't merely an opportunist in invoking the same principle four years later. The key thing, as he rightly saw, was to prevent the selection of "a Pseudo-president."

And future Senate presidents will be in a better position to follow Jefferson's principle without indulging in his devious tactics. The 1787 Constitution had forced Jefferson into a race against time. Adams's term ran out on March 4, and a constitutional flaw threatened to engulf the nation in civil war if a new president was not selected by then. Happily, this Founding blunder no longer haunts us. It was papered over by the Twentieth Amendment to the Constitution in 1933, which explicitly gave Congress the power to name an interim president if the new one has not yet been designated by inauguration day.[12]

This gives the president of the Senate much more leeway. When facing his March 4 deadline, Jefferson couldn't be blamed for failing to send a fact-finding mission to Georgia—given the miserable winter roads, there was little chance that they could investigate, and report back, in time. Future Senate presidents won't face similar constraints. With a provisional president minding the store in the interim, it won't be catastrophic if an election contest isn't resolved by inauguration day.

Of course, it will remain important to resolve election contests expeditiously. Yet it won't be so important that it will make sense to resolve them in the Jeffersonian manner—by guessing about the underlying facts. However fierce the snowstorm, it won't take weeks to send a fact-finding team to the troublesome state. While the rising forms of electronic voting won't be error-free, the time required for a comprehensive and impartial recount shouldn't be excessive. The calculus of constitutional statesmanship has changed in two respects: the speed of an impartial recount has increased, while the costs of missing inauguration day have been reduced. It may have been statesmanlike of Jefferson to make his best guess about Georgia in 1801, but it would be sheer willfulness for some future Senate president to make a similar plunge in the dark.

Even after a couple of centuries, it remains too "early a day" to connive in the selection of "a Pseudo-president." Yet it is no longer appropriate to pursue Jefferson's great principle by aping his tactics. The Senate president should commit himself to follow the recommendations of a special fact-finding panel, and should take pains to constitute the panel in a way that assures the broader public of its impartiality. The aim should be to determine who really did win in the contested state(s), and in a way that sustains public confidence. "Surely in so great a case," as Jefferson declared to Madison, "substance & not form should prevail."

From Jefferson to Roosevelt

The first legacy of 1800 is paradox—out of political success came constitutional failure. Though the protagonists managed to reach a statesmanlike solution to the crisis of February 1801, they failed to rewrite the Constitution in a way that would avoid future crises.

The second legacy is no less paradoxical. While Jefferson gained the acquiescence of the Federalist House of Representatives in February 1801, he never reached a similar understanding with the Federalist Court over the next decade. Our story ends with Jefferson and Marshall still scheming to destroy the other's ascendancy. This continuing tension was constitutionally productive, bringing about a constitutional synthesis that expressed both Federalist and Jeffersonian values. This dynamic between the Court and the political branches, moreover, serves as a Founding model that reverberates through American history.

One or another president, claiming a mandate from the People, seeks to repudiate chunks of the nation's constitutional tradition. But he doesn't take the path marked out by the Philadelphia Convention. He doesn't ask Congress and the states to formulate and ratify the new principles in formal constitutional amendments.

Instead, he takes the path blazed by Jefferson in his confrontation with the Marshall Court. He successfully urges Congress to enact legislation that sweeps away established understandings, and he challenges the Supreme Court to a life-and-death struggle if it resolutely defends the traditions he seeks to repudiate. Despite the brinksmanship, both sides somehow regain equilibrium—and over time, the Court manages to integrate a good-faith interpretation of the new popular mandate into preexisting traditions, creating a pattern of living constitutional meanings that sustain a sense of political order for the next generation and beyond. Call this the model of presidential leadership.

In that model's checkered history over the past two hundred years, a single episode has the most to teach us—Franklin Roosevelt's challenge to the Supreme Court over the New Deal. At first glance, my pairing of Jefferson with Roosevelt may seem surprising. The substantive visions of the two presidents could not be more different: while Jefferson sought to weaken the federal government by dismembering the judiciary, Roosevelt took a centralizing course, building up a powerful administrative apparatus that intervened in new areas of life formerly dominated by the states. And when we look at the Supreme Court there is a similar reversal: the Marshall Court sought to preserve federal authority against Jefferson's assault, but the New Deal Court tried to preserve the authority of the states against Roosevelt's vision of a strong central government.

Despite these great substantive variations, the institutional dynamics between president and Court during the two episodes are remarkably similar. And if this is so, we may be on our way to isolating a crucial aspect in the grammar of American constitutional law: a distinctive pattern that organizes the responses of presidents and courts during periods of fundamental change, *regardless of the substance of the changes.*

A second advantage of the New Deal story is that it is seventy years old—far enough in the past to provide some historical distance, yet recent enough to permit insight into the ways in which the relationship between president and Court has evolved since the early republic. If I chose an example closer to the present day, it would be too easy for historical analysis to degenerate into political partisanship. A case study that invites a certain degree of dispassion can provide a precious resource in the inevitably more contentious effort to define the constitutional meaning of recent events.

All this supposes that a comparison between the dynamics unleashed by the elections of 1800 and 1932 can yield genuine insights. Isn't it unlikely that the Founding exchanges between Jefferson and the Marshall Court still resonated 130 years later, when Roosevelt confronted the Supreme Court led by Charles Evans Hughes?

Consider the striking parallels. In both 1800 and 1932 a president enters office with a popular mandate for fundamental change, and Congress, within its first hundred days, enacts sweeping legislation repudiating chunks of the constitutional status quo. As in the 1800s, so in the 1930s, the justices flirt with resistance, then reluctantly accept the legitimacy of major presidential initiatives. But the president remains unsatisfied and goes on the attack: Jefferson tries to tame the Federalist Court by impeaching Chase, Roosevelt tries to tame the Republican Court by packing it with New Dealers.

Both presidentialist efforts fail in crucial Senate votes. While the Senate sustains the Court's claims to institutional independence, it doesn't prevent the president from reshaping constitutional development over the longer term. As justices die or retire, the Senate confirms the president's replacements, who begin to elaborate key shifts in the reigning jurisprudence. After a decade or so, in both cases, the Court is reworking doctrine to express major new themes affirmed by the presidentialist exercise in popular sovereignty. The new judicial doctrine doesn't amount to total repudiation of the past. On both occasions, the Court synthesizes new and old in ways that sustain a sense of constitutional legitimacy.

So much for the similarities.[13] Of course, there are important differences as well, which alert us to historical trends that continue to the present day. So let me retell the story more slowly, and with a more discriminating eye.

The Changing Nature of the Presidency

In both 1800 and 1932 the presidency was the focus of two-party competition of a kind the Framers had not anticipated. But in the intervening century-plus, the nature of political parties, and their relationship to formal institutions, changed substantially, as did the role of the presidency in the constitutional dynamic.

The Jeffersonian "party" lacked the institutional machinery and professionalism of later political organizations. It was, first and foremost, an ideological movement of like-minded notables, who collaborated in the election of the president and who also voted with great discipline when elected to Congress. To mark this point, I have called the Republicans a *movement-party,* and this matters in assessing the role of its movement-president, Thomas Jefferson (see Chapter 1).

Jefferson's authority was based on a unique combination of factors— past service to the republic, political craftiness, but also intellectual leadership. As the author of the Declaration of Independence and many other important writings, he was the dominant movement-intellectual of his time. At a later point in our history, a president with Jefferson's intellectual firepower would have used it to launch well-timed appeals to the People to push his program through Congress and the Court.

This was not Jefferson's way. He didn't even use the formidable network of Republican newspapers to issue partisan pronunciamentos in his own name. Despite the key role he had played in organizing the movement-party during the 1790s, he remained profoundly attached to nonpartisan norms of proper public behavior. He vastly preferred to appear in public as a figure who transcended party politics, while acting behind the scenes to organize his loyalists in the House, the Senate, and the press to make the Republican case to the nation. Though he used the presidency as the principal *engine of government,* transforming the Republican vision into the law of the land, he did not use it to propel him forward as his *party's principal spokesman to the nation.*

Roosevelt took on this second role with enthusiasm. Perhaps he had little choice. In contrast to Jefferson, Roosevelt could not rely on his collaborators in Congress to provide ideological coherence for the New Deal. The Democrats who swept into power in 1933 did not resemble the Republicans of 1801. They were not members of a movement-party but of a "patronage-party." Both southern white supremacists and northern party bosses called themselves Democrats. This party label, however, did not imply a common ideology or much of anything else—except a long history of opposing Republicans and a profound desire for power and patronage. If anybody was going to give any sort of political coherence to the New Deal, it would have to be the president.

Franklin Roosevelt seemed unsuited for this task. In contrast to Jefferson, he was nobody's idea of an intellectual; in fact he was often compared unfavorably in this respect with Herbert Hoover.[14] Nevertheless, he was eager to try.

His first act as party nominee made this plain. Until Roosevelt broke the mold, presidential candidates did not attend their party's nominating convention. They left the dirty business of wheeling and dealing to others and remained modestly at home, awaiting an official delegation to inform them of the convention's choice. All this was an empty ritual: candidates were in close contact with the campaign managers who got them their nominations in smoke-filled rooms. But it had long seemed important to sustain a ceremony that cast the nominee as a latter-day Washington, reluctantly heeding the nation's call to service.

Roosevelt put an end to all that. Upon winning the nomination, he jumped on an airplane and flew to Chicago to address the convention directly, electrifying the crowd with his pledge of a "new deal" to combat the Depression: "[W]hile the [Republicans] prate of economic laws, men and women are starving. We must lay hold of the fact that economic laws are not made by nature. They are made by human beings."[15]

As president, Roosevelt provided an institutional home for a "Brains Trust," gathering together leading academics and policy entrepreneurs to organize his reform initiatives. And he regularly projected his voice into the nation's living rooms in fireside chats—serving as the principal interpreter of his party's promise of a New Deal for the American people.

Unlike Jefferson, Roosevelt was obliged by the ideologically disparate character of his patronage-party to create a direct relationship with the

American public, using the presidency to give voice to diverse movements for social change engaged by the New Deal. His relations with Congress were also different. The professional politicians leading the Democrats in Congress were much more entrenched than their counterparts had been in the early 1800s, and they proved more resistant to presidential pressure as time went on.

These differences should not obscure key similarities. In both 1800 and 1932, two-party competition transformed the race for the presidency into an ideological contest that shattered the Framers' expectations. And in both cases, the out-party's victory was popularly understood as a mandate for a fundamental challenge to the status quo. But in 1932 the president would be taking a much a more public role in the contest over constitutional meaning.

A Changing Court

And he would be facing a much stronger Court. The Federalist tribunal that Marshall inherited in 1801 was a ramshackle affair—without a great tradition of achievement, occupying itself largely with circuit riding, it had seen three chief justices come and go in its first twelve years. During the fierce election campaign, the Federalist justices had incensed the triumphant Republicans by using the Federalist Sedition Act as a weapon against Republican newspaper editors. The justices were in hot water, and they knew it: it is entirely unsurprising that the Court quickly buckled before the Jeffersonian assault on the circuit judges, contenting itself with a symbolic affirmation of judicial independence in Marbury v. Madison.

The Court confronting Roosevelt was a more formidable force. It had suffered some notable defeats since Marshall's day—its defense of slavery in *Dred Scott* and its assault on progressive taxation in the *Income Tax Cases,* for example. Despite these setbacks the Court had managed to prosper, and in 1932 it had not suffered a crushing defeat for decades.

The justices had also escaped the onerous circuit riding that Jefferson had imposed upon them. The traumatic repeal of the Federalist judiciary act had preserved circuit riding for a remarkably long time. Only in 1891 did Congress permit the justices to stay in Washington on a full-time basis, creating a new set of intermediate courts of appeal throughout the country. And in 1925 Congress had given the Court a vote of confidence by granting it broad new powers to control its appellate docket.[16] In confronting the New Deal, the justices would no longer be in a position of deciding key issues without face-to-face discussion. They could deliberate together at length, and they could choose the timing of their decisions.

Little wonder that the Hughes Court displayed greater self-confidence than its Marshallian predecessor. Like Jefferson, Roosevelt immediately pushed a bill through Congress that launched a frontal assault on existing constitutional understandings. The National Industrial Recovery Act (NIRA), the centerpiece of the early New Deal, responded to the Great Depression with a centralized regime of industrial planning, managed by the national executive. The new legislation was a body blow to the established constitutional tradition emphasizing free markets and states' rights.

But in contrast to its early days, the Supreme Court headed by Chief Justice Charles Evans Hughes was not obliged to respond to this assault with blinding speed. It deferred its decision on the NIRA until 1935, when popular enthusiasm for central planning had abated quite a bit. Then, after discussing the pros and cons, the Court struck down the NIRA by a vote of 9 to 0.

This self-confident act of resistance might have had a disastrous impact if Roosevelt, like Jefferson, had been at the head of a movement-party. He might have had a tough time controlling his party's ideologues in Congress, if they had insisted on reenacting the NIRA with only small changes, thereby challenging the Court to an all-out struggle over central planning.

Since the Democrats were largely a patronage-party, Roosevelt had much greater leeway in developing a reply to the initial judicial rebuff. His "Second New Deal," passed in the aftermath of the Court's decisions of 1935, elaborated a philosophy of activist government that contrasted sharply with the NIRA. Instead of central planning, the new statutes offered up a vision of regulated capitalism. The exemplars were the National Labor Relations Act, granting sweeping rights of union organization to labor, and the Social Security Act, guaranteeing government pensions to the elderly.

Once again, the Supreme Court could safely remain on the sidelines while challenges to the new legislation percolated through the lower courts. In the meantime, Roosevelt returned to the voters in 1936 in search of a renewed mandate for his changing vision of activist national government. When challenges to the Labor Act and Social Security Act finally reached the Court in 1937, the justices faced a different political reality. The Second New Deal now had been massively endorsed by landslide victories in the presidency and Congress, and continued judicial resistance would have placed the Court's continuing independence at serious risk. The judges were, finally, on the brink.

Here is the point where the similarities, rather than the differences, between the two eras become salient. Just as the Marshall Court beat a retreat in Stuart v. Laird, so did the Hughes Court in its great 1937 cases upholding the Labor Act and the Social Security Act—NLRB v. Jones & Laughlin and Steward Machine Co. v. Davis.[17]

This famous "switch in time" inaugurated the modern era of constitutional law, and scholars have endlessly debated why the justices chose this particular moment to retreat. Judicial psychoanalysis is not my specialty. I am more concerned with the very public processes by which presidents and courts create constitutional meanings over time. From this vantage, the conflict between Roosevelt and his judicial antagonists bears witness to the remarkable endurance of the patterns initiated during Jefferson's presidency. The substantive issues provoking the institutional conflict were very different: Jefferson was repudiating the Federalists' vision of active national government by striking down their system of powerful federal courts; Roosevelt was repudiating the then-traditional vision of limited federal government by creating a powerful administrative apparatus to regulate the problems of a modern industrial life. Once we look beyond these substantive differences, however, the institutional dynamics seem pretty similar: on both occasions, transformative presidents and preservationist courts were locked in a sustained struggle until the courts stepped back from the brink and accepted the legitimacy of the president's central initiatives.

In both eras, this was the moment of maximum vulnerability for the Court. Its headlong retreat had discredited it before large portions of the public. And it had raised serious questions within legal circles: If the Court was willing to contradict established legal principles to save itself, was there *anything* left that looked like law?

Enter Marbury v. Madison. If one simply reads the Court's opinion, it is hard to guess that the justices were reeling before the Jeffersonian on-slaught. Within the serene confines of legal space, legal doctrine reigns supreme, with great clarity and confidence. As we have seen, Marshall created this impression by refusing to order the Jefferson administration to do anything, thereby making it impossible for his antagonists to demonstrate the Court's powerlessness by flouting its orders. If the chief justice had attempted to invade the space of political or social life, he would only have succeeded in emphasizing his irrelevance to the living Constitution.

By limiting himself to the realm of legal space, Marshall prevented the judicial retreat from becoming a total defeat. The opinion's confident reasoning suggested that the Court's crushing encounter with political reality had not utterly destroyed its hopes for constitutional law. By presenting a legally powerful rationale for judicial review, *Marbury* suggested that it was only a matter of time before the Court would become a consequential political actor.

Of course, it was impossible to know in 1803 whether *Marbury*'s prophecy would be fulfilled, or whether the opinion would be lost among the endless pages of the *United States Reports*. Nevertheless, Marshall's emphatic legal gestures suggested that it was too soon to write the Court's obituary, and that was no small thing.

Remarkably enough, the Hughes Court executed precisely the same maneuver in the midst of the New Deal crisis. It too reasserted its continuing relevance at its darkest hour, though this time around, it did not indulge in the magisterial prose of a Marshall opinion. Instead, the Court contented itself with producing a footnote that turned out to be one of the most famous utterances in constitutional history—Footnote Four of the *Carolene Products* case of 1938.[18] Like the opinion in *Marbury,* the footnote was written amid the wreckage of the old order; like *Marbury,* it sketched out a bright vision for judicial review; and like *Marbury,* it elaborated this vision in purely legal space, without any effort to provoke a real-world confrontation by ordering the Congress or the president to do anything. Its entire point was to provide the justices with a rationale for judicial review that might appeal to a broad public in the future struggle for institutional authority.

Although *Carolene* was similar to *Marbury* in its timing and function, it differed in its rationale for judicial review. Moving beyond *Marbury*'s emphasis on the written Constitution, the New Deal justices elaborated a distinctively modern mission.[19] The *Carolene* Court reimagined itself as the ultimate guardian of democracy, asserting the need to protect citizens who were deprived of the vote or otherwise cut out of the democratic process.[20] Judicial vigilance was particularly required when pervasive prejudice threatened to undermine the political influence of "discrete and insular minorities."

This guardianship rationale has proved enormously influential over time,[21] but here I wish to emphasize the *Marbury*-like character of the moment when it was announced. Although the *Carolene* Court was reeling before a president speaking for the People with maximum credibility, it artfully waved the flag of judicial review in a direction that pointed to a durable project for a new age of constitutional law. It had converted a disastrous rout into a strategic retreat.

The Model of Presidential Leadership

It is time to turn from the Court to the presidency in our exploration of the parallels between the Founding and the New Deal. As before, the challenge is to move beyond the obvious differences in the substantive visions championed by Jefferson and Roosevelt, and consider the striking similarities in the way they managed the process of constitutional change.

Recall that Jefferson refused to call a truce with the Marshall Court even after the justices had offered an olive branch in Stuart v. Laird and formally accepted the Republican purge of the lower courts. He pressed onward with an impeachment campaign, trying to sweep the Federalist justices out of office and replace them with men who could be counted on to elaborate a compelling Republican vision of constitutional law.

Stuart v. Laird proved effective in ultimately deflecting this presidential initiative. By accepting the purge of the lower judiciary, it bought precious time for the Court, and when the moment of truth came at Chase's impeachment trial in the Senate, it made it a lot easier for some Republicans to defect and save the Court from a crippling blow to its independence. By de-escalating its conflict in *Stuart,* the Court provided independent-minded senators with the breathing room they needed to cast a vote for judicial independence.

Like Jefferson, Roosevelt was not a man who was easily pacified by a strategic judicial retreat. Despite the Court's switch in time, he too pushed for a radical change in the Court's personnel. Only this time he used a different technique. He did not try to impeach his most strident judicial opponents. Instead he proposed to "pack the Court," asking Congress for the statutory authority to add six new justices to the bench, expanding the number of seats from nine to fifteen.[22]

Court-packing is different from impeachment, but the presidential aim remained the same—to seize immediate control over the only remaining branch of government dominated by holdovers from the old regime. As Roosevelt explained on March 4, 1937, in an address at the Democratic victory dinner commemorating his second inauguration, the "three horse team of the American system of government [cannot function] if one horse lies down in the traces or plunges off in another direction." And he believed he had earned the right to whip the errant steed into line: "In three elections during the past five years great majorities have approved what we are trying to do. To me, and I am sure to you, those majorities mean that the people themselves realize the increasing urgency that we meet their needs now."[23]

"The people themselves" versus the Court—this is the way court-packing would have been remembered if Roosevelt had pushed his statute through Congress. But the Hughes Court's dramatic acceptance of New Deal initiatives during the spring of 1937 represents its *Stuart* moment: making it politically possible for Democratic fence-sitters to wonder whether such extreme measures were really necessary. By the time court-packing legislation came before the Senate that summer, the Court's switch gave enough Senate Democrats the political space they needed to desert the president and defeat court-packing. Like the Senate's acquittal of Chase, the Senate's rejection of court-packing is now interpreted as a cautionary tale—even in the wake of a sweeping reelection victory, a president and his party do not have an *unlimited* mandate to change the Constitution in the name of the American people.

At this point the Jefferson/Roosevelt story takes another common turn. Once the Court's independence is reaffirmed by the defeat of impeachment/court-packing, the Court doesn't counterattack and try to destroy the political coalition that pushed it to the brink of destruction.

Instead it takes the path of accommodation: slowly but surely, it begins to incorporate the rising constitutional vision into the higher law of the United States.

There is no mystery here: as time goes by, the old justices leave, giving the sitting president the chance to reshape constitutional doctrine by appointing judges who are willing and able to push the law in new directions. Both Jefferson/Madison and Roosevelt exploited this opportunity, but Roosevelt showed greater discipline and determination. This is surprising, since Jefferson and Madison were the deeper thinkers with the clearer political philosophies. Nevertheless, the famously pragmatic Roosevelt drew the line when it came to making Supreme Court appointments. Perhaps it was his bitter experience with the Old Court, perhaps it was his political insight into the deeper dynamics of American government, but he was not a man to allow a Joseph Story onto the bench for a lifetime of judicial sabotage. Only once did he permit patronage or personalities to trump ideological commitment in making his selections—in 1941 he gave James Byrnes a Supreme Court seat as a consolation prize for losing the vice presidency, but Byrnes found the job uncongenial and resigned very quickly.[24] The enthusiastic New Dealers on the Court, in contrast, stayed and stayed to write their vision of activist government into the law of the land.

And there were lots of them. Jefferson and Madison made four appointments in sixteen years; Roosevelt made eight in thirteen. But he was obliged to endure four long years of judicial resistance before making the first in his long string of nominations. By the time he placed Hugo Black on the bench in 1937, he was thoroughly convinced of the imperative need to create a Court that would elaborate a compelling constitutional vision of activist national government.[25]

As a consequence, the New Deal revolution in judicial doctrine was far broader and deeper than its Jeffersonian predecessor. Yet the same presidentialist dynamic was operating, and at about the same pace. In both cases, a reconstituted Court was proclaiming large new constitutional meanings within a dozen years of the initial presidential victory: cutting back on federal powers by 1812, increasing their scope by 1945.

And finally, both Courts sought to synthesize the new themes into a larger vision of the Constitution that embraced the earlier historical achievements of the American people. For the Marshall Court, this involved weaving Jeffersonian threads into the basic fabric of Federalist constitutional understanding. The New Deal judicial synthesis was much more ambitious. The Court's affirmation of activist national government and democratic self-rule provided a new framework for a radical reinterpretation of the constitutional tradition. While the New Deal Court sought to integrate the great constitutional achievements of prior generations, these efforts invariably bore the mark of its large new understanding of the powers and democratic promise of the national government.[26]

To put this complex point in a single line: the Republican judicial synthesis of the early republic accepted the Federalist principles as a baseline, modifying but not supplanting them with Jeffersonian themes; in contrast, the New Deal synthesis created a new twentieth-century foundation for constitutional thought, and incorporated prior achievements only when they were compatible with this modern framework. This is a large difference, but it should not conceal an even more important similarity: in both cases, the Court did not produce a jurisprudence that either erased the constitutional past or ignored the constitutional present; in both cases, it took on the arduous task of creating a living constitutional law that sustained a conversation between the present and the past, in never-ending dialogue.

We are now in a position to glimpse a recurring institutional dynamic, from beginning to end:

Election of the people's president → Congressional assault on the old Constitution → Supreme Court resistance, and then a switch in time → Continued electoral victories → Senate support of judicial independence → New judicial appointments → New judicial synthesis.

This was the pattern of the early nineteenth century, during the birth agony of the plebiscitarian presidency and judicial review. This was the pattern of the twentieth century, during the birth agony of the New Deal and the modern constitutional order. Some variation on this pattern may well arise repeatedly in the twenty-first century—when future presidents and their parties successfully establish a mandate from the People for fundamental change.

Or maybe not. I am no prophet. My aim has been to provide a deeper understanding of the constitutional past, and hope that it will better prepare us to confront the future.

*   *   *

The standard story of the Founding celebrates the men of 1787 who wrote the Constitution, but ignores the men of 1801 who repaired the Enlightenment machine when it threatened to explode. I have been trying to right this imbalance.

By all means, let us praise the Philadelphia Convention for its great gamble on the Enlightenment. If the Framers had been intellectually conservative folk, they would never have launched their unprecedented experiment in government on a continental scale. There were simply too many untested theories behind their initiative, too many reasons to suppose that Madison was wrong in speculating that a big republic was a good republic. And yet the men of Philadelphia convinced the country to gamble on their speculative political science, committing America to a vision of government that has stood the test of time.

But we should also praise the statesmen who picked up the pieces when the gambles went wrong. The Framers' misunderstanding of the presidency was the biggest of their mistakes, and their speculations required a massive dose of statesmanship if their Constitution was going to survive and prosper. Conventional wisdom ignores this point in highlighting Marbury v. Madison as the only memorable contribution of the early 1800s to the Founding heritage. If we take *Marbury*'s paean to the written Constitution out of historical context, we are well on the way to a worshipful relationship to the demigods who wrote the Constitution at Philadelphia. We are tempted to believe that the republic will remain on track to greatness so long as all of us follow the instructions handed down by the miracle workers at Philadelphia.

This is a fatal mistake. The Constitution is not a miraculous "machine that would go of itself."[27] It is an ongoing dialogue between the inspiring speculations of one generation and the worldly experience of the next, between the visionary initiatives of popular sovereignty and the sober adaptations of statesmanship.

This is the Founding inheritance, and we abandon it at our peril.

Horatius's Presidential Knot

This essay by "Horatius" does not explicitly name John Marshall. It simply advocates the statutory creation of an interim presidency to resolve the electoral college crisis. But Marshall's stake in the matter would have been obvious to all contemporary readers.

When Horatius insists that Congress can only designate an "officer of the United States" as interim president, he effectively eliminates most contenders for the position, privileging the claims of the most senior "officer[s] of the United States": the secretary of state, the senior member of the executive branch; and the chief justice, the senior judicial officer. At the time of publication, Marshall was secretary of state and the chief justiceship was vacant.

Apart from general stylistic affinities with Marshall's prose, the text expresses two great themes that he elaborated later as chief justice. First, it proposes an expansive interpretation of a narrow provision to serve the larger purpose of strengthening the national government. Second, it emphasizes the special constitutional status of officials who have received "their commissions and appointments from the President." The first theme anticipates cases like McCulloch v. Maryland; the second, Marbury v. Madison.

A skeptic might note that Horatius strikes an un-Marshallian pose in refusing to rely on a sweeping interpretation of the "necessary and proper" clause. But, as Horatius suggests, relying on this clause was both unnecessary and unwise. Unnecessary, because the interim presidency might be fully justified on other constitutional grounds; unwise, because a broad reading of the "necessary and proper" clause might give Congress the power to authorize the "interim" president to "continue in office for the whole term of the ensuing four years, or perhaps longer."[1]

The Presidential Knot

Information has been received from all the states concerning the election of President and Vice-President, and it is considered certain that Mr. Jefferson and Mr. Burr have an equal number of votes, each seventy-three votes. On the second Wednesday in February, the House of Representatives, voting by states, are to give their votes by ballot, before they adjourn, for the one or the other of these gentlemen; and a majority of the states, which cannot be less than nine states, must concur in the choice of one or the other, or neither will be elected. It is extremely to be desired that a majority of the states may be found in favor of one of the candidates; but upon a view of the present representation in that house, serious doubts may be entertained whether either Mr. Jefferson or Mr. Burr will unite nine states in his favor. Such being a possible event, it will be proper for Congress before the second Wednesday in February, to provide by law for the vacancy in the office of the President that may be so occasioned, and to declare what officer shall act as President until a President shall be elected in the manner prescribed by the constitution.

Mr. Jefferson coming from a southern state, and being considered unfriendly to the measures of commercial defence which have been adopted, and hostile to the general tenor of the Washington administration, which has been continued by his successor, will not in all probability obtain the vote of either of the six following states, viz.

New-Hampshire, Massachusetts, Connecticut, Rhode-Island, Delaware, and South-Carolina, each of which will be inclined to prefer Mr. Burr.

The states of Georgia, Tennessee, N. Carolina, Kentucky, Virginia, Pennsylvania and New-York, seven in number, may be reckoned certainly in favor of Mr. Jefferson.

New-Jersey is uncertain, but most probably will prefer Mr. Burr, who is said to be a native of that state[.] Vermont is represented by two members, who almost without an exception are opposite to each other in every vote, consequently being equally divided Vermont will give no vote on the question.

The representatives from the state of Maryland are eight in number, of whom five are federalists. It is therefore probable that this state will either vote for Mr. Burr, or be equally divided, and give no vote.

Thus, of sixteen states, fourteen may be expected to vote, of whom seven are sure on the side of Mr. Jefferson, and six sure on the side of Mr. Burr, and one uncertain; and if this one shall vote for Mr. Jefferson, yet he will not have the votes of nine states, and without the votes of nine states, he cannot be elected President.

The constitution has enjoined that the certificates of the electors shall be opened, and their votes counted *in the presence of the Senate, and House of Representatives,* and "if there be more than one person who have a majority of the votes of the electors appointed, and have an equal number of votes, then the House of Representatives shall *immediately* chuse, by ballot, one of them for President." The choice is required to be *immediately made,* in order that the result may be declared in the presence of the Senate, and to prevent the possibility of intrigue and corruption. The choice must be therefore made before the house adjourns or disperses, and after the convention of the Senate and House of Representatives terminates, the house cannot at a future day act upon this subject.

What will be the consequence if no choice is made? Will the government of the United States be stopped in all its operations, or may it be continued until a President shall be elected in pursuance of the constitution?

Some gentlemen, overzealous for the success of Mr. Jefferson, utter threats that unless he is elected the government shall be at an end. Menaces of this kind are always unbecoming and at no time to be regarded, and the writer of these observations, being by no means inclined to give the preference to Mr. Burr, regrets that they were not repressed.

There are two clauses in the constitution which may be supposed worthy of attention in this enquiry.

The last clause of the 8th section of the first article is in the following words—"Congress shall have power to make all laws which shall be necessary for carrying into execution the foregoing powers, and *all other powers vested in this constitution in the government of the United States,* or any department or officer thereof."

A clause in the 1st section of the same article is in the following words—"In case of the *removal* of the President from office, or of his death, resignation or inability to discharge the power and duties of the said office, the same shall devolve on the Vice President, *and the Congress may by law provide for the case of removal, death, resignation or inability of both President and Vice-President, declaring what officer shall then act as President, and such officer shall act accordingly until the disability be removed or a president shall be elected."*

In the interpretation of the words of a statute and more strongly in the interpretation of a written constitution or form of government, that interpretation is never to be made which will frustrate the end of the statute or constitution. If therefore the words of the constitution be susceptible of two constructions, one which in a particular event, reasonable and probable in itself, will put an end to all its operations, and the other which will continue its existence, the latter must undoubtedly be preferred— such is believed to be the present case.

The second article of the constitution is occupied with regulations and provisions relative to the person who should exercise the supreme executive power. From the nature of the powers vested in the President for a limited time, it is manifest that a President or an office authorised to perform his functions should always be in existence. By the constitutional tenure of their offices, both the President and Vice-President are to cease their functions at the same time, and both those offices may become vacant every fourth year. If a majority of the electors appointed are not in favor of some one man, the states as represented in the house of representatives, are to choose one out of the five highest on the list, and a majority of the states is necessary to a choice. The variety of considerations likely to operate on the electors, rendered it probable that a majority of them would rarely concur in favor of one man; consequently that it would frequently devolve on the house of representatives to choose the President. But the representation from the several states in that house, was as likely to consist of an even as of an odd number, so that it was probable some states would not vote on the question, their representatives being equally divided, while other states who should vote, would differ in their opinion relative to the candidates—Hence it was reasonable to expect the case would sometimes, if not often happen, when neither the majority of electors nor a majority of the states would give their votes to any one person in exclusion of all others. For such a state of things the constitution ought not to be understood to be unprovided, or it will be understood to be without the means of self preservation. In the clause which was last cited, congress are authorised to provide by law for the *case of the removal, death, resignation or inability both of the President and Vice-President, declaring what officer shall then act as President, and such officer shall act accordingly until the disability be removed or a President be elected*. The words here used are comprehensive enough to embrace every vacancy, and if they are construed not to embrace the case of removal by virtue of the constitutional terms of the offices of President and Vice-President, they will not embrace the vacancy most probable to happen, while they are admitted to embrace the vacancies that are very improbable. That the President and Vice-President should both die, or resign, or be disabled in the course of four years, or be removed by sentence of impeachment, will be a very rare occurrence.[2]

In carrying into execution this power, the act of congress proposed 1st March 1792, has authorised the President of the Senate protempore, and in case there be no President of the Senate, then the Speaker of the House of Representatives for the time being to act as President of the United States until the disability be removed, or a President shall be elected.

A serious doubt is entertained whether this provision of the act be constitutional—upon the impeachment of William Blount, a distinction was taken between an officer and a Member of Congress, and it was held that a Senator was not an officer of the United States, and therefore was not liable to impeachment. Upon this ground the Majority of the Senate would not hold cognizance of that impeachment.

Congress are empowered by the constitution to provide and declare by law, *what officer* shall in case of removal of the President & Vice-President act as President, and such *officer* shall act accordingly, till a President shall be elected.—Therefore, if a Senator be not an *officer,* he is not a person qualified to be charged with the presidential duties. A senator who is chosen President of the Senate protempore, is an officer of that house, as is the clerk of the Senate, but not an officer of the United States. It was said in Blount's case, that *the officers* of the U. States receive their commissions and appointments from the President, according to which criterion the President of the Senate protempore is not an officer.

These remarks apply with equal force to the Speaker and other members of the house of representatives. Moreover there is obvious danger in admitting that a member of Congress is capable of being raised to the Presidency by means of *a law.*

In a system of government so complex as the American, where many and various parts of the machinery have an opportunity of embarrassing the movements, a doubt should not be permitted concerning the rightful title of him to whom the temporary discharge of the presidential duties shall be committed—Under this impression it seems necessary for Congress to revise the existing law on this subject, and by a new law to declare *what officer* shall act as President, in case of a vacancy in the offices of President and Vice-President at the same time, occasioned either by removal, death, resignation or disability, until the disability be removed or a new President be elected: And in the new law it may be expedient to exercise the sense that the word *removal,* in the clause cited, comprehends the case where neither the electors nor the house of representatives shall elect a successor to the President whose time expires by virtue of the constitutional limitation.

No reliance is placed on the clause giving Congress power to make all laws necessary and proper for carrying into execution all the enumerated powers, and all other powers vested by the constitution in the government of the United States, or in any department or officer thereof, for supporting the constitutionality of the law proposed to be passed.[3]

1st. When in the article exclusively occupied upon the subject of the President, in fixing his powers and duties, in prescribing the manner of his election, in limiting his duration in office, we see a clause expressly authorising Congress to appoint by law some officer to act as President in case of the removal, death, resignation, or inability both of the President and Vice President, until the disability is removed, or a President shall be elected, it is reasonable to infer that the legislative power of Congress to fill a vacancy in the office of President is derived only from this particular clause.

2d. There is a manifest distinction between a power in Congress to make laws for carrying into execution all the powers vested in the government, or in any department or officer, and a power in Congress to provide a President by legislative act.

3d. If the general power of passing laws is construed to enable Congress to appoint a President in case of no election of President and Vice President, a President so appointed by legislative act, may be chosen out of their own body, and may continue in office for the whole term of the ensuing four years, or perhaps longer, if the law shall so direct; for the exercise of the general power is subject to no particular restrictions, but is to be governed by the discretion of Congress. Yet in the second article, when the constitution vests the power of supplying a vacancy in the office of President, by a legislative declaration, we find it can only be supplied till the disability be removed, or a President shall be elected, and the appointment of Congress is limited to the officers of government.

4th. Upon the same principle of construction of this clause of the first article, Congress would have power to supply vacancies in the Senate when the state legislature shall make default in choosing their senators; for a Senate is as indispensably requisite for carrying on the government as is a President.

From these observations it is apparent that under the first article of the constitution, Congress have no power to supply any vacancy in the office of President, but that they derive all their power upon this subject from the second article, and that their power is completely adequate in pursuance of this article, to provide by law for the vacancy that may happen by the removal of both the President and Vice President on the 3d of March next, and the non-election of a successor in the manner prescribed by the constitution.

HORATIUS

Judge Bassett's Protest

Judge Bassett appeals to the Supreme Court to disobey Congress's command to resume circuit-riding, and urges it to strike down the congressional statute that destroyed his court.

The *Protest* is written in the form of a judicial opinion that fits squarely within the jurisprudential framework later developed by Marshall in Marbury v. Madison. For Bassett, as for Marshall, the Constitution's claim to higher law status is grounded in the will of the People, not on natural law. For both men, courts are drawn into the business of judicial review as part of their obligation to decide concrete cases according to law.

But Marshall makes these points in connection with a lawsuit brought by a mere justice of the peace claiming a five-year office under a congressional statute. Bassett is a federal judge claiming life tenure under the express terms of the Constitution. As a consequence, he reflects more deeply on the separation of powers and the nature of judicial independence. Perhaps this is the sort of opinion Marshall might have written if he had successfully persuaded his fellow justices to defy Congress?

Bassett's text allows us to explore the road not taken by the Court in Stuart v. Laird, and to appreciate how readily an opinion might have been written by a Court that chose the path of institutional confrontation, rather than collaboration, with the political branches of government.

Given the nature of his case, Bassett makes stronger claims than those made by Marshall in *Marbury*. He calls on the Supreme Court justices to refuse to "participate in the overthrow of the Constitution" by riding circuit and conducting trials without an appropriate judicial commission. In contrast, the justices in *Marbury* refrained from taking any action in the real world that challenged Jefferson's authority.

On the jurisprudential level, Bassett is also more aggressive in claiming that the Supreme Court is the final arbiter of all constitutional controversies, subject only to constitutional amendment. Although *Marbury* is consistent with this strong view, it does not make any explicit claim to sweeping judicial supremacy. Marshall's opinion is also compatible with a more modest judicial role, in which the Court only seeks to bind the parties in the case before it, and recognizes that the other branches have the authority to follow their own interpretations of the Constitution.

Nevertheless, both Bassett and Marshall are plainly proceeding from the same matrix of Federalist constitutionalism, and the *Protest* provides a unique insight into the range of choices that the legal culture of the time opened up to the Marshall Court if it had not chosen the path of collaboration with Jefferson in Stuart v. Laird.[1]

Protest of the Honorable Judge Bassett, of Delaware, Against the acts repealing the Judiciary Law

The question is, indeed, simple in its terms, but all important in the solution.—Are the *offices* of the judges, composing the Circuit Courts, created by the act of the 13th of February, ABOLISHED by the late acts of the 8th of March and 29th April, 1802? or do those "OFFICES" exist in full force, under the constitution of the United States?

Recurring both to the positive letter and clear spirit of the constitution of the United States, my mind never doubted.—Yet, on a subject so interesting to the present, and so big, with consequences to future generations, it became me to review the grounds, of my own conviction, and to examine the evidences opposed to it.

This has been done; and after the most careful deliberation and most anxious solicitude to arrive at TRUTH—I am bound to DECLARE, that in my solemn judgment those acts of the 8th of March and 29th of April, 1802, have *not abolished* the offices of the judges of the Circuit Courts of the United States, created and perfected under the act of February, 1801; but that they do exist in full force, as at first, protected against legislative destruction, by the constitution of the United States.

And, in my *judicial* character, and under the highest obligation of supporting that constitution, I am constrained to *pronounce* those acts, because of their design and intent to abolish the said offices, and to transfer them to other judges, so far *null* and *void*.

It would exceed the necessary limits of this DECLARATION, to enumerate the various reasons which concur in support of the foregoing opinion.

The subject has been recently exhausted, it is not to be expected, from human powers, to add to the number or force of the proofs, which wisdom and eloquence have arrayed on the side of the constitutional *position,* that the Judges of the U. States cannot be *deprived* of their offices by the *Legislative* body; or in any other way than on *impeachment* before the Senate, and conviction there of MISBEHAVIOUR in office.[2]

I shall, as briefly as possible, state the *grounds* to my judgment, with such illustrations, and recurrence to objections, as may serve to obviate difficulties.

And here it is important for me to remark, that my opinion, however fortified by considerations of sound policy and general good consequences, flows not from those *extraneous* sources: I rest it upon the words and expressions of the *People* contained in the constitution, as it came from their hands; and upon the plain, natural and accepted meaning of those words and expressions.

The constitution of the United States, by *three* several *articles,* each following the other, has formed *three* distinct *powers of government:*—the *Legislative* power, the *Executive* power, and the *Judicial* power. Each of these governing powers, derives its title to *existence* and *duration,* by the same words of grant or conveyance, from the people. By the first article it is enacted, "that all legislative *power* herein granted, shall be *vested* in a congress of the United States, to consist of a Senate and House of Representatives."

Having thus established the Legislative power it proceeds to direct *how* the Congress, who is to exercise it, shall be brought into, and continued in existence.

For this end, elections are to be made in the several States. The people are to choose the Representatives and the Legislatures to appoint the Senators. Then follow the clauses fixing the *duration* of the congressional office, determining that the Representatives shall be chosen for two years and the Senators for six years.

By the second article it is enacted, "that the Executive power shall be vested in a President of the United States of America;" and fixes the *duration* of his appointment, by declaring that he "shall hold his office during the term of *four* years." The manner of choosing him is then prescribed, and this is to be done by electors appointed in the several states.

By the third article it is enacted, that "the Judicial power of the United States shall be vested in one supreme court, and such inferior courts as Congress may from time to time ordain and establish."

Having thus vested the judicial power in *national* courts, or courts of the U. States, just as the legislative power was vested in a Congress, and the executive power in a President, the article proceeds to fix the *duration* of the offices of *those* who were to exercise the judicial power: and for that purpose, declares, "that the JUDGES both of the supreme and inferior courts shall HOLD THEIR OFFICES, during good behaviour."

From the *structure,* then, of the constitution, and by, indeed, a natural order, each department is to be distinct. The *manner* of bringing those departments into *operation* is then pointed out;—and when the persons are selected, either by elections or under laws, to fulfil those three distinct powers of government, the constitution *fixes,* by positive grant and limitation, the *duration* of their respective offices.

It was not left to the people of the several states, or to their legislatures, *how long* a Representative or Senator in Congress should serve them after chosen; nor to the United States, how long their President and Vice-President should serve them; nor to the Congress, how long the Judges, appointed under their laws, should hold their commissions, and enjoy the powers and salaries annexed to them.

The people of the several states are allowed a *free choice* of representatives; to the legislatures is given a *free choice* of Senators; to the United States a *free choice* of President and Vice President; to Congress full time and *free* power, to ordain and establish, from time to time, such courts as they shall see fit; and the President and Senate *free* discretion in the selection of Judges. But as far as respected the *duration* of those several offices, when once conferred or vested, no power to revoke, diminish, extend or abolish, is granted to the people of the several states, or to the state legislatures, or to the Congress of the United States—THE WHOLE PEOPLE OF THE UNITED STATES did, themselves, in the original charter of government, expressly and positively determine, that *when* chosen a *representative* should HOLD his appointment for TWO *years:* that a Senator should hold his appointment for SIX *years:* that the *president* and *vice-president* should hold their offices for FOUR *years:* and that the judges should hold their offices DURING GOOD BEHAVIOUR.

In regard to all the *other* offices, or appointments, which are spoken of in the constitution, or contemplated as necessary to execute the public measures, the *duration* of them is *not* fixed by the *People,* but left to the *discretion* of the *Government.*

The reason and necessity of this *distribution* of power, and *duration* of office are obvious.

The *three great powers* of government were essential to its *existence.*

There could be no freedom at all without them. It became necessary for the *People,* therefore, in order to secure their liberties, so to *construct* each of those departments as that one might not be subject to the *will* and *pleasure* of the other; or what is the same thing, that the *officers* composing one department should not be exposed to the dismission, or dependence on the other.[3]

That would defeat all the benefits of divided power. It would have enabled *one branch* to swallow up the other, and *consolidate* government. There could then be no *constitution,* but the uncontrolled and capricious *will* of the victorious department.

This great evil, which has poisoned and finally destroyed all the forms of free government in the world, was that[4] to be effectually curbed, by the provisions of the constitution, whereby each branch is made *Independent* of the other, by having granted to its *officers,* under that instrument, a *fixed* and unalterable *term of office;* or a right to exercise their appropriate and vested powers.

This was the best security which could be devised to preserve free, distinct and permanent, the legislative, executive, and judicial powers; the separation and independence of which, have been agreed by all writers, as essential to the preservation of *civil Liberty.*

But I shall not enter the field of political reasons and consequences. They are indeed at hand, and leave no doubt of the wisdom and foresight of the *People* and *States,* who adopted the present form of government.

I am considering a matter of *fact,* and not choosing between *theoretical* opinions. The question is, not what *might* or *ought* to have been done, but what IS DONE? If the CONSTITUTION does, in fact, contain an explicit declaration, that the JUDGES, when chosen under it, and whether Supreme or Inferior, "*shall hold their offices during good behavior,*" then no authority to *alter* the *tenure* or *abolish* the office exists. The *people* only, resorting to *amendments* in the way which they have prescribed, can *change* the form of government.

The Legislative, the Executive, and Judicial departments are the *creatures* of the Constitution. They *must be satisfied* with what is granted to them, and refrain from every encroachment on the *Independence,* and *rightful* limits of *power* and *office,* holden by each, under that sovereign LAW of the *people.*

Whatever *is* granted, to each department, *may* be exercised, even to *abuse.* Whatever is denied *must* be abstained from, though ever so *desirable.* Whatever is *regulated* and *fixed* by the Constitution, *must* bind, though ever so *grievous.* It is possible, nay probable, that some *defects,* on experience, will be found attached to the national Government. These, however great and obvious, must be borne, until the *People* and States shall see fit by *amendments,* to redress them.

If the *Executive* or *Legislative* Department or both, shall *assume* this power under *pretexts* ever so plausible, or popular, nay, though every man in the United States could *wish* for their right to do it, in the particular case, it is plain we shall have *no* Constitution but what every successive Congress shall see fit to make.

The authorities, then, constituted by and under the Federal Government, must look to, and be bound by its provisions. They are not to speculate about their wisdom, or attempt to supply their defects; but ought faithfully and virtuously to *adhere* to the WILL *of the* PEOPLE as they *find it expressed* in the great national CHARTER.

Taking the Constitution for our guide, what real doubt can be raised on the question under consideration? The WORDS are, "Article III, The Judicial power of the United States, shall be vested in *one Supreme Court,* and in *such inferior Courts,* as Congress may from time to time *ordain* and *establish:* The JUDGES, *both* of the Supreme and Inferior Courts, *shall* HOLD THEIR OFFICES DURING GOOD BEHAVIOUR: and *shall* at stated times recive [*sic*] a *compensation* for their services, which *shall not be diminished* during their continuance in office."

What terms could have been devised in the English language, more *decisive?* It is not said, they shall hold their offices against the will of the *President;* or against the power of Congress; but simply and *universally,* that they shall *hold their offices,* during good behavior.

The Legislature, then, can annex no new conditions, and say; "you shall hold your offices, *until* we repeal the law creating them; or, *until* we abolish them; or, *until* we create *new courts,* and invest, with your power, *other judges,* who may suit us better; or, *until* there shall appear to us no further *necessity* for your courts; or, you shall hold *so long* as we think it eco-nomical to pay your salaries. No power is given to *Congress* of terminating judicial offices at all.

It was easy to foresee, that if power had been given to the *Legislative body,* to dismiss the *judges on such like* grounds, that the JUDICIAL POWER would be no longer *independent;* but the *judges,* whose province it is to determine, according to the law and the *constitution,* would thereby be-come the *dependents* of men in power, and often the mere instruments of vengeance in the hands of *political majorities.* The framers, therefore, of the constitution, knowing the invaluable benefit of *judges,* who are *depen-dent* for their offices and salaries, on *good behaviour* only; have invested them with office on that single *condition;* and have appointed a fixed and independent court, the *Senate,* which only can remove judges on proof that they have *misdemeaned themselves* in *office* and so *broken* the condition on which they hold it.

As before observed, the offices of *President* and *Vice-President* are held under *similar* words.

(TO BE CONTINUED)

Continued, Sept. 3, 1802

By article 2. The executive power shall be vested in a President of the United States of America. He shall *hold his office* during the term of "four years, and together with the Vice President chosen for the same term, be elected as follows," &c.

As well might the Legislature attempt to repeal or abolish the office of the Vice-President or even the President himself, on the ground that they were too expensive or unnecessary, as of the Judges after their appoint-ment. There is no constitutional restriction upon them, in the one case, which does not exist in the other.

Each *holds his office* by the *same words,* under the constitution, differ-ing only in *duration.*

So Representatives and Senators from the States, have no other security for the continuance of their offices for two and six years, than those words in the constitution, which say they shall be chosen for two and six years. No *restriction* is put on Congress, against increasing or diminishing the *duration* of their appointments, because none was necessary: For the PEOPLE having prescribed, in that instrument, *how* long Representatives and Senators, the President and Vice-President, and the Judges should hold their offices, it would follow, that as soon as their appointments were legally completed by the *lawful means,* the *right* of *exercising them,* in point of *duration* vested in them under the constitution which protects the office and its exercise so long, against any power but that of the people and states, acting in their original character, by amendments.

It has been asked, shall judges hold their offices and be paid their salaries for life; even tho' the legislative body might from fair motives of public convenience and economy, be desirous of removing them? The answer is found in the constitution of the country.

The people, in *that,* empowered Congress to erect courts, and apportion out among them the judicial powers of the government.

But when ordained and established by Congress, it is declared, the *judges* shall *hold the offices,* thus created, *during* their *good behaviour.*

The people had to choose between the *possible,* but comparatively trifling, inconvenience of maintaining the office of Judges when once appointed, until their decease, provided they behaved well; and the immense and never ceasing evils, resulting to liberty and justice, from placing their judges under the controul, and at the *will* of the Legislative department. They well understood, that all the *checks* and limitations introduced into the *charter* of Government, respecting the rights and obligations of the several States, or in favour of the citizens, would become nugatory the moment that the offices and compensations of the judges were to be holden at the pleasure of majorities in the legislature. It was easy to perceive that a legislative body which held in its hands the offices and livings of those who were to decide whether their *acts* were contrary to the *constitutional* law, would at any time *command* the constitution, and make it yield to their wishes and views. If their law was resisted by the judiciary, as violating the superior law of the constitution, there would be no difficulty in asserting that the *obnoxious* judges were unnecessary, or too *expensive,* or that a *better system* could be framed: And judges would be soon found more pliant to the governing powers.

Thus all the advantages of an independent judiciary would be lost: lost to the people and to the constitution.

But, as I have before said, thus it is written in the charter of government. If the people can be persuaded, that in creating an INDEPENDENT JUDICIARY they have *no* security; if, on experience, they shall find the courts too inconvenient, or the judges too expensive, the remedy is plain and expeditious. Let amendments be proposed in the manner provided in the fifth article of the constitution. They can be obtained, if such is the real wish of the people, almost as soon as the passage of an act of Congress.

Until recourse is had to this method of abolishing *existing judicial offices,* I am bound to say, that no judge can be deprived of his office, but on impeachment for, and conviction of misbehaviour in office. Until then he remains clothed with inviolability, the *independent* and fearless expounder of the laws, and the guardian of the constitution.

It has been said, that what is *created* by *law,* may be *abolished* by law; that the power of the legislature must be the same to both purposes; and therefore as the judicial offices in question arose out of the law of Feb. 1801, a law of March, 1802, may repeal or extinguish it.

This would be true, if Congress was an absolute legislature, possessing power without control.

But Congress is the agent and *creature* of the constitution; like the executive and judiciary, it must act within the bounds prescribed to it by the fundamental law.

The constitution is a charter of grants and reservations. It grants to the Legislative power the right of creating judicial offices; but it reserves the right of fixing the duration of those offices when created under the constitution. It has, in fact, *prescribed* their duration. As soon as Congress have executed their power of establishing the court and the officer is appointed, the provision in the constitution respecting his *continuance* attaches upon their law. It is identified with it; and secures the office to the possessor by his own immutability.[5]

Nothing appears more obvious. It would be easy to shew, that a Legislative Body, acting *under* the controling provisions of a standing and fixed Constitution, may often possess the power to create or grant by *law,* and yet by no act afterwards can repeal or abolish the interest or office arising out of the first law. The Senators from each State may be, and frequently are *appointed by law;* yet a repeal of the law by the *same* legislature, and even another law appointing a substitute, would not abolish the first office. The repeal and the new appointment would be void; because the constitution annexed to the first appointment the term of office, and the officer will hold for his six years, however much dissatisfied the legislature, which made the law, may be with the officer.[6]

By the 2d article of the constitution, it is provided, that Congress, in case of vacancy in the offices of President and Vice-President, "may, by law, declare what officer shall then act as President, and such officer shall act accordingly, until the disability be removed, or a President shall be elected."

In this case the office is filled by a mere *Legislative* act; and yet in virtue of the expression in the Constitution, that the officer so appointed, "should act accordingly, *until* the disability be removed, &c." it will be admitted, that Congress would not have the power to repeal such law, or to appoint by a new law, another person to exercise the powers of President.

It may be remarked here, that the words of "tenure" in regard to this officer to be appointed by *Law,* are not so solemn and explicit as those words in the Constitution respecting *judicial* officers created under a law of Congress.

Many other instances might be put, which readily suggest themselves to the mind, where Legislative *creation,* is not followed with right or power of legislative repeal or extinction.

The repeal of laws under which *grants* have been made, and interests vested, would not rescind the estate or benefit, even though no *constitutional* security existed in favor of the donee or grantee.

And however prejudice may be wrought upon, or ignorance deceived, the *grant* of an office and salary, under the law and constitution, is equally sacred and inviolable as any other interest which can by conveyed by one party and accepted by another.

And when it is considered too, that this covenant, between the government and the officer, is *founded* on the great political principle, of maintaining an INDEPENDENT JUDICIARY, the contract should derive from thence a superior sanction.

The case of other officers, who do not accept appointments under any particular terms of *continuance in office,* is widely different.—They take and hold at the will and pleasure of the President or Congress. This is known to them at the time. The *constitution* has not fixed the conditions or duration of such offices; and, of course, being created by the mere will of the President, or by Congress, may be abolished by the same power.

And yet, if the position be true, that judges have no more permanent interest or estate in *their* offices, and compensations than others, it follows, that those words in the constitution, "that *they,* when appointed, shall hold their offices *during good behavior,* and shall receive for their services a compensation not to be diminished," are wholly insignificant. The *Executive* or *Legislative* may dismiss them, at any time, and for any cause.

But the truth is, that the provision in the Constitution is wise and necessary; and whether it is so or not, while it remains there, the office of a judge, and the compensation annexed to it, are fixed as the charter itself, if he continues to behave well.

The Constitution announces, in explicit terms, that he who is appointed a judge, "shall hold his office during good behaviour, and receive a *certain compensation.*"

The Legislature, when they *create* the office, do it under this constitution. The person who is nominated and appointed by the President and the Senate, receives a commission under the *seal* of the United States, in which he reads these express words, "That he is appointed a judge of the Circuit Court of the United States for the third circuit; and is authorized and empowered to *execute* and *fulfil* the duties of that office, according to the Constitution and laws of the United States; and then follows, words of absolute *grant,* "TO HAVE and to HOLD the said office, with all the powers, privileges and emoluments of the same of right appertaining—DURING HIS GOOD BEHAVIOUR."

With this commission and grant in his hand; with the *law* of Congress, *creating the office* and fixing the *compensation,* to authorize it; and with the *constitution* of the United States before him, positively assuring him, that *the office and the salary* shall be holden by him *during* his *good behaviour,* he accepts it upon the terms offered. And shall he be deprived of *both office and salary* the next month or year? or whenever the *legislature,* who is but *one* out of *three* parties to this solemn covenant, shall be pleased to say, "you are no longer *necessary* or *agreeable,* we can find *judges* to exercise your offices cheaper, or who will be more subservient to our wishes!"

If such principles as these shall be finally sanctioned by American judicatures, if the *people*, the moral, virtuous, and dignified people of the United States, tempted by momentary passion or parsimony, can be brought to sanction them, then will *language* have lost its *meaning*, and the most solemn and sacred contracts made between the *public* and *its citizens*, their obligation.

The ruin of *individuals* and their families, who may have surrendered comfortable livings and lost honorable and lucrative offices, upon the *plighted faith* of the United States, ought to arrest such destructive tenets.

But the *preservation of political freedom* itself is concerned in the rejection of such doctrines. Let it once be decided by *legislatures* and *courts of justice*, that words mean nothing when applied to *judges* and their compensations, and the constitution is at an end. They have equal right and power to say, and when the *temptation* occurs will say, that they mean *nothing* in any *other* case. Surely it deserves to be *considered*, whether the *adoption* of such principles must not gradually impair *all confidence* in *public* institutions and *public* faith; and in the end, *vitiate* the *public* morals beyond the reach of reformation.

It has been made a question, whether the *judiciary* can lawfully decide, that a *legislative act is contrary to the constitution*, and for that reason hold it void. It has been said, that it must be *obeyed*; that the *judges of the United States* are bound to yield to it and execute it.

I deem it quite unnecessary to range after proofs, shewing the error and danger of such an opinion. Perhaps it no where exists.

This power can, however, be demonstrated by a train of reasons and consequences, drawn from the *nature* of a *limited* legislature, and the *peculiar* province of a national *judiciary*, in a manner incapable of refutation. It will be sufficient for me, however, to rest my answer to such an objection upon the TERMS of the *constitution*, and the natural and necessary effect of them.

By the third article and in the second section it is declared, that the JUDICIAL POWER shall extend to all cases in *law* and equity arising *under* the CONSTITUTION, the LAWS of the United States, and TREATIES.

Whensoever, then, a case shall be brought before the *judges of the United States*, wherein, on *one side* it is contended that a *particular act* of the legislative body is void, as being contrary to the constitution of the United States, and, on the other, that it is not contrary to it, *that* will be a *case arising* both under the constitution and law of the United States; and, of course, by the express terms of the constitution, falls under the *judicial* power.

By the sixth article it is expressly provided and declared, "that this *constitution*, and the *laws* made in *pursuance* thereof, &c. shall be the *supreme law* of the land." Hence it follows that the *constitution* is the *supreme law*, and the particular *acts* of the *legislative body* are only supreme when made *pursuant* or in conformity to that, which is the fixed and overruling STAT-UTE enacted by *all the people*, and only to be changed, altered, or opposed by the power that made it.

If then the *constitution* is the *supreme law*, the *judicial* department, in whom is *vested* by the same instrument the *right* and duty of expounding and enforcing the *law*, must necessarily be *governed* by it.

Whenever *any question*, however, or wherever, it may *originate* comes before the judges, they *must* decide according to *law*.

If the controversy happen to turn upon the *opposing* terms of the *constitution*, and the *act* of the Legislative body, still the judges must decide, and decide *according to law*.

The *Executive* or *Legislative* may err; they may, like other men, from inadvertency, from error of opinion, from some too prevalent bias, or from design, commit an *unconstitutional act*. Every *citizen*, and every *state*, is entitled to the benefits of the *constitution*, which is declared the *supreme* law, and the *judicial* power of the United States is that organ and independent branch of the government whose duty and right it is, to pronounce and execute the *law*.

Whenever a question arises, which is law? or what is the law? whether it arises out of doubtful or conflicting acts of the legislature or between the words and provisions of the legislative, the *judicial* department *decides* the controversy.

If one side insists upon the *act of Congress*, and the other upon the *act of the people* as contained in the constitution, the judges are required by the *nature* of their office, by a positive oath and by *express articles* in the latter *instrument* to support it as the *supreme* or governing law; and to reject and declare *void* whatever is *contrary* to it, in the act of the Legislative body, or other authority, *subordinate* to the Constitution.

It can be said, that the *judges* may err, and determine measures and acts to be contrary to the constitution which are not so.

Certainly the *judicial* department *may* decide wrong.[7]

All human tribunals are liable to error. The executive may err, and the Legislative often err. But there must be *somewhere,* a power to determine what *is the law of the land,* and thereby to settle and quiet, whether right or wrong, legal *rights* and *constructions.* Force and the sword, or some CIVIL JURISDICTION must finally adjust these domestic controversies.

Wise and free *people* with free forms of Government, have confided this important, but *essential* power, to their JUDICIAL institutions.[8] They endeavour to compose those institutions of their most *experienced* and learned men.—These they render *permanent* in office, and *insure* to them *fixed* and adequate *compensations* whilst they *behave well.* In short, they render them *independent* of *hope* or *fear;* and as free from *undue influence,* as the lot of mortality will admit.

They subject them to trial, loss of office and disgrace for *misconduct.* With so many public precautions to ensure wisdom and perfect rectitude, and with so many motives operating upon the judges to act well, human society can frame no *higher security* for the preservation of justice and the laws. *Error,* with all these guards against it, may *possibly,* after every grade of revision and appeal, be ultimately sanctioned by the SUPREME COURT of the union. This will indeed but rarely happen, yet, because there *must* be some *umpire,* to settle *"what is law,"* the judicial branch, in the last resort, is that which decides without appeal.

The *people,* indeed, by a *constitutional act,* may, if the occasion demands it, *correct* an error even here. But *until* then, every *department,* every officer, every *citizen* of the United States is *bound* to yield to the sentence of the judicial department, *judicially* declaring what *is the* law.

If we look only into the Constitution for one moment, and see the various *checks* and *limitations* upon Legislative power, and in favor of the *states* and *citizens,* all declared to be the *supreme law of the land,* and consider, for a moment, the *nature* of the *judicial power,* to which is expressly delegated the right of deciding *all* questions *arising* under the *constitution* and *laws* of the United States; and that without this power in the *judiciary* to extend to the states and citizens the benefits of the *constitution* as a *supreme law,* they can only be obtained through force and blood; no rational doubt can be entertained that it is the *right,* and indeed the highest duty of the *judges,* if convinced that a law of Congress, is opposed to the *laws of the people,* as enacted in the constitution, to pronounce it, for that reason a nullity and void.

These are my views of the judicial power. I never entertained the least scruple upon this point; considering it as clear as the constitution itself. *Judicial determinations* too, of the highest authority, have placed this question, or ought to have placed it at rest. On the *pension* law, the *judges of the supreme court* agreed, that it was unconstitutional, and *Congress,* acquiescing in the determination, repealed so much as was by them held void.

On the *carriage tax,* the question was brought, by a citizen of Virginia, before the *supreme court,* on the *very point,* that the law was *unconstitutional.* The judges determined it was *not contrary* to the constitution; but their *power* and *right* to determine *otherwise* were never questioned; and they *affirmed the law,* not on the ground that they were *obliged* to execute a *law of Congress,* but on the principle of its *conformity* and being *pursuant* to the constitution.

These are the *general* grounds and reasonings upon which *my* judgement is founded, that the acts of Congress of the 8th March, and 29th of April, 1802, do *not abolish the offices* of the *judges,* under the law of the 13th February, 1801. I hold those acts, so far as they are designed to *abolish the offices* of those judges, *void,* because directly *contrary to the Constitution of the United States,* which established them *in the judges,* when once created and vested, *during their good behaviour.*

I feel myself called upon, in this place, to notice an opinion, which some entertain, who hold, that *Congress,* by no act, can deprive a *judge* of his *judicial capacity,* and the *salary* annexed to his *original office:* But that Congress *may* abolish the particular *court,* of which he is the judge, and *transfer* the judicial powers, which were exercised in that court, to any *other* existing courts and judges of the United States; or may *create other* courts of the same or different name and territorial limits, and vest the same powers in those courts, to be composed of newly created judges, or judges already appointed, belonging to any other court of the United-States.

That *Congress* can, by no *lawful* means, deprive a judge of his judicial *capacity,* or commission, and if by *their act,* and not by his own neglect, refusal, or misbehaviour, he is *left* without any judicial services to perform, they are bound to pay him the stipulated compensation, unless he voluntarily relinquishes it, cannot well be doubted by any, who take the *constitution as a law,* or *moral obligation* for a *principle* of human action. And so far I agree in the foregoing opinion, that the *commission* to *hold* such a court remains, and the salary annexed to it:—But the *constitution* of the United States, by that clause which secures to judges their *office* during good behaviour, was surely designed to answer *much higher purposes* than merely to entitle him to the *name* and technical qualities and *capacities* of a *judge,* and to the *compensation* stipulated between him and the public.

It was plainly and principally designed to secure to *him* the substantial *exercise* of the *judicial powers and rights* annexed to the office, at its creation; but *beyond* that the *great and important end* of the provision was to *render the judge* INDEPENDENT of *legislative* and *executive* power, for the benefit of the *people* and the *States,* in the administration of the laws.

Once abandon *this ground,* and allow that Congress may *strip the judges of the courts* of the United States of *all* their *judicial powers,* by *abolishing the courts* which they are *commissioned to fill,* and by giving the *whole* of their jurisdiction to *other* courts and judges, (provided only the *capacity* of judge, and the *salary* in virtue of that, and the contract, is continued) I say, once establish *this,* and the *most important* and most obvious *intent* of the constitution is defeated.

The judiciary is compleatly, and if the foregoing opinion be true, constitutionally DEPENDENT on the *will* of the *legislative* department. If a judge or any set of judges become obnoxious, because they will not bend to the dominant party, or execute acts however *opposed* to the constitution, and they may be removed from the *exercise of their offices,* and their powers be *lawfully* transferred to others, it is in vain to talk of an *independent* judiciary. Successive legislatures will find or make judges to answer their views; and those who are *dismissed* (as in the case that has happened) may not only be *left* without any *judicial powers* of office, but even without *subsistence* itself!

It is said in the constitution, "that *courts* shall be established and that *the judges,* both of the supreme and inferior *courts,* should *hold their offices* during good behaviour."

What is *meant,* what can be meant by this, but that when courts are *established,* and judges are *appointed* for those courts, those judges shall have a *right,* and are *vested* with an indefeasible power, during their good behavior, to *hold* courts and to *exercise in them* some judicial powers.

Can it be seriously contended, that the *judges,* under the act of Feb. 13, 1801, do "*hold the office* thereby created and expressly granted to *them in their commissions,* within the meaning of those words in the constitution? *When,* at the same time, it is maintained, that *all* their *courts* are *rightfully* abolished, and all the *judicial powers* annexed to those courts, in their creation, and every action and proceeding in those courts, *rightfully* transferred to *other* courts of the *same name* and nature, and composed of judges who are to *execute* those identical powers.

"Holding their offices," according to the *manifest intent* of the constitution, in my apprehension means nothing short of the full *right* of *continuing in, and exercising,* the *judicial powers* attached to the court they compose.

If we *execute* those powers, we *hold the office.* If others *execute* them, they *hold the office.* The only question is, to whom, of *constitutional right,* does it *belong to execute them?*

Those who maintain the great and salutary principle of an independent judiciary, *resulting from the constitutional tenure of office during good behaviour,* and who are not prepared to resign it for an empty *name,* must, I apprehend, be brought to this, as the only sound and satisfactory conclusion—That the *judges of a court* once ordained and established by congress, have, in virtue of their office, and as *essentially constituting the office itself a vested title,* under the *constitution,* to hold the *court* and *exercise* the *judicial powers attached to it.*

I deem it superfluous to consider what *congress* may or may not do lawfully in modifications and amendments, by altering the *sessions,* varying *territorial* limits of jurisdiction, changing the *style* of courts and judges, *adding* to and *diminishing* the stock of judicial *powers* and *duties* in the same court.

It is said, that should it be construed, that the *office of a judge* "consists in an *exclusive* right to exercise *"all the judicial powers"* attached to it, in its creation and no others, this might prove *inconvenient;* I answer, that if this *is* the sound construction, or the one attended with the *least* bad consequences inasmuch as it complies with the *words* of the constitution, and *maintains* the *independence* of the judges (its favorite object) it *ought to prevail,* leaving the inconveniences, if they exist, to *constitutional,* and not to *legislative* amendment.

In *practice* it has not been found necessary to make any essential changes or alterations of jurisdiction in civil or criminal cases in the courts of justice hitherto established.

But it need not be contended, that the legislature are prevented under the construction which I give to the constitution in this particular, from adding to, diminishing, or altering the judicial powers and duties of the established courts. The offices of the judges will not be destroyed; they will still "hold their offices," provided they *hold courts* and *exercise judicial powers.* If it be said, that this being admitted, *congress* may, if so disposed, as effectually *reduce the offices* of the judges and their *independence,* by circumscribing their limits of territory and subjects of jurisdiction, to a mere sound; or by imposing *impracticable duties,* drive them from office; I answer, that such open *abuses* are not to be presumed, and *when* they happen, the act producing them would be *void.* It would be a *fraud* on the office of the judge and on the constitution, and would be held up so by all judges bound to support the constitution as the Supreme Law.

The *line* which divides rightful authority from abuse of it, so as to become *unconstitutional,* cannot and need not be defined or conjectured. When the occasion furnishes ground for the question, the *judges* will exercise a *judicial discretion* upon it. There can be no other or safer criterion.

But, to whatever length or extreme of *abuse* an act of congress might *lawfully* go in this particular, still, however, leaving to the judges *courts* and the *exercise* of *judicial powers,* what I contend for is; that a *law* which abolishes the *courts,* and *all the judicial powers* of one set of judges *lawfully appointed,* and transfers to *new courts,* and to other judges the same judicial powers, leaving the first without *any official* rights, or provision for their salaries, is unconstitutional and void. *Such* a law or laws carry on the *face* of them indubitable signs and evidence of a *design* in the legislature to *take away from the first judges their offices,* and are therefore manifestly contrary to the letter and the spirit of the constitution.[9]

Such an act made and operating against the words, the true intent, and obvious policy of the *Constitution,* is not to *prevail.*

The judges, to whom the same office, in *effect,* is transferred, will not *accept the legislative commission,* nor, by executing the act, participate in the overthrow of the Constitution. Taking *that* as the *supreme law* of the people they are bound to reject, as *void,* every measure which if *carried into effect* by them would directly or indirectly defeat any of its provisions.

The abolition of the *courts and the exercise of all the judicial powers of the judges,* and the *deprivation of their salaries,* furnishes a *case* which seems to involve no question of "*degree,*" to which the legislative body may rightfully invade the *offices* of the judges. It attempts to abolish *both office and judge entire*. The true question is, whether such an act with *such* intent and operation is not unconstitutional?

The judges who are called in to *execute* such an act in *any way,* are bound to consider whether it was *constitutional*. If they are of opinion it was not, then they are to refuse any *cooperation,* which would effectuate, or *tend* to effectuate the *consequences* and designs proposed by the prohibited act of the Legislature.

The *repealing act* of the 3d of March, 1802, of itself, designing to abolish the *courts* and *judges* created by that of February, 1801, was prohibited by the constitution; it was void, and the judges still retain their *rights* of office.

The *judges* designated to execute the repealing act of the 8th of March, 1802, and the amending act of 29th of April, 1802, or, in other terms, the judges called upon to *assist* and *sanction* the usurpation and illegality, if such is the opinion they entertain of those acts must necessarily refuse to participate or aid in their design and consequences.

It has been said, that the act of February, 1801, inasmuch as it abolished the *circuit courts* under the act of the 24th of September, 1789, justifies the opinion that *Congress* may *abolish courts,* and *transfer all the judicial powers and jurisdiction* of those courts, to newly erected courts of the same name and nature, to be composed of newly appointed judges.

A short and decisive answer presents itself. The cases are *dissimilar.*

No Judges were ever *appointed* and *commissioned* to exercise the judicial powers and duties attached to the *first circuit courts.*

These were performed by the judges of the *supreme* and *district courts,* who were directed to hold them by *law,* having no *executive* commissions *as judges of those courts.*

Congress, in abolishing those courts abolished no *judges or offices.* No judicial *tenure of office* was in the least affected. The judges of the *supreme* and *district courts* still contintinued [*sic*] in possession of *their proper respective courts* and *salaries.* They merely officiated in the *circuit courts,* under a kind of *legislative commission,* which *attached* these duties to their proper and distinct judicial offices. *Congress* might, of course, lawfully *discharge* them from those duties, leaving them in *full* possession of their original and *appropriate jurisdictions.*—Should *all* the judges of a court die or resign, Congress, by abolishing such courts, would effect no judicial tenure of office.[10] The *circuit courts* of 1789, were in a similar case. No judges *belonged to them,* or exercised the judicial powers in *right of constitutional office during good behaviour.* The abolition therefore of these courts was unattended with any invasion of *judicial office or compensation.* As to the abolition of the *district courts of Tennessee and Kentucky* by the act of Feb. 1801, that neither, if properly viewed, will justify the attempt which has been made to abolish *judges and their offices.*

The act does not *abolish a single judicial power* before exercised by the district judges. It *increases* their powers and also their salaries. It does not *abolish* their *judicial offices* but continues them in full *exercise* of their rights and duties, as *judges.*[11] It *preserves* to them their official name of district judges. The only essential operation of the act was to change the name of the courts, in which they were to exercise their offices, with some territorial alterations and regulations, tending to render the *exercise of their offices* more convenient.

It is not pretended that the *name* of a court is unchangeable, or that any other alterations may not be made, consistent with the *holding of the substantial rights of office and compensation annexed to the judge at his creation.*

After these observations, it remains only, that I should conclude with a *distinct* exhibition of my *opinions, resolutions,* and *motives.*

And First: For the reasons assigned, I maintain, as my deliberate, solemn, and judicial opinion, that the acts of March and April, 1802, designing and operating *substantially to abolish* the *offices and salaries* of the judges under the law of the eleventh of February, 1801, are so far *unconstitutional,* and for that reason *void.*

And further, that the *judges* of these courts respectively do of right still *"hold their offices,"* as at first.[12]

Secondly, nevertheless, those acts of March and April, 1802, create many *impediments* which oppose the *execution* of our offices.

The discontinuance of our *compensations,* the destruction of our *sessions,* as to time and place, the privation of *officers,* and other *evident* embarrassments occasioned by the operation of those acts, on subjects of mere *legislative organization,* must create, a *suspension* of the *exercise* of our powers of office *until* Congress shall, by law, provide the *means* necessary to their execution. We shall respectively stand acquitted under such circumstances, if no attempt is made to *hold* our Courts, which might be productive of disorder, unseemly conflict and error.

Should the opinion herein delivered, on this important question, *finally* prevail, no doubt can be entertained, but that the *legislative body* will with alacrity and good faith, pass such *laws* as may cure the *discontinuance* of the courts, and enable them to *resume* their usual and constitutional functions.

Thirdly: In the *interim,* I hold it my bounded duty to *claim* the office thus appertaining to me, and publickly to PROTEST against the acts of all *persons* and *authorities,* who are *designated* by the laws of the 8*th of March* and 29th *of April* 1802, who may in any wise interfere with, or prevent, or tend to prevent, the restoration and full exercise of my office, as one of the judges of the circuit courts of the United States for the 3d circuit.[13]

Fourthly. In circumstances so peculiar, and in a case of such *magnitude,* I conceive it an obvious *right* to give *publicity* to the foregoing opinions and reasons.[14]

The *judges,* under the act of February 1801, have been left without any *other means* of declaring and making known *their* sentiments and claims.

To those who know the course of my life, the time at which it has arrived, and the *principles* which professedly (and I trust really) govern it, will acquit me of any views inimical to the peace of my country, or to its constituted authorities. I have spent the best of my years in *efforts,* at least, to attain and secure *true civil liberty:* and the stations I have filled, by the favour and confidence of my fellow-citizens, have afforded me the highest opportunities, in public situations, of being useful to the extent of my humble abilities, yet the *act* which I shall now subscribe, is far the most important of my life, with reference to human obligation.

If any *difference* of opinion, between me and my *associates* in office, exists, it relates merely to the *point of time* for expressing our sentiments. I can confidently assert, that on deliberation, they *coincide* with me in other respects.

But whatever deference was justly due to the ideas of others, my *own conscience* and judgment, after weighing every consideration, dictated the present line of conduct.

I have delivered my thoughts for the benefit of those who are called to reflect on this interesting subject. They are feebly expressed; perhaps erroneously conceived; they are however *sincere.*

My most ardent wish is that the *termination* of this conflict may produce *safety* to our Country, and CONSTITUTION.

I have done what I deemed a sacred duty in SUPPORT OF THAT CON-
STITUTION. I have done it *now*, because my *life* may not be spared till tomorrow.

I commit all to those who must *ultimately* DECIDE, satisfied that
honor, intelligence, and *independence* will guide and sanction their judgment.

RICHARD BASSETT.

Dated at Bohemia, the 14th
day of August, 1802.

NOTES

Abbreviations

Annals	United States Congress, *Annals of Congress* (1857–1861).
AHA Report	*Annual Report of the American Historical Association* (1913).
Burr	Mary Jo Kline and Joanne Wood Ryan, eds., *Political Correspondence and Public Papers of Aaron Burr* (1983).
Elliot	Jonathan Elliot, ed., *The Debates in the Several State Conventions on the Adoption of the Federal Constitution* (1836).
Farrand	Max Farrand, ed., *The Records of the Federal Convention of 1787* (1911).
Gallatin	Henry Adams, *The Life of Gallatin* (1879).
History	George Lee Haskins and Herbert A. Johnson, *Foundations of Power: John Marshall, 1801–1815* (1981). Oliver Wendell Holmes Devise History of the Supreme Court of the United States, vol. 2.
Hist Docs	Michael Nelson, ed., *Historic Documents on Presidential Elections, 1787–1988* (1991).
Jeff	Andrew A. Lipscomb and Albert Ellery Bergh, eds., *The Writings of Thomas Jefferson* (1905).
LC	Library of Congress.
LJM	Albert Beveridge, *The Life of John Marshall* (1916–1919).
Mad	David B. Mattern et al., eds., *The Papers of James Madison* (1991).
PJM	Charles F. Hobson et al., eds., *The Papers of John Marshal* (1987).
PAH	Harold C. Syrett et al., eds., *The Papers of Alexander Hamilton* (1976).
WJA	Charles Francis Adams, ed., *The Works of John Adams* (1850–1856).
WOM	Stanislaus Murray Hamilton, ed., *The Writings of James Monroe* (1898–1903).
WPF	Bruce Ackerman, *We the People: Foundations* (1991).
WPT	Bruce Ackerman, *We the People: Transformations* (1998).
WTJ	Paul Leicester Ford, ed., *The Writings of Thomas Jefferson* (1896).

PART ONE Introduction: America on the Brink

1. *Washington Federalist,* Feb. 12, 1801.
2. 5 U.S. (1 Cranch) 137 (1803).

3. See *WPT* 212–218; Gordon Wood, *The Creation of the American Republic, 1776–1787*, ch. 8 (1969).

4. The Eleventh Amendment, enacted in 1798, is generally—and wrongly—treated as if it were a detail for specialists, rather than a chapter in the big story. This is even truer of the Twelfth Amendment, dealing with reform of the electoral college, which I will be discussing in due course.

5. In fact, the starring role currently assigned to *Marbury* is a creation of conservative elites during the early twentieth century. Before then, *Marbury* played a minor role in legal understanding. See Davison Douglas, "The Rhetorical Uses of Marbury v. Madison: The Emergence of a 'Great Case,'" 38 *Wake For. L. Rev.* 375, 387–407 (2003). As Douglas demonstrates, the canonization of *Marbury* was part of a larger effort to celebrate the Court as the ultimate bastion of property rights against the populist threat of regulation and redistribution. This book is also part of a more general reinterpretation. But this time the key question isn't *Marbury's* relationship to the protection of private property, but its relationship to the ideal of popular sovereignty in general and presidential leadership in particular.

6. The two books whose authors most closely share my ambition are Stephen Skowronek, *The Politics Presidents Make* (1997) and James Ceasar, *Presidential Selection* (1979). I have been greatly influenced by both, and in ways that particular notes cannot acknowledge.

1. The Original Misunderstanding

1. From this vantage, Seymour Martin Lipset's *The First American Nation*, 1–99 (1963), deserves far more attention than it has received recently.

2. See *WPT*, chs. 2–3.

3. Lewis B. Namier, *The Structure of Politics at the Accession of George III* (1929). While Edmund Burke had begun to question the traditional view of parties, Richard Hofstadter couldn't find anybody in late eighteenth-century America who took Burke's proposal seriously. See Hofstadter, *The Idea of a Party System*, 29–35 (1969).

4. See Hofstadter, *Idea of a Party System*, 1–39.

5. For a more elaborate reading of Federalist thought see *WPF*, ch. 7. See also Hofstadter, *Idea of a Party System*, 40–73; Daniel Sisson, *The American Revolution of 1800*, 23–69 (1974); Gordon S. Wood, *The Creation of the American Republic 1776–1787*, 559–560 (1969).

6. For a blow-by-blow account see Bernard A. Weisberger, *America Afire*, chs. 3–11 (2000).

7. See Jeffrey Palsey, "1800 as a Revolution in Political Culture," in James Horn, Jan Lewis, and Peter Onuf, eds., *The Revolution of 1800*, 121, 135–141 (2002).

8. See John Hoadley, *Origins of American Political Parties, 1789–1803,* 144 (1986).

9. Noble Cunningham, *In Pursuit of Reason,* 223–225, 224–226 (1987).

10. On the 1796 vice-presidential contest see Roy F. Nichols, *The Invention of the American Political Parties,* 194–198 (1967). In a world without professional politicians, party loyalty was obtained largely through appeals to norms of honor and gentlemanly conduct. But this did not make it any less effective. See Joanne Freeman, *Affairs of Honor,* ch. 5 (2001).

11. See Joanne Freeman, "The Election of 1800: A Study in the Logic of Political Change," 108 *Yale L. J.* 1959, 1975–78 (1999).

12. See Palsey, "1800 as a Revolution," 144–147; Hoadley, *American Political Parties,* 186. Consider, for example, Samuel Purviance's appeal for support in a congressional race in North Carolina in 1800: "To those of my Fellow-Citizens with whom I have not a personal Acquaintance, and who may not therefore be informed of my Political Principles, it may be necessary to state, that I am what the Phraseology of Politicians has denominated a FEDERALIST. But, although I am the Friend of Order, of Government, and of the present Administration, I will not pledge myself to support in Consequence of a selfish, or a bigoted Policy, any Governmental Measure which I might think pernicious to the General Welfare of our Country, or the particular Interests of yourselves." Quoted in Noble Cunningham, ed., *The Making of the American Party System: 1789 to 1809,* 137 (1965).

13. The rise of political parties in the 1790s has been the subject of ongoing scholarly debate since Charles Beard took it up in his *Economic Origins of Jeffersonian Democracy* (1915). This note relates my discussion of the scholarly literature.

Important work of the mid-twentieth century presented the Federalists and the Republicans as if they were the creators of a "first party system" similar to those established by later generations. For a useful survey, see William Chambers, ed., *The First Party System: Federalists and Republicans* (1972). The most notable contributions include Joseph Charles, *The Origins of the American Party System* (1956), Noble Cunningham, *The Jeffersonian Republicans* (1957); and Manning Dauer, *The Adams Federalists* (2d ed., 1953). This work contributed greatly to historical understanding, but flirted with anachronism.

More recent historians, notably Ronald Formisano, provided a needed corrective. See his "Deferential-Participant Politics: The Early Republic's Political Culture, 1789–1840," 68 *Amer. Pol. Sci. Rev.* 473 (1974); "Federalists and Republicans: Parties, Yes—System, No," in Paul Kleppner et al., eds., *The Evolution of American Electoral Systems,* 33–76 (1981); and The *Transformation of Political Culture* (1983).

I follow Formisano on two points. First, he rightly cautions against characterizing the 1790s as involving a two-party "system"—since this word tempts us to suppose that the two parties believed that rotation in office was to be expected and desired. Nothing could be further from the truth. Second, he rightly emphasizes that "Federalists" and "Republicans" were the names of rival groups of notables whose political activities flowed naturally from their general dominance in community life. There were no statewide organizations controlled by professional politicians concerned with winning elections and managing patronage. Since strong party organization was lacking, the rivalry between the two parties ebbed and flowed—bursting into the open during periods, like 1797–1801 and 1811–1815, when great issues agitated local and national elites, but subsiding at times when ideological questions seemed less pressing. If, following Formisano, one defines a "political party" as an enduring and autonomous organization, one might well doubt whether "Federalists" and "Republicans" qualified as "parties" in many places outside the capital cities of Philadelphia and Washington.

I reject Formisano's stipulative definition. My notion of a "movement-party" elaborates the type of formation that disrupted the nation's political life in ways that the Founding document failed to anticipate, and did much to exacerbate. Indeed, the absence of nuts-and-bolts political organization may well account for the ferocity of party conflict. The bitterness of the antagonisms might have been diluted by the admixture of more practical political types concerned with bread-and-butter issues. (As we shall see in Chapters 4 and 5, Congressman Bayard's interest in patronage was an important factor in ending the constitutional crisis peacefully.)

More broadly, a fixation on the weakness of specialized political organizations serves to obscure the many other ways in which the rise of political parties "in the years between 1789 to 1803 [was] nothing short of remarkable." Hoadley, *American Political Parties*, 190. Hoadley's book contains the most rigorous empirical investigation undertaken thus far, and provides evidentiary support for my approach to the subject. See also the summary in Richard McCormick, *The Second American Party System*, ch. 2 (1966).

14. "Farewell Address," in Janet Podell and Steven Anzovin, eds., *Speeches of the American Presidents*, 21–22 (2d ed., 2001).

15. On both the politics and substance of the Address see Stanley Elkins and Eric McKitrick, *The Age of Federalism*, 489–497 (1993).

16. Lance Banning puts the proviso well: "In an age when political factions were universally condemned, when persistent opposition to the government in power aroused suspicions of disloyalty to the state, resistance to constitutional degeneration—and that almost alone—could transmute members of a political faction into patriotic defenders of the common good. Men who joined together to resist a threat to liberty, who stood against a governmental plot, were something other than a band of factional politicians." Banning, *The Jeffersonian Persuasion*, 206 (1978).

17. 14 *Mad* 197 ("Parties," Jan. 23, 1792).

18. Id., 370, 371–372 (Sept. 22, 1792).

19. See, e.g., Jefferson to Mazzei, Apr. 24, 1796, in 7 *WTJ* 72, 75–76 (Federalists were an "Anglican[,] monarchical, & aristocratical party").

20. The excesses of the French Revolution did not diminish Jefferson's ardor. He considered the beheading of Louis XVI an "absolute necessity," and he discounted the Reign of Terror: "My own affections have been deeply wounded by some of the martyrs to this cause, but rather than it should have failed, I would have seen half the earth desolated. Were there but an Adam and an Eve left in every country, and left free, it would be better than as it now is." See Conor Cruise O'Brien, *The Long Affair, 1785–1800,* 38–68, 113–151 (1996), for a scandalized commentary (he quotes Jefferson's remarks on Adam and Eve at 145).

21. See generally Banning, *Jeffersonian Persuasion.*

22. See Lipset, *First American Nation.*

23. For a summary of this story, see Weisberger, *America Afire,* 200–224.

24. On the Convention's difficulties, see Jack Rakove, "The Political Presidency: Discovery and Invention," in Horn, Lewis, and Onuf, eds., *Revolution of 1800,* 30. For more detail, see the outstanding essay by Shlomo Slonim, "The Electoral College at Philadelphia: The Evolution of an Ad Hoc Congress for the Selection of a President," 73 *J. Amer. Hist.* 35 (1986). I am also indebted to James Ceasar's *Presidential Selection: Theory and Development,* ch. 1 (1979). John Roche, "The Founding Fathers: A Reform Caucus in Action," 55 *Amer. Pol. Sci. Rev.* 799, 810–813 (1961), is also stimulating but underestimates the basic constitutional values at stake in the clever engineering.

25. The Brearley group was selected on August 31. 1 *Elliot* 280.

26. 2 *Farrand* 505–531.

27. 2 *Farrand* 501 (James Wilson, Sept. 4, 1787).

28. Id. See also id.: "the increasing intercourse among the people of the States would render important characters less & less unknown" (Mr. Baldwin, Sept. 4).

29. George Mason was the most emphatic, asserting that the electoral college would fail to select a winner "nineteen times out of twenty." 2 *Farrand* 500 (Sept. 4), 512 (Sept. 5).

30. 2 *Farrand* 512 (Sept. 5). Morris was Pennsylvania's representative on the Brearley Committee, which did not make a formal report in support of its recommendations on presidential selection. His arguments were probably representative of the Committee, since they echo similar points made earlier by other members. See the remarks of Hugh Williamson, Gouverneur Morris, and James Madison, id., 113–114 (July 25).

31. U.S. Const., art. II, §1, cl. 3.

32. 2 *Farrand* 494.

33. The phrase is Hugh Williamson's, id., 524. See also 527 (remarks of Williamson, Sherman, and Mason).

34. In 1800 Virginia had 22 representatives in the House. U.S. Census Bureau, *Historical Statistics of the United States,* 13, 693 (1960).

35. The Senate retained the power to select a vice president if the leading candidates were tied after the House selected the president.

36. "Mr. Madison considered it as a primary object to render an eventual resort to any part of the Legislature improbable." 2 *Farrand* 513 (Sept. 5). Later in the day, Madison moved to enable the electoral college to name the president if "1/3 of the Electors should vote for the same person." Id., 514. Hamilton wanted to eliminate the backup procedure entirely by awarding the presidency to the electoral college winner regardless of his number of votes. Id., 525 (Sept. 6).

37. The anxieties of the small states provided a leitmotiv for the Convention's interminable discussions of presidential selection. See Slonim, "Electoral College," 48–50, 51, 55–56. When Madison made his proposal to dilute the required electoral college majority, he immediately encountered the objection that his amendment "would put it in the power of three or four States to put in whom they pleased." 2 *Farrand* 514 (Elbridge Gerry, Sept. 5). His proposal lost by a vote of 2 to 9. Id.

38. On August 24 the Convention was considering a plan under which the president would be elected by a joint session of the House and Senate, each member casting a single ballot: "Mr. Read moved 'that in case the numbers of the highest in votes should be equal, then the President of the Senate shall have an additional casting vote,' which was disagreed to by a general negative." 2 *Farrand* 403.

39. On the partisan dynamics, see Rakove, "Political Presidency." For more detail, see Tadahisa Kuroda, *The Origins of the Twelfth Amendment,* 72–82 (1994).

40. Kuroda, *Twelfth Amendment,* 83–98.

41. See James Lewis Jr., "'What Is to Become of Our Government?': The Revolutionary Potential of the Election of 1800," in Horn, Lewis, and Onuf, *Revolution of 1800,* 3, 13.

42. As Jefferson explained to Burr immediately after learning of the tie vote: "It was badly managed not to have arranged with certainty what seems to have been left to hazard. It was the more material, because I understand several of the high-flying federalists have expressed their hope that the two republican tickets may be equal, and their determination in that case to prevent a choice in the House of Representatives, (which they are strong enough to do,) and let the government devolve on a President of the Senate. Decency required that I should be so entirely passive during the late contest that I never once asked whether arrangements had been made to prevent so many from dropping votes intentionally, as might frustrate half the republican wish; nor did I doubt, till lately, that such had been made." Jefferson to Burr, Dec. 18, 1800, 4 H. W. Washington, ed., *Writings of Thomas Jefferson,* 340 (1854).

43. After an admirably thorough study of the 1798 elections, Dauer concluded

that it "resulted in the choice of 63 Federalists to 43 Republicans." See Dauer, *The Adams Federalists*, 233 (1953). While his analysis is basically sound, party labels don't inexorably predict voting behavior. Nine of Dauer's 63 "Federalists" voted against their party half the time or more during the second session of Congress: Alston, Dent, Goode, Gray, Huger, Jones, Nott, Parker, and Taliaferro. Three had been replaced by Republicans by the time of the lame-duck session: Foster by Lincoln, Hartley by Stewart, and Marshall by Tasewell.

Republicans demonstrated greater solidarity. Only Samuel Smith of Maryland showed signs of wavering allegiance during the first session of Congress, but he had returned to the fold in the second session.

These shifts imply a significant shrinkage of the Federalist majority by February 1801. But the party still effectively commanded at least a four-vote majority in the House. (See Dauer, id., app. 3, 317–325, for the roll-call data.) As a consequence, they easily won some preliminary procedural skirmishes dealing with the House runoff (see Chapter 4).

44. Jefferson to Monroe, Dec. 20, 1800, Jefferson Papers 18511, LC, available at *http://memory.loc.gov/ammem/mtjhtml/mtjser1.html*.

45. 10 *Annals* 1028.

46. Aristides, "On the Election of the President I," *National Intelligencer*, Dec. 24, 1800.

47. Aristides, "On the Election of the President II," id., Jan. 15, 1801. Aristides was presenting an argument from principle. In fact, the "one state–one vote" rule had the paradoxical consequence of enhancing Jefferson's strength in the House (see Chapter 4). But Aristides did not stoop to this strategic point in denouncing any House effort to displace the popular judgment.

48. "A Plain Fact," *New England Palladium*, Jan. 20, 1801. For other articles to similar effect, see *Columbian Centinel* (Boston), Dec. 24, 1800; *Philadelphia Gazette*, Dec. 31, 1800, Jan. 2, 1801; *United States Chronicle*, Jan. 1, 1801; *New England Palladium*, Feb. 27, 1801. Garry Wills develops this theme with great cogency in *"Negro President": Jefferson and the Slave Power*, 47–89 (2003).

49. Linda Kerber, *Federalism in Dissent*, 23–66 (1970); Paul Finkelman, "The Problem of Slavery in the Age of Federalism," in Doron Ben-Atar and Barbara Oberg, eds., *Federalists Reconsidered*, 135–156 (1998).

2. John Marshall for President

1. Gallatin to his wife, Jan. 15, 1801, in *Gallatin*, 252. For a vivid description see James Young, *The Washington Community*, 1–7 (1966).

2. Gallatin to his wife, Jan. 22, 1801, *Gallatin*, 255.

3. Pickering to Rufus King, 3 King, *The Life and Correspondence of Rufus King,* 366 (1896). See also James Truslow Adams, *The Living Jefferson,* 300 (1936); 2 *LJM,* 539.

4. Jefferson to Judge Breckenridge, Dec 18, 1800, 7 *WTJ* 469.

5. For a useful overview of the constitutional and unconstitutional possibilities, see James Lewis, "'What Is to Become of Our Government?' The Revolutionary Potential of the Election of 1800," in James Horn, Jan Lewis, and Peter Onuf, eds., *The Revolution of 1800,* 3 and figs. 1.1 and 1.2 (2003). But Lewis does not provide a legally nuanced account of the historical debate surrounding these options. Garry Wills does better, but he omits some options entirely and gives short shrift to others. See his *"The Negro President": Jefferson and the Slave Power,* ch. 2 (2003).

6. 1 Stat. 239 (1792). These provisions were changed in 1886, when a new statute authorized Congress to decide whether to call a special election to pick a new president. Ch. 4, §1, 24 Stat. 1 (1886). The possibility of a special election was not eliminated until 1947. See 3 U.S.C. §19 (2000). The Twenty-fifth Amendment, effective in 1967, provides a procedure for replacing the vice president in a rapid fashion, making the 1947 statute irrelevant in most cases.

7. If the Federalists had invoked this default option, who would have been their pick as president pro tem? Abigail Adams provides this answer in a letter of January 3, 1801, to her son Thomas: "If there should be no choice—I presume Mr. Ross is the only man in Senate who can wisely be fixed upon as president pro tem." Adams Family Papers, Massachusetts Historical Society, Reel 400.

8. Jefferson to Madison, Dec. 19, 1800, 7 *WTJ* 470. Jefferson's report is confirmed by letters written by leading Federalists, such as this one: "[T]here is manifestly an alarm in the minds of our republican Brethren, lest there should be an equi-vote. In that case, there may be three alternatives, either the Union must for one year, (unless we can agree in designating the Man) be without any other President, than the President of the Senate, or Mr. Jefferson must have it and Mr. Burr lose it, or Mr. Burr have it & Mr. Jefferson lose it." Elizur Goodrich to Roger Baldwin, Dec. 19, 1800, Baldwin Family Papers, Yale University, series I, box 7. See also Timothy Pickering to Rufus King, Jan. 5, 1801, in 3 King, *Life and Correspondence,* 365.

Gouverneur Morris was more judgmental: "It was propos'd to prevent any Election and thereby throw the Government into the Hands of a President of the Senate, it even went so far as to cast about for the Person. This appear'd to me a wild Measure and I endeavored to dissuade those gentlemen from it who mentioned it to me; it seems now to be given up. The Object with many is to take Mr Burr & I should not be surpriz'd if that Measure were adopted." Morris to Hamilton, Dec. 19, 1800, 25 *PAH* 267. Hamilton agreed with Morris in his reply of Jan. 9, 1801,

25 *PAH* 304, but both turned out to be wrong—as we shall see, this scenario proved to be very much alive to the very end of the crisis.

9. Jefferson to Madison, Dec. 26, 1800, *WTJ* 344.

10. Madison to Jefferson, Jan. 10, 1801, 17 *Mad* 453.

11. Nowadays Madison is often viewed as a conservative thinker, akin to Burke or Hume, but this is a serious mistake. See *WPF* ch. 7 and Ackerman, "Revolution on a Human Scale," 108 *Yale L. J.* 2279, 2299n29 (1999).

12. Here is the report of an outraged Federalist on January 9: "[R]evolutionary opinions are gaining ground . . . I have Seen a letter from Mr. Madison to one of the Virginia Representatives, in which he Says that in the event of the present House of Representatives not Choosing Mr. Jefferson President that the next House of Representatives will have a Right to Choose . . . ; and that the nature of the case, aided with the support of the great body of the people will Justify Jefferson and Burr *Jointly* to call together the Members of the next House of Representatives previous to the 3d of Decr. Next, for the express purpose of Choosing a President, and that he is Confidant *they* will make a *proper* Choice." James Gunn to Hamilton, Jan. 9, 1801, 25 *PAH* 303.

13. Under ordinary conditions, the chief justice might also seem an obvious candidate to serve as interim president, but this office was vacant when Horatius's article appeared. Adams had offered the job to John Jay—though it was broadly recognized that the elderly Jay would probably turn it down (see Chapter 6).

14. For Federalist allegations of Republican Jacobinism, see Alexander DeConde, *The Quasi-War,* 10–12, 28, 41 (1966).

15. Akhil Amar and Vikram Amar, "Is the Presidential Succession Law Constitutional?" 48 *Stan. L. Rev.* 113 (1995).

16. There is evidence of a broader, if more private, constitutional discussion on the available options. According to the Maryland congressman Samuel Smith, in response to inquiries by "a high tory fed," an (unnamed) Supreme Court justice asserted that a law appointing an interim president "would comport with the Constitution and might be passed but that it was inexpedient for the same result would follow from any new election and might irritate the people. That his opinion was that the instruction of the Electors was Mr. J[efferson] and that it would be prudent to follow their instruction." Smith to Burr, Jan. 11, 1801, Samuel Smith Papers, LC.

17. In a letter of February 4, Adams acknowledges Marshall's letter of acceptance of the chief justiceship, and asks him to "continue to discharge all the Duties of Secretary of State, until ulteriour Arrangements can be made." 6 *PJM* 73–74. Note that Adams asks Marshall to remain in his *existing* position and does not ask him to resign and accept a new appointment as acting secretary of state. As a consequence, Marshall would have qualified as acting president if the Federalists, fol-

lowing Horatius's advice, had passed a new statute that named either the chief justice or the secretary of state as acting president.

18. 2 *LJM* 541.

19. Donald Dewey, *Marshall v. Jefferson: The Political Background of Marbury v. Madison*, 43–44 (1970).

20. Hobson to Ackerman, via e-mail, June 8, 1999. Even if Professor Hobson had concluded that Beveridge was unreliable, he should have mentioned Marshall's possible authorship of Horatius at 6 *PJM* 49, as a prod for future scholarship.

21. 2 *LJM* 514n2.

22. For a couple of years I worked with the linguist Roger Shuy to see whether contemporary computer techniques could help establish Marshall's authorship. But alas, the Horatius essay is only 2,500 words long, and compelling statistical proof requires longer texts.

23. This is, at any rate, the moment when Jefferson began writing letters agonizing about the problem. See, e.g., Jefferson to Burr, Dec. 18, 1800, in 4 H. A. Washington, ed., *Writings of Thomas Jefferson*, 340 (1854).

24. I will describe this episode shortly. It is enough to say here that Marshall began writing his nine newspaper essays about June 17, 1819, and that the essays were published from June 30 to July 15. See Gerald Gunther, "John Marshall, 'A Friend of the Constitution': In Defense and Elaboration of McCulloch v. Maryland," 21 *Stan. L. Rev.* 449, 453–454, n19 and n3. In estimating the writing interval, one must allow for the fact that Marshall had to post his essays to Justice Bushrod Washington, who then handed them on to the printer.

25. David McCullough, *John Adams*, 541–543, 548–551 (2001).

26. See Constance McLaughlin Green, *Washington: Village and Capital, 1800–1878*, 19, 21 (table 1).

27. And he was at home to serve as a host to John Adams on the latter's return to Washington in the late fall of 1800. McCullough, *John Adams*, 543.

28. Virginiensis [Charles Lee], *Defence of the Alien and Sedition Laws* (1798). Lee also wrote some law reports, which "it is unlikely that Lee ever intended to publish." See W. Hamilton Bryson, *Miscellaneous Virginia Law Reports*, 2 (1992). Bryson has published them, however, and they are very primitive documents that give no evidentiary support to the suggestion that Lee might have written the Horatius essay.

29. Justice Bushrod Washington was a resident of Alexandria and a good friend of Marshall's. He also actively campaigned for Adams while on the bench. But he was much inferior to Lee in his juristic capacities, and I found no evidence that he engaged in newspaper polemics. Both Oliver Wolcott and William Cranch were permanent residents of the new capital city, but their writings do not display the le-

gal panache of Horatius. Of the Federalists arriving in Washington in November, I scrutinized the newspaper writing and pamphleteering of John Adams and of Gouverneur Morris, a senator from New York and a leading force at the Philadelphia Convention. Once again, the stylistics don't seem to match, but all such judgments are contestable.

A more likely suspect is Justice William Paterson—another strong Federalist, and a much abler constitutionalist than Justice Washington. Better yet, Paterson actually used the pseudonym Horatius in nine essays in the New Brunswick *Genius of Liberty* in 1795, and he wrote as Hortensius as well. See John E. O'Connor, *William Paterson: Lawyer and Statesman,* 239 (1979) (Horatius); Richard P. McCormick, *The History of Voting in New Jersey,* 107n53 (1953) (Hortensius). I have studied the manuscript version of Paterson's Horatius essays and they seem quite distant stylistically. More objective facts also lead me to discount him: Paterson lived in New Jersey, and was not in Washington at the time. Given the logistics, it would have been tough for him to arrange for a timely publication in the two newspapers. I have discounted Justice Chase, who seems to have been in Baltimore, for the same reason. Best of luck to future sleuths!

30. The only other paper then publishing in Washington was the Republican *National Intelligencer.*

31. See Gunther, "John Marshall, 'A Friend of the Constitution.'"

32. Snowden's name appears on the masthead for the issue carrying Horatius's essay, Jan. 2, 1801, and for all the issues carrying essays written by a "Friend of the Constitution": *Alexandria Gazette and Daily Advertiser,* June 30, July 1, 2, 3, 5, 6, 9, 14, 15, 1819. The paper became the *Alexandria Daily Gazette* in 1808, then went through several name changes before appearing as the *Alexandria Gazette and Daily Advertiser* in 1819.

33. Marshall to Washington, June 17, 1819, Miscellaneous Manuscripts, New-York Historical Society, cited in Gunther, "John Marshall, 'A Friend of the Constitution,'" 451–452.

34. Id., 499.

35. See Jean Edward Smith, *John Marshall: Definer of a Nation,* 174 (Aristides), 582n32 (Gracchus) (1996).

36. Id., 242–251.

37. A year after publishing the Horatius essay, Rind used his paper to advertise Marshall's forthcoming biography of George Washington, reporting that it "is now in the work-shop of an artist eminent for his erudition, and possessed of the materials which were collected by Washington himself. The public are therefore requested to defer subscriptions to the daily proposals for lives of this great man, as the editor has authority to state that an accurate and elegant performance on this subject will very shortly be presented to the world." *Washington Federalist,* Mar.

27, 1802, cited in 6 *PJM* 106n3. Note that Rind does not mention Marshall by name but clearly states that he is authorized to act as his agent.

38. Monroe to Jefferson, Jan. 18, 1801, in 3 *WOM* 256.

39. James Haw, *Stormy Patriot: The Life of Samuel Chase,* 203 (1980).

40. Hortensius [George Hay], *Richmond Examiner,* Feb. 9, 1801. Lucius, "Letter I to General Marshall," id., Feb. 10, 1801. See also Lucius, "Letter II to General Marshall, Esq.," id., Feb. 13, 1801.

41. *Washington Federalist,* Feb. 12, 1801.

42. Jean Edward Smith, for example, claims that "Marshall took no part" in schemes to appoint an interim president, citing only Beveridge's biography in support—a curious choice, since it is Beveridge who attributes the Horatius letter to Marshall. See Smith, *John Marshall,* 14. The other major recent biography, R. Kent Newmyer, *John Marshall and the Heroic Age of the Supreme Court* (2001), despite its admirably comprehensive scope, passes over the entire issue in silence.

Marshall's correspondence contains three relevant letters. Each suggests an antipathy to Jefferson or a guarded preference for Burr, but none speculates that anybody else might become president, and all profess detachment from day-to-day politics. But it would be a mistake to read too much into these silences. It would have been terribly imprudent for Marshall to commit anything embarrassing to paper, especially when the mails were easily compromised, and his presence in Washington made it possible for him to politick without leaving a paper trail. Marshall certainly had very particular reasons to keep his cards close to his vest in dealing with two of his interlocutors—Hamilton and Pinckney. The third letter is to Edward Carrington, his wife's brother-in-law, and seems motivated by business transactions, but concludes with a suggestion of partiality to Burr and a fear that Marshall "will be compeld to remain till the 3d of march at this place." All in all, slim pickings, but tea-leaf readers are invited to inspect the letters at 6 *PJM* 41, 44, 46.

3. Jefferson Counts Himself In

1. This chapter is based on a lengthy research project that I undertook with David Fontana. For further analysis and documentation, see Bruce Ackerman and David Fontana, "Thomas Jefferson Counts Himself into the Presidency," 90 *Va. L. Rev.* 551 (2004). For a more popular version, see Bruce Ackerman and David Fontana, "How Jefferson Counted Himself In," 293 *Atlantic Monthly* 84 (March 2004).

2. 2 *Farrand* 537.

3. U.S. Const. art. I, §3.

4. U.S. Const. art. II, §4.

5. U.S. Const. art. I, §3, cl. 6.

6. Article I, §3, clause 5 does authorize the Senate to choose other officers, including a president pro tem, and implicitly authorizes the latter to preside "in the absence of the Vice President"—allowing the vice president voluntarily to vacate the chair during his impeachment trial, but nothing in the text so requires. Even if the vice president passed the gavel to the president pro tem, this senator might be a blatant partisan.

Others have noted this absurdity. See, e.g., Michael J. Gerhardt, *The Federal Impeachment Process: A Constitutional and Historical Analysis,* 64–65 (1996); Stephen Carter, "The Role of the Courts in Separation of Powers Disputes," 68 *Wash. U. L. Q.* 669, 675 (1990). But see Akhil Amar and Vikram Amar, "Is the Presidential Succession Law Constitutional?" 48 *Stan. L. Rev.* 113, 122n59 (1995) (arguing that unwritten conflict-of-interest principles prevent vice presidents from presiding over their own impeachment trials).

7. The Founders were entirely aware of the dangers of self-interested judging. See, e.g., "Federalist no. 10," in Clinton Rossiter, ed., *The Federalist Papers,* 47 (James Madison) (1999).

8. See Joanne Freeman, *Affairs of Honor,* 213–227 (2001).

9. 3 *Annals* 1544 (1797).

10. See Ackerman and Fontana, "Jefferson Counts Himself into the Presidency," 583–584.

11. While the new House would be strongly Republican, the Jeffersonians would gain control of the new Senate only through some strategic miscalculations by the Federalists (see Chapter 6).

12. The Federalists consistently used their congressional majorities during the lame-duck session to ram through legislation and appointments (see Chapters 4 and 5). There is no reason to suppose any different motivation in this case.

13. U.S. Const. art. II, §1, cl. 3.

14. Act of Mar. 1, 1792, ch. 8, §2, 1 Stat. 239. The electors were actually instructed to create three copies of the relevant documents. One set was personally delivered, and one was mailed, to the president of the Senate; the third went to a local federal district judge for safekeeping. Id., §2. Likewise, the state executive was instructed to prepare three copies of the certificate of ascertainment and include one copy in each set of electoral documents. Id., §3.

15. The Library of Congress was good enough to prepare a microform of these early electoral votes at my request, and I have placed my copy on file at the Yale Law School Library as Electoral Vote Records, film no. 189 [hereinafter cited as Electoral Vote Records].

16. U.S. Const. art. II, §1, cl. 3.

17. The original documents have been inspected at the National Archives.

18. U.S. Const. art. II, §1, cl. 3.

19. I have inspected every vote certificate submitted by the state electors in the first six elections. See Electoral Vote Records. All are in perfect order, except for some problems arising at the first election, held in 1788, which preceded the first session of Congress as well as the Act of 1792. These deviations were very minor. The Act of 1792 seems to have codified preexisting practice.

20. The signatures of the electors appear below this statement. See Electoral Vote Records.

21. The text simplifies in one particular. Remember that the statute required the preparation of three sets of documents—two to be delivered to the president of the Senate and one to a local federal district judge. See note 14 above.

22. C. Peter Magrath, *Yazoo*, 7 (1966).

23. Id., passim.

24. Perhaps some might be tempted to go further and use the envelope's certification as the basis for an argument that Georgia had in fact complied with all constitutional requirements. On this view, the Constitution's requirement that the electors "sign and certify" is satisfied by the writing on the envelope, while the requirement of a "list of all the Persons voted for" is satisfied by the document inside the envelope.

But, as we have seen, it was a serious question whether the envelope's certification that a "list of the votes . . . for President and Vice President [is] contained therein" was in fact referring to the document in the envelope or whether it was referring to some other document that had been removed by a fraudster intent on falsifying the ballot. Rather than inviting a decisionmaker to make this inference, the constitutional text is best read as requiring the ballot itself to contain the requisite certification—especially since the Constitution only refers to the ballot, and does not impose any requirements on the envelope containing it.

Suppose, however, that this commonsense interpretation is rejected. Even then, the episode remains constitutionally problematic. Only now the problem focuses on Jefferson's decision to seize the authority to make the requisite finding that no fraud had occurred on the basis of the certification on the envelope. As we have seen, the constitutional text does not clearly give the Senate president the authority to engage in contestable fact-finding without inviting Congress to share in this responsibility.

25. In the months leading up to the election there was some uncertainty about the Georgia result. See, e.g., *Columbian Museum and Savannah Advertiser*, May 9, 1800, 2 (predicting 4 votes for Jefferson, 4 for Pinckney), and *Gazette of the United States*, Nov. 11, 1800 (Philadelphia) (2 for Jefferson and Burr, 2 for Adams and Pinckney), though there were other, more accurate predictions, see *Columbian Museum and Savannah Advertiser*, July 22, 1800, 3.

After November 19 the papers consistently put all of Georgia's votes in the Republican column. See, e.g., *Louisville Gazette and Republican Trumpet,* Nov. 19, 1800, 3; *Augusta Herald,* Nov. 26, 1800, 3; *Gazette of the United States* (Philadelphia), Dec. 26, 1800, 3 ("Electors of President and Vice-President in the State . . . [of] Georgia, have given a unanimous vote for Mr. Jefferson and Mr. Burr").

26. Jefferson's confidence in Georgia is also suggested by an administrative matter. To ensure timely delivery of all electoral votes, the governing statutes authorized the secretary of state, then John Marshall, to "send a special messenger" if any state's electoral certificates had not arrived by the "first Wednesday in January." Act of Mar. 1, 1792, ch. 8, §4, 1 Stat. 239. The states were sending their ballots to Jefferson, in his capacity as president of the Senate. On December 28 he wrote to Marshall that no special messengers would be required. Jefferson to Marshall, 6 *PJM,* 45, 45–46.

27. 2 Matthew L. Davis, *Memoirs of Aaron Burr with Miscellaneous Selections from His Correspondence,* 71–73 (1836).

28. A search of the principal archives containing Davis's papers, and those of the tellers, has failed to uncover further evidence.

29. Davis was sharply critical of Jefferson's victory in 1800. See Davis to Gallatin, Jan. 2, 1801, Matthew Livingston Davis Papers, New York Historical Society; Davis to Livingston, Feb. 4, 1804, Livingston Collection, New York Historical Society. He frequently criticized Jefferson for his "lack of good character" and "unethical impulses." See id. His partisanship was further inflamed by Jefferson's rejection of his candidacy for the lucrative position of naval officer for the New York City Custom House. See Howard Lee McBain, "De Witt Clinton and the Origin of the Spoils System in New York," 140–144, rpt. in 28 *Studies in History, Economics, and Public Law* 1 (1907). On Davis's alliance with Burr, see Freeman, *Affairs of Honor,* 199–205.

30. Here is the precise report from the Philadelphia *Aurora and General Advertiser,* Feb. 16, 1801, 2: "The Tellers declared there was some informality in the votes of Georgia, but believing them to be the true votes, reported them as such." As a strongly Republican newspaper, the *Aurora* had no interest in fabricating facts that cast doubt on Jefferson's decision. In any event, its report was copied verbatim in Boston, New York, Philadelphia, and even Savannah, by newspapers of every political stripe. *Columbian Centinel* (Boston), Feb. 21, 1801, 2; *Columbian Museum and Savannah Advertiser,* Feb. 27, 1801, 3; *Pennsylvania Gazette* (Philadelphia), Feb. 18, 1801, 2; *Philadelphia Gazette and Daily Advertiser,* Feb. 14, 1801, 3; *Spectator* (New York), Feb. 18, 1801, 3. Boston's *Mercury and New-England Palladium,* Feb. 24, 1801, 2, varied the language slightly: "The votes from Georgia, were rather informal—but accepted." To further enhance verisimilitude, all the newspapers reported that the event took place at a precise moment: "half past 3 o'clock, P.M."

31. Davis is incorrect, however, in asserting that the Georgia ballot "merely stated in the inside that the votes of Georgia were, for Thomas Jefferson *four,* and for Aaron Burr *four,* without the *signature of any person* whatsoever." As Figure 2 shows, the document does contain signatures, but the signatories do not specify that they are casting an electoral ballot, much less certify their ballot in the standard way.

32. Quoted in David McKnight, *The Electoral System of the United States,* 65, 293 (1878).

33. Hamlin also differs from Davis in reporting the facts about Georgia's ballot with perfect accuracy. Despite the passage of seventy-five years, he says—correctly—that the Georgia envelope contained a certificate of ascertainment, but that the ballot "had nothing on its face to show that the votes were given for anybody." His invocation of "tradition" points to sources independent of the hearsay reported by Davis, which was erroneous in significant respects.

34. Immediately after the Georgia incident, on February 14, 1800, a bill was introduced to provide statutory definition of the tellers' duties: "[T]o receive the certificates of the Electors from the President of the Senate, after they shall have been opened and read, and to note in writing, the dates of the certificates, the names of the Electors, the time and place of their meeting, the number of votes given, and the names of the persons voted for; and also, the substance of the certificates from the Executive authority of each state, accompanying the certificates of the Electors." A Bill Prescribing the mode of deciding disputed elections of President and Vice President of the United States, S., 6th Cong. (1800), microformed in 6th Congress, 1799–1801: Senate Bills (LC). For reference to the date of introduction, see House Spec. Comm., Counting Electoral Votes, H.R. Misc. Doc. no. 44–13, at 16 (1877); S. Jour., 6th Cong., 1st sess., 23, 31 (1800).

This text grants strictly ministerial authority. It failed to pass Congress, Tadahisa Kuroda, *The Origins of the Twelfth Amendment,* 72–82 (1994), but the date of its introduction suggests that it was a response to the procedural weaknesses revealed by the Georgia incident.

35. None of the published reports indicates that Jefferson paused or sat down to give others a chance to protest. House Spec. Comm., Counting Electoral Votes, 30–31, 33; 10 *Annals* 1023 (1801); H. Jour., 6th Cong., 1st sess., 796–799 (1801); S. Jour., 6th Cong., 1st sess., 124–125 (1801); 2 Thomas Borden, ed., *Abridgment of the Debates of Congress,* 531 (1857); McKnight, *Electoral System,* 393; *Presidential Counts,* xxii, 11, 16 (1877). Jefferson's aggressive conduct contrasts with John Adams's greater deliberation in 1797. During that vote count, Vice President Adams faced a similar controversy over the Vermont ballot, which had awarded him four votes. Instead of shutting down the debate, he gave his opponents an opportunity to raise a legal challenge before declaring himself the win-

ner. See Ackerman and Fontana, "Thomas Jefferson Counts Himself into the Presidency," 567–581.

36. 10 *Annals* 1023–24 (1801) (emphasis added).

37. Taliaferro is listed as a Federalist in Manning Dauer, *The Adams Federalists*, 323 (1953). James Jones, Georgia's other congressman, had died before vote-counting day. On the Senate side, Gunn seems to have been a Federalist. See Gunn, James, 1753–1801, at *http://bioguide.congress.gov/scripts/biodisplay.pl? index=G000526* (last visited Jan. 30, 2004). Josephine Mellichamp, *Senators from Georgia*, 23 (1976) does not list Gunn's partisan affiliation, but reports his duel with the state's leading Republican, James Jackson.

38. McKnight describes the likely behavior of the tellers: "We all know that the custom of the tellers at a meeting is for one to count out aloud the votes as they are given and for the others to record them; this is undoubtedly what they did here on this extraordinary and unique occasion." McKnight, *Electoral System*, 292. See also *Presidential Counts*, xiii.

39. James Sharp, *American Politics in the Early Republic*, 267 (1994).

40. Clifford Lord and Elizabeth Lord, *Historical Atlas of the United States*, 79 (1944).

41. Recall that the 1792 Act required the electors to send another envelope, containing a copy of their ballot and the certificate of ascertainment, to a local federal district judge. These documents probably contained the same defects as those delivered to Washington, but we have not been able to locate them.

42. For more on the Vermont matter, see Ackerman and Fontana, "Jefferson Counts Himself into the Presidency," 567–581.

43. Madison to Jefferson, Dec. 25, 1796, 16 *Mad* 435.

44. Jefferson to Madison (Jan. 16, 1797), 16 *Mad* 461.

45. Governor Jackson to Baldwin, Dec. 5, 1800, Abraham Baldwin Papers, University of Georgia, Athens. The outcome is also confirmed by a series of newspaper reports: see *Louisville Gazette and Republican Trumpet*, Nov. 19, 1800, 3; *Georgia Gazette*, Jan. 8, 1801, 3; *Augusta Herald*, Dec. 13, 1800, 3, Dec. 27, 1800, 2, Jan. 3, 1801, 3, Jan. 17, 1801, 2, and Jan. 28, 1801, 2.

46. Manning Dauer reports the party affiliation of each House member in *The Adams Federalists*, 288–331. Assuming all Federalists voted for the leading Federalist candidate in the five-man runoff, it is easy to predict the result: 8 states vote Federalist (Connecticut, Delaware, Georgia, Maryland, Massachusetts, New Hampshire, Rhode Island, and South Carolina); 6 states vote Republican (Kentucky, New Jersey, New York, Pennsylvania, Tennessee, and Virginia), and 2 states are evenly split (North Carolina and Vermont). In the two-man runoff that actually took place, 8 states voted for Jefferson, 6 voted for Burr, and 2 tied. Even my five-candidate scenario does not generate a Federalist victory, since it only

yields 8 Federalist votes and the Constitution requires 9 for victory. This leads me to speculate about Pinckney's potential emergence as a dark-horse compromise. Of course, my five-candidate scenario is based on Dauer's formal party affiliations, and so provides only a rough approximation. I provide a more intuitionistic analysis at note 49 below.

47. Marvin R. Zahniser, *Charles Cotesworth Pinckney*, 47–70, 87–96, 136–164 (1967). Vans Murray to Adams, Mar. 22, 1799, in American Historical Association, 1912 *Annual Report*, 529, 530 (1914).

48. In the runoff, South Carolina was the only southern state that did not vote for Jefferson.

49. Given the voting patterns revealed in the two-man runoff, several states might well have opted for a compromise on Pinckney in a five-candidate race. For example, South Carolina, which consistently voted for Burr, would probably have been happy to shift to Pinckney, a favorite son. Pinckney also had obvious attractions for North Carolina, whose delegation was split five to five along party lines. While the state cast its vote for Jefferson in the two-man runoff, a southerner like Pinckney was far more attractive than Burr. The same is true of Georgia. Benjamin Taliaferro had been elected as a Federalist but often voted with the Republicans, see Dauer, *The Adams Federalists*, 297–331, and voted for Jefferson over Burr in the runoff, *National Intelligencer*, Feb. 13, 1801. Nevertheless, he would have been under intense pressure from the Federalist establishment to vote for Pinckney as a compromise candidate.

At this point, Pinckney would have been only one state shy of the requisite 9 (North Carolina + Georgia + the 6 that voted for Burr). Support most plausibly would have come from a southern state like Maryland (splitting 4 to 4 between Jefferson and Burr) or Tennessee (1 to 0 for Jefferson). New Jersey was also a possibility (3 to 2 for Jefferson, with 1 Republican teetering). See Morton Borden, *The Federalism of James A. Bayard*, 88 (1955).

50. But perhaps the operation of another constitutional gimmick might have saved the situation. If the House had selected Adams or Pinckney, it would have been up to the Senate to select the vice president under yet another set of rules. The Constitution generally gives this office to the defeated presidential candidate with the most votes, but the Senate is authorized to choose among candidates "who have equal votes" after the president has been selected—Jefferson or Burr in this case. U.S. Const. art. II, §1, cl. 3. If the Senate had consoled Jefferson with the number-two spot, a national crisis might have been avoided if President Pinckney (or Adams) had resigned voluntarily, allowing Vice President Jefferson to become the fourth president of the United States.

51. As we have seen, the Constitution replaces the Senate president with the chief justice in the analogous case involving presidential impeachments.

52. See generally R. Kent Newmyer, *John Marshall and the Heroic Age of the Supreme Court* (2001); James Simon, *What Kind of Nation* (2002).

53. Pinckney often corresponded with Marshall, discussing the best ways to promote Federalist interests. Marshall to Pinckney, Nov. 20, 1800, Pinckney Family Papers, LC, and 6 *PJM* 16, 16–17.

4. On the Brink

1. Art 2, sec. 3.

2. Rule 5th, in 10 *Annals* 1010 and in *Hist Docs,* 77–78. See also Samuel Tyler to James Monroe, 9 Feb. 1801, 1 *Wm and Mary Q.,* 1st ser., 102 (1892) (noting that "the Feds had a majority of six votes" and had little difficulty getting their version of the rules adopted).

3. Rule 4th, 10 *Annals* 1010 and *Hist Docs* 77–78.

4. See Rule 6th, *Hist Docs,* 78–79.

5. James Lewis presents a very different interpretation of these rules. He suggests that the Federalists made a great concession in requiring the vote to continue without adjournment "until a choice is made." This "seemed to eliminate solutions of questionable constitutionality, such as providing by law for a transfer of power to the president pro tempore or for a new election. What was left were the two clearly constitutional options—electing Jefferson and electing Burr—and many clearly unconstitutional options." Lewis, "'What Is to Become of Our Government?' The Revolutionary Potential of the Election of 1800," in James Horn, Jan Lewis, and Peter Onuf, eds., *The Revolution of 1800,* 3, 19 (2002). But Lewis adopts much too wooden an interpretation of "until a choice is made." If the Federalists had successfully driven the House into an impasse, it would have been perfectly appropriate for the Federalist Speaker to declare that it was impossible to make "a choice" between Jefferson and Burr, and that the time had come for the House and Senate to consider further legislative action. As we shall see, this is precisely where things stood by the weekend.

6. James Sharp, *American Politics in the Early Republic,* 267 (1994).

7. Under the House rules, each member of a state delegation cast a secret ballot. However, a Republican newspaper, the *National Intelligencer,* published a list which attributed votes to individual members and reported that Jefferson won by a margin of 55–49 on the first ballot, but that five defections occurred on the second and subsequent ballots, which would seem to give Burr a majority of 54–50, until Dickson of North Carolina switched his vote to Jefferson on the thirty-second ballot (without changing the state-by-state vote). *Hist Docs,* 85 (table 1), 86, 87.

Given the prevailing partisanship, I treat the *Intelligencer*'s count cautiously. But since it was a Republican paper, it had no interest in exaggerating the shift in the Federalist direction. The erosion of support is confirmed by a confidential (hence more trustworthy) letter from Samuel Tyler to James Monroe: "On the first vote, Virginia gave 16 for J., and the State of N. Carolina gave 9 for J., one Burr. On the second Virga. gave 14 for J., 5 Burr; N.C.:6–4." *Hist Docs,* 104. See also a breakdown of the vote by the Federalist Robert Goodloe Harper in a letter his constituents, reporting that members of the House divided 53 for Burr to 51 for Jefferson. Letter of Feb. 24, 1801, 2 *AHA Report,* 132, 133–134. For a similar assessment, see Daniel Sisson, *The American Revolution of 1800,* 427 (1974).

8. Bayard to Hamilton, Mar. 8, 1801, 25 *PAH* 344–345. I think that the "not incorruptibles" were probably Smith of Maryland and Linn of New Jersey. I suspect that Edward Livingston of New York is the "blockhead."

The letter quoted was written a month after the crisis was resolved, but contemporaneous letters from Bayard contain similar appraisals. See, e.g., Bayard to his son Andrew, Jan. 26: "It is however certainly within the compass of possibility that Bur [*sic*] may ultimately obtain nine States," *AHA Report,* 120, 121; Bayard to his son-in-law Bassett, Feb. 16: "Burr has acted a miserable paultry part. The election was in his power, but he was determined to come in as a Democrat, and in that event would have been the most dangerous man in the community," *AHA Report,* 126. In 1806 Bayard recalled that Republican congressmen from New York, New Jersey, Vermont, and Tennessee had been "more disposed to vote for Mr. Burr than Mr. Jefferson" but voted for Jefferson on the first ballot "out of complaisance to the known intentions of the party." See 1 *Burr* 482.

Hamilton also detected weaknesses among the Jeffersonians, and since he was adamantly opposed to Burr, he was not engaging in wishful thinking. Hamilton to Gouverneur Morris, Jan. 13, 1801 (Tennessee vulnerable and Edward Livingston may swing New York to Burr), 25 *PAH* 314.

9. 10 *Annals* 1027 (1801). Some say the House called it quits earlier in the morning, but I follow Congressman Roger Griswold's unequivocal statement in a contemporaneous letter: "The balloting has continued from yesterday afternoon until this hour, which is about one OClock in the afternoon . . . and I have not slept since the night before last, we have now however agreed to suspend the ballot untill tomorrow at eleven Oclock, & shall retire of course to our lodgings. The issue cannot be conjectured." Griswold to Matthew Griswold, Feb. 12, 1801, Yale University, Manuscripts and Archives.

10. See Rule 4th, *Annals.* In a letter to his constituents of Feb. 24, 1801, Harper explains: "In the morning the members, by general consent, *but without a regular adjournment,* separated till next day, to take rest and refreshment" (emphasis supplied). *AHA Report,* 132, 135.

11. But one member from North Carolina did change his vote to Jefferson on the thirty-second ballot.

12. Gallatin to James Nicholson, 14 Feb. 1801, 8 o'clock, afternoon, in *Gallatin*, 261.

13. Gallatin to Henry Muhlenberg, May 8, 1848, id., 248. The plan is reprinted in Henry Adams, ed., 1 *The Writings of Albert Gallatin*, 18–23 (1879) [hereinafter cited as *Balloting Plan*]. The plan does not contain an explicit date, but internal evidence suggests that it was written between January 27 and February 5. The earlier date represents the confirmation of John Marshall as chief justice, which the Balloting Plan treats as a fait accompli. But the writer does not know of President Adams's request that the Senate meet in special session on March 4, while Gallatin's letter to his wife of February 5 recognizes that Adams has taken this fateful step. I have not uncovered any evidence that tells us when the plan was approved by the Republican caucus.

14. Id., 18.

15. Id., 22.

16. Tadahisa Kuroda, *The Origins of the Twelfth Amendment*, 83, 89–91 (1994).

17. Gallatin to his wife, 22 Jan. 1801, in *Gallatin*, 255, 256 (1879). Here is how Gallatin describes the problem in the list of "dangers" he tendered to the caucus: "The risk of losing the election of President, by their [the Federalists'] fixing a period sufficiently early to prevent the effect of a renovation of the Senate in New York, Maryland, Pennsylvania, and South Carolina, and thereby possibly neutralizing the votes of those four States." *Balloting Plan*, 22. Gallatin is brief because the problem would have been obvious to other politicians.

18. *Balloting Plan*, 23.

19. Id.

20. Adams to Gerry, Feb. 7, 1801, 9 *WJA* 98.

21. S. Jour., 7th Cong., special sess., 30 Jan. 1801, 147.

22. S. Jour., 3rd Cong., special sess., 4 Mar. 1793; id., 5th Cong., 1st special sess., 4 Mar. 1797.

23. *Balloting Plan*, 20.

24. *Philadelphia Aurora*, Feb. 12, 1801.

25. See Editorial Note, "The Electoral Tie of 1801," 1 *Burr* 481, 486. The Republicans did not leave their strategizing to the last minute. As early as January 14, 1801, the *National Intelligencer*, a Republican paper, published an essay written by "an American" urging Jefferson to stick to his chair in the Senate and prevent the Federalists from naming a president pro tem. To do otherwise would make Jefferson "the worst of accessories to usurpation," and indeed transform him into a "criminal." See also *Philadelphia Aurora*, Jan. 10, 1801.

26. Goodrich to Simeon Baldwin, Jan. 6, 1801, Baldwin Family Papers, Yale University, series I, box 7.

27. See Point 4 of Gallatin's action plan, quoted earlier, under which Republicans would "secede from any illegal meeting of the Senate." I take it that Gallatin considered the meeting "illegal" because its purpose was to elect a president pro tem—it is difficult to believe that he challenged the bare right of the Senate, as a continuing body, to meet for other purposes.

28. Gallatin provides an informed guess on what the Federalist-Republican balance in the Senate would be in a letter to his wife on February 5: "Mr. Adams has very improperly called Senate for the 4th of March next, at which time the three new Republican Senators from Kentucky, Georgia, and South Carolina cannot, from their distance, be here; the new Republican Senator from Pennsylvania instead of Bingham will not be appointed . . . ; the same with a new Senator from Maryland; Charles Pinckney has also dislocated his shoulder. The fact is that in December next the Senate will be 16 to 16, or at worst 15 to 17. And on 4th March only 8 or 9 republicans against 17 or 18." *Gallatin,* 260. In fact, there were 18 Federalists in the Senate on March 4. I describe the remarkable way in which the Federalists lost their majority in Chapter 6.

29. These basic constitutional points have been ignored by many distinguished historians. I have learned more about the Federalist era from Stanley Elkins and Eric McKitrick's *The Age of Federalism* (1994) than from any other single source. Nonetheless, their treatment of the crisis is flawed: "The possibility that other means of designating a president might be found—e.g. appointing a president pro tempore of the Senate, who might then take power in the event of a continued deadlock, or passing a special law—was removed when Jefferson showed he intended to remain in his seat as the Senate's presiding officer until the end of the session, and when the House resolved to do no business until a President should be chosen." Id., 906n154.

This analysis is defective. For starters, their point about Jefferson is defeated by the Senate's constitutional standing as a continuing body—which enabled the Federalists to appoint a president pro tem on March 4 after Jefferson's term as vice president had expired. Their second point about the House resolution "to do no further business" is equally misguided. The House always had the power to pass a new resolution declaring that it had reached an irresolvable deadlock in the presidential balloting, and that it would now proceed to the business of enacting a new succession statute. Since such a resolution was not subject to the special "one state–one vote" rule required for the House to elect a new president, the standing Federalist majority was legally capable of enacting it.

30. Franklin Sawvel, *The Anas of Thomas Jefferson,* 240 (1903). This is an entry from Jefferson's diary dated April 15, 1806, precipitated by a recent (and personally disturbing) visit from Burr. As Joanne Freeman perceptively argues, this "diary" was undoubtedly intended for eventual publication as part of Jefferson's effort to vindicate himself and his party to posterity. Freeman, *Affairs of Honor,* 63–

66, 103–104 (2001). Jefferson provided a similar version of events in a letter to Benjamin Rush of Jan. 16, 1811: "When the election between Burr and myself was kept in suspence by the federalists, and they were meditating to place the President of the Senate at the head of the government, I called on Mr. Adams with a view to have this desperate measure prevented by his negative. He grew warm in an instant, and said with a vehemence he had not used toward me before, 'Sir, the event of the election is within your power. You have only to say that you will do justice to the public creditors, maintain the navy, and not disturb those holding offices, and the government will instantly be put into your hands. We know it is the wish of the people it should be so.'—'Mr. Adams,' said I, 'I know not what part of my conduct, in either public or private life, can have authorised a doubt of my fidelity to the public engagements. I say however I will not come into the government by capitulation. I will not enter on it but in perfect freedom to follow the dictates of my own judgment' . . . 'Then,' said he, 'things must take their course.' I turned the conversation to something else, and soon took my leave." 9 *WTJ* 297. This version does not include Jefferson's threat of "resistance by force," but it clearly states that the interview took place "[w]hen the election between Burr and myself was kept in suspence."

31. This letter was found in the French diplomatic archives in 1967, and is reproduced in Sisson, *Revolution of 1800,* 463–468.

32. There are many minor errors in the dispatch, and so its assertions should be treated cautiously.

33. *American and Daily Advertiser,* Feb. 14, 1801 (Baltimore; Republican), rpt. in *Philadelphia Aurora* (Republican), Feb. 16, 1801. See also *Philadelphia Aurora,* Feb. 19, 1801, reprinting a report from the *Baltimore Telegraph* ("The city [Washington] is crowded with persons from all parts of the union"); *Poulson's American Daily Advertiser* (Philadelphia; Federalist), Feb. 27, letter dated Washington, Feb. 19 ("Great numbers of persons from the surrounding States were waiting the issue.—Both parties held a steady and imposing look"). For more evidence, see Sisson, *Revolution of 1800,* 427–437; Sharp, *Politics in the Early Republic,* 269–273.

34. *Federal Gazette and Baltimore Daily Advertiser,* Feb. 16, 1801 (Federalist). See also New York's *Federalist Daily Advertiser,* Feb. 28, 1801, printing a letter from Washington dated Feb. 18: "It may be proper to state, that during the late balloting in Congress, no means were left untried to awe the Federalists into the measures of the faction. Letters were written to the members, threatening them with assassination; and several of them were frequently stopped on their way from the House to their lodgings, and most daringly insulted. For several days previous to the decision, men of the most abandoned and profligate characters flocked to the city: and it is the opinion of every sensible man here, that if the recent accommodation had not taken place, violent measures would have been resorted to, to thrust Mr. Jefferson into the chair."

35. Gallatin to Muhlenberg, May 8, 1848, in *Gallatin,* 248, 249 (emphasis supplied). Written 47 years after the event, when Gallatin was 87, this letter raises special problems of interpretation. Speaking broadly, Gallatin's account portrays the Republicans as "the most sincere and zealous supporters of the Constitution" and downplays the more revolutionary pronouncements of Jefferson and others. I agree with Sharp that this apologetic element of the letter should be discounted. By 1848 the elder Gallatin was "embarrassed by the radical and disunionist sentiments that had been expressed by some Republicans in 1800 and 1801," and consciously or unconsciously was seeking to disassociate his generation of Jeffersonians from more recent secessionist currents. See Sharp, *Politics in the Early Republic,* 275. But this point doesn't apply to my use of Gallatin's letter. To the contrary, given his general tendency to whitewash the Jeffersonians, Gallatin should be believed when he inserts telltale facts—like the one I have italicized in the text—that suggest a very different story from the one he is trying to tell. For further corroboration of death threats, see Chapter 9.

36. In the Introduction to Part One I quoted the *Washington Federalist* threatening the Republican militias of Virginia and Pennsylvania with a counterforce of 60,000 Massachusetts militiamen. This article precipitated chest-thumping across the nation, with Federalist and Republican editors impugning the other side's military capabilities. See, e.g., *Washington Federalist,* Feb. 16, 1801; *Philadelphia Aurora,* Feb. 17, 19, 1801; *New York Daily Advertiser,* Feb. 18, 20, 1801.

37. Gallatin to Muhlenberg, May 8, 1848, in *Gallatin,* 248, 249.

38. The proclamation, issued on January 20, was printed in the *Aurora* on February 12, 14, and 21. A second proclamation, ordering a comprehensive canvass of the state's military resources, was issued on January 24 and printed in the *Aurora* on February 6 and 13.

39. McKean to Jefferson, Mar. 19, 1801, Thomas McKean Papers, Historical Society of Pennsylvania. This is a revised version of a letter drafted by McKean during "the height of the crisis," see Sharp, *Politics in the Early Republic,* 269, but Jefferson seems to have received only the March version. Michael Bellesiles dismisses McKean, saying that "[n]othing came of his preparations other than rhetorical broadsides," but he gives no evidence in support of his confident rejection of Governor McKean's probity. See Michael Bellesiles, "The Soil Will Be Soaked with Blood," in Horn, Lewis, and Onuf, *Revolution of 1800,* 75 and n81.

I have uncovered further evidence in an 1849 biography of General Peter Muhlenberg, written by his nephew: "During the pendency of this contest, an event occurred which is not generally known, and in which General Muhlenberg was one of the prominent actors. It was the nearest approach to a revolution which has ever threatened this country, and for that reason probably all papers connected with it have been destroyed, and the very existence of the project is almost unknown . . . The government, after finding that no choice was made by the House of Representatives between Jefferson and Burr, desired the passage of a law declaring the election null and void, and vesting the chief executive power in some officer, probably the Chief Justice. This outrageous violation of the constitution would have secured their position to the party in power for another presidential term; and with so easy an example before them, of nullifying an election, it may well be doubted whether any other would ever have taken place . . . General Muhlenberg was selected as the head of the military force necessary, and the militia of Pennsylvania under his command were to march immediately upon the capitol and depose the usurping government, whilst the states called a convention to amend the constitution . . . The dangerous nature of the scheme probably prevented any part of it being committed to writing, the extract from Jefferson's letter being the only documentary evidence the writer has been able to find; the other facts above stated were related by General Muhlenberg himself to his nephew, shortly after their occurrence." Henry A. Muhlenberg, *The Life of Major General Peter Muhlenberg of the Revolutionary Army*, 327–330 (1849). Since Muhlenberg believes that his uncle's involvement is "to be deprecated," it is unlikely that he fabricated his story to blacken the family name. There is good reason to believe that he was indeed reporting "facts . . . related by General Muhlenberg himself . . . shortly after their occurrence." Note that Muhlenberg mentions Marshall as the most likely president pushed by the Federalists.

40. Sharp, *Politics in the Early Republic*, 269, 269n74. Bellesiles recognizes these points, but as in the case of Pennsylvania, he downplays the threat on the ground that military conflict posed an unacceptable risk of slave rebellion to the Virginia slaveocracy. See Bellesiles, "The Soil Will Be Soaked with Blood," 75–78. He has a point about this perennial southern anxiety, but if he is right, Monroe was certainly playing a convincing game of bluff. Private correspondence among leading Federalists confirms a serious concern with this threat: "And it appears to be an alarming fact, that while the question of Presidential Election was pending in the House of Rs. parties were organized in several of the Cities, in the event of there being no election, to cut off the leading Federalists & seize the Government." Alexander Hamilton to James Bayard, Apr. [16–21], 1802, 25 *PAH* 608.

41. Jefferson to Monroe, Feb. 15, 1801, 4 H. A. Washington, ed., *Writings of Thomas Jefferson*, 354–355 (1854). A day earlier Jefferson had rooted his proposal of a convention more explicitly in the theory of popular sovereignty, telling Benjamin Barton that if "the government should expire on the 3d of March by the loss of it's head, there is no regular provision for reorganizing it, nor any authority but in the people themselves. They may authorize a convention to amend the machine." Letter of Feb. 14, 1801, id., 353. The following month Jefferson sharply distinguished between the election of Burr and a Federalist effort to appoint a provisional president: "Had [the election] terminated in the elevation of Mr. Burr, every republican would, I am sure, have acquiesced in a moment; because, however,

it might have been variant from the intentions of the voters, yet it would have been agreeable to the Constitution. No man would more cheerfully have submitted than myself, because I am sure the administration would have been republican, and the chair of the Senate permitting me to be at home eight months in the year, would, on that account, have been much more consonant to my real satisfaction. But in the event of an usurpation, I was decidedly with those who were determined not to permit it [the election of an interim president]. Because, that precedent once set, it would be artificially reproduced and would soon end in a dictator. Virginia was bristling up, I believe. I shall know the particulars from Governor Monroe." Jefferson to McKean, Mar. 9, 1801, 10 *Jeff* 221.

42. Jefferson presented another variation on the convention theme in a letter to Joseph Priestly of Mar. 21, 1801, saying that if the Federalists had refused to yield the presidency "[a] convention, invited by the republican members of Congress, with the virtual President and Vice President, would have been on the ground in eight weeks, would have repaired the Constitution where it was defective, and wound it up again. This peaceable and legitimate resource, to which we are in the habit of implicit obedience, superseding all appeal to force, and being always within our reach, shows precious principle of self-preservation in our composition." 4 Washington, ed., *Writings of Jefferson*, 374. Note that Jefferson is adapting Madison's earlier unconventional suggestion that he and Burr assume power as "the virtual President and Vice President"—with the difference that Madison was proposing that "the virtual" executives summon the newly elected Seventh Congress, not a constitutional convention. See Chapter 2. As to Jefferson's claim that the call for a convention would "supersed[e] all appeal to force," recall that Gallatin had rejected any assumption of executive authority on the ground that it risked "civil war." *Balloting Plan*, 20.

43. After some grand Enlightenment derivations from the mortality tables, he later concluded that a new convention should meet "every nineteen or twenty years" to allow each generation a chance to govern itself. Jefferson to Samuel Kercheval, July 12, 1816, 15 *Jeff* 32–44.

44. See Conor Cruise O'Brien, *The Long Affair*, 49–56 (1996).

45. Jefferson to Madison, Feb. 18, 1801, 4 Washington, ed., *Writings of Jefferson*, 355–356.

5. What Went Right?

1. R. Kent Newmyer, *John Marshall and the Heroic Age of the Supreme Court*, 148 (2001) (on Marshall's snub); David McCullough, *John Adams*, 564 (2001)(on Adams's departure).

2. Jefferson to Madison (Jan. 16, 1797), 16 *Mad* 461.

3. See Michael Bellesiles, "The Soil Will Be Soaked with Blood," in James Horn, Jan Lewis, and Peter Onuf, eds., *The Revolution of 1800,* 59 (2002).

4. Id., 348.

5. Richard Kohn, in *Eagle and Sword,* ch. 11 (1975), supplies a note at 229 that usefully distinguishes the variety of distinct armies established by the Federalists under different statutes in 1798.

6. The only scholar I've found who appreciates this point is Morton Grodzins; see his "Political Parties and the Crisis of Succession in the United States: The Case of 1800," in Joseph La Palombara and Myron Weiner, eds., *Political Parties and Political Development,* 303, 319–320 (1966).

7. 2 Charles Adams, *The Life of John Adams,* 214–219 (1968); Ralph Brown, *The Presidency of John Adams,* 90–113 (1975).

8. See Tadahisa Kuroda, *The Origins of the Twelfth Amendment,* 90 (1994).

9. Ron Chernow, *Alexander Hamilton,* 616–626 (2004). As a technical matter, Hamilton did not come out squarely against Adams. Instead, he conspired to manipulate the electoral college to enable the Federalist's vice-presidential candidate, Charles Cotesworth Pinckney, to come out ahead.

10. See Joanne Freeman, *Affairs of Honor,* 218–220, 239–241 (2002).

11. Alexander Johnston, "The Essex Junto," in 2 John Lalor, ed., *Cyclopaedia of Political Science, Political Economy, and of the Political History of the United States,* 109 (1883).

12. There was a political logic behind Adams's angry break with Hamilton after the loss in New York. Since the "Northern strategy" looked bleak, it made more sense to appear as a "third force" between Hamilton and Jefferson, and so pick up a few votes in the South.

13. Jefferson to Benjamin Rush, Jan. 16, 1811, 9 *WTJ* 296–297.

14. Hamilton to Bayard, Jan. 16, 1801, 25 *PAH* 319, 323, 323–324.

15. Though Jefferson considered himself the only legitimate choice, it is important to distinguish between two grades of illegitimacy in his thinking. Selection of Burr by the House was one thing; selection of Marshall or some other Federalist as an interim president was another. While Jefferson would have bitterly denounced Burr's rise to the presidency as an affront to the popular will, I have found no indication that he threatened violence in response; in contrast, he did explicitly threaten military action if the Congress selected Marshall or another Federalist as interim president (see Chapter 4). This is an important difference, and it suggests the continuing power of the constitutional text to play a constructive role. Jefferson's restraint in the case of Burr reflects the fact that Burr's selection would have been accomplished through plainly constitutional procedures; his threats of armed rebellion reflect the greater constitutional uncertainty surrounding the power of the Federalist Congress to select an interim president—though, as we saw in

Chapter 2, Horatius presented perfectly plausible legal arguments in support of such a move.

Of course, Jefferson's restraint in the matter of Burr was never put to the ultimate test, and it is perfectly possible that he would have allowed the Republican governors of Virginia and Pennsylvania to unleash their militias in this case as well. We will never know.

16. Burr to Smith, Dec. 16, 1800, quoted in 1 *Burr* 471. The initial date of publication in Baltimore was Dec. 27. Id., 491n1.

17. Burr to Smith, Dec. 29, 1800, quoted in 1 *Burr* 478–479. Burr and Smith met face to face in Philadelphia in early January. There is no contemporaneous record, but a letter from Gabriel Christie to Smith, written in 1802, recalls Smith's description: "at length you enquir'd of Col Burr what was to be done if the Foederal Members would not give, in that case no president would be Elected— Col Burr (greately as you sade to your surprize) told you that at all events the House could and ought to make a choice, meaning if they could not get Mr Jefferson they could take him you told Col Burr that that could not be done for the republicans would not give up on any terms, you had little or no more conversation on the Subject. you told *us* you came away much moritifyd as whin you went up to Philadelphia you expected that Col Burr would give you full authority to say that he would not serve if Elected President by the House of Representatives of the U.S. but instead of that gave you to believe that it would be best not to rise without making a choice even if that choice should be him." Christie to Smith, Dec. 19, 1802, quoted in 1 *Burr* 484.

18. See 1 *Burr* 500–501n1.

19. The original letter has been lost, but Burr confirms its essential contents in his response to Gallatin of February 12: "My letters for ten days past had assured me that all was setled . . . I am therefore utterly Surprized by the Contents of your's of the 3d." 1 *Burr* 500. Generally speaking, it took about four days for mail to go from Washington to Albany, though it sometimes took a good deal longer. Burr to Livingston, Feb. 16, 1801, 1 *Burr* 504. It is likely, then, that the letter arrived a few days before Burr's response to Gallatin. Even if it arrived on February 12, Burr had enough time to get to Washington before the impasse was broken on the 17th. Moreover, once he was on the road, the Federalists would have probably awaited his arrival before conceding.

It is unlikely that Gallatin, a Republican stalwart, would have told Burr to go to Washington to sabotage Jefferson's chances. Mary Jo Kline suggests that Burr may have misread the letter, and that Gallatin was urging Burr to the capital to help bring about Jefferson's election. 1 *Burr* 500–501. This seems doubtful: given the letter's importance, it was probably reread many times. It is more likely that Gallatin simply reported the facts, and that Burr himself inferred that this new report meant he should go to Washington. It should be noted, however, that some scholars have placed greater trust in the account, asserting that Gallatin's "surprising suggestion" was based on the possible understanding that Burr was "the one man who could obtain enough support from each party" to "prevent a civil war." Herbert Parmet and Marie Hecht, *Aaron Burr*, 164–166 (1967).

One minor detail of the account is incorrect: Townsend is wrong to suggest that Smith of Maryland was partial to Burr, although he is right in identifying Livingston and Lynn as potential swing voters.

20. See Freeman, *Affairs of Honor*, 247–250.

21. Tennessee was the only other state with a single Representative, William Claiborne. According to his biographer, Federalist leaders tried to seduce him with an offer of a military position, but he stood firm. Joseph Hatfield, *William Claiborne*, 19–40 (1976).

22. Morton Borden, *The Federalism of James A. Bayard*, 90 (1954) (quoting John Cotton Smith describing Bayard's position before the caucus).

23. Bayard to Hamilton, 8 Mar. 1801, 25 *PAH* 344–345.

24. Franklin B. Sawvel, ed., *The Anas of Thomas Jefferson*, 209–210, entries of Feb. 12 and 14, 1801 (1903). The latter entry quotes Gouverneur Morris as asking: "How comes it . . . that Burr who is four hundred miles off, (at Albany) has agents here at work with great activity, while Jefferson, who is on the spot, does nothing?" And see id., 223–228, entries of Jan. 2 and 26, 1804.

25. In his recent account of the election crisis, John Ferling recognizes that Burr refused to bargain directly for the presidency. But he does not consider this self-restraint a token of Burr's statesmanship, calling it a "stumbling performance." Ferling, *Adams v. Jefferson*, 193–195 (2004).

26. Bayard to Adams, Feb. 19, 1801, "Papers of James A. Bayard, 1796–1815," 2 *AHA Report*, 129–130. Other Federalists expressed Bayard's fears: "It being at length ascertained, after 35 trials, and five days consumed in balloting, that the supporters of Mr. Jefferson had come to a determination, *which was known to have been solemnly made, and was publicly avowed, to risk the constitution and the union rather than give him up*, and that no probability existed of a change in any of them, those who had voted for Colonel burr, and who preferred the constitution and the peace of the country to their own wishes, thought it time to preserve those great and invaluable objects, by suffering Mr. Jefferson to be chosen." R. G. Harper to his constituents, Feb. 24, 1801, id., 136 (emphasis supplied). A similar anxiety motivated border-state senators like John Crittenden to make desperate efforts in 1860 to avoid civil war. See *WPT* 128–129.

27. For a blow-by-blow account see Borden, *Federalism of Bayard*, 91–93.

28. See Sawvel, *Anas of Jefferson*, 237–241, entry of Apr. 15, 1806. Freeman, *Affairs of Honor*, 250–252, contributes an insightful discussion of the episode.

29. Ferling suggests that Jefferson did indeed make a deal with Bayard and the Federalists, *Adams v. Jefferson,* 189–194. Though we will never know for sure, I find his analysis rather convincing.

30. On Feb. 25 Burr wrote to Gallatin, "The Feds boast aloud that they have compromised with Jefferson, particularly as to the retaining certain persons in office." 1 *Burr* 509. Borden, *Federalism of Bayard,* 92, quotes Bayard's "tell-tale letter."

31. *Philadelphia Aurora,* Feb. 20, 1801. Also see 10 *Annals* 1028 (1801). The quotation in the text combines material from two different articles, though both were written by the editor and appear on the same page.

PART TWO   Introduction: Constitutional Brinksmanship

1. Jefferson's First Inaugural Address, Mar. 4, 1801, Jefferson Papers, box 8, LC.

2. See James Ceasar, *Presidential Selection,* ch. 2 (1979); Ralph Ketcham, *Presidents above Party* (1984); Stephen Skowronek, *The Politics Presidents Make,* ch. 4 (1997).

3. For thoughtful explorations of Federalism after its defeat in 1800, see Linda Kerber, *Federalists in Dissent* (1970); Doron Ben-Atar and Barbara Oberg, eds., *Federalists Reconsidered* (1998). But much more needs to be done.

4. Jefferson to John Dickinson, Dec. 19, 1801, 10 *Jeff* 302. Jefferson's special grievance is further evidenced by his charming letter to Abigail Adams in response to her letter of condolence on the death of his daughter in 1804. Jefferson used the occasion to suggest that his friendship for John Adams endured, despite the partisanship of the past few years: "and I can say with truth, that one act of Mr. Adams' life, and one only, ever gave me a moment's personal displeasure. I did consider his last appointments to office as personally unkind. They were from among my most ardent political enemies, from whom no faithful co-operation could ever be expected; and laid me under the embarrassment of acting through men whose views were to defeat mine, or to encounter the odium of putting others in their places." Jefferson to Mrs. Adams, June 13, 1804, 11 *Jeff* 29.

5. For a multifaceted discussion, reviewing the voluminous scholarly debate, see the essays on judicial review before John Marshall by Philip Hamburger, Renee Lettow Lerner, Matthew Harrington, Maeva Marcus, and Arthur Wilmarth, in 72 *Geo. L. Rev.* 1–197 (2003).

6. See, e.g., *History,* chs. 5–6; Louise Weinberg, "Our Marbury," 89 *Va. L. Rev.* 1235 (2003).

7. See, e.g., Edward Corwin, *John Marshall and the Constitution* (1919); Robert McCloskey, *The American Supreme Court* (1994).

6.   Federalist Counterattack

1. The Convention did discuss the length of congressional terms, but this never led it to focus on the potential dangers of lame-duck authority.

2. Art. I, sec. 4, cl. 2.

3. On the ratification process, see Bruce Ackerman and Neal Katyal, "Our Unconventional Founding," 62 *U. Chi. L. Rev.* 475, 537–539 (1995).

4. Resolution of Sept. 13, 1788, 34 *J. Cont. Cong.* 523 (1937).

5. 1 *Annals* 100–101, 16–17 (1789).

6. 1 Stat. 239, 241, sec. 12 (1792).

7. As its first session lasted into the summer, Congress was not anxious to return to New York City quickly, and it passed an ad hoc statute postponing the second session to January 1790. But there was no discussion of the lame-duck problem.

8. Motion for Adjournment, 2 *Annals* 1766 (1790). Congress did debate whether it should move from New York to Philadelphia for its final session, 2 *Annals* 1679–82, and voted in the affirmative. At no point did it consider whether, given the lame-duck character of the session, it was appropriate to meet at all. During the debate, Congressman Smith did say that "it is certain that the present Congress will hold another session," id., 1679, but this innocuous remark doesn't suggest a serious confrontation with the lame-duck problem.

9. Under emergency conditions, most notably during Reconstruction, the outgoing Congress passed a special statute summoning its successor to Washington on March 4 so that it could immediately take up the task of government. See *WPF* 201. While some Congresses convened early, none refrained from meeting after the next election made them lame ducks.

10. See John Hoadley, *Origins of American Political Parties*, ch. 6 (1986).

11. See 1 Stat. 96, 198, 267, 370, 507 (special sessions beginning the first Monday in Jan. 1790, Oct. 1791, and Nov. 1792, 1794, and 1797).

12. See John Nagle, "The Lame Ducks of *Marbury*," 20 *Con. Comm.* 317, 319–331 (2003), for a chronology of lame-duck Federalist actions in connection with the judiciary.

13. See, e.g., Washington's Address to Congress, 6 *Annals* 1592–97 (1796).

14. Adams received Ellsworth's letter on December 15; see Kathryn Turner, "The Appointment of Chief Justice Marshall," 17 *Wm. & Mary Q.,* 3d ser., 143n3 (1960). He sent Jay a letter offering the job on December 19; see Frank Monaghan, *John Jay: Defender of Liberty,* 424 (1935). My discussion is broadly consistent with the story provided by Turner, and I am much indebted to her splendid research.

15. Monaghan, *John Jay,* 406, 424.

16. Dec. 23, 1800, Adams Papers, Massachusetts Historical Society.

17. Dec. 28, 1800, Adams Papers, id.

18. Dec. 19, 1800, 9 *WJA* 91–92.

19. Jay to Adams, Jan. 2, 1801, in H. P. Johnston, ed., 4 *Correspondence of John Jay*, 284, 286 (1991).

20. Id., 285.

21. See Kathryn Turner, "Federalist Policy and the Judiciary Act of 1801," 22 *Wm. & Mary Q.*, 3d ser., 3, 11n89 (1965).

22. Stoddert to Adams, Jan. 19, 1801, in 4 Maeva Marcus, ed., *Documentary History of the Supreme Court of the United States*, 686 (1985) (emphasis supplied).

23. John Adams, ed., *Autobiographical Sketch by John Marshall*, 29–30 (1937). Note that Marshall suggests that Adams had an objection to Paterson, but most other evidence points in the opposite direction.

24. See Judiciary Bill, 10 *Annals* 915 (1801). Federalists Taliaferro, Dent, Alston, and Gray voted with the Republicans. No Republicans voted for the bill.

25. See Turner, "Appointment of Marshall," 156–160. The judiciary bill passed from the House to the Senate on January 21, the day after Marshall's nomination. The Senate approved Marshall on January 27, and on January 29 the judiciary bill came to the Senate floor. Id., 160.

26. Turner, in "Appointment of Chief Justice Marshall," reaches the same conclusion (at 155) and provides more evidence. My contribution, such as it is, is to place Turner's analysis in larger constitutional context.

27. See Jean Edward Smith, *John Marshall: Definer of a Nation*, 245 (1996).

28. From 1789 through 1819 the salary of the chief justice was $4,000—a substantial sum for a part-time job, but not an enormous amount for a full-time position, considering that leading lawyers could make $10,000 or more. See 3 G. Edward White, *History of the Supreme Court: The Marshall Court and Cultural Change, 1815–1835,* 163n29 (1988).

Louise Weinberg speculates that Marshall took the job because he saw its potential for constitutional leadership. See Weinberg, "Our Marbury," 89 *Va. L. Rev.* 1235 (2003). She may well be right in part, though there is no hard evidence, but she fails to consider the more obvious attractions of a job that then looked like a sinecure. Donald Dewey shows far great realism in *Marshall versus Jefferson,* 20 (1970), suggesting that leisure time on the bench would permit Marshall to write his *Life of Washington*, which he hoped would greatly enrich him.

29. Originally, two justices rode together and joined the local district judge to create a three-judge circuit court, but this was changed in 1 Stat. 333, 334, sec. 1 (Mar. 2, 1793), to save the justices from some of the remorseless wear and tear. Thereafter, only a single justice was required join the local district judge to form a two-man circuit court. See Felix Frankfurter and James Landis, *The Business of the Supreme Court,* 22 (1928).

30. See, e.g., Act of July 5, 1797, 1 Stat. 526 (N.C.); Act of Dec. 24, 1799, 2 Stat. 3 (Pa.).

31. Act of Mar. 2, 1793, 1 Stat. 334. In 1802 the Republicans amended the provision to allow any party to certify a question to the Supreme Court in the event of disagreement. Act of Apr. 29, 1802, 2 Stat. 156, 159–161.

32. Kathryn Turner details the series of failed proposals in her fine essay "Federalist Policy and the Judiciary Act of 1801."

33. Most important, the new version created 16 new judgeships, in contrast to the 25 proposed previously. See id., 11–15. Only one new judgeship was created for the frontier states of Tennessee and Kentucky in the Sixth Circuit. This new circuit judge would conduct most trials sitting with two district judges.

34. Jefferson to Madison, Dec. 26, 1800, in Marcus, *Documentary History of the Supreme Court*, 663.

35. Even today, political partisans exploit lame-duck authority in ways that should be unacceptable. See Nagle, "Lame Ducks of *Marbury*," 317, 331–337; Bruce Ackerman, *The Case Against Lameduck Impeachment* (1999). But the actions of the Federalists remain beyond the pale—it is unthinkable that modern lame ducks would pass major legislation that provided a permanent retirement home for the party faithful.

36. Bingham to Peters, Feb. 4, 1801: "Such is the critical state of the Votes in the House, arising from the accession of Several Members, who are adverse to the Bill, that it is Supposed it will be in imminent danger, if it Should return to the House and be placed within their Power—The committee therefore to whom it was referred, altho desirous of introducing Several Modifications, have reported the Bill without Amendment, and I am inclined to believe that we shall be compelled to take it,–for better and for worse–or totally reject it . . . the federal party wish the appointments to be made under the present administration . . . the Importance of filling these Seats with federal characters, must be obvious." Peters Papers, Historical Society of Philadelphia. See also Federalist Senator Dwight Foster to Timothy Pickering, Feb. 4, 1801: "Efforts are making to pass this Bill in its present crude State *without Amendments* . . . One argument strenuously urged is that if it now passes Mr. Adams will have the Nomination of the Judges to be appointed." 4 Marcus, *Documentary History of the Supreme Court*, 710 (emphasis supplied).

37. Thomas Truxton to Hamilton, Mar. 26, 1802, 25 *PAH* 577–579.

38. Smith to Dayton, Jan. 30, 1801, Gratz Collection, box 5, Historical Society of Pennsylvania.

39. For Stockton's high reputation, see Charles Warren, *History of the American Bar*, 114 (1911).

40. Letters from Stockton to Adams, Jan. 17, 1801, Adams Papers, Massachu-

setts Historical Society, Boston; from Adams to Stockton, Jan. 27, 1801 in 9 *WJA* 94–95; from Stockton to Adams, Feb. 2, 1801, Adams Papers, Massachusetts Historical Society, Boston.

41. Adams's effort to fill the jobs for the southernmost Fifth Circuit was a total failure—all three of his appointees turned down the offers. See Levi Lincoln to Jefferson, Mar. 21, Apr. 9, Apr. 16, 1801; copies in Lincoln Family Papers, American Antiquarian Society, Worcester, MA, box 1, folder 4. This allowed Jefferson to nominate replacements; see *History*, 132n129.

42. There is no evidence, either way, as to whether Marshall knew of Stockton's fears. But there can be no question that he was reading the Washington newspapers, which already contained Republican threats to repeal the Federalist judiciary act.

43. Adams chose Wolcott over Jonathan Sturges, who was then a judge on the Connecticut superior court. See Turner, "Midnight Judges," 504. Wolcott's lack of professional experience was well known. Congressman James Hillhouse gave it as a reason why the more experienced Egbert Benson was given the job of chief judge of the circuit: "it would in some measure place you in a situation to be protected from the mistakes and errours to which you might be exposed, until you should have had an opportunity to make yourself acquainted with the technical rules of proceeding." Hillhouse to Wolcott, Feb. 19, 1801, in 2 Gibbs, *Memoirs of the Administrations of Washington and John Adams*, 493 (1846).

44. This was the only nomination that provoked the Republican minority to demand a formal division of the Senate. Key was approved in a party-line vote of 20–9. 1 *Sen. Exec J.* 383 (Feb. 20, 1801).

45. Bayard to Bassett, Feb. 10, Feb. 12, Feb. 16, 1801, in Elizabeth Donnan, ed., *Papers of John Bayard: 1796–1815,* 124, 125, 127 (1915).

46. 1 *Sen. Exec. J.* 381 (Feb. 18, 1801).

47. Perhaps Bayard was misunderstanding or misrepresenting his dealings with Adams, though I rather doubt it. Adams never had occasion to comment on this aspect of the story, but recall that Jefferson did deny Bayard's account of his dealings with him in connection with the electoral college crisis (see Chapter 4). In his next letter to Bassett, dated February 22, Bayard confirms the president's change of heart: "You are appointed one of the Judges of the circuit Court, but not the Chief Judge . . . The President changed his mind after the date of my last letter to you. He had then determined to appoint you Ch. Just." Donnan, *Papers of Bayard,* 130. This report is not particularly informative, but it doesn't suggest anything particularly deceitful in Bayard's report of the incident.

48. Bassett immediately resigned his governorship to accept the judgeship. See Turner, "Midnight Judges," 513.

49. Brown to Adams, Feb. 19, 1801; see also letters of Davis and Fowler to Marshall, Feb. 18, 1801, Adams Papers, Massachusetts Historical Society.

50. For the details of Humphrey Marshall's nomination, see Ruth Wedgewood, "Cousin Humphrey," 14 *Con. Comm.* 247 (1997).

51. *Kentucky Gazette* (Lexington), Mar. 30, 1801. The fears of nepotism were very real. District judge Harry Innes not only opposed the McClung appointment in a letter to Adams but expatiated at length to Jefferson, calling McClung "a mere creature to party & faction" and a failure at the bar: "I fear if he meets with the appointment he will be governed by family influence." Innes to Jefferson, Feb. 10, 1801 ("recd. Mar. 6"), in 109 Jefferson Papers, series 1, LC.

52. 1 *Sen. Exec. J.* 383–384 (Feb. 23, 1801) (nominating the judges of the Fifth and Sixth circuits).

53. Morris to Livingston, Feb. 20, 1801, in 3 Jared Sparks, ed., *The Life of Gouverneur Morris,* 153–154 (1832).

54. Bingham to Peters, Feb. 23, 1801, Peters Papers, Historical Society of Pennsylvania.

55. Turner, "Midnight Judges," 510. 1 *Sen. Exec. J.* 386 (messages of Feb. 26 and 27, 1801). Charles Warren describes Edward Tilghman as "the consummate Pennsylvania authority on all points connected with estates, tenures, uses and remainders," and calls William "a master of Equity Jurisprudence." Warren, *History of the American Bar,* 245n2, 246n1 (1911).

56. Bingham to Tilghman, Feb. 27, 1801, box 32, Gratz Collection, Historical Society of Pennsylvania.

57. 1 *Sen. Exec. J.* 389 (Mar. 2, 1801).

58. The chief judge of the newly created court was to receive an annual salary of $2,000 and the others, $1,600. Act of Feb. 27, 1801, §10, 2 Stat. 103, 106–107.

59. Marshall to James Marshall, Mar. 18, 1801, 6 *PJM* 90–91.

60. 1 *Sen. Exec. J.* 388 (Mar. 2, 1801).

61. J. A. C. Grant, in "Marbury v. Madison Today," 23 *Am. Pol. Sci. Rev.* 673, 678–679 (1929), seems to have been the first scholar to bring this issue up. For further discussion, see Chapter 8.

62. See Turner, "Federalist Policy and the Judiciary Act of 1801," 21–22.

63. The salaries of federal district judges ranged from $1,000 to $1,800 in 1801. See 1 Stat. 72, ch. 18; 2 Stat. 423, ch. 35; 2 Stat. 121, ch. 29. Promotion to a circuit judgeship earned them a raise to $2,000, which was the uniform salary throughout the nation.

64. The other district judges were Benjamin Bourne, John Lowell, Samuel Hitchcock, and Thomas Bee—all Federalists. Turner, "Midnight Judges," 521.

65. In addition to Senators Greene and Paine, Congressman Jacob Read of South Carolina received a district judgeship.

66. Gunn to Hamilton, Dec. 13, 1800, in 25 *PAH* 254. Gouverneur Morris found the picture less clear: "On counting over the Senate after March next it ap-

pears that out of thirty two there will be fifteen of each Party with two feeble Members on whom no Dependence can be placed." Morris to Hamilton, Jan. 26, 1801, id., 329.

67. Though both Greene and Paine had already accepted judicial commissions, they did not immediately resign from the Senate, as required by the Constitution's explicit stricture against congressmen holding any other "office of the United States." Art. I, sec. 6. cl. 2. Greene resigned from the Senate on March 5, 1801, 1 *Sen. Exec. J.* 381 (1800–1801). Paine resigned on September 1, Congressional Quarterly, *Biographical Directory of the American Congress, 1774–1996,* 1121 (1997). Greene's unconstitutional retention of office occasioned explicit comment. In the 1802 debate over the repeal of the judiciary act, John Rutledge recalled that "the friends of the [new] Administration objected to his keeping it [his Senate seat]; they said he was a judge, as appeared by the journals of the Senate." 11 *Annals* 751 (1802).

68. Maryland's first senator, Republican John Henry, had resigned in 1797 and been replaced by another Republican, James Lloyd. Maryland's legislature had then gone over to the Federalists, and Lloyd was clinging to his place. In the first week of October 1800, however, Republicans won a majority in the House of Delegates, although the Federalists retained control of the Senate. See Frank Cassell, *Merchant Congressman in the Young Republic, 1752–1839,* 92 (1971); Frank F. White, *The Governors of Maryland, 1777–1970,* 318 (1970).

On December 1 Lloyd resigned his seat, and the divided legislature settled on Federalist William Hindman to fill out the term. Congressional Quarterly, *Guide to United States Elections,* 795 (3d ed., 1994). It failed to settle on a permanent senator, and the Federalist governor appointed Hindman to retain the seat until the legislature should agree on a permanent choice. A Republican victory in elections for the state Senate empowered the legislature, at long last, to fill the seat with a senator from the majority party, and on November 19 it elected a Republican, Robert Wright, to the term that had begun on March 4—eight months late, but two weeks before the start of the first real session. Congressional Quarterly, *Biographical Directory of Congress,* 2094–95. The seating of Senator Wright spelled the end of Federalist dominance in the United States Senate, which in turn virtually guaranteed the repeal of the Federalist judiciary act.

69. In its fall elections, Vermont returned a Federalist governor but a Republican House of Representatives. The governor and his council agreed with the House that each would vote simultaneously for a senator to fill the seat vacated by Paine. In case they failed to agree, they would vote by joint ballot. That is exactly what happened: the governor and council, for their part, chose Federalist William Chamberlin by a majority; the House chose Republican Stephen R. Bradley by a majority. A Joint Committee of the Whole was convened to compare the results

and proceeded to elect Bradley. See 4 *Records of the Governor and Council of the State of Vermont*, 296–298 (1973).

When Greene resigned his Senate seat, Rhode Island elected Republican Christopher Ellery on May 6. See Congressional Quarterly, *Guide to U.S. Elections*, 805. Rhode Island then became solidly Republican. When another vacancy opened in October 1802, the Federalists did not think it "worth while to set up a candidate with a certainty of being beat." Bourne to Wolcott, Nov. 1, 1802, Oliver Wolcott Papers, Connecticut Historical Society, box 16, folder 73.

70. See 1 *Sen. Exec. J.* 381 (Feb. 18, 1801). In the same message, Adams also announced his nominations for the three-judge panels for the Second, Third, and Fourth Circuits. His special concern with New England politics was further suggested by his handling of Charles Lee's nomination to the Fourth Circuit. Since Lee was then serving as attorney general, this nomination opened up a vacancy, which Adams proceeded to fill by nominating Theophilus Parsons of Massachusetts. This designation was honorific only, since Parsons would be replaced as soon as Jefferson came to power. But the gesture suggests that Adams's mind had turned homeward, and that he was concerned with "setting things right" with the leading personalities of New England.

71. Id., 383 (Feb. 20, 1801). The Senate approved not only all the nominations from New England but those from the other three circuits as well. Given the time pressure, the national implications of the Greene appointment as district judge might easily have eluded senators from these regions, who would have been more concerned with their own circuit courts. In fact, the only nomination that generated serious debate was that of Philip Key, who had served on the wrong side during the Revolution. All other nominations passed without a formal division, with the 8 Republicans then in the chamber formally voting against, and the 18 Federalists voting in the affirmative. Id.

72. 1 *Sen. Exec. J.* 384 (Feb. 24, 1801).

73. 1 *Sen. Exec. J.* 386 (Feb. 25, 1801).

74. Federalist Rhode Island cast one of its four electoral votes for John Jay, 10 *Annals* 1023 (1801).

75. Madison to Monroe, Feb. 28, 1801, in 22 Madison Papers, LC, quoted in Turner, "Midnight Judges," 519n159.

7.   Republican Triumph

1. I develop these themes at greater length in Bruce Ackerman, "The New Separation of Powers," 113 *Harv. L. Rev.* 633 (2000).

2. James Young, *The Washington Community*, 29 (1966) (table 1). I exclude the 161 members of Congress, the presidency, and the Supreme Court.

3. Senate turnover was also high. Id., 90 (table 4). Since many members of Congress continued their political careers on the state level, turnover was a tribute, among other things, to the punitive conditions of life in the nation's frontier capital.

4. See Introduction to Part II.

5. See Richard Ellis and Stephen Kirk, "Presidential Mandates in the Nineteenth Century," 9 *Stud. Am. Pol. Dev.* 117 (1995); Jeffrey Tulis, *The Rhetorical Presidency* (1987); James Ceasar, *Presidential Selection*, ch. 2 (1979).

6. Stephen Skowronek, *The Politics Presidents Make*, 69–77 (1993).

7. See David Bushnell, ed., *El Libertador: Writings of Simon Bolivar* (2003); for a thoughtful essay on Bolivar's style of presidentialism, see José Rivera, *En Pos de la Quimera,* ch. 5 (2000).

8. Randolph won a seat in Congress in 1799, at the age of 26. Henry Adams, *John Randolph,* 28 (1898). Given the enormous turnover of membership, his youth did not disqualify him from a leadership position. But Jefferson was careful to diversify his leadership portfolio, giving important roles to Joseph Nicholson, William Branch Giles, and Samuel Smith. For example, Giles, and not Randolph, took the lead in the repeal of the Federalist Judiciary Act. It was only after Giles and Smith left the House in 1803 (Giles temporarily leaving politics on account of illness, and Smith winning election to the Senate) that Randolph began to move more visibly to the forefront. Id., 83–84.

9. Young, *Washington Community,* 195.

10. Id., 190. Young's discussion has greatly influenced me—to the point where I should indicate one key point of disagreement. Though he occasionally recognizes the plebiscitarian aspect of Jefferson's presidency, this is not a major theme. He tends to speak broadly of the "Jeffersonian Presidencies" in a way that includes the entire group who served during the period between 1800 and 1828. This broad term disguises the extent to which the victory won by Jefferson and his movement-party in 1800 gave him a plebiscitary legitimization that his successors lacked. See generally Chapter 9.

11. Id., 90 (table 4).

12. Pauline Maier, *American Scripture,* 170–175 (1997).

13. Young, *Washington Community,* 168, 169.

14. Jefferson to Giles, Mar. 23, 1800, 4 Henry Washington, ed., *Writings of Thomas Jefferson,* 380–381 (1854). See also Jefferson to Benjamin Rush, Mar. 24, 1801, id., 382–384, and sources cited in Chapter 8.

15. The shock was reported to Jefferson by his New England attorney general, Levi Lincoln. See letters of June 15 and July 28, 1802, Lincoln Family Papers, American Antiquarian Society, Worcester, MA, box 1, folder 4.

16. As the Republican Congress was gearing up for repeal of the judiciary act, the *Washington Federalist* returned to the constitutional lessons of the Greene

case. It contended on December 16, 1801, that Jefferson's actions were not "a matter of mere malignancy" but "a direct violation of the constitution . . . The nomination was approved by the Senate. This constitutes the *appointment*. The constitution says the President *shall* commission him." The *Federalist*'s recollection of Greene appeared in the newspaper one day before *Marbury* was first considered in the Supreme Court. Id., Dec. 18 [misdated 17], 1801. *Marbury* also concerned the constitutional status of judicial commissions, and its relationship to Greene's case will be explored further in Chapter 8.

17. 1 *Sen. Exec. J.* 389 (Mar. 2, 1801).

18. Though Marbury has hogged the historical spotlight, three other disappointed JPs—Dennis Ramsay, Robert Hooe, and William Harper—joined him in the lawsuit. Many other JPs accepted their loss without further protest.

19. Jefferson to Knox, Mar. 27, 1801, 8 *WTJ* 35–37. See generally David Forte, "Marbury's Travail: Federalist Politics and William Marbury's Appointment as Justice of the Peace," 45 *Cath. U. L. Rev.* 349, 394–397 (1996).

20. *Aurora* (Philadelphia), Dec. 30, 1801.

21. Some scholars emphasize *Marbury*'s role in provoking the Republicans' decision to repeal the judiciary act. See Dean Alfange Jr., "Marbury v. Madison and Original Understandings of Judicial Review," *Sup. Ct. Rev.* 329, 354–360 (1993); Richard Ellis, *The Jeffersonian Crisis,* 42–45 (1971). Though *Marbury* was a provocation, I believe that Jefferson was bent on repeal in any event. One thing is clear: it was Jefferson who made the decision, and it is very doubtful that the Republicans in Congress would have done it on their own. See id., 51.

22. 1 James Richardson, ed., *Messages and Papers of the Presidents,* 326, 331 (1898).

23. 11 *Annals* 26. Breckenridge refers to "an army of judges" at id., 98.

24. Jefferson to John Dickinson, Dec. 19, 1801, 10 *Jeff* 302. See also Jefferson to Rush, Dec. 20, 1801, 8 *WTJ* 126–128 (endorsing plans to "lop[ ] off the parasitical plant engrafted at the last session on the judiciary body").

25. For examples of technocratic argument, see 11 *Annals* 92–93 (Breckenridge); 104 (Baldwin); 112–113 (Wright); 600–601 (Giles). A subsidiary line of argument praised the virtues of circuit-riding, on the ground that it enabled the justices to gain an intimate understanding of state law and practices. See, e.g., id., 102 (Baldwin).

26. Id., 658.

27. See, e.g., id., 34 (Mason); 118 (White); 174 (Ogden). This theme was echoed in the House by Stanley; id., 570–572.

28. See, e.g., id., 34 (Mason); 174 (Ogden). Similar arguments were made in the House by Hemphill and Bayard; id., 534, 624.

29. In the Senate, Morris argued that the judges cost each citizen only one cent

per capita; id., 37. See also Wells's elaborate technocratic critique, 134–136. In the House, see, e.g., Hemphill, id., 534, and Bayard, id., 626.

30. Morris emphasized the imperative nature of the provision's language. The term "establish," in his view, implied the permanent vesting of power, id., 39 and 87; see also 175 (Ogden). In the House, see Hemphill, id., 539–540. Mason looked to the language of the second sentence, stating that judges "shall hold" their offices during "good behavior." This implied, he argued, that the offices themselves could not be eliminated, id., 33. Henderson presented a similar argument in the House, id., 525.

31. Breckenridge was the first of many to stress that Congress's power to establish inferior courts "from time to time" implied the further power to destroy and reorganize these courts. Id., 27–28. In the House, see, e.g., Thompson, id., 549; Bacon, 562; Giles, 592; Smith, 694–695. In a parallel move, many Republicans urged that the judicial guarantee of life tenure "during good behavior" served only as a safeguard against arbitrary removal by the executive, and did not apply to judicial reorganizations enacted by the legislature. See, e.g., Giles, id., 587.

32. At early stages in the debate, the Republicans professed a bit of uncertainty on this point. Breckenridge, their leader in the Senate, sometimes vigorously asserted that the judges' commissions were worthless: "What likeness is there between the salary of the judge and the national debt? . . . Is that a vested right? Is that a debt to which the community have received an equivalent? It is neither." Id., 96. But at other times he left the matter open: "If the judges are entitled to their salaries under the Constitution, our repeal will not affect them; and they will, no doubt, resort to their proper remedy. For where there is a Constitutional right, there must be a Constitutional remedy." Id., 30. See also Stone, id., 74, Baldwin, 107, Bacon, 563. But as the debate proceeded it took on a more fiercely partisan tone, and the Republicans increasingly shed their hesitations. See, e.g., id., 556.

33. Bayard, for example, provided a lengthy analysis of the defects of the old circuit-riding system, id., 618–621, and the improvements promised by the reform, id., 623–626.

34. Id., 39. See also Senator Bradley's trenchant critique: "You admit that the dismission of sixteen judges, by name, would be unconstitutional. What difference is there between this and your bill, which declares that the circuit courts shall no longer be held by the present judges, but by certain other men? You do not destroy the office of circuit judge, for you still retain the circuit courts. You remove the office from one set of men who now hold it, and give it to another set that pleases you better. Then you contend that this operation, being a removal of offices from men, is not a removal of men from offices, as if your purpose was not as effectually attained by inverting the order of the words as without it . . . Surely so barefaced an evasion, so undisguised an usurpation of power, can deceive no man

who is not already resolved to be deceived." Id., 164. Bradley's point would return to haunt the justices of the Supreme Court in responding to the Republican demand that they resume circuit-riding in the face of the outstanding commissions held by the ousted circuit judges (see Chapter 8). For other statements in favor of judicial independence, see Goddard, id., 730–731; Rutledge, 754, 760.

35. Id., 597. Giles's speech set the tone for much of the House debate, with the Federalist Huger characterizing him, quite properly, as the "*premier, or prime minister* of the day." Id., 666.

36. Id., 67–68, 581 (Giles), 660, 664 (Randolph).

37. Id., 67.

38. Id., 628. See also 80, 90 (Morris); 121 (White).

39. Id., 659.

40. Contrast, for example, the opposing narratives dealing with the 1790s provided in the great set speeches by Giles and Bayard that framed the debate in the House. Compare id., 580–583 (Giles) with 606–614 (Bayard).

41. Even Representative Huger, a strong Federalist who presented a powerful speech against repeal, recognized this point: "I will not undertake to say, sir, that those who passed the law, now so much deprecated, were totally exempt from party feelings; nor will I deny that it was adopted at a late stage of the last session, and carried by no very large majority, either in the Senate or the House of Representatives. I do contend, however, that the measure cannot, in fairness and candor, be attributed to mere party motives, distinct from all public advantage; that the defects of the old system have been for years back complained of; . . . and that the most important change . . . has been heretofore warmly advocated by gentlemen of the very political sect which now raise such a clamor against it." Id., 670–671.

42. Id., 650.

43. Bayard elaborated on his charge: "I consider this business wholly as a Presidential measure. This document and his Message, show that it originated with him; I consider it as now prosecuted by him, and I believe that he has the power to arrest its progress, or to accomplish its completion." Id., 627.

44. Here is a characteristic invocation of presidential authority from Senator Wright: "As to the point of its being unconstitutional: It will be recollected that the President himself has recommended the repeal of this law; an evidence of its constitutionality of so high authority with the enlightened people of America, that if it stood singly on that, it would require a *federal host* to shake it; but we know that there are honorable gentlemen on this floor not disposed to *confess* their respect for that authority on this occasion." Id., 113; see also 161 (Mr. Bradley). Representative Macon, a strong Republican, denied undue presidential influence, but in a manner that seems hollow and formulaic (to me at least), id., 714. I find further corroboration in the remark of the Federalist Rutledge, id., 743, com-

menting on the "unpleasant[ness]" experienced by his opponents in "call[ing] this an Executive measure."

45. For those interested in exploring the debate further, I recommend James O'Fallon, "*Marbury,*" 44 *Stan. L. Rev.* 219, 221–239 (1992).

46. The most notable exception is a thoughtful speech by Huger—a Federalist, and therefore more open to the idea of legitimate party rotation: "It is but too true, we know it, sir, that parties do exist in our Government; that shades of political difference do unfortunately divide the American people. In free Governments this must ever be the case. Still, however, let it not be forgotten that we are citizens of one and the same country, and have a common interest in the public and general welfare. Would it not then be wise and prudent, would it not tend to do away, in a great measure, the baneful effect of party, and to promote harmony among our fellow-citizens, if in the changes of men and of parties, which must necessarily take place in the administration of public affairs, we accustomed ourselves to act with some little delicacy towards each other, and to pay some little respect to the measures of those who have immediately preceded us?" 11 *Annals* 677.

47. The defector was John Colhoun of South Carolina. Id., 149. For a good description of the situation, see Ellis, *Jeffersonian Crisis,* 46–47.

48. 11 *Annals* 148. The threat to the Republican initiative was compounded by the selection of members to the special committee. Though Breckenridge was the Republican leading the campaign for repeal, he failed to obtain a seat on the committee by a margin of a single vote. Id., 150.

49. Id., 150.

50. On Monday, February 1, just five days after the bill was returned to committee, Senator Breckenridge gave notice of his intention to bring the bill back to the floor the next day. Id., 152. When he did so on February 2, he acknowledged the presence of "some gentlemen now in the Senate who were not present during any part of the discussion." Id., 154. The newly arrived senator was Republican Senator Bradley. Federalist protests were predictable. Senator Tracy: "Does not the state of parties, for parties there are, require that we should heal instead of irritating their wounds?" Id., 159. Just as predictably, the Republicans ignored these protests, and swept the bill onward to passage.

51. There were a few exceptions that proved the rule: Edwin Gray was a Federalist who voted in favor. William Eustis and Thomas Tillinghast were Republicans who voted against. Federalist Henry Woods is listed as voting both yea and nay. Id., 982.

52. Many newspapers published substantial sections of the debates verbatim. In Boston, see the *Mercury and New England Palladium* and the *Columbia Centinel and Massachusetts Federalist.* In New York, see the *American Citizen,* the *Spectator,* and the *Gazette of the United States.* In Philadelphia, see the *Gazette of the*

United States, the *Philadelphia Gazette and Daily Advertiser,* and *Poulson's American Daily Advertiser.* In Washington, D.C., see the *National Intelligencer and Washington Advertiser* and the *Washington Federalist.*

53. 11 *Annals* 1306 (appendix).

54. Matoon to Thomas Dwight, Feb. 11, 1802, quoted in Wythe Holt, "If the Courts Have Firmness Enough to Render the Decision," in Wythe Holt and David Nourse, eds., *Egbert Benson,* 9 (1987).

55. "Farewell a Long Farewell to All Our Greatness," *Washington Federalist,* Mar. 3, 1802. For similar sentiments, see Z., "To the Judges of the Supreme Court of the United States," *Gazette of the United States* (Philadelphia), Apr. 7, 1802.

56. See Holt, "If the Courts Have Firmness Enough," 9–13. Even before Congress passed the repeal, Gouverneur Morris was enlisting Hamilton in a campaign to mobilize public opinion. Hamilton responded by calling a meeting "of a small number of leading Federalists" in Washington in early May to generate a "systematic and persevering effort by all Constitutional means to produce a revocation of the precedent, and to restore the Constitution." Hamilton to Pinckney, Mar. 15, 1802, 25 *PAH* 562–563. We do not know whether this meeting took place, but Hamilton did launch an aggressive newspaper campaign, writing as "Lucius Crassus." See "The Examination No. XXVIII," 25 *PAH* 589–597.

57. Rutledge to Bayard, Mar. 26, 1802, Collery Collection, Historical Society of Delaware. Wythe Holt made an important contribution in bringing this letter to scholarly attention for the first time in Holt, "If the Courts Have Firmness Enough," 10. While I quibble with certain aspects of his account at later points, his essay marks a breakthrough in historical understanding.

58. Wolcott to Griswold, Mar. 23, 1802, Lane Collection, Yale University.

59. In the following year the justices formally decided that they could not legally act as commissioners under the act. "United States v. Yale Todd," 13 *Howard* 52 (1851) (note inserted by Chief Justice Taney).

60. Hayburn's Case, 2 U.S. 408, 410 (1792).

61. Id.

62. 11 *Annals* 252–253 (1802). During the floor debate, the only reason given for the change in the court's schedule was efficiency: it was easier on the justices to come to Washington once a year and meet for a longer time. But as Bayard pointed out, canceling the upcoming session was in fact inefficient: "He considered this provision as predicated on injustice. It operated to continue the suits for more than a year. This is the effect of this mighty potchery of legislation! Where suitors are entitled to trial in six months, they are denied even a hearing for fourteen months. He believed this was unprecedented in this or any other country. Will gentlemen say why these causes cannot be decided in June? As the justices expected to meet, as the suitors expected to have their causes tried in June next, if

hereafter we are to have only one session, why interpose by a new repealing law, to affect a law which is not at present to be repealed till the first of July?" Id., 1211. These questions went unanswered. The next line of the *Annals* simply reports the defeat of Bayard's motion to strike the special section of the act abolishing the June 1802 term. See also Bayard to Hamilton, Apr. 12, 1802: "You have seen the patchwork offered to us as a new judicial system. The whole is designed to cover one object which the party consider it necessary to accomplish—The postpone-ment of the next session of the Supreme Court to Feby following. They mean to give the repealing act its full effect before the Judges of the Supreme Court are al-lowed to assemble." 25 *PAH* 600–601.

63. 11 *Annals* 1229.

64. Monroe to Jefferson, Apr. 25, 1802, 3 *WOM* 341–344.

65. See 2 Stat. 156, 167 (Apr. 29, 1802).

8. Marbury v. Stuart

1. Morris, Diary, Apr. 5, 1802, LC. It isn't clear whether Ross's report is based on recent word from Marshall or whether he is merely repeating the intelligence provided by Rutledge two weeks before. Rutledge visited Marshall at Ross's re-quest, and Ross may simply be reassuring Morris, on the basis of old news, that their defeat in the Senate does not imply that all is lost. The importance of Mor-ris's diary entry was first noted by Wythe Holt in "If the Courts Have Firmness Enough to Render the Decision," in Wythe Holt and David Nourse, eds., *Egbert Benson,* 12 (1987).

2. The bill passed the Senate by a vote of 16–10. 11 *Annals* 257 (1802).

3. Rutledge to Bayard, Mar. 26, 1802, Collery Collection, Historical Society of Delaware.

4. Marshall to Wolcott, Apr. 5, 1802, 6 *PJM,* 104.

5. Marshall to Cushing, Apr. 19, 1802, id., 108. See also his letters to Paterson of Apr. 6 and May 3, id., 105, 106, 117.

6. Marshall plainly believed that the circuit judges' commissions remained valid, and that the limited commissions of the Supreme Court justices did not au-thorize them to ride circuit. But his views on the power of Congress to abolish the circuit courts aren't entirely clear. Bayard tells Hamilton that Marshall accepts the constitutionality of repeal, 25 *PAH* 614 (Apr. 25, 1802), but this is hearsay, and if it is true, Marshall's views became more extreme over time. As an old man, asked for his opinion when serving as a delegate at the Virginia Constitutional Conven-tion, he responded that the repeal statute "could never be admitted as final and conclusive." 2 Bruce Dickson, ed., *Debates of the Virginia States Convention of*

1829–30, 481, 872 (1830). Republicans quickly rose to disagree, including the elderly William Giles, who had been instrumental in getting the act passed. Marshall remained steadfast: "Mr. Marshall observed, that the present was not the first example which had occurred . . . where gentlemen held opinions directly opposite to each other." Id., 873.

7. Id.

8. Consider the account presented in Jean Edward Smith's biography, *John Marshall: Definer of a Nation* (1996). Smith omits Marshall's early assurances to Federalist politicians of his intention to engage in judicial resistance. He then says that Marshall "expressed no concern" about the repeal in his letter to Wolcott of April 5—but in fact Marshall regrets the cancellation of the June meeting. Turning next to his April 6 letter to Paterson, Smith says that "Marshall was unconcerned about Congress's repeal of the Act of 1801"—but in this letter, Marshall "confess[es] I have some strong constitutional scruples." Smith then turns briefly to Marshall's April 19 letters to Cushing and Paterson, but focuses mainly on the passages leaning toward riding circuit, and ignores the stronger passages that advocate striking. He also bungles his discussion of Bayard's reports on Marshall, citing a letter of April 17 when he seems to be talking about a letter of April 24, and fails to put the letter in context. See generally Smith, id., 305–306.

Wythe Holt makes a fundamental contribution to the subject, but his interpretation of the correspondence is also highly selective. He reads nonexistent arguments into the letter of April 6: "Marshall was writing to Justice Paterson that, despite his 'strong constitutional scruples' about repeal, Congress nevertheless had plenary constitutional power to assign the various duties of the federal judges, including reassignment of the duties of existing Circuit Judges and Supreme Court Justices . . . Marshall concentrated solely upon the issue of Congressional power to reassign judicial duties." But Marshall's letter does not contain this concession. Holt recognizes that Marshall "waxed a bit stronger in his constitutional objections" in his second letter to Paterson. But he believes Marshall, intimidated by the political dangers, had already made up his mind, and fails to consider why, if this is so, Marshall was still holding out the prospect of a defiant meeting in his third letter to Paterson of May 3. See Holt, "If the Courts Have Firmness Enough," 12–14. Richard Ellis's briefer discussion also emphasizes the conciliatory aspect of Marshall's conduct, see Ellis, *The Jeffersonian Crisis,* 61–65 (1971).

Kent Newmyer's treatment is by far the most perceptive of the modern commentaries: "a strictly legal analysis of the Repeal Act led [Marshall] to conclude that the justices should not ride circuit," and he concludes that the Court's retreat was motivated by institutional statecraft, not compelling legal conviction. See R. Kent Newmyer, *John Marshall and the Heroic Age of the Supreme Court,* 155 (2001). But he treats the entire episode, culminating in Stuart v. Laird, as a sideshow without any fundamental relationship to Marbury v. Madison. Id., 152–157.

In emphasizing the link between *Marbury* and *Stuart,* I am drawing on earlier historiography. In his classic biography, Albert Beveridge says: "When the Republicans repealed the Federalist Judiciary Act of 1801, Marshall had actually proposed to his associates upon the Supreme Bench that they refuse to sit as circuit judges, and 'risk the consequences.' By the Constitution, he said, they were Judges of the Supreme Court only; their commissions proved that they were appointed solely to those offices; the section requiring them to sit in inferior courts was unconstitutional. The other members of the Supreme Court, however, had not the courage to adopt the heroic course Marshall had recommended. They agreed that his views were sound, but insisted that, because the Ellsworth Judiciary Act had been acquiesced in since the adoption of the Constitution, the validity of that act must now be considered as established. So Marshall reluctantly abandoned his bold plan." 3 *LJM* 122.

Much earlier, the *New York Review* of 1838, in an homage to the late chief justice, had no trouble identifying his role in the affair: "When [repeal] was passed, Mr. Chief Justice Marshall addressed a circular letter to all the other judges of the supreme court, stating, that upon full examination and consideration, he had come to the conclusion that the judges of the supreme court could not constitutionally be required to hold any other sessions than those of the Supreme Court; that they were by their commissions appointed solely as judges of the supreme court and could not be compelled to sit in any other inferior court; and he accordingly stated to his brethren, that if they concurred in that opinion, he would decline to sit in the circuit court, and risk the consequences. His brethren all returned answers fully agreeing with him in the opinion, that the judges of the supreme court could not constitutionally be required to sit in any other court; but they advised him to go to the circuits, considering that the question had been put at rest by the acquiescence of the judges going the circuits up to the year 1801. He accordingly followed their advice, and went the circuits." 3 *New York Review,* 328, 347 (1838).

These early accounts contain errors of detail, but they avoid the hagiographic tendency of much modern scholarship.

9. My analysis is supported by a contrast with the letter Marshall sent Paterson two weeks earlier: "I confess I have some strong constitutional scruples. I cannot well perceive how the performance of circuit duty by the Judges of the Supreme Court can be supported. If the question was new I shoud be unwilling to act in this character without a consultation of the Judges; but I consider it as decided & whatever my own scruples may be I am bound by the decision. I cannot however but regret the loss of the next June term. I could have wishd the Judges had convend before they proceeded to execute the new system." 6 *PJM* 108, 109. Marshall is clear about his own "strong constitutional scruples" against circuit riding, but the later letter makes it clear that he is not willing to let Congress win

without a struggle, and that he is continuing his epistolary campaign to persuade his fellow justices.

10. Marshall's letter to Chase does not survive, but Chase's response begins with an acknowledgment of "your letter of the 19th instant," and it seems reasonable to suppose that Marshall's letter was similar in style and substance to the one written to Paterson.

11. Though Chase begins by saying he will give three reasons, he never explicitly identifies the third part of his argument. I think this is what he had in mind.

12. *History*, 172–177n182 (1981); also 6 *PJM* 109–116.

13. Chase also goes beyond Marshall in suggesting that a statute authorizing the grant of a second commission to the justices would be unconstitutional. But this claim was not necessary to resolve the case at hand: the justices didn't have a second commission, and they were legally required to go on strike if their first commission did not cover the conduct of trials in the circuit courts.

14. Marshall to Paterson, May 3, 1802, 6 *PJM* 117–118.

15. I do not suggest that the meeting would have been strictly illegal. The new statute did not explicitly prohibit the justices from making personal contact. It simply postponed the next plenary session of the court until February 1803.

16. Notice that Marshall does not ask Paterson to poll Justice Washington, nor does he suggest that he will poll Washington himself. He seems to be operating on the assumption that Washington's opposition isn't necessarily dispositive. As late as May 28, according to Stoddert, Chase still believed that there would be a face-to-face meeting: "I saw Judge Chase on my way. He says there will be a meeting of the Judges in Washington before the New Law goes into operation—the object to determine whether they will aid in the execution. I do not believe he will, should all the rest be against him. People's minds are preparing—are indeed already prepared to sanction what the judges shall do." Stoddert to Wolcott, May 28, 1802, New York Historical Society. Stoddert was reliable, but Chase wasn't, so the credibility of this report is open to doubt.

17. Paterson to Cushing, Massachusetts Historical Society. Chase sent a copy of his full analysis to Cushing in early June, but the precise date is not provided in the covering letter now in the archives.

18. Paterson's original letter does not survive, but he apparently sent a copy to Cushing, whose wife, Hannah, copied it out in a letter to Abigail Adams, which survives in the Adams Papers in Massachusetts. The key passage is printed at 6 *PJM* 118n6.

19. *History*, 177, citing letter from Cushing to Paterson, June 8, 1802, Miscellaneous Manuscripts, Cushing, New York Historical Society. Cushing expresses similar sentiments in a letter to Chase of June 11, now in the Massachusetts Historical Society. Moore's response does not survive.

20. I analyze later historical episodes involving unconventional threats in *WPT,* parts 2–3.

21. See William Casto, *Oliver Ellsworth and the Creation of the Federal Republic,* 105–107 (1997); William Casto, *The Supreme Court in the Early Republic,* chs. 2–4 (1995).

22. Justices Chase and Washington had been particularly active, often leaving the bench to campaign for Federalist candidates. See *History,* 161.

23. The meeting was called by the judges of the Third Circuit, see Holt, "If the Courts Have Firmness Enough," 16, and while it generated a lot of correspondence—I have discovered, for example, a treasure trove of constitutional writing from Oliver Wolcott in the Connecticut Historical Society—only four judges actually convened in Philadelphia in early July. Bassett, one of the Third Circuit judges, was present, and his Protest describes his relationship to his colleagues: "If any *difference* of opinion, between me and my *associates* in office, exists, it relates merely to the *point of time* for expressing our sentiments. I can confidently assert, that on deliberation, they *coincide* with me in other respects." *New England Palladium,* Sept. 3, 1802, 2.

24. Bassett was James Bayard's father-in-law, and Bayard may well have written the Protest in whole or in part. I disagree with historians who disparage the Protest as "long, tedious and often convoluted," Holt, "If the Courts Have Firmness Enough," 16.

25. "Old South," LXXI, quoted from the slightly revised text in Benjamin Austin, Jr. ["Old South"], "Constitutional Republicanism," in *Opposition to Fallacious Federalism,* 295–296 (1803).

26. See Holt, "If the Courts Have Firmness Enough," 16–18.

27. 1 *Sen. Exec. J.* 381 (Feb. 18, 1801).

28. 1 *Sen. Exec. J.* 385 (Feb. 25, 1801).

29. Plumer to Edward Livermore, Dec. 21, 1802, Microfilming Corp. of America, *The William Plumer Papers, 1778–1854,* LC. A search of the relevant archives in Virginia and Philadelphia has uncovered the formal papers in the case, but no trace of Marshall's opinion.

30. See, e.g., *New York Commercial Advertiser,* Aug. 24 and 25, 1802; *Centinel of Freedom* (Newark, N.J.), Sept. 7, 1802. Holt, "If the Courts Have Firmness Enough," 62.

31. *Independent Chronicle,* Sept. 2, 1802, 1.

32. 3 Donald Bacon et al., eds., *Encyclopedia of the U.S. Congress,* 1556 (1995).

33. Adams originally appointed sixteen circuit judges, but all three from the southernmost Fifth Circuit rejected the positions, see Levi Lincoln to Jefferson, Mar. 21, Apr. 9, Apr. 16, 1801; copies in Lincoln Family Papers, American Antiquarian Society, Worcester, MA, box 1, folder 4; and John Lowell, the chief judge

of the First Circuit, died on May 2, see *Independent Chronicle,* Oct. 11, 1802. One of the remaining twelve, McClung, was the sole midnight judge for the frontier Sixth Circuit, and seems to have been out of the loop.

34. For the full text of the memorial see *History,* 179–180.

35. 12 *Annals* 430.

36. Id., 438, 440–441.

37. Id., 52.

38. Id., 60, 78.

39. See, e.g., id., 434 (Mr. Griswold).

40. Id., 52–53.

41. Id., 52.

42. In the course of the debate, some of the Republicans denied the constitutional propriety of congressional authorization. Congressman Richardson, for example, remarked that it was "a little surprising that this application should be made," since the Federalists had previously contended that the Court had the power of judicial review independently of congressional authorization: "If they [the judges] have this right we need not confer it; if have it not, we cannot give it them. If the petitioning judges can bring their case before the Supreme Court, let them do so; my consent shall never authorize it." Id., 437–438. See also id., 59 (Senator Wright). But, as the snippet from Richardson suggests, the argument was made in a tone of defiant confidence born of the Republican electoral victory.

43. See 1 Charles Warren, *The Supreme Court in United States History,* 272n1. Warren's sources include the *Charleston Courier,* May 9, 1803; the *Washington Federalist,* May 13, 1803; and the *New England Palladium,* Apr. 19, 1803.

44. 3 Joseph Story, *Commentaries on the Constitution of the United States,* 495, 495n2 (1833) (emphasis supplied). I have drawn the first two sentences of this quotation from Story's text at page 495, the remainder from a footnote. If anything, this selection understates the strength of conviction with which Story presents his arguments.

45. St. George Tucker, for example, condemned the views of his fellow Republicans as "calculated to subvert one of the fundamental pillars of free governments." 1 St. George Tucker, ed., *Blackstone's Commentaries: With Notes of References to the Constitution and Laws of the Federal Government of the United States and of the Commonwealth of Virginia,* 360–362 (1803).

46. Jefferson to Johnson, June 12, 1823, in 4 Thomas Randolph, ed., *Memoir, Correspondence, and Miscellanies, from the Papers of Thomas Jefferson* 373 (1829).

47. Lee began his argument in *Stuart* on February 23, and continued on February 24, after *Marbury* was announced. See National Archives Microfilm Publications, *Minutes of the Supreme Court of the United States,* series 215, reel 1, page 134, left column (1954). I shall be emphasizing arguments made by Lee late in

his oral presentation, which suggests that he made them after *Marbury* was announced. The court records do not make this absolutely clear, and there is an outside chance that Lee made them during his first day of argument—in which case, he had a preternatural sense of the path that Marshall would follow in *Marbury*.

48. Marbury v. Madison, 5 U.S. 137, 154–162.

49. 5 U.S. 137, 163.

50. Id., 163.

51. Article III grants original jurisdiction to the Supreme Court only in cases in which a state is a party and cases involving foreign diplomats.

52. Stuart v. Laird, 5 U.S. 299, 304–305 (1803) (argument of Charles Lee).

53. Id., 305.

54. Here is the Reporter summarizing Lee's argument: "[Congress] may modify the courts, but they cannot destroy them, if they thereby deprive a judge of his office . . . The words *during good behaviour* cannot mean *during the will of congress*." Id., 303–304.

55. Id., 308–309.

56. Charles Hobson denies that the Court was "compelled to sacrifice sound constitutional doctrine in either *Marbury* or *Stuart*," see Hobson, "Marshall, the Mandamus Case, and the Judiciary Crisis," 72 *Geo. Wash. L. Rev.* 289, 298 (2003), but he reaches this conclusion only by ignoring the key point of doctrinal contradiction: if, as *Marbury* insists, the Supreme Court justices could not constitutionally exercise original jurisdiction except in very special circumstances, how did their commissions give them legal authority to preside over trials as circuit judges? Hobson fails to confront this question and imagines that he successfully resolves the contradiction by pointing out that *Stuart* did not need to reach the "larger constitutional question . . . whether Congress . . . could deprive the judges of their lifetime appointments." But even if the answer to this question were yes, *Marbury* implies that it was unconstitutional for the justices to take up the slack without receiving new and distinct commissions.

57. *History*, 652.

58. Individual justices issued seriatim opinions in almost one-fifth of the 63 reported cases before 1801. These generally involved the more important decisions, including Georgia v. Brailsford, 2 Dall. 402 (1792); Chisholm v. Georgia, 2 Dall. 419 (1793); Bingham v. Cabot, 3 Dall. 19 (1795); Penhallow v. Doane's Administrators, 3 Dall. 54 (1795); Talbot v. Janson, 3 Dall. 133 (1795); Hylton v. United States, 3 Dall. 171 (1796); Ware v. Hylton, 3 Dall. 199 (1796); Fenemore v. United States, 3 Dall. 357 (1797); Calder v. Bull, 3 Dall. 386 (1798); Cooper v. Telfair, 4 Fall. 14 (1800); and Bas v. Tingy, 4 Dall. 37 (1800).

59. Stuart v. Laird, at 308. Johnson notes the exceptional character of *Stuart*,

but uncritically accepts the reason given by the Reporter for Marshall's selective silence. See *History*, 383–384.

60. See 6 *PJM* 371.

61. See, e.g., Talbot v. Seeman, 5 U.S. (1 Cranch) 1 (1801) (Washington); Mason v. Ship Blaireau, 6 U.S. (2 Cranch) 240 (1804) (Chase).

62. Hepburn & Dundas v. Ellzey, 6 U.S. (2 Cranch) 445 (1805) (Marshall). The case involved a suit between a citizen of the District of Columbia and a citizen of a state. The question was whether the circuit court had jurisdiction by virtue of the diversity of citizenship of the litigants. Writing for the Supreme Court, Marshall held that the District of Columbia was not a "state" in the relevant sense, and that the court lacked jurisdiction. *Hepburn* was similar to *Stuart* in raising an issue involving the jurisdiction of the court—except that it was an infinitely less important issue. If Marshall didn't recuse himself in 1805, he didn't have to do it in 1803—except, of course, that recusal provided him a face-saving way to avoid explaining why the Court wasn't following *Marbury*.

I should note, however, that Marshall does seem to have generally followed the practice of recusal through 1817 or so, even after the Court explicitly renounced it in 1808. Marshall may have continued to recuse himself in order to pacify colleagues who wished to write opinions. It allowed him to give others a chance to shine without ceding his claim to serve as the principal author of opinions of the Court. See Johnson's interesting discussion in *History*, 572–573. However this may be, Marshall's opinion in *Hepburn* establishes that he had no principled objection to participating in cases he decided below.

63. See Rose v. Himley, 8 U.S. (4 Cranch) 241 (1808) (three of the six judges present had given opinions below, and recusal would leave the Court without a quorum); Shirrs v. Caig, 11 U.S. (7 Cranch) 34 (1812) (confirming official abandonment of recusal practice, even when not demanded by necessity).

Modern readers will undoubtedly be disturbed by a practice in which justices regularly participated in appeals from their own decisions, and may be surprised to learn that the Court embraced the practice in 1808, rather than move in the direction suggested by modern notions of fairness. But there were real administrative problems involved if every case required the withdrawal of one or more of the justices. One should also consider that English high court judges regularly participated in the decision of cases at Westminster which they had already heard when riding circuit. See 1 James Oldham, *The Mansfield Manuscripts and the Growth of English Law in the Eighteenth Century*, 131 (1992).

64. For a classic statement of the maxim, see 2 Thomas Cooley ed., *Blackstone's Commentaries on the Laws of England*, 21–23 (2003).

65. Madison declined to certify "the nomination of the applicants and of the advice and consent of the Senate." 5 U.S. at 138 (1803).

66. Id., 146.

67. Some have interpreted these events as indications of a conspiracy by Marshall and his brother to create a feigned case from the very beginning. See John Garraty, "The Case of the Missing Commissions," in Garraty, ed., *Quarrels That Have Shaped the Constitution,* 1 (1962). But I think Newmyer is right in dismissing this possibility. See Newmyer, *Marshall and the Heroic Age,* 160.

At the other extreme, Hobson argues that it is anachronistic to hold Marshall "accountable to stricter modern canons of judicial conduct . . . He could not have perceived—or suspected that others might perceive—that he had an interest in that case that could influence his judgment." Hobson, "Marshall, the Mandamus Case, and the Judiciary Crisis," 293. I disagree: His brother's affidavit clearly suggested that Marshall should be serving as principal witness, not judge, rather than relying on his brother's say-so; and Madison's boycott emphasized the imperative need for the Court to establish a compelling appearance of impartiality. See Dean Alfange Jr., "Marbury v. Madison and Original Understandings of Judicial Review," *Sup. Ct. Rev.* 329, 392–393 (1993). See also William Van Alstyne, "A Critical Guide to Marbury v. Madison," 1969 *Duke L. J.* 1, 8 (1969).

68. One of the weirder moments in *Marbury* is Marshall's description of his plight as a judge, given Madison's boycott of the proceedings: "After searching anxiously for the principles on which a contrary opinion may be supported, none have been found which appear of sufficient force to maintain the opposite doctrine. Such as the imagination of the court could suggest, have been very deliberately examined, and after allowing them all the weight which it appears possible to give them, they do not shake the opinion which has been formed." 5 U.S. 137, 158.

Marshall confessed to a certain unease about *Marbury* in his later years. Responding in 1830 to the recent publication of Jefferson's correspondence, Marshall wrote to Henry Lee: "The parts of my conduct which form the subject of [Jefferson's] most malignant censure are in possession of the public, and every fair mind must perceive in them a refutation of the calumnies uttered against me. To unfair minds any thing I could urge would be unavailing and probably unread. Nothing is unknown or can be misunderstood by intelligent men *unless it be the motives which compelled the court to give its opinion at large on the case of Marbury v. Madison.*" Oct. 25, 1830, 11 *PJM* 73 (emphasis supplied).

If Marshall had recused himself, the Court would have had a temporary problem: only three other justices were in Washington, not enough for a quorum in a tribunal containing six judges. But Justice Moore arrived shortly afterward, and a brief postponement of the case would have solved this problem. There was no rush. (Justice Moore arrived in time to hear *Stuart,* when Marshall did recuse himself.)

69. Philip Weinberg ed., *Compendium: The Supreme Court,* 441 (1990). The constitutional case was Ogden v. Saunders, 12 Wheaton 213 (1827).

70. Plumer to Livermore, Dec. 21, 1802, *William Plumer Papers, 1778–1854,* LC (spelling modernized).

71. The index to the relevant volume of Laurence Tribe's leading treatise contains 63 page references to *Marbury* and not one to *Stuart.* Compare 1 Laurence Tribe, *American Constitutional Law,* xcii, with cxii (2000). Leading casebooks consign *Stuart* to a footnote, without inviting students to reflect on its fundamental constitutional significance. See Gerald Gunther and Kathleen M. Sullivan, *Constitutional Law,* 12n1 (1997).

72. See Donald Dewey, *Marshall v. Jefferson,* 74 (1970) (quoting original sources). Dewey is a rare modern historian who appreciates the significance of *Stuart,* but his analysis deals with politics, not law. My friends Jack Balkin and Sandy Levinson have recently taken up the cause in their essay "What are the Facts of Marbury v. Madison?" 20 *Con. Comm.* 255, 259–264 (2003), which relies on an earlier version of the present chapter.

73. See Sylvia Snowiss, "Text and Principle in John Marshall's Constitutional Law," 33 *John Marshall L. Rev.* 973 (2000).

74. Marbury v. Madison, 5 U.S. 137, 175–176.

75. I develop the larger implications of this view in *WPT.*

76. Jefferson to Dickinson, Mar. 6, 1801, 9 *Jeff* 216–217.

77. I interpret Madison's views on this matter in *WTP,* ch. 7, and in Bruce Ackerman, "Revolution on a Human Scale," 108 *Yale L. J.* 2279, 2299n29 (1999).

78. Nevertheless, this scholarship breaks important new ground. See Sylvia Snowiss, *Judicial Review and the Law of the Constitution* (1990); Snowiss, "Text and Principle in Marshall's Constitutional Law"; Larry Kramer, *The People Themselves* (2004). Among recent commentators, James O'Fallon's strength is his insistence on reading Marbury as a response to the Jeffersonian revolution. See O'Fallon, "Marbury," 44 *Stan. L. Rev.* 219 (1992). But he also suggests that Marshall's self-conscious defense of judicial review is a relatively unimportant aspect of the opinion. I agree with Dean Alfange that this is a regrettable failing of O'Fallon's enlightening essay, see Alfange, "Marbury v. Madison and Original Understandings," 331–332.

79. For compelling critiques along these lines, see Alfange, "Marbury v. Madison and Original Understandings," 368–372, 393–406; O'Fallon, "Marbury," 243–259; and Van Alstyne, "Critical Guide to Marbury v. Madison." I am not persuaded by Louise Weinberg's effort at refutation in "Our Marbury," 89 *Va. L. Rev.* 1235, 1303–10 (2003).

80. Robert McCloskey, *The American Supreme Court,* 26–27 (1994)

81. McCloskey takes note of *Stuart*'s existence, id., 30, but he only deals with its political implications. By contrast, Dean Alfange properly emphasizes *Stuart*'s doctrinal importance in "Marbury v. Madison and Original Understandings," 362–364, 371, 391–392, but fails to develop an affirmative interpretation of the enduring meaning of the *Marbury-Stuart* pair. I am indebted to him for raising key questions that provoked my own effort.

82. I have tried, but failed, to come up with evidence of an explicit decision by the circuit judges to desist from further legal action in the wake of *Marbury*.

83. See Susan Bloch, "The Marbury Mystery: Why Did William Marbury Sue in the Supreme Court?" 18 *Const. Comm.* 607, 627.

9. Presidential Purge

1. See Herbert Johnson, "Impeachment and Politics," 63 *So. Atl. Q.* 552, 556 (1964) ("The impeachment of Pickering was but the first step in the Republican program."). Even Jefferson's very sympathetic biographer, Dumas Malone, cautions that his hero "cannot be fairly held responsible for all the words and actions of the Republican leaders in Congress, . . . the Federalists regarded [Pickering's] impeachment as a measure of the administration, and party discipline was clearly manifest in connection with it." 4 *Jefferson and His Time,* 463 (1970). This account by a Jeffersonian admirer falls far short of a straight denial of the president's role as principal motivator of the impeachment campaign.

Republicans in Pennsylvania had begun a similar campaign against the Federalist justices of the state supreme court, successfully removing William Addison in 1802 and pressing onward unsuccessfully for the next few years. Jefferson's appointee as U.S. attorney, Alexander Dallas, prosecuted the Addison case, and the president expressed approval. "The Republicans had drawn the sword of 'dangerous tendency' from the forge; it remained to be seen whether the blade would cut thicker necks than Addison's." Peter Hoffer and N. E. H. Hull, *Impeachment in America,* 205 (1984). See also 3 *LJM* 164 and nn1–3.

William H. Rehnquist takes a different view, characterizing Jefferson's decision to impeach Chase as "a fit of pique" that was not rooted in "the implementation of a carefully planned strategy to purge all the Federalist justices from the Supreme Court." *Grand Inquests,* 53 (1992). But he does not seriously consider the countervailing evidence.

2. "Farewell, a Long Farewell to All Our Greatness," *Washington Federalist,* Mar. 3, 1802, 2. These fears had substance. William Branch Giles, a leading Republican senator from Virginia, wrote to Jefferson on June 1, 1801, advocating "an absolute repeal of the whole Judiciary . . . terminating the present offices and

creating a new system." Quoted in Richard Ellis, "The Impeachment of Samuel Chase," in Michal R. Belknap, ed., *American Political Trials,* 57, 61 (1981).

3. Jefferson's request is reprinted in *History,* 212. Senator Plumer provides an account of Jefferson's views on January 5, 1804: "I dined this day with President Jefferson—I was at his house near an hour before the other gentlemen—Speaking of the impeachment of Pickering, I observed I had no doubt that the judge was insane, & asked him whether insanity was good cause for impeachment & removal from office. He replied, 'If the facts of his denying an appeal & of his intoxication, as stated in the impeachment are proven, that will be sufficient cause of removal without further enquiry.'" Everett Brown, ed., *William Plumer's Memorandum of Proceedings in the United States Senate, 1803–1807,* 100 (1923) (hereinafter *Memorandum*). Joseph Nicholson, another congressional leader, was in close contact with Jefferson, and "knew that Jefferson had hinted that the judge had to go." Hoffer and Hull, *Impeachment,* 208; see also Robert Johnstone, *Jefferson and the Presidency,* 181 (1978).

4. The House initially did not draft formal articles of impeachment, sending Randolph and Nicholson over to the Senate to convey the impeachment orally and to demand Pickering's immediate appearance. After the Federalists balked, the Senate deferred action until the House had tendered formal articles. 12 *Annals* 267–268 (Mar. 3, 1803); Lynn Turner, "The Impeachment of John Pickering," 54 *Am. Hist. Rev.,* 485, 491–492 (1949).

5. 13 *Annals* 364 (Mar. 12, 1804).

6. Id., 365.

7. Id., 362. The motion was defeated by a vote of 19–9. Id., 363.

8. Id., 366. Three were Republicans: John Armstrong (New York), Stephen Bradley (Vermont), and David Stone (North Carolina). The two Federalists, Samuel White (Delaware) and John Dayton (New Jersey), did not even stick around to record their votes of "not guilty," though they had already made their objections clear. Id., 366; see also Hoffer and Hull, *Impeachment,* 217–218.

Three other Republicans failed to vote. Pierce Butler (South Carolina) left the capital earlier for personal reasons, but John Brown (Kentucky) excused himself several days earlier because he was "inclined to vote against convicting of [Pickering]; but being . . . unwilling to offend his party, obtained leave of absence for the residue of the session." *Memorandum,* 173.

Aaron Burr may well have skipped town to avoid dealing with the question: "Now that the excitement of the chase was finished, Burr also found his presence at home imperative, and left abruptly." Turner, "Impeachment of Pickering," 503.

9. Quoted in Turner, "Impeachment of Pickering," 505.

10. *History,* 234.

11. 13 *Annals* 1171–81 (Mar. 12, 1804).

12. *History,* 222.

13. For the entire grand jury charge see 14 *Annals* 673–674.

14. Letter of May 13, 1803, quoted in *History,* 219. Since Jefferson wrote to Nicholson, not Randolph, why did the latter take the lead? Nicholson was a Marylander like Chase, and a likely successor on the Court if the impeachment succeeded. His confidantes had counseled him to avoid too large a role in the impeachment campaign. Nathaniel Macon to Nicholson, July 26, 1803, quoted in *History,* 220. The president's decision to target Nicholson does suggest his reluctance to rely on Randolph as his principal sword-bearer.

15. See 14 *Annals* 83–84, 13 *Annals* 1171.

16. 13 *Annals* 1180 (Mar. 1804).

17. *Federal Gazette,* Apr. 11, 1804.

18. 13 *Annals* 89 (Nov. 1803) (Smith).

19. Federalist Senator Hillhouse response to these remarks is revealing: "As to what he had heard about cutting off heads, he supposed that could not have been meant as a threat; in his part of the country such a crime could not take place. The gentleman [Smith], however, must be supposed to know his neighbors better than he did, but he could not suspect such danger from a valiant people." Id., 130. Hillhouse was from Connecticut; Smith, from Maryland. For a reluctant Federalist concession that a statutory solution to the problem of presidential succession might well have been in the works, see the remarks of Senator Tracy, id., 169.

20. 13 *Annals* 120 (Nov. 1803).

21. An example suggests the complexity of the Republicans' strategic dilemma. Suppose, as actually happened, that Jefferson dumped Burr and the Republican caucus selected another New Yorker, George Clinton, to serve as his running mate; and that the new Republican ticket confronted the Federalist team of Pinckney and King. To avoid a replay of 1800, some of the Republican electors would have had to waste their second ballot by voting for another candidate—say, James Madison. Only in this way could Jefferson have won the presidency without ending in a dead heat with Clinton.

At this point, however, the Republicans would have confronted a dilemma. Suppose that only one of their electors wasted the second ballot on Madison; in this case, the Federalists could deprive Jefferson of the presidency by instructing two of *their* electors to vote for Clinton instead of King, thereby putting the New Yorker one vote ahead of Jefferson in the electoral college tally. To avoid this result, the Republicans would have to waste a lot of votes on Madison: if the Federalists won X electoral votes, the Republicans would be obliged to award Clinton X minus 1 votes. This strategy would guarantee Jefferson the presidency, but it might well deprive Clinton of the vice presidency—since, under this scenario, at least one of the Federalist candidates could get X votes and come in second.

22. 13 *Annals* 178 (Dec. 1803) (Tracy).

23. Id.

24. Id., 90 (Nov. 1803) (Hillhouse).

25. Id., 186 (Taylor).

26. For an exception, see Akhil Amar, *America's Constitution: A Biography* (Random House, forthcoming). I have mined the debate for themes central to my larger argument. For a detailed account of the political climate, see Tadahisa Kuroda, *The Origins of the Twelfth Amendment*, 127–161 (1994).

27. See James Lewis, *The Louisiana Purchase*, 61–68 (2003). See also Peter Castor, *The Nation's Crucible: The Louisiana Purchase and the Creation of America*, 47–48 (2004).

28. Hume, "Review of Jefferson's Administration," no. 9, *Massachusetts Spy* 1 (Aug. 15, 1804). Hume's 27 essays were originally published in the *Columbian Centinel*. He returned to the subject in his 23rd essay with interesting variations on his theme: "Already has the nation witnessed the destruction of the circuit judges. To effect this, the democrats acknowledged that the judges of the supreme court could not be removed, unless convicted of misconduct on impeachment. They consequently so far committed themselves, that they thought it imprudent to resort to their former mode of depriving the judge of his office, and then refusing to pay him any salary, because he had performed no duty. No way therefore remained to destroy the highest tribunal of justice in the nation, but to raise a committee, though no complaint had been preferred, to ransack the whole of a man's public life to find something, which might give color to an impeachment . . . Judge Chase is selected as the first victim, not for real misconduct, but because he is presumed the most unpopular of any of the judges of the Supreme Court. The rest must fall in quick succession." Id. (Nov. 28, 1804). For a similar understanding of the election's relationship to the Republican campaign, see Hoffer and Hull, *Impeachment*, 237.

29. Taylor, *A Defence of the Measures of the Administration of Thomas Jefferson*, 37 (1804). Taylor originally published the *Defence*, under the pseudonym "Curtius," as a series of articles in the *National Intelligencer*, which were widely republished by other Republican papers before they came out as a book. The centrality of the *Defence* is suggested by the frequent efforts of the Federalist press to respond to its arguments.

30. Id., 37–38.

31. Johnson suggests that the Republicans expressly sought to delay the impeachment trial until after the November 1804 presidential election. See Herbert Johnson, *The Chief Justiceship of John Marshall, 1801–1835*, 64 and n25 (1997) (citing letter from Uriah Tracy to Robert Goodloe Harper, Mar. 13, 1804). This is likely, but I note that Johnson's correspondents are both Federalists, and therefore prone to place their antagonists in an unsympathetic light.

32. John Quincy Adams to John Adams, Mar. 8, 1805, in 3 Worthington Ford, ed., *Writings of John Quincy Adams, 1801–1810*, 110–111 (1914).

33. See Hoffer and Hull, *Impeachment*, 189, 231–252. Caesar Rodney, one of Randolph's fellow managers, presented the most compelling elaboration of the "popular will" conception at the trial. 2 Samuel Smith and Thomas Lloyd, eds., *The Trial of Samuel Chase*, 365–450 (1805).

34. Senator William Branch Giles was a strong advocate of the "popular will" theory of impeachment. See Hoffer and Hull, *Impeachment*, 188–189. He was also a central player, constantly consulting with Randolph in public view of other senators and serving as a liaison to the president, who was a close friend.

35. Id., 238.

36. Randolph was never a practicing lawyer although he had attended some lectures in law. See Henry Adams, *John Randolph*, 20 (1883); Lemuel Sawyer, *A Biography of John Randolph*, 10, 12 (1844).

37. I do not attempt a full elaboration of the charges against Chase or the conduct of the trial. The best summary is provided by Hoffer and Hull, *Impeachment*, ch. 12. See also David Currie, *The Constitution in Congress: The Jeffersonians*, 31–38 (2001).

The merits of the Senate's decision remain controversial. Compare the harsh condemnation of Chase's conduct by Raoul Berger, *Impeachment*, 242–251 (1973), with the sympathetic indulgence of Stephen Presser, *The Original Misunderstanding* (1991). This disagreement generated a spiraling controversy: Berger, "Justice Samuel Chase v. Thomas Jefferson: A Response to Stephen Presser," 1990 *BYU L. Rev.* 873 (1990); Presser, "Et Tu Raoul, or The Original Misunderstanding Misunderstood," 1991 *BYU L. Rev.* 1475 (1991); Berger, "The Transfiguration of Samuel Chase: A Rebuttal," 1992 *BYU L. Rev.* 559 (1992).

The debate is too adversarial for my taste—as if the protagonists were legal advocates aiming for decisive victory in the court of history. For my purposes, it is enough to establish that the charges against Chase were well within the realm of constitutional plausibility, and therefore require consideration of the structural factors that facilitated his acquittal.

In addition to the account by Hoffer and Hull, I am indebted to Keith Whittington's "Reconstructing the Federal Judiciary: The Chase Impeachment and the Constitution," 9 *Stud. Amer. Pol. Dev.* 55 (1995). But I disagree with his suggestion that the conviction of Chase would "have served to immunize the rest of the judiciary" from further impeachment campaigns. Id., 113. Whittington bases this conclusion on his belief, which I share, that many Republicans in the Senate refused to view impeachment as an all-purpose tool for discharging judges at will, and insisted that it be reserved for cases involving "gross improprieties." But he fails to recognize that Marshall's decision to participate in *Marbury* represented a "gross impropriety" that was comparable to those charged against Chase. And, as a midnight appointment made after the election of 1800, Marshall was an especially appropriate target, so far as Jefferson was concerned.

38. First Article of Impeachment, 1 Smith and Lloyd, eds., *Trial of Chase*, 5.

39. For Plumer's comment on the pardon, see *Memorandum*, 280. For Henry Adams on Randolph's reaction, see Adams, *John Randolph*, 144–145.

40. See Hoffer and Hull, *Impeachment*, 230.

41. Fourth Article of Impeachment, Smith and Lloyd, *Trial of Chase*, 6.

42. See James Haw, Francis F. Beirne, Rosamond Beirne, and R. Samuel Jett, *Stormy Patriot: The Life of Samuel Chase*, 228–229 (1980).

43. Robert Goodloe Harper was the mastermind of Chase's legal defense. Here is part of his final argument to the Senate: "It is not necessary for me to contend that this offence must be an indictable offence. I might safely admit the contrary, tho' I do not admit it: and there are reasons which appear to me unanswerable for the opinion, that no offence is impeachable, unless it be also the proper subject of an indictment. But it is not necessary to go so far; and I can suppose cases where a judge ought to be impeached, for which I am not prepared to declare him indictable. Suppose, for instance, that he should constantly omit to hold court; or should habitually attend so short a time each day as to render it impossible to dispatch the business. It might be doubted whether an indictment would lie for those acts of omission; although I am inclined to think that it would. But I have no hesitation in saying that a judge in such a case ought to be impeached. And this comes within the principle for which I contend; *for these acts of culpable omission, are a plain and direct violation of the law.*" 2 Smith and Lloyd, *Trial of Chase*, 254–255 (1805) (emphasis supplied). For all the lawyerly zigzag, Harper concedes that an indictable offense is not a necessary condition for impeachment.

44. Caesar Rodney, Closing Argument, 2 Smith and Lloyd, *Trial of Chase*, 387.

45. Alexander Hamilton, "Federalist no. 65," in Jacob Cooke, ed., *The Federalist Papers*, 439 (Mar. 7, 1788) (1961).

46. This basic Republican claim is solidly based on the historical materials. See Hoffer and Hull, *Impeachment*, part 3. While these authors' treatment of Chase's trial is outstanding, they give undue emphasis to the managers' assertions that Chase's actions warranted impeachment simply because they had a "dangerous tendency" to undermine republican institutions. This thread of argument was certainly visible, but many of the managers' charges did not require this open-ended appeal to "dangerous tendency," and fit comfortably within more traditional rubrics focusing on a palpable abuse of the public trust.

47. See Whittington, "Reconstructing the Judiciary," 90–92, for a collection of statements from the House managers that elaborate on Chase's inappropriate partisanship.

48. See the work of Presser, cited above, for an elaboration of this view.

49. Pickering's conviction was announced on March 12, 1804. The first of many debates on Yazoo began on March 7, 1804.

50. C. Peter Magrath, *Yazoo*, 7, 38, 39–45, 46–48 (1966).

51. Richard Ellis, *The Jeffersonian Crisis*, 103 (1971). Ellis contributes another valuable discussion in his "Impeachment of Samuel Chase." I part company, however, when he says that "the president's unwillingness to become involved, even behind the scenes, with the Chase impeachment must be included as a decisive factor contributing to the final verdict." Id., 68–69. There are many telltale signs of Jefferson's involvement behind the scenes.

52. See Thomas Fleming, *Duel*, 357 (1999).

53. Id., 359. Burr's leading biographer seems bemused by these developments: "For three years, Burr's patronage recommendations had for the most part been ignored. All at once, his wishes in this regard became the Administration's command." Milton Lomask, *Aaron Burr: The Years from Princeton to Vice-President, 1756–1805*, 364 (1979). Plumer observed in late December that Jefferson has "shown more attention & invited Mr. Burr oftener to his house within this three weeks than ever he did in the course of same time before. Mr. Gallatin . . . has waited upon him more often at his lodgings . . . The secretary of State, Mr. Madison . . . accompanied him on a visit to . . . the French minister." Quoted id., 364. For further evidence of Jefferson's involvement, see *History*, 224–225, 243.

54. See 3 *LJM* 181n3.

55. See Johnstone, *Jefferson and the Presidency*, 184 and n49; see also Norman K. Risjord, *Thomas Jefferson*, 139 (1994).

56. See Chapter 7. And see generally Jeffrey Tulis, *The Rhetorical Presidency*, chs. 1–2 (1987).

57. Dumas Malone suggests that public intervention might have led to charges of impropriety by Federalists and, perhaps, by some Republicans. See Malone, 4 *Jefferson and His Time*, 467. But he does not suggest that these uneasy Republicans would have deserted the president when push came to shove. It was not instrumental concerns that restrained Jefferson from publicly condemning Chase, but his belief that demagoguery was beyond the pale of respectability.

58. This is not the place to chart the tumultuous Randolph-Jefferson relationship. The conflict came to a climax in 1807, when Jefferson engineered Randolph's removal as chairman of the House ways and means committee and Randolph went into permanent opposition as the leader of a small group of "old republicans." See Adams, *John Randolph*, 194–195, 209–212; Noble Cunningham, "Who Were the Quids?" 50 *Miss. Valley Hist. Rev.* 252 (1963).

59. Adams, *John Randolph*, 152–154.

60. During most of Jefferson's first term, Randolph was "a hard-working and even disciplined party member as long as he was convinced that Jefferson meant

what he said about reforming the government." Robert Dawidoff, *The Education of John Randolph*, 179 (1979).

61. Adams, *John Randolph*, 91–93.

62. For example, one historian considers it unlikely "that there would ever have been an open rebellion against the administration but for the character of one man—Randolph of Roanoke." Norman Risjord, *The Old Republicans*, 33 (1965).

63. See James Madison, "Federalist no. 63," in Cooke, ed., *Federalist Papers*, 428–430 (Mar. 1, 1788).

64. 1 Smith and Lloyd, *Trial of Chase*, 254–261.

65. Marshall's letter is dated January 23, 1804, but I follow Hobson's suggestion that Marshall had made the common January mistake of forgetting that the year had changed. See 6 *PJM* 347, 348n1 (1990). The date of 1805 is also supported by the fact that Chase was himself very pessimistic about the outcome of his trial at that time. Haw et al., *Stormy Patriot*, 225 (quoting letter from Chase to William Tilghman, Jan. 28, 1805).

66. 6 *PJM* 347.

67. The article impeaching him for excluding the Taylor evidence did, however, garner 18 affirmative votes. 14 *Annals* 666.

68. This was not the last time in American history when an override provision like Marshall's could be seen hovering visibly in the wings. See *WPT*, 320–333 (describing similar proposals during the New Deal court-packing controversy).

69. Haskins's account serves as the paradigm case, see *History*, but a recent essay by Louise Weinberg outdoes Haskins in Federalist partisanship. Weinberg, "Our Marbury," 89 *Va. L. Rev.* 1349–88 (2003).

70. Edward Corwin, *John Marshall and the Constitution*, 66 (1919).

71. See *WPT*, 227–229 (Senate acquittal of Andrew Johnson during Reconstruction), 329–337 (Senate rejection of court-packing during the New Deal).

10.   Synthesis

1. 14 *Annals* 1213 (Mar. 1, 1805).

2. John Quincy Adams to John Adams, 8 Mar. 1805, Worthington Ford, ed., *The Writings of John Quincy Adams*, 106, 118 (1917).

3. Everitt Brown, ed., William Plumer, *Memorandum of Proceedings in the United States Senate, 1803–1807*, 101–102 (1923).

4. Randolph finally broke with Jefferson in March 1806, with his outspoken opposition to the administration's proposed $2 million payment to France to avoid war. See Jefferson to William Duane, Mar. 22, 1806, 10 *WTJ* 241; J. Q. Adams, *Writings*, 177–190. Lemuel Sawyer, a House colleague of Randolph's, attri-

butes the break to less worthy matters involving petty personal affront. See Sawyer, *A Biography of John Randolph,* 26 (1844). Both motivations might have been in play.

5. 15 *Annals* 502 (Feb. 24, 1806).

6. The vote was 81–42—just short of the two-thirds needed to pass. At that point, a motion to defer further consideration to the next Monday was unanimously accepted. Id., 504.

7. Nathan Schachner, *Aaron Burr,* 260 (1937).

8. Jefferson to Hay (the prosecutor in the case), June 12, 1807, 11 *WTJ* 228. Some commentators claim that Jefferson refused to comply with Marshall's subpoena, but the correspondence with Hay seems to establish the opposite. See also letters of June 17 and June 23, id., 231, 253–254.

9. Edward Corwin condemns Marshall's conduct of the trial as "the one serious blemish in his judicial record" in *John Marshall and the Constitution,* 111 (1919), arguing that key decisions were lawless and motivated entirely by personal hatred. I do not accept this view. I think Marshall's decisions were legally plausible and quite brave, given the hysteria against Burr, see Robert Faulkner, "John Marshall and the Burr Trial," 53 *J. Am. Hist.* 247 (1966). But certainly there were a lot of contestable legal judgments involved, and Marshall easily could have come out in a way more pleasing to Jefferson. For a fine presentation of the case against Marshall see Charles Haines, *The Role of the Supreme Court in American Government and Politics, 1789–1835,* 279–288 (1943)—an outstanding book that deserves a scholarly revival.

10. Haines, *Role of the Court,* 283.

11. Jefferson to Giles, Apr. 20, 1807, 11 *WTJ* 191. Jefferson also wrote to General Wilkinson that "[The scenes which have been acted at Richmond"] . . . will produce an amendment to the Constitution which, keeping judges independent of the executive, will not leave them so, of the nation." Sept. 20, 1807, 11 *WTJ* 375.

12. Jefferson, "Annual Message to Congress," 17 *Annals* 18 (Oct. 27, 1807). Jefferson's message was followed up by a sustained campaign against Marshall in the *Philadelphia Aurora.* See, e.g., "To the Congress of the U. States," *Aurora,* Nov. 15, 1807 (column by "The People" calling for Congress to respond to Jefferson's invitation to remedy the "defect" that "enabled A. Burr and his accomplices, to turn into a *farce*" the treason proceedings); and *Aurora,* Nov. 18, Nov. 21, Nov. 25, Nov. 28, and Dec. 1, 1807. The author of the series concludes: "I now, sir, take my leave of you, I hope forever. In doing this, I will not suppress the wish of my heart—that you may cease to occupy a station the duties of which, I conscientiously believe you have not discharged 'to the best of your knowledge and ability,' but have used as engines to injur your country."

13. See 17 *Annals* 21–22 (Nov. 5, 1807) (Tiffin proposes to limit judicial tenure

to a term of years and to allow for removal by president on address of two-thirds of both houses of Congress); 99 (Jan. 25, 1808) (instructions from Vermont legislature on same subject); 133 (Feb. 22, 1808) (similar to Tiffin proposal); 331 (Apr. 12, 1808) (similar to Tiffin proposal). These proposals were referred to a select committee, but nothing came of them. See id., 99. Similar activity was taking place in the House, see 18 *Annals* 1525 (Jan. 30, 1808), 1680–82 (Feb. 24, 1808).

14. See William Casto, *The Supreme Court in the Early Republic*, ch. 6 (1995).

15. See id., 126–129, 247–249.

16. *Richmond Enquirer,* Nov. 25, 1806, 3.

17. This is a leading theme of *History.*

18. In urging a Republican of "sufficient talents to be useful," Treasury Secretary Gallatin described Jefferson's problem: "I am told that the practice is as loose in Georgia as in New England and that a real lawyer could not easily be found there. But South Carolina stands high in that respect, at least in reputation." Donald Morgan, *Justice William Johnson,* 49 (1954).

19. Id., 50.

20. Plumer to Sheafe, Mar. 22, 1804, and Plumer to Smith, Mar. 23, 1804, Plumer Papers, LC, quoted id., 51.

21. Henry Abraham, *Justices and Presidents,* 85 (2d ed. 1985).

22. See 1 Leon Friedman and Fred Israel, eds., *The Justices of the United States Supreme Court,* 389–391 (1969). Livingston's credentials were further burnished by the Republican commitments of his powerful family. Robert Johnstone, *Jefferson and the Presidency,* 188–189 (1978). It is unlikely that Jefferson or his advisers actually studied his judicial opinions, which in fact reflected an eclectic mix of Jeffersonian and Federalist sentiments. Id., 391–394.

23. Abraham, *Justices and Presidents,* 86.

24. Article I, sec. 6. See Randolph to Nicholson, Feb. 17, 1807, Joseph H. Nicholson Papers, LC: "You must know that we have made a new Circuit consisting of the three Western States, with an additional Associate justice. A caucus (excuse the slang of politics) was held, as I am informed, by the delegations of those states for the purpose of recommending some character to the President . . . An attempt was made by the honorable aspirant himself [Campbell] so to amend the bill as to get around the constitutional barrier to his appointment. Can you conceive a more miserable or shameless prevarication."

25. The Senate confirmed Todd on March 3, 1807; the Embargo Act was passed early in the next Congress, on December 22, 1807. All but two of the senators and representatives from Kentucky, Ohio, and Tennessee voted for the embargo (Ohio's Sen. Smith was absent). See 17 *Annals* 50–54, 1215–23.

26. Jefferson to Madison, Oct. 15, 1810, 9 *WTJ* 282. For a fuller account, though with a Federalist bias, see 1 Charles Warren, *The Supreme Court in United States History,* 400–419 (1926).

27. Jefferson to Granger, Oct. 22, 9 *WTJ* 286.

28. The embargo was detested by New England Federalists, see Louis Sears, *Jefferson and the Embargo,* 143–196 (1927), but it also generated a great deal of Republican infighting, 4 Irving Brant, *James Madison,* 469–482 (1953).

29. See James Young, *The Washington Community,* 202–205, 230–231 (1966).

30. See Morgan Dowd, "Justice Joseph Story and the Politics of Appointment," 9 *Am. J. Leg. Hist.* 265 (1965).

31. See id., 275–276; John Maltese, *The Selling of Supreme Court Nominees* 34 (1995); 1 Warren, *Supreme Court in U.S. History,* 412–413.

32. See Marie Hecht, *John Quincy Adams,* 148–149, 173–174, 180–181 (1972).

33. See Paul Nagel, *John Quincy Adams,* 198–199 (1997).

34. Granger's problem was his long championship of New England interests in the Yazoo controversy, which made him unpopular in many other circles. 1 Warren, *Supreme Court in U.S. History,* 408–409.

35. Madison's connections with Isaac Story went back to their days at Princeton, see Friedman and Israel, *The Justices,* 438.

36. Abraham, *Justices and Presidents,* 89.

37. See 1 Friedman and Israel, *The Justices,* 422–423.

38. See 2 *History,* 652; Donald Morgan, "The Origin of Supreme Court Dissent," 10 *Wm & Mary Q.* 353, 369 (1953).

39. Johnson to Jefferson, Dec. 10, 1822, Jefferson Papers, LC, reprinted id., 369.

40. See Morgan, "Supreme Court Dissent," 365–367, 367n55. The reports don't indicate Marshall's absence. Bushrod Washington spoke for the Court in Pierce v. Turner, 5 Cranch 154 (1809), and William Cushing in Marine Insurance Company of Alexandria v. Young, 5 Cranch 187 (1809). The only Republican justice to do so was Livingston, in Keene v. United States, 5 Cranch 304 (1809), and Hudson v. Guestier, 6 Cranch 281 (1810). I should also mention the opinion for the Court written by William Johnson in Marshall v. Currie, 4 Cranch 172 (1807), involving Marshall's relative Humphrey Marshall. Though the report is not explicit, I assume that the chief justice recused himself.

41. Between 1813 and 1822 Marshall spoke for the Court an average of 15 times a year, and other justices accounted annually for 21 opinions. Morgan, "Supreme Court Dissent," 367n56.

42. For a rich blow-by-blow account see 2 William Winslow Crosskey, *Politics and the Constitution in the History of the United States,* 770–784 (1953). Crosskey presents the story as if it were a conspiracy designed (by Jefferson himself?) to create a case that would allow the Supreme Court to destroy the criminal jurisdiction of the federal common law. But this suggestion is utterly implausible. From the beginning of the Connecticut proceedings in 1806 up to the appointment of Duvall

in late 1811, there was a solid Federalist majority on the Court, generally predisposed to common law criminal jurisdiction. When the Connecticut Republicans started the case, and for many years after, they had every reason to suppose that the Supreme Court would uphold their prosecutions, not—as Crosskey suggests—discredit their effort.

43. See Leonard Levy, *Emergence of a Free Press,* 306–307 (1985).

44. See Gary Rowe, "The Sound of Silence," 101 *Yale L. J.* 919, 936–939 (1992), upon which I rely throughout.

45. Jefferson to Randolph, Aug. 18, 1799, 9 *WTJ* 73.

46. See Haines, *Role of the Court,* 306.

47. 20 *Annals* 77, 78, 86, 89 (1809).

48. See Madison's report in Marvin Meyers, ed., *The Mind of the Founder,* 359–362 (1981).

49. See Rowe, "Sound of Silence," 926n32.

50. United States v. Hudson and Goodwin, 11 U.S. 32, 33 (1812).

51. The traditional view holds that the vote was 4–3. See 2 Crosskey, *Politics and the Constitution,* 782–783; Stewart Jay, "Origins of Federal Common Law," 133 *U. Pa. L. Rev.* 1003, 1012 (1985). Rowe doubts this tally, citing an unpublished circuit opinion in which Johnson says "that Judge Washington alone, if any one, at that time dissented from the opinion." Rowe, "Sound of Silence," 927.

I suspect that Johnson was exaggerating the support for his position. Joseph Story suggests as much in another circuit decision of 1813, where he disparages *Hudson* as decided "by a majority only of the court," United States v. Coolidge et al., 25 F. Cas. 619, 621 (1813). When Story's case reached the Court in 1816, the justices' reception indicates a deeper division than Rowe suggests.

52. 6 Cranch 87 (1810).

53. See Donald Roper, "Judicial Unanimity and the Marshall Court: A Road to Reappraisal," 9 *Am. J. Leg. Hist.* 118, 119 (1965). See Chapter 8 for Marshall's antipathy to dissent.

54. Kathryn Preyer suggests that Marshall's commitment to common law crime was shaky by the latter part of the decade, see her "Jurisdiction to Punish: Federal Authority, Federalism and the Common Law of Crimes in the Early Republic," 4 *Law & Hist. Rev.* 223, 246–247 (1986). But she does not claim that he had clearly repudiated the concept, and I read the cases more cautiously. Marshall also expresses firm support for common law jurisdiction, at least where crimes against the law of nations are concerned. See his letter to St. George Tucker, Nov. 27, 1800, 6 *PJM* 23–25. I also place some weight on the behavior of Marshall's new collaborator on the Court, Story, who set out to convince the Court to overrule *Hudson.* I don't think the young man would have gone public if he had thought his chief dis-

approved. Even if I am wrong, and Marshall was prepared to join Johnson on the merits, he must have been repelled by the strongly Jeffersonian reasoning of the Court's opinion.

55. 6 *PJM* 32.

56. Rowe, "Sound of Silence," 920.

57. United States v. Coolidge et al., 25 F. Cas. 619, 621, 620 (1813).

58. 1 Warren, *Supreme Court in U.S. History,* 439.

59. United States v. Coolidge, 14 U.S. 415 (1816).

60. Id., 416.

61. The conventional wisdom is on display in the Holmes Devise histories of the Court. Three scholars have written about *Hudson and Goodwin* but none appreciates its significance in the president-court dynamic. See *History,* 354–356 (Haskins), 633–646 (Johnson); G. Edward White, 3 *History of the Supreme Court: The Marshall Court and Cultural Change 1815–35,* 137–138, 865–867 (1988). Only Haskins considers Stuart v. Laird at length, but in the spirit of a Federalist partisan, without reflecting upon the larger themes involved in the rise of the plebiscitary presidency. *History,* 180–181, 383–384.

62. 10 U.S. (6 Cranch 87) (1810). While the Court used the case to strike down a state statute, the winners did not actually gain effective relief until 1814. See Peter Magrath, *Yazoo,* 97 (1966). Another early—if less significant—judicial intervention in state affairs occurred in New Jersey v. Wilson, 7 Cranch 116 (1812), discussed in *History,* 598–600.

63. See generally Larry Kramer, *The People Themselves* (2004); for a fine case study, see Gary Rowe, "Constitutionalism in the Streets," 78 *S. Cal. L. Rev.* 401 (2005).

64. For more on normal politics, see *WPF,* chs. 7–9.

11. Reverberations

1. I have considered the fate of other transformative presidencies in *WPF, WPT,* and Bruce Ackerman and David Golove, *Is NAFTA Constitutional?* (1995). I criticize contemporary presidentialist patterns in "The Broken Engine of Progressive Politics," *American Prospect* 34 (May–June 1998), and in "The New Separation of Powers," 113 *Harv. L. Rev.* 633 (2000).

2. Some of these patches have taken the form of constitutional amendments, some have involved Congress enacting statutes, and I will be noting their relevance at appropriate points. For more comprehensive discussions, see Stephen Siegel, "The Conscientious Congressman's Guide to the Electoral Count Act of 1887," 56 *Fla. L. Rev.* 541 (2004); Bruce Ackerman and David Fontana,

"Thomas Jefferson Counts Himself into the Presidency," 90 *Va. L. Rev.* 551, 629–643 (2004).

3. See Siegel, "Conscientious Congressman's Guide," 625–634.

4. 3 U.S.C. §15 (2000).

5. U.S. Const. art. II, §1, cl. 3.

6. The Senate president's authority has come into play on other occasions, but never when his decision could change the outcome of the election. As a consequence, Senate presidents have tended to frame their rulings narrowly to avoid the underlying constitutional questions. The principal incidents are usefully summarized in Vasan Kesavan, "Is the Electoral Count Act Unconstitutional?" *80 N. Car. L. Rev.* 1653, 1679–94 (2002). I find Kesavan's substantive interpretations of the Constitution entirely unpersuasive, but he provides an admirably exhaustive review of the relevant literature.

During the electoral college crisis precipitated by the Hayes-Tilden election of 1876, Congress passed a special statute to short-circuit the authority of the Senate president. It created a special electoral commission to judge the returns that were then in dispute, and required the Senate president to follow the commission's decisions. I discuss this important precedent in Ackerman and Fontana, "Jefferson Counts Himself into the Presidency," 634–640.

7. See Chapter 3.

8. Even today, a challenge to an electoral vote requires at least one senator and one representative to come forward and make their objections explicit. Otherwise, the president of the Senate counts the vote.

9. 10 *Annals* 1024 (1801).

10. See Wilbur Howell, ed., *The Papers of Thomas Jefferson,* 2d series: *Jefferson's Parliamentary Writings,* 337–426 (1988).

11. Jefferson to Madison, Jan. 16, 1797, in James Smith, ed., *The Republic of Letters: The Correspondence between Thomas Jefferson and James Madison, 1776–1826,* vol. 2: *1790–1804,* 958–959 (1995). For more detail see Chapter 3.

12. See Twentieth Amendment, sec. 3 (1933).

13. This stylized presentation builds on my account of New Deal dynamics in *WPT,* 255–382. My interpretation of this episode has provoked a lot of commentary; those wishing to explore further might begin with the symposium "Moments of Change: Transformation in American Constitutionalism," 108 *Yale L. J.* 1917 (1999).

14. Walter Lippmann famously said of Roosevelt that he was "a pleasant man who, without any important qualifications for the office, would very much like to be President." *New York Herald-Tribune,* Apr. 28, 1932. Even a sympathetic historian like Arthur M. Schlesinger Jr. concedes that FDR's "intellectual processes had always been intuitive rather than logical. He often thought lazily and

superficially." *The Age of Roosevelt: The Crisis of the Old Order, 1919–1933,* 407 (1957).

15. See *WPT,* 283–284.

16. See generally Felix Frankfurter and James M. Landis, *The Business of the Supreme Court: A Study in the Federal Judicial System,* ch. 3 (1928). As a technical matter, a vestigial legal structure regulated circuit riding until 1911, when it was formally eliminated. See 36 *Stat.* 1087 (1911).

17. 301 U.S. 1 (1937) and 301 U.S. 548 (1937).

18. United States v. Carolene Products Co. 304 U.S. 144, 152–153n4 (1938).

19. The Court did not renounce *Marbury's* theory of judicial review. The guardianship rationale announced in *Carolene* has served as a modern complement to *Marbury,* not as a replacement.

20. See *WPF,* 127–129, and *WPT,* 366–368; see also Bruce Ackerman, "Beyond Carolene Products," 98 *Harv. L. Rev.* 713 (1985).

21. For the canonical statement of *Carolene's* constitutional theory, see John Hart Ely, *Democracy and Distrust* (1980).

22. Roosevelt's court-packing initiative did not absolutely require the Court's membership to expand from 9 to 15. This would be up to the individual decisions of the justices. Whenever a justice insisted on staying on the Court after he turned 70, the plan would have increased the size of the Court to allow for the appointment of a younger justice. If all justices resigned at retirement age, this would have kept the Court's membership at the traditional number of 9. *WPT,* 317–320.

23. Samuel Rosenman, ed., *The Public Papers and Addresses of Franklin D. Roosevelt,* 116, 120 (1937).

24. See Walter Brown, *James F. Byrnes of South Carolina,* 124 (1992).

25. See Frank Freidel, *Franklin D. Roosevelt: A Rendezvous with Destiny,* 221–239 (1990).

26. See, e.g., *WPF,* ch. 6.

27. See Michael Kammen (quoting James Russell Lowell), *A Machine That Would Go of Itself,* 18 (1986).

Horatius's Presidential Knot

1. The text reproduced here is the one that appeared in the *Alexandria Advertiser,* Jan. 2 and Jan. 3, 1801. Notes point to divergences from the version published in the *Washington Federalist,* Jan. 6, 1801.

2. Part I in the *Alexandria Advertiser,* Jan. 2, 1801, ends here. Part II was published one day later.

3. This sentence appears only in the *Washington Federalist,* not in the *Alexandria Advertiser.*

Judge Bassett's Protest

1. Though Bassett signed the Protest, one scholar has suggested that it was ghostwritten by his son-in-law, Congressman James A. Bayard of Delaware, and a contemporaneous report from Boston's Republican newspaper, the *Independent Chronicle,* says that "this work is considered as the product of Bayard and Bassett united." See Wythe Holt, "If the Courts Have Firmness Enough to Render the Decision," in Wythe Holt and David Nourse, eds., *Egbert Benson,* 16 (1987).

The text reproduced here is from the *New-England Palladium,* Aug. 31 and Sept. 3, 1802. I compared this version with those in three other newspapers—the *New York Commercial Advertiser* (August 24–25, 1802), the *Federal Ark* (Dover, Oct. 19 and 26, Nov. 2, 9, and 16, 1802), and the *Gazette of the United States* (Philadelphia, Aug. 21, 1802). Notes indicate minor divergences from the *Palladium* version. I have omitted a few introductory paragraphs in which Bassett explains why he cannot remain among the "indifferent spectators of the debates."

2. The *New England Palladium* says "to *and* to the number or force of the proofs"—an obvious typographical error. Since other versions say "add," which makes sense, I have made the appropriate change in the text.

3. Other versions say "should not be exposed *to dismission.*"

4. The *New York Commercial Advertiser* says "was *thot* to be effectually curbed," while the *Federal Ark* and the *Gazette of the United States* say "was *thought* to be effectually curbed."

5. Other versions say "*its* own immutability."

6. Other versions say "*annexed* to the first appointment."

7. Other versions combine this sentence and the next paragraph.

8. Other versions start a new paragraph after this sentence.

9. Other versions say "contrary to the letter *and spirit* of the constitution."

10. Other versions say "would *affect* no judicial tenure of office."

11. Other versions say "in *the* full exercise of their rights and duties."

12. Other versions reverse the order of this paragraph and the next.

13. Other versions say "I hold it my *bounden* duty."

14. Other versions say "the foregoing *opinion* and reasons."

ACKNOWLEDGMENTS

This book started life as a chapter of *We the People,* a never-ending work in prog-ress. I published the second volume in that series in 1998, and immediately began work on the third, which confronts the problem of constitutional interpretation—and where else to begin but Marbury v. Madison?

Seven years later, I emerge with more and less than I expected. More: this book moves far beyond *Marbury* to propose a thoroughgoing revision of the great events that ring down the curtain on the Founding of the republic. And less: it rep-resents a painfully small step toward the promised third volume of *We the People.* But there is still time left, I hope, to make it past the finish line.

My thanks, first and foremost, to the Yale students who have helped so much throughout the years, David Fontana above all. In my initial review of the original sources, I came across rumors claiming that Jefferson, acting as president of the Senate, counted his Federalist rivals out of the House runoff during the electoral college crisis of 1801. Over the last four years, David has pursued this question with great imagination, energy, and discipline, collaborating with me to establish the facts authoritatively and to place them in larger context. The fruits of his labors are best displayed in our article "Thomas Jefferson Counts Himself into the Presi-dency" in the *Virginia Law Review,* but Chapter 3 builds on his work as well. I also want to single out Jed Shugerman. His creative research helped establish John Marshall as the likely author of a crucial newspaper essay, discussed in Chapter 2, that signaled a dangerous escalation of the electoral college crisis. Many other Yalies made significant contributions, including John Bronsteen, Benjamin Bur-man, Andrew DeFilippis, Caitlin Fitz, Jeff Green, Bill Jewett, Anil Kalhan, Anand Kandaswamy, Anita Krishnakumar, Maya Lester, Daniel Levin, Sam McGee, John Pellettieri, Jessica Roberts, Andrew Sepielli, Greg Silbert, Leigha Simonton, Phil Spector, Felix Valenzuela. My secretary, Jill Tobey, and the faculty librarian, Gene Coakley, have also been terrific—helping in countless ways that made my task manageable.

I am grateful to my colleagues at Yale and elsewhere who have provided aid and inspiration during the long hard slog: Akhil Amar, Joyce Appleby, Jack Balkin, Mirjan Damaska, David Davis, Owen Fiss, Robert Gordon, Paul Kahn, Sandy Levinson, Jerry Mashaw, David Mayhew, Jack Rakove, Jed Rubenfeld, Stephen Skowronek, Ted White, and James Whitman. Tony Kronman was exceptionally supportive, both as dean and as intellectual provocateur.

And then there is Roger Shuy, professor of linguistics emeritus at Georgetown. For several years we struggled to establish, by statistical means, the author-ship of the essay by "Horatius" that plays a significant role in this book. We failed, but it wasn't for want of trying, and Shuy was a vastly informative teacher to a class of one.

As always, it is my wife, Susan Rose-Ackerman, who has been the indispens-able ally: her gentle spirit and her sharp mind pushing me forward, despite false starts and blind alleys.

INDEX

Adams, Abigail, 327n4

Adams, John, 3, 4, 19, 38, 46, 76, 246; anti-party consciousness, 100–101; Bayard and, 331n47; Constitution and, 121; creation of a military balance of power, 94; in 1801 deadlock crisis, 22, 69, 81, 99; in 1796 election, 58, 72; in 1800 election, 95, 97, 98, 113, 122, 124–125; foreign policy, 101; Fries case and, 209–210; Hamilton and, 20, 97, 99, 104, 122; as incumbent president, 85; interim presidency and, 88; Jefferson and, 87–88, 98–99, 131, 136–137, 320n29, 327n4; judicial nominations and appointments, 37, 126–127, 131–133, 137–140, 194, 331nn41,42, 334n70, 345n33; Judiciary Act of 1801 and, 130–131, 152; judiciary for District of Columbia and, 135; lame-duck nominations and appointments, 7, 8, 126–127, 134, 137–138, 140–141, 147–148, 174–175, 215, 327n4; legalistic views, 85–87, 102; moral and strategic blunders, 130, 141, 142, 156; newspaper writing and pamphleteering, 308n29; pardon by, 210; refusal to attend Jefferson's inauguration, 93, 99; role in transfer of power in 1801, 94; sedition law and, 235; State of the Union Address, 129; statesmanship, 78, 113; Vermont ballot problem in 1797 and, 313n35; as vice president, 118, 313n35; war between France and England and, 95–101, 107, 141

Adams, John Quincy, 208, 225, 232, 242

Adams, Thomas, 124

Addison, William, 351n1

Alexandria Advertiser, 47

Alien and Sedition Acts, 47, 74, 236

American Revolution, 24, 25, 28, 96, 101

Aristides (author of political tracts), 33

Armstrong, John, 352n8

Articles of Confederation, 4

Assembly leadership model, 12

Balance of power, 78, 139

Balloting Plan (Gallatin), 80–85, 86–87, 145, 318n13, 319n27

Barnes, David, 148

Bassett, Richard, 133, 172–173, 176–177, 179, 366n1; judicial appointment of, 331n48; protest against the Judiciary Act, 276–297, 345n23; relationship to colleagues, 345n23

Bayard, James, 4, 80, 99, 104–107, 142, 159, 177, 247, 317n8, 340n62; Adams and, 331n47; circuit-riding debate and, 337n33; defense of lame-duck authority, 155, 156; Jefferson and, 106, 331n47; judiciary nominations and, 132–133; as leader of the House Republicans, 153–154; as possible author of Bassett's protest, 366n1

Benson, Egbert, 331n43

Beveridge, Albert, 45, 46, 307n20, 309n42, 343n8

Bill of Rights, 12, 13

Bill of Rights (England), 11

Bingham, William, 135

Black, Hugo, 264–265

Blount, William, 43, 273

Bradley, Stephen R., 333n69, 337n34, 339n50, 352n8

Brearley, David/Brearley Committee, 27, 29, 30, 302n30

dent, 310n6; wars, 224. *See also* Chase,
Samuel; Pickering, John
Ingersoll, Jared, 123, 124, 127, 134–135
Innes, Harry, 332n51

Jackson, Andrew, 112, 243
Jackson, James, 61, 314n37
Jackson, Samuel, 13
Jay, John, 40, 55, 69, 123, 306n13; rejects
chief justiceship, 124–125, 127, 128
Jefferson, Thomas, 12, 20, 72, 74, 102,
146, 246; Adams and, 87–88, 98–99,
320n29, 327n4; in American Revolution, 101; assault on judiciary, 9–10,
113–114, 149, 159, 161, 175, 176,
200, 206, 214, 228, 241–242, 254,
258, 261; basis for authority of, 256;
Bayard and, 106, 331n47;
brinksmanship of, 112–113; Burr and,
105–106, 213, 226–227, 357n53; campaign against Federalists, 199; campaign
against Marshall, 75, 147, 198, 215,
227, 254, 359n12; campaign to reorganize judiciary, 144, 206; campaign to reorganize presidency, 206; circuit-riding
debate and, 172; claim of mandate from
the People, 5, 6, 9, 22, 39, 44, 79, 88,
94, 101–102, 111, 197, 208, 214; comparison with Roosevelt, 263–264; confrontation with Supreme Court, 254;
Constitution and, 194, 224, 262; control over Congress, 143; in 1801 deadlock crisis, 3, 4, 30, 32–33, 34, 37, 40,
43, 46, 57, 58, 66, 71, 73, 75, 77, 86–
87, 102, 120, 130, 214, 269–270,
324n15; on 1801 deadlock crisis, 101–
102, 303n42; Declaration of Independence and, 190, 256; in 1796 election,
72; in 1800 election, 4, 6, 7, 12, 14,
34–35, 59, 63, 66, 73, 77, 78, 83, 91–
92, 94, 106–107, 111, 113, 116, 128,

139, 190, 192, 251, 253, 312n29,
335n8; failure to call constitutional convention, 107; on Federalist party, 112;
Federalist party and, 73, 90–91, 112;
first term events, 143; foreign policy,
231, 232; French Revolution and,
302n20; Gallatin and, 357n53; Georgia
ballot problem and, 66, 67–69, 71, 73,
74, 77, 311n24, 312n26; governing
strategy, 145, 146–147; Greene affair
and, 148; Hamilton and, 19; impeachment campaign against Chase, 202,
214–215, 255, 262, 351n1; impeachment of Pickering, 200, 201; inaugura-
tion/Inaugural Address, 93, 99, 111,
138, 144; judicial appointments, 10,
224, 229–232, 263, 264; Judiciary Act
of 1801 and, 130, 147, 150, 161,
336n21; lame-duck appointments, 8,
147–148, 193; as leader of Republican
movement, 146, 256; Madison and, 24,
91, 191, 231, 357n53; Marbury v. Madison and, 149, 182, 183, 190, 191, 195;
plebicitarian presidency, 335n8; popular
sovereignty and, 322n41; on possible selection of Burr, 324n15; as president of
Senate, 56, 130, 247; proposed payment
to France, 358n4; public persona and
social style, 145, 147, 155, 256; purge
of judiciary, 181, 188, 193–194, 222–
223; Randolph and, 212–213, 216–217,
219, 357nn58,60; relations with Supreme Court, 75–76, 193–194, 195,
198, 277; on Republican party, 111–
112; Republican principles of, 20; resources of presidential leadership, 143–
147; in 1801 runoff, 55, 69–71, 76;
State of the Union Address, 142, 150;
statesmanship, 70, 73, 74, 76, 251, 253;
Stuart v. Laird and, 262; threat of strike
by justices and, 162; threat to use violence, 94, 96, 214; use of power, 56; as